Writing Food History

Writing Food History
A Global Perspective

Edited by
Kyri W. Claflin and Peter Scholliers

BERG

London • New York

English edition

First published in 2012 by
Berg
Editorial offices:
50 Bedford Square, London WC1B 3DP, UK
175 Fifth Avenue, New York, NY 10010, USA

Berg is an imprint of Bloomsbury Publishing Plc.

Library of Congress Cataloging-in-Publication Data

Claflin, Kyri W.
Writing food history : a global perspective /
edited by Kyri W. Claflin and Peter Scholliers.
p. cm.
Includes bibliographical references and index.
ISBN 978-1-84788-809-9—ISBN 978-0-85785-217-5—
ISBN 978-1-84788-808-2   1. Food habits—History.
2. Food preferences—History.   3. Dinners and dining—
History.   I. Scholliers, Peter.   II. Title.
GT2850.C54   2012
394.1'2—dc23   2012010556

British Library Cataloguing-in-Publication Data

A catalogue record for this book is available from the British Library.

ISBN 978 1 84788 809 9 (Cloth)
978 1 84788 808 2 (Paper)
e-ISBN 978 0 85785 217 5 (individual)

Typeset by Apex CoVantage, LLC, Madison, WI, USA.
Printed in the UK by the MPG Books Group

www.bergpublishers.com

Contents

Notes on Contributors

Amy Bentley teaches Food History and Culture at New York University. She is editor of *A Culture History of Food in the Modern Era* (2012) and author *of Eating for Victory: Food Rationing and the Politics of Domesticity* (1998). Her book on the history of infant food and feeding practices in the United States is forthcoming from the University of California Press.

Jonathan Brumberg-Kraus has published numerous articles on food and Judaism. He was on the steering committee of the Society of Biblical Literature Seminar on Meals in the Greco-Roman World. Brumberg-Kraus is currently working on a book entitled *Jewish Food* about what makes Jewish food "Jewish." He has taught a freshman seminar on "The Rituals of Dinner" for the past decade.

Yujen Chen received her Ph.D. degree from Leiden University (2010) with a dissertation entitled "Embodying Nation in Food Consumption: Changing Boundaries of 'Taiwanese Cuisine' (1895–2008)." She has published several articles on Taiwanese culinary culture in historical and anthropological journals. Her research interests include national cuisine, the social history of food, and the cultural history of Taiwan.

Kyri W. Claflin is the author of numerous articles and chapters including "La Villette: The City of Blood, 1867–1914" in *Meat, Modernity and the Rise of the Slaughterhouse* (2008) and "Les Halles and the Moral Market: Frigophobia Strikes in the Belly of Paris," in the Oxford Symposium volume *Food & Morality* (2008). She teaches courses on the culture and cuisine of France and a survey course on the history of food. Her research interests include provisioning Paris, food and wartime, and the history of cookbooks.

Katarzyna Cwiertka is the author of *Modern Japanese Cuisine: Food, Power and National Identity* (2006) and *Cuisine, Colonialism and Cold War: Food in Twentieth Century Korea* (2012). She has also edited several volumes with a larger geographical focus, including *Asian Food: The Global and the Local* (2002), *Critical Readings on Food in East Asia* (2012), and *Food and War in East Asia* (forthcoming).

Paul Freedman's most recent book is *Out of the East: Spices and the Medieval Imagination* (2008). He edited the award-winning collection of essays *Food: The History of Taste* (2007). He is Professor of Medieval History at Yale University.

James C. McCann is Professor of History and Director, *ad interim,* at Boston University's Pardee Center for the Study of the Longer Range Future. His many publications include books on agriculture and environmental history in Africa. His last book was the prize-winning *Maize and Grace: Africa's Encounter with a New World Crop, 1500–2000* (2005). He has written a book on African cuisine, *Stirring the Pot: A History of African Cuisine* (2009), which won the "Best in the World" award from *Gourmand* Magazine at a ceremony at the Folies-Bergère in Paris in March 2011.

Nawal Nasrallah was Professor of English and Comparative Literature at the universities of Baghdad and Mosul before coming to the United States in 1990. Her published works as an independent scholar and food writer include *Delights from the Garden of Eden: A Cookbook and a History of the Iraqi Cuisine* (2003), an English translation of Ibn Sayyar al-Warraq's tenth-century Baghdadi cookbook *Annals of the Caliphs' Kitchens* (2007), and *Dates: A Global History* (2011).

Jeffrey M. Pilcher teaches classes on the history of food and drink at the University of Minnesota. His books include *¡Que vivan los tamales! Food and the Making of Mexican Identity* (1998), *Food in World History* (2006), *Planet Taco: A Global History of Mexican Food* (2012), and an edited volume, the *Oxford Handbook of the History of Food* (2012).

Krishnendu Ray is the author of *The Migrant's Table: Meals and Memories in Bengali-American Households* (2004). Before coming to New York University, he taught at the Culinary Institute of America for a decade. He is currently working on a book-length project tentatively titled *Taste, Toil and Ethnicity*. Most recently, he co-edited *Curried Cultures: Globalization, Food and South Asia* (2012).

Özge Samancı is a historian whose research interests include Ottoman and Turkish food history. She is the author of publications including "Culinary Consumption Patterns of the Ottoman Elite during the First Half of the 19th Century" in *The Illuminated Table, the Prosperous House* (2003), "Pilaf and Bouchées: The Modernization of Official Banquets at the Ottoman Palace in the Nineteenth Century" *in Royal Taste* (2011), and several articles on Ottoman culinary culture in *Yemek ve Kültür,* a Turkish journal about food culture where she is a member of the editorial committee. She is also the co-editor of *Turkish Cuisine* (2008), an inclusive book about the Turkish culinary culture.

Peter Scholliers is a Professor of History whose research interests include the standard of living in Western Europe. He is the author of many publications and the editor of numerous volumes of essays on various aspects of the history of food. Most recently, he is the author of *Food Culture in Belgium* (2008) and the editor (with Fabio Parasecoli) of *A Cultural History of Food* (2012).

John Wilkins is Professor of Greek Culture and works on topics related to food, medicine, and culture in antiquity. He has a book in press on Galen's treatise on nutrition, and he brought out *Food in the Ancient World* (with Shaun Hill) in 2006. He has co-edited several volumes on topics in the history of food, including *Food in Antiquity* (1995) and *Athenaeus and His World* (2000).

Introduction
Surveying Global Food Historiography

Peter Scholliers and Kyri W. Claflin

Consuming Food and Its History

The history of food fascinates a large and varied public. Television programs, historical cooking classes, websites, exhibitions, and a flood of general-interest books attest to the widespread attention. In addition to, and sometimes overlapping with work that attracts a general audience, a growing body of scholarly literature focuses on food history. Such academic interest should surprise no one, given the welcome bequeathed to food as a topic of serious study by university departments in the past ten to fifteen years. University publishers and grant-giving institutions support food history, and a number of graduate programs focus on the culture of food.[1] Peer-reviewed journals devoted to food and foodways are multiplying at an astounding pace,[2] along with regular conferences on one or another specialized topic.[3] Perhaps even more striking, and certainly confirming the trend, food history turns up more and more often at general history meetings.[4]

The history of food is a source of knowledge about how and why food, cultures, and societies have changed over time. It is true that media attention to and writing about food as a historical subject are frequently embedded in nostalgia and a romanticized past. However, understanding how the choices made by previous generations contributed to today's culinary heritages helps consumers cope with present-day insecurities. At the same time, such understanding reinforces individual and group identity, amplifies a sense of community, and augments feelings of food safety and prestige.[5] Moreover, societies today must make critical food decisions. Knowledge about past foods, foodways, and food crises will help ensure that those decisions are wise ones.

This intensified awareness of food history and food studies reflects today's heightened anxiety about the industrial systems that get our food from farm to plate. Food historian Florent Quellier puts it this way, "Food history writing deals with two big concerns of present-day Western society: food fears and the crisis of identity."[6] In his native France, since the 1990s the public and the government have faced serious outbreaks of BSE (bovine spongiform encephalopathy, or mad cow disease) and the proliferation of unwanted GMOs (genetically modified organisms). In many parts of the world (including France), globalization is thought to threaten traditional habits and cultural differences, and much of the blame falls on American popular culture and industrialized fast food. From production to consumption, modern food chains produce as well as respond to rapid and radical changes in the way we eat.

The multiplication of intermediaries and political agendas that accompany complex food chains place many decisions about our food beyond our control, leaving us with deep concerns about the unhealthy ingredients lurking in processed foods and all-too-frequent outbreaks of foodborne illnesses. Social psychologists and sociologists have suggested that ever-lengthening food chains lead to distrust, alienation, and more uncertainty about who we are because we no longer know where precisely our food comes from.[7] Consumers are reacting against the ills of food chains in countries across the globe. Witness the rising popularity of the Slow Food movement, organic foods, *produits de terroir*, and culinary tourism in search of a taste of "authenticity."[8] Not the least of these new enterprises is food history.

The Goals of This Book

Academic food historians tend to begin their work by situating their topic and approach in the field, reviewing and evaluating the literature on their subject. Books may devote an entire first chapter to historiography.[9] This work of contextualization directs our attention to the emergence of the topic in question within an ongoing historical tradition, the contribution of the new work, and the importance of the author's questions and methods for comprehending historical change. To date, however, only a few specialized surveys devoted to food historiography have been published, and these are limited in scope. There are reviews of the historiography of food in nineteenth- and twentieth-century Europe,[10] as well as American food historiography since the eighteenth century.[11] The review essay, with its reflections on several related books on food history, is another place to find comment about methodologies, approaches, and results.[12] Naturally, reviews of single books can also include historiographical observations.[13] Alongside surveys by historians, research notes in other disciplines, notably anthropology, often contain historical references.[14] Some encyclopedias dealing with food history open their columns to historiographical information, but, regrettably, this is done only occasionally.[15] Importantly, there is a long tradition of bibliographies on food history, often helpfully annotated, which have been published by agricultural historians, nutritional sociologists, cookbook specialists, and scholars in other fields.[16]

Over the past several years, the Internet has become a crucial resource for food historians with listings of food bibliographies and other resources. Two university Internet sources illustrate the immense amount of information available online that is of interest to food history, gastronomy, and food studies: the *Gastronomy and Food Studies Library* website at the University of Adelaide[17] and the comprehensive "Gastronomy" research guide on Boston University's Mugar Library website.[18]

Since publishing costs are not a concern, electronic media encouraged diversity in the proliferation of online bibliographies. *The Food Bibliography,* launched in 2007 by the Institut Européen de l'Histoire et des Cultures de l'Alimentation (IEHCA), is searchable by author, title, and theme; it currently has 17,500 entries.[19] Another site, primarily concerned with anthropological work, but with significant interest for historians, is *World Food Habits*, which conveniently groups books by themes.[20] Individual scholars worldwide set up websites to list their own and other works related to their particular research interests.[21]

Until the present book on global food historiography, there has been no broad and systematic overview of intellectual trends in food history. Admittedly, "global" is a big claim. Still, our aim is to bring together a selection of historiographical essays that address a wider range of times and places than has been gathered together in one secondary source. After roughly three decades of sustained scholarly attention (in and out of academia), research, and publishing in numerous countries, the present affords an opportune moment to assess achievements and note lacunae in food history.

Writing Food History: A Global Perspective takes stock of the writing of food history past and present. While this book is primarily concerned with food historiography, it also considers the contribution of the practice of history to food studies. Like cultural studies and women's studies, almost by definition and certainly by necessity, food studies is an interdisciplinary field. Yet most of us who work and teach in this field know full well just how strong disciplinary conventions can be. Interdisciplinarity is about crossing boundaries, not eliminating them. We look forward to the dialogue in food studies as a result of the efforts of our contributors to closely examine and synthesize what has gone on in a single discipline—history—through the framework of historiography.

Historian Jeffrey Pilcher reminds us of the value of food historiography: "Greater attention to historiography will help us all to learn from existing scholarship, to draw comparisons between different regions and time periods, and most importantly, to strike out in new directions with innovative research that will advance our knowledge of the history of food and society."[22] While we certainly agree that historiography can guide researchers as they look to new subjects and sources for food history, we also want to learn to what extent food history today is *already* connecting with disciplinary and interdisciplinary traditions. Are researchers engaging with other work in food history as well as with ideas, debates, and theories circulating in the larger historical community? Or have food historians been so intoxicated by the myriad possibilities for new topical studies that we come up against fragmented and unrelated research projects? On the whole, we are pleased that the research reported in this book shows a fruitful and responsible engagement with other disciplines. More exciting still, the chapters reveal an important and growing body of secondary texts in the field of food history (and in food studies more generally) that have virtually attained canonical status.[23]

Historians inevitably share an interest in how people conduct historical research, how they approach writing, and what theories and methods they have found useful.

Historiography emphasizes key works, important debates, and changes over time in how and why history is written. These are considerations we have asked our contributors to highlight. Anyone who reads all of the chapters will come across areas of overlap with multiple mentions of notable scholars' names and groundbreaking secondary works (see also the index to this book). Different national traditions of food history writing come from common roots: sociology early in the twentieth century, economics with its emphasis on prices and demographics, the history of everyday life with the French *Annales* school from the 1950s onward, social history as a distinct field separate from political history, cultural anthropology, and cultural history. However, each chapter stands on its own, and we have left these references as our authors have framed them in their individual analyses.

The original questions that prompted the book were big ones. How have historians written the history of food? Which other disciplines inform historical writing about food? We found, eventually, that this was a false dichotomy. Food history, like its parent field social history, has always been firmly rooted in interdisciplinary borrowings. We have already noted the contributions of sociology and anthropology to the history of food (as well as to the practice of history in general). Since the linguistic turn, historians fruitfully borrow from poststructuralist theories and literary criticism. Historians have been accused of borrowing theoretical concepts from the social sciences and then getting them all wrong.[24] We shall stay clear of that debate, but the sentiment may indicate that historians borrow from the social sciences by adapting their methods and approaches into traditional historical methodology to create particularly historical perspectives on theories used in other disciplines. "Poaching" and incorporating successfully work in both directions. Sidney Mintz's historical anthropology and Stephen Mennell's historical sociology are prime examples of social sciences borrowing from history. The relationship between archaeology and food history research, noted in several chapters, promises valuable methodological collaboration in the near future. Since roughly the 1960s, sociologists, anthropologists, economists, and natural scientists have been studying past foodways, and, more recently, communication scientists, literary scholars, social geographers, art historians, and journalists have joined in. In so doing, all of these disciplines called on historical expertise. It is revealing that a journal launched by psychologists in 1981, *Appetite: Multidisciplinary Research on Eating and Drinking*, which specializes in behavioral nutrition and the cultural, sensory, and physiological influences on choices and intake of food and drinks, has broadened its coverage and opened up its pages to history.[25] Thus, food history continues to attract the attention of a growing range of professionals from various disciplines, as well as many nonacademic enthusiasts and popular writers.

We asked the authors to situate current trends in food history in the larger context of when and why food emerged as a field of research in the early- to mid-twentieth century. Our authors investigate the themes, times, and places that have received the most attention. They ask about the new insights and approaches the field has

generated, and they assess the roles of other disciplines and (new) theoretical constructs in the development of the study of food history.

In light of all of the interest in and activity around the history of food among the
general public and in a variety of university departments, what, we wanted to know,
has been the response of historians of food who have seen their field of specialization
being encroached on by a continuous influx of studies emerging from very different
angles. No doubt, some cast a very critical eye on ways that nonprofessional historians use sources, ignore historical context, or flout historical method. But, here again,
we find that, generally, food historians applaud contributions by nonhistorians. As
we have indicated, the food historiography in the following chapters notes debts to
numerous outstanding works originating in other disciplines, as well as from outside
academia. In addition to Mintz and Mennell, who were already mentioned, we can
add anthropologists Clifford Geertz, Jack Goody, and Mary Douglas; sociologists
Pierre Bourdieu and Priscilla Ferguson; and geographers Jean-Robert Pitte, Peter Atkins, and Susanne Freidberg. Other historical fields have contributed a great deal to
food history, including economic history (e.g., Hans-Jürgen Teuteberg), environmental history (e.g., William Cronon), colonial history (e.g., Rebecca Earle), women's
history (e.g., Sheilagh Ogilvie), and the history of medicine (e.g., Emma Spary). Outstanding nonacademic contributions appear in the annual proceedings of the Oxford
Symposium, the biannual edited volumes of the Leeds Symposium, and *Petits Propos
Culinaires*, to name just the most obvious sources. All of these publications present
the work of professional academics and nonacademics side by side. Laura Mason,
Peter Brears, Laura Shapiro, and the late Alan Davidson are a few out of many nonacademic food writers whose food history writing has been exemplary. Putting together this volume showed us the unsettled state of the language we use to identify
the status of the variety of people who do food history. The relationship between
scholars and writers of popular food histories also appears to be fraught with uncertainty about where they overlap and where each goes a different way. Ideally, the
language that describes the larger community of food historians will be as inclusive
as possible. Food history and food studies benefit from welcoming all excellent work.

The Role of History in Food Studies

What contributions do historians make to food studies as an interdisciplinary field?[26]
More properly, we should inquire about the relationship of the past and the present.
History is a mode of inquiry for understanding the past. It works with a notion of
temporality that, in general, the social sciences do not share.[27] Where social scientists aim at establishing predictive models, historians emphasize the particularity
and chronology of their inquiry.[28] Historian Peter Burke pointed to another feature
of the historian's craft, "the task of mediating between two cultures, the past and the
present, of setting up a dialogue between the two systems of concepts, of translating
from one language to the other."[29] Simply put, the practice of history is the way we

make the past legible. How important is the study of the past to producing knowledge that is relevant now? While historians may disagree on why we should write history, most agree that history affords context for and perspective on who we are today and how we got here. History helps us understand why societies and cultures evolved over time in the ways they did. Like food and foodways, history adds a vital ingredient to our individual and communal identities.

Historians have not always been very keen on incorporating theoretical concepts in their work. It was not stressed in our training (although this seems to be changing), which has remained true to rigorous source criticism. While historical questions and objects have changed over the years, historical methodology—archival research and empiricism—remains much the same. In recent years, greater stress on inter- and multidisciplinarity has produced new thinking about writing history, which pushes the historian to include theoretical frameworks from the social sciences. The following chapters testify that borrowing from our colleagues in the social sciences has many precedents, from the "new social" history to the "cultural turn." And we have not yet seen the end of "new" histories and the last of the "turns."

We do not yet hear in food studies programs calls for the erasure of disciplinary boundaries or an abandonment of methodological differences. Academic disciplines still train students in their own methods, techniques, and "insider" language. Food studies as a field occasionally experiences tension among the disciplines because, as William H. Sewell Jr. observes, we are still seeking what has turned out to be an elusive "dialogue between historians and social scientists."[30] In the 1930s, historian Eileen Power acknowledged the poor relations between disciplines—"the historians are so hard on the sociologists, and the economists are so rude to the historians"[31]— yet the conception she shared with Marc Bloch of interdisciplinarity as a method for greater understanding of society, both past and present, is one of the principal ideas that underpins food studies today.

Understanding between the disciplines sometimes appears not to have progressed very much since Power's day, perhaps not least because we lack a common language. The ongoing challenge in food studies as an interdisciplinary endeavor is to elaborate just such a language. It is not out of place to think systematically about how to reap for ourselves and our students the greatest benefits from the multidisciplinarity of the field. We may even begin to imagine what food as a postdisciplinary study might look like.

Notes

We sincerely thank Priscilla Ferguson for comments, suggestions, and support.

1. For example, the joint Master in Storia e cultura dell'alimentazione (Barcelona-Bologna-Brussels-Tours), the Master of Liberal Arts in Gastronomy (Boston University), and the Master's Program in Food Studies (New York University).

For a complete list, see Association for the Study of Food & Society (ASFS), n.d.

2. *Gastronomica* (2001) and *Food & History* (2003), which joined older journals like *Petits Propos Culinaires* (1979), *Food and Foodways* (1984), and *Food, Culture & Society* (1996).

3. Two examples are the annual meeting of the Oxford Symposium on Food and Cookery (since 1981) and the biennial symposium of the International Committee for the Research into European Food History (since 1989).

4. For example, the 123rd annual meeting of the American Historical Association (New York, January 2009) included six sessions on food history, and the 21st International Congress of Historical Sciences (Amsterdam, August 2010) had a session on the history of food and clothing ("Specialized Theme").

5. Johnston and Baumann, 2007.

6. Quellier, 2007, 11. "Ainsi l'histoire de l'alimentation répond-elle à deux grandes inquiétudes des sociétés occidentales actuelles: les peurs alimentaires et une crise identitaire."

7. Kjaernes, Harvey, and Warde, 2007, 2–3.

8. Other ways that consumers seek assurance of safety and healthfulness is by supporting small local farms, taking up gardening, and educating themselves with books, magazines, food blogs, and television programs.

9. For example, Meyzie, 2010, chap. 1.

10. Teuteberg, 1992; Scholliers, 2007.

11. Oliver, 2006.

12. For example, Super, 2002; Spary, 2005; Ferguson, 2005.

13. See, for example, the review sections in *Food & History*, *Food and Foodways*, and *Gastronomica.*

14. Camp, 1982; Mintz and Dubois, 2002.

15. For example, Kiple and Ornelas, 2000. Although both volumes contain quite apt bibliographies per item, little or no attention is paid to the history of writing history.

16. See Cleary, 1988 (on French agriculture); Finlay, 2001 (on German agriculture); Wilson, 1973 (on "habits"); Duran, 2000 (on dietary studies prior to 1940); Driver, 2008 (an annotated list of Canadian cookbooks); and Bloisy and Hoel, 2008 (on [mostly present-day] work conditions on the work floor). See also Thomas Gloning's "Bibliographical Notes on the History of Cookery, Food, Wine, etc." (Gloning, n.d.).

17. University of Adelaide Library, n.d.

18. Boston University Libraries, n.d.

19. Grieco, n.d.

20. Dirks, n.d.

21. For example, Carlin, n.d. The Internet now presents lists of "best food blogs" (in and out of the academic world), for example, *The Foodblog.Com, A Healthy Serving of Food Blogs*, http://www.foodblogblog.com/ (started in 2007).

22. Pilcher, 2010, 325.
23. E.g., Flandrin and Montanari, 1999; A. Davidson, 1999; Mintz, 1985; Appadurai, 1988. See also Nestle and McIntosh, 2010.
24. Sewell, 2005.
25. In 2007, social geographer Peter Atkins and historian Peter Scholliers joined *Appetite*'s editorial board, which also consists of psychologists, physicians, psychiatrists, biologists, and nutritionists.
26. Interdisciplinarity itself is not without ongoing resistance within disciplinary departments. Smail, 2011.
27. Sewell, 2005, 1–21.
28. Sewell, 2005, 3.
29. Burke, 1992, 6.
30. Sewell, 2005, 1–2.
31. Power, 1934, 13–14.

Part I. The West

-1-

Food and Drink in the Ancient World

John Wilkins

Like Sinologists and Indologists, Classicists and Ancient Historians study societies that flourished a very long time ago but also interest us now. The Greeks and Romans provide models for scenes of dining made by 20th Century Fox and MGM and enjoyed by millions. They are in some ways alien cultures, but their antiquity often presses us to harness them to provide origins for modern needs and preoccupations. Thus the Greeks may provide our earliest model for the cookbook in Europe,[1] the Persians the model of hierarchical dining, the Romans the orgy, and the Hellenized Egyptians Cleopatra. But to what extent were the Greeks and Romans really like us, consuming an early version of the Mediterranean diet, recommended by the World Health Organization, and displaying power at banquets like Louis XIV or the Queen of England? Were they not, rather, "desperately foreign," to revert to a key debate in the field of ancient history?

These questions play out in studies of society, warfare, and empire; they play out too for those who wish to taste the food of ancient Rome. Characteristic flavors, after all, were fermented fish sauce, like those of Southeast Asia, and resins made from silphium and asafetida, two members of the giant fennel family more reminiscent of Indian cooking. For some it can be done;[2] for others the Greeks and Romans shared our physiology but not our tastes. And whose taste are we talking about? That of Alexander the Great and Julius Caesar, or the great mass of the population who are not considered in many of the literary historical texts but are attested in some, particularly in Galen's writings on nutrition, in archaeological contexts such as the drains of Herculaneum, in the inscriptions on stone dedicating meals to citizens in cities in Asia Minor,[3] or in the records of professional guilds in Rome.[4] The point may most strikingly be made by contemplating the great temples of antiquity, such as the Parthenon in Athens or the remains at Paestum or Agrigento. The tourist marvels at the vastness and sophistication of the architectural structures but must remember to add to the scene the animals being slaughtered at the altars outside and the vast complexes of dining rooms and tented areas outside where all participants shared the meat. Schmitt-Pantel's *La Cité au Banquet* (1992) is particularly good at putting together literary texts, such as an elaborate scene of a sacrificial feast at Delphi in Euripides' tragedy *Ion*, with decrees inscribed in stone. One example would be the Athenian democracy decreeing the personnel compose a sacrificial procession at the annual feast of Athena. Another would be a benefactor in one of the Greek cities of Asia Minor setting out exactly what each citizen will receive on a particular day. She has recently prepared a second edition (2011) with an extended bibliography.

The student of food in the ancient world could do worse than wandering around the buildings of the agora and acropolis of central Athens with Thompson and Wycherley's *The Agora of Athens* (1972), those of Rome with Claridge's *Rome* (1999), or those of Pompeii with Laurence's *Roman Pompeii: Space and Society* (1994). Why were there so many bars and fast-food shops in Pompeii and Herculaneum? Answer: there were limited cooking facilities in the apartments and homes of ordinary citizens. Why was it so important for Greek cities to have a *prytaneion*, or hospitality building holding the central hearth of the city?[5] Answer: the city offered hospitality to its honored guests in a way that kings had done in pre-polis times, such as those described in the Homeric epics. What were Roman markets like? There are many architectural descriptions in Claridge to set beside literary denunciations of merchants (not respectable people but worth investing in for the elite) and literary praises of Rome as the metropolis of the world.[6]

Questions of origins and models are not new in the field of ancient history. Under the Roman Empire, numerous authors asked similar questions about foods and dining. Athenaeus of Naucratis is a particularly important example of this, writing in the second to third century C.E. and reviewing, from the imperial world enjoyed by his contemporary Aelius Aristeides (117–181 C.E.), grand dining back through the Greek world to the courts of Assyria, Babylon, and Persia, taking in along the way additional influences from the Egyptians, Celts, and nomadic peoples of the steppes to the north and the Libyan deserts to the south, not to mention India to the east and the strange peoples of the Red Sea. The study of food belonged to ethnographies and royal histories. A further powerful approach that preoccupied Athenaeus and many of his sources, such as Plato, Polybius the historian of Rome, and Athenaeus's contemporary Plutarch, was luxury and the idea that uncontrolled desire was a threat to the individual and to the community. This idea runs powerfully through much ancient thought about food and focuses on the excessive elaboration of the fundamental human needs of nourishment, shelter, and reproduction.[7] Unrestrained desire was much more likely to be linked with food than alcohol in antiquity, for cultural reasons mentioned later on. Athenaeus provides an excellent example of the tension in ancient thought between models of progress from primitive human cultures and models of decline from better times. These are linked not only with notions of identity, so that in the Rome of Athenaeus's day (about 200 C.E.) wealthy people reclined at mealtimes, a practice inherited by many Mediterranean peoples from the Assyrians and Persians, but also through assertion of the purity of their own past in the rural simplicity of Republican Rome where fish (and all foreign influences) were unknown and people ate bacon and emmer wheat porridge. These were part of the mythology of the imperial capital, which, as already noted, benefited from all of the goods of the known world.[8] In the Greek version of this mythologizing of identity (Athenaeus wrote in Greek, as did Galen and Plutarch), Homer provides the model of pristine simplicity, and in fact invented the symposium centuries before the development of the polis where the symposium is now thought to have originated.

Athenaeus is also a major example of the encyclopedic, all-embracing use of knowledge that characterized the Roman Empire in the second and third centuries C.E. Reviewing the past and collecting endless examples from great authors of Greek culture such as Plato, Aristotle, and Homer were important for Athenaeus[9] and similar writers such as Plutarch and Galen.[10] This respect for the authority of the past stimulated such collections in the fourth century C.E. as the medical compilations of Oribasius, which were mainly quotations from Galen, and the cookbook of Apicius.[11] The former quotes Galen and other authorities almost word for word on many different kinds of foods, while the latter is a fascinating collection of recipes that combine showy luxury items, such as flamingos, with ways of cutting corners in the kitchen. It is a composite work from numerous sources written in the later Latin of the fourth century C.E. Full of interest, it barely reflects the luxurious lifestyle of its supposed author, who lived three or more centuries earlier, depending on which "Apicius" we are talking about (he was already a legendary gourmet in Athenaeus). Both "Apicius" and Athenaeus are difficult authors to evaluate because of the composite nature of their works, but this did not hinder the interest they generated in the Renaissance and beyond[12] (for example, among those at the courts of the pope or the Holy Roman Emperor who might wish to understand and possibly imitate the great eaters of antiquity[13]).

As Athenaeus had approached ancient dining with encyclopedic aims, so the German classifiers of antiquity in the late nineteenth century gave reviews of such key issues as sacrifice and cookbooks,[14] while chroniclers of Roman life gave in some detail accounts of kitchens, mealtimes, and foods.[15]

Approaches to Food in Ancient History

Those who wish to understand food and drink in antiquity not with a specific question but in need of general approaches and orientation can best begin with Garnsey's *Food and Society in Classical Antiquity* (1999), a stimulating overview that is attuned to modern preoccupations and has an excellent bibliographical essay. This volume is to be read with three other works by Garnsey, "Les raisons de la politique" (1996), *Cities, Peasants and Food in Classical Antiquity* (1998), and a volume containing some of his collected essays, *Famine and Food Supply in the Greco-Roman World* (1988). In *Food in Antiquity* (1969), Brothwell and Brothwell offer a more archaeologically focused account. A more Greek focus is available in Dalby's *Siren Feasts* (1996), with a strong emphasis on terminology, both ancient and modern. He took this further in his *Food in the Ancient World from A to Z* (2003), which does not offer the same historical synthesis, but rather a glossary with indispensable summaries of ancient and secondary sources. Wilkins and Hill, in *Food in the Ancient World* (2006), offer a Greco-Roman synthesis, with a particular interest in nutrition and medical sources, particularly Galen (on the connection between nutrition and cooking in ancient thought see the following). A further general overview is Auberger's *Manger en Grèce classique* (2010). These studies may be supplemented with collections of essays, such as Longo and Scarpi's *Homo Edens* (1989) and Slater's *Dining in a Classical Context* (1991). *Food in Antiquity* (1995), edited by Wilkins, Harvey, and Dobson, is divided into six sections, on cereals and staples, meat and fish, social and religious questions, societies beyond the Greeks and Romans, medicine, and literature, with thirty-two contributors and bibliographies. Wilkins and Nadeau's *Blackwell Companion to Food in the Ancient World* (forthcoming) is a further overview with some thirty-five contributors. Erdkamp's *A Cultural History of Food in Antiquity 800 BCE–500 CE* (2011) offers a cultural history of food.

Murray's *Sympotica* (1990), supplemented by Murray and Tecusan's *In Vino Veritas* (1995), provides a milestone opening up the study of the symposium in a new way by bringing together the drinking practices depicted in the Homeric poems, in archaic poetry, and on vases with archaeological, historical, and social studies to show the power of the institution of the symposium in the formation of the early classical city, the training of young men, and the control of wine. In this volume the symposium is seen as an institution of the elites in both archaic Greece (750–480 B.C.E.) and classical Greece (480–323 B.C.E., the Greece of Plato's *Symposium*). This view has been challenged for the classical period by Fisher's essay "Symposiasts, Fish-Eaters and Flatterers: Social Mobility and Moral Concerns" (2000), which uses archaeological and literary evidence to show that the ritualized drinking of the symposium spread further down the social scale into medium-sized homes and was also practiced in the public buildings of the Athenian democracy.[16]

During the twentieth century, political questions dominated much research in food studies and into the food supply of Rome and Athens in particular. Supplies of grain to these imperial cities were a modern interest (see Steele's *Hungry City*, 2008), even though Athens was not a city large enough to act as a prototype for a modern metropolis. Rome, however, was. Important studies on Athens are Gernet's *L'Approvisionnement d'Athènes en blé au V et IV siècle* (1909), Gallo's "Alimentazione et Classi Sociali" (1983), and Oliver's *War, Food and Politics in Early Hellenistic Athens* (2007); on Rome, Rickman's *The Corn Supply of Ancient Rome* (1980), Garnsey's *Famine and Food Supply in the Greco-Roman World* (1988, with bibliography), Garnsey and Rathbone's "The Background to the Grain Law of Gaius Gracchus" (1985), Erdkamp's *The Grain Market in the Roman Empire* (2005), and Alston and Van Nijf's edited volume *Feeding the Ancient Greek City* (2008, with bibliographies). Sharp's "The Food Supply in Roman Egypt" (1998) shows that much grain came to Athens and Rome from Egypt, and also from the Black Sea, North Africa, and Sicily.[17] In "The Roman Military Diet" (1971), Davies explores how the Roman army managed to deal so effectively with provisions and supplies in terrains as diverse as Egypt and the fort of Vindolanda on Hadrian's Wall in Britain.

A further important area relating to food and politics is to be found in great architecture, in particular the temples like the Parthenon mentioned earlier. These temples expressed powerful messages to the nineteenth-century European imperial powers (notably the Pergamon altar, taken to Berlin, and the "Elgin marbles," taken to London), but the sacrificial purpose of the structures has survived less clearly. The sacrificial procession is depicted on the Parthenon frieze, but the eating of meat to express religious solidarity tends to be less the focus of modern discussion than the imperial context and exquisite artwork. Power as expressed in dining rituals that distribute the meat of sacrifice (among other foods) within the ruling hierarchies is explored in Vössing's *Mensa Regia: Das Bankett beim hellenistischen König und beim römischen Kaiser* (2004), Stein-Hölkeskamp's *Das römische Gastmahl, Eine Kulturgeschichte* (2005), Donahue's *The Roman Community at Table during the Principate* (2004), Briant's *Histoire de l'Empire perse* (1996), Amigues's "Pour la table du Grand Roi" (2003), and the volume *Le Banquet du Monarque dans le Monde antique: Orient, Grèce, Rome* (forthcoming), edited by Grandjean, Hugoniot, and Lion. These studies demonstrate how the bread and circuses of Rome had a long ancestry back to Near Eastern systems of distribution based on the imperial cities of the Fertile Crescent.[18] The *prytaneion* mentioned earlier in this chapter is important in this political context also.[19]

Away from the political arena there are many discussions around species, names, and varieties of plants, animals, and foods in the ancient world. Cereals and beans were hard for Galen to identify, and the problems remain.[20] Dalby's *Food in the Ancient World from A to Z* is a good place to start for an ancient and modern bibliography on this. On plant identifications, see especially André's *Les Noms des Plantes dans Rome Antique* (1985) and Amigues's *Théophraste: Recherches sur les plantes, livre IX* (2006). Nor are foods always what they seem. Barley is most likely to be eaten not as flatbread but as "cake" or "porridge," a preparation of more or less moistness depending on how it is to be eaten. Much barley flour was mixed with water or milk, dried, and reconstituted in the winter when needed.[21] Carrots were not our orange, Afghan variety, but an apparently less tasty European variety; rice was known, but only as an exotic Asian plant. Above all, little meat appears to have been eaten, and much of that was in a ritualized fashion attached to sacrifice. This has been strongly argued for Greek practice,[22] but a similar case has been made too for Rome,[23] where many have thought the level of meat eating so high as to indicate much commercial slaughter.

The best investigations into the detail of ancient consumption combine textual evidence with archaeology. Dalby's *Siren Feasts* is a good example, as is Garnsey's *Food and Society in Classical Antiquity* (1999). Archaeological reports now include floral and faunal remains, as they once did not. The contribution of archaeology is now great. A good starting point remains Renfrew's *Palaeoethnobotany* (1973), for she establishes the idea of plants moving, specifically of the olive, the vine, and the peach moving westward into Europe, as eggplant and oranges were to do in postclassical times. Mylona's *Fish-Eating in Greece from the Fifth Century BC to the Seventh Century AD* (2008) reviews extensive evidence of fish and shellfish in texts and archaeological remains. Sparkes's "The Greek Kitchen" (1962) remains an exemplary review of the utensils and practices of the ancient kitchen, if so it can be called. His study derives from the finds in the Athenian agora excavations extensively cataloged by the American School of Archaeology. Other evidence comes from sewers, in particular those currently being investigated by the Herculaneum Conservation Project.[24]

Patterns of eating in the home depend on our understanding of houses and apartments in ancient cities.[25] In general, kitchens were not separate rooms, unlike storerooms, and cooking was often conducted outside where possible. Earlier Greek houses appear to have separated male rooms for the symposium from the women's part of the house, but the evidence can be read in many ways.[26] Public and private were not imagined in the ancient world in the same way as in the modern West. There is much material on Rome and Pompeii,[27] and the wealthy villas of the Roman elite deserve further investigation, following Dunbabin's *The Roman Banquet: Images of Conviviality* (2003), which surveys the mosaics surviving in the Roman Mediterranean. At the top end of villa culture, the imperial residence at Piazza Armerina in Sicily is instructive. In addition to the layout of the rooms, many of these buildings reflect the interior and exterior worlds of the diners in paintings and mosaics.

Further valuable images that imitate the practices of the symposium are to be found in Greek vase paintings, which are closely linked to the rituals of the occasion and poetry recited at them: see in particular Lissarrague's *Un flot d'images* (1987). The vases with images of the symposium are a small subset of all the drinking cups and mixing vessels, in which the Greeks and Romans mixed wine with water. The huge range of subjects, from daily activities like bathing and water carrying to images of Greek comedy and tragedy, illustrate what the Greeks and Romans expected to look at on their dining tables (which were normally individual tables placed beside the dining couch, for those wealthy enough to be able to afford the space and the furniture). Until recent decades, the images were much more studied than the uses of the vases, but now that sympotic studies have taken off (see the preceding on Murray's *Sympotica* and Corner's 2010 article "Transcendent Drinking: The Symposium at Sea Reconsidered"), practice and belief systems, not to mention chemical residues of wine and food in the vases, are also of interest.

The study of the symposium may be divided into social practice, the cultural place of wine, and the literature that was produced in a sympotic context. The first, imported from the Near East,[28] involved reclining on couches to eat and drink as an expression of maleness in Greek culture and hierarchy in Roman culture. This is best explored in the essays in Murray's *Sympotica* and Murray and Tecusan's *In Vino Veritas*. The symposium was a training ground for male youths to learn the values of the city, and a way for citizens, especially wealthy ones, to express their commensality. Wine served this purpose more fully than food, and the broad idea was to tread a road between sobriety and drunkenness with ritual drinking, games, and tests of skill and balance.[29] As for the cultural place of wine, Murray's edited collection, *Sympotica*, and Davidson's *Courtesans and Fishcakes* (1997) suggest that the wealthy drank in this ritual fashion, while the vast majority of the population drank either on a commercial basis, buying wine from bars, or on the basis of family networks. It does not seem likely that the majority of the ancient populations of Greek cities drank in a nonritualized fashion since so much of their lives was ritualized and subject to religious framing.[30] Wine, like meat, was consumed in forms strongly marked by ritual at a number of city festivals and presided over by the god Dionysus.[31] It is unlikely that the god who dissolved hierarchy in ancient thought reinforced it by excluding the majority of the population from ritualized drinking. As for practical matters, studies of wine production and distribution[32] and the connection between wine and wealth[33] can be matched with much local detail across the Roman Empire.

The literature of the symposium was originally the poetry of lyrics by poets such as Alcaeus and of elegiacs by poets such as Theognis.[34] These were transformed into prose forms by Plato, most notably in his brilliant *Symposium*, one of the pearls of world literature, and thenceforth into a series of literary forms, including *The Deipnosophistae* of Athenaeus and numerous works of Plutarch, which are explored in Romeri's *Philosophes entre Mots et Mets* (2002) and Whitmarsh's *Ancient Greek Literature* (2004). How later forms blended into the Christian cultures of later antiquity is explored in D. E. Smith's *From Symposium to Eucharist* (2003) and König's *Saints and Symposiasts* (forthcoming, with bibliography).

Food and wine played a large part in Greek and Roman literature, as in that of many other cultures. In Greek genres under the auspices of Dionysus, such as tragedy and comedy, wine and food are distinctive in their presence[35] and absence,[36] though tragedy embraces extremes of eating (cannibalism) in plays such as Aeschylus' *Agamemnon* and Sophocles' *Tereus*. Food and drinking are prominent in the earliest Greek literature we have, the epic poems of Homer, in which civilized values are expressed in sharing food, especially meat, and barbarity by eating one's enemy and being ignorant of the key plants of Greece, the olive and the vine. Vidal-Naquet's "Land and Sacrifice in the Odyssey" (1981) explores the eating codes of the *Odyssey* to powerful effect, and Hitch's *King of Sacrifice* (2009) the role of sacrifice in the *Iliad*. In the fourth century B.C.E., Greek cities developed a burlesque form of epic that plays up the role of fish, which was notably absent in the Homeric poems (see later). One notable example is the *Attic Dinner* of Matro;[37] another is *The Life of Luxury* of Archestratus (Europe's earliest cookbook), translated and discussed in Wilkins and Hill's *Archestratus: The Life of Luxury* (1994) and, with extensive discussion of the Greek text, in Olson and Sens's *Archestratos* (2000).

In Roman literature, meanwhile, Gowers showed in an influential study, *The Loaded Table* (1993), that food is often linked with the less grand genres of comedy, satire, and satiric poetry. *The Dinner of Trimalchio* is a satiric tour de force of Petronius,[38] with much use of colloquial Latin and humor against lower-class freedmen in the Bay of Naples, while Juvenal rehearses metropolitan grossness at table in contrast with Republican frugality. In Rome, the patrons made sure that their dependent clients knew their place at table.

The twentieth century saw prodigious advances in the study of food beyond philology and archaeology to embrace anthropology and sociology. In the latter, Nadeau studied the rituals of dining in *Les Manières de Table dans le monde gréco-romain* (2010a) after Norbert Elias and Stephen Mennell, to demonstrate that the model of Elias does not work in antiquity. Nadeau finds many processes of change but no clear development of civilized manners in ancient thought. Decline into decadence was as likely an analysis as progress in manners. In comparative anthropology, Forbes and Foxhall have shown in "*Sitometreia*: The Role of Grain as a Staple Food in Classical Antiquity" (1982) how ancient peasant farmers followed strategies for survival similar to those in twentieth-century Crete and the Peloponnese. Most powerful have been studies of anthropology in the Centre Gernet in Paris, after the work of Lévi-Strauss. Detienne and Vernant edited a series of essays entitled *La cuisine du sacrifice en pays grec* (1979) on sacrifice and the understanding of meat and cooking in antiquity. Vernant in particular shows how the early poet Hesiod presented the myth of Prometheus as a cultural paradigm in which the acquisition of fire brought agriculture, marriage, and a fatal divide between gods and mortals (a version of the Garden of Eden in Genesis). Sacrifice was thus an ambiguous blessing, not only giving humankind high-status meat from herds they tended, but also identifying their mortality in contrast with gods. The gods received the smoke and incense of sacrifice, while the human beings ate the mortal flesh and entrails. In a similar study, *Les jardins d'Adonis* (1972), Detienne contrasted the rituals of the eastern god Adonis with those of the Greek goddess Demeter. The latter brought the technology of cultivated cereals to the Greeks and festivals in her honor tried to maintain her favor over the crops. The myth of her daughter Persephone, abducted by Hades, represented the life of the corn that was buried in the soil in winter and returned as a sprouting plant in the spring. The women of the city in particular worshipped the goddess at the Thesmophoria festival with sacrifices of roast pork. She made the women, as well as the fields, fertile. In contrast to these citizen women, sex workers worshipped Adonis, the lover of Aphrodite who died in his youth. They represented his life by putting on rooftops potted herbs and spices, which wilted in the sun's heat. Detienne's structuralist analysis of female sexuality and plants works well in the context of Greek myth, but not perfectly, since dramatic texts attest citizen women worshipping Adonis. The key point is the intersection of myth, human being, plant, and animal in a single cultural system: unlike in our thought world, women could be changed into plants and rocks, gods could take on human appearance, and human beings lived in a coherent if frightening cosmos.

There are numerous other ancient theories of sacrifice with the most important being set out by Burkert in *Griechische Religion* (1977); he writes in a tradition that sees the guilt of killing an animal as a vestige of hunter-gatherer societies dating from before the agricultural revolution. Sacrifice marks out Greco-Roman identity and their relationship to eating meat. An impersonal abattoir on the edge of town was not normally their way of killing animals. In principle they shared the killing and the meat, confronting the need for such contained violence in human society. This placing of cooked meat within a cultural system of sacrifice and civilization resembles the Hippocratic account of cooking at the heart of human development and progress. It is important to know that the Hippocratic term for digestion was *pepsis*, or cooking. In Hippocratic thought, preparing food in the kitchen simply prepares food for human digestion. There is an impressive anthropological account of this in the Hippocratic text *Ancient Medicine*, chapter 3. The Hippocratic texts formed the basis for most medical thought on nutrition from 400 B.C.E. until 1850 C.E. Other culture myths explained how Dionysus brought wine from the East and how Hercules brought animals to the Greco-Roman world from an island in the Atlantic.[39]

In many respects, eating was a key mark of identity in antiquity. Fasting was known to the Greeks and Romans (at the Thesmophoria[40]), but was particularly linked with the Jews.[41] The Jews, unlike the Greeks and Romans, had many eating taboos, though the Greeks had a notion of religious pollution that might attach to foods.[42] Those most alert to taboos were vegetarians,[43] in particular the Pythagoreans and a mystery religion known as Orphism. Pythagoras was influential in philosophy, but he is known more for his mathematics and music than his vegetarianism; he had little impact on mainstream life after the fourth century B.C.E., before which Pythagorean cities may have flourished in southern Italy. Pythagoreans avoided beans and meat and belonged more clearly to a counterculture than do vegetarians in Western culture. Detienne explores purist and less pure versions of the philosophy, which determined how alternative the belief might be in the ancient city (where not eating meat meant in effect not belonging to the city). Pythagoreanism appealed to Plutarch,[44] Ovid, and the neo-Platonist Porphyry.[45]

Within less radical philosophical thought food was essential (Plato, Aristotle, Epicurus), but there was great need to restrain the desire for too much.[46] This idea was developed in the fasting regimes among early Christians awaiting Armageddon.[47]

All of these systems of belief operated against the background of the ecology of the ancient Mediterranean world, most fully explored in Hordern and Purcell's *The Corrupting Sea* (2000). This was a world of microclimates and great regional variation against which all the generalizations set out in the preceding must be judged. See, for example, Mitchell's book *Anatolia I* (1993) on Asia Minor, Cool's *Eating and Drinking in Roman Britain* (2006), and Luce's *Paysage et Alimentation dans le monde grec* (2000) on southern France. In general, the ancient Mediterranean could not sustain its population with any regularity. Garnsey's *Famine and Food Supply in the Greco-Roman World* (1988), Halstead and O'Shea's *Bad Year Economics* (1989),

Sallares's *Ecology of the Ancient Greek World* (1991), and Gallant's *Risk and Survival in Ancient Greece* (1991) all show that, outside the cities, which commanded the best food supplies, farmers and country dwellers regularly faced hunger in the spring and (according to Galen) were forced down the food chain into less desirable foods normally fed to animals. In *A Fisherman's Tale* (1984), Gallant tried to show that fish supplies were less than claimed in ancient sources, but the attempt to construct statistics from ancient evidence seems misguided. Shoals of fish appear to have arrived with varying regularity, resulting in gluts and scarcity, but with enough of the former to sustain extensive production of fish sauce, particularly in the Black Sea region and Spain.[48] Fish complemented meat as first-class protein, but meat supplies before the Roman Empire were never extensive and were tied to the demands of the sacrificial year.[49] Both meat and fish had a much larger place in the ancient imagination than is justified merely by the supply.[50]

The salting of fish and the production of fish sauce were as close as ancient food producers came to an industrial scale. But many ancient texts (such as Cato, Columella, and Pliny the Elder) give abundant technical descriptions of farming and other practices, which have been discussed in Curtis's *Ancient Food Technology* (2001), Dalby's *Cato: On Farming* (1998), and Frayn's *Subsistence Farming in Roman Italy* (1979).

Finally, a word is needed on a further technical area, the expansion of nutritional and medical studies. Galen and his Hippocratic predecessors wrote extensively on physiology and nutrition. In both *Famine and Food Supply in the Greco-Roman World* (1988) and *Food and Society in Classical Antiquity* (1999), Garnsey shows the value of Galenic materials, since in his treatise on nutrition and in a related treatise on the humors, Galen focuses on peasants and the effects of food shortages, a topic rarely addressed in other ancient texts. Poor people in the countryside tended to go hungry in the spring, as Galen observes on a number of occasions. Galen is interested in the physiological impact of foods that were eaten by necessity when peasants had too little to eat. Examples are bitter vetch, which in better times they fed to their animals, and acorns, which were suitable for pigs, but nutritious, if bitter, for human beings.[51] Once the foods were understood, the patient needed to integrate them properly into his or her daily life. Galen sets this out, predominantly for the city dweller, in his treatise on "Hygiene."[52] These studies explore the place of food in the ancient healthy diet with more sympathy to the author than is to be found in Romano's "La Dietetica di Galeno" (2000), which takes its cue from the 1931 article "Antike Diëtetik" by Edelstein, a great medical historian who, however, believed with Plato that worrying about lifestyle is a sign of a rich hypochondriac. Galen's healthy diet follows such predecessors as the author of Hippocrates *Regimen* II,[53] Mnesitheus of Athens,[54] and Diocles of Carystus.[55] The ancient material often connects with modern concerns: Gourevitch's "L'Obésité et son traitement dans le monde romain" (1985) deals with obesity, which was largely considered a disease of excess among the powerful who were unable to restrain their appetite along with all their other desires. In *Medicine and the Making of Roman Women* (2000), Flemming gives an interesting perspective on women, who, while underrepresented in Galen, are widely discussed in Hippocratic authors and Soranus of Ephesus. In *Food and Society in Classical Antiquity* (1999), Garnsey explores the incidence of modern conditions relating to malnutrition among ancient skeletons, finding that women tended to be undernourished even during pregnancy, while Griffin and colleagues, in "Inequality at Late Roman Baldock, UK: The Impact of Social Factors upon Health and Diet" (2011), have analyzed dental and other remains in the United Kingdom, discovering that those buried in Roman graves may have had better dental health and nutritional indicators than those not. A final medical note is needed on ancient drugs, the vast majority of which were based on plants and animals in more concentrated form than their equivalents as food.[56] The pharmacology of Dioscorides and the medicine of Galen were among the most influential of ancient texts from 400 C.E. right through the Renaissance until the nineteenth century.

As for future directions, work is beginning on later antiquity and the Byzantine world.[57] There is enormous potential in archaeology, including much in regional detail to add to the general picture. In two journal articles, Pitts shows, for example, that local elites in Britain followed Roman drinking practices before the invasion, after which drinking vessels became less ornate; there are developments in the Black Sea area, too, with access now to Russian and Soviet material.[58] Much too may come from zooarchaeologists such as Paul Halstead and from new techniques of chemical and other analysis. There is much in literature and in cultural studies, especially such rich bodies of work as Galen and Oribasius, where a large number of treatises are still to be translated and explored in a medical system that is based on cooking and diet. Much remains to be done on the food links between Greco-Roman culture and the peoples of the Near East.[59] This is the area that played such a vital role in domesticating plants and animals and in setting up the first city cultures in the West and Near East.

Notes

1. Archestratus, in Wilkins and Hill, 1994; Olson and Sens, 2000.
2. Dalby and Grainger, 1996; Grainger, 2006; Giacosa, 1999; Faas, 2003.
3. Mitchell, 1993; Schmitt-Pantel, 1992.
4. Donahue, 2004.
5. Details in S. Miller, 1978.
6. Aelius Aristeides, *Oration* 26 (on markets outside Rome see Frayn, 1993).
7. J. Davidson, 1997.
8. On food and identity, see further chapters by Roller, Purcell, and Wilkins in Gold and Donahue, 2005; Nadeau, 2010c; Beer, 2010.
9. Zecchini, 1989; Braund and Wilkins, 2000; Jacob, 2001.

10. König and Whitmarsh, 2007.
11. Flower and Rosenbaum, 1958; André, 1974; Grocock and Grainger, 2006.
12. Flower and Rosenbaum, 1958, 9–15; Arnott, 2000; Bancroft-Marcus, 2000.
13. See index in Riley, 2007, s.v. "Apician flavour."
14. Wissowa, 1893–1972.
15. Metcalfe, 1844; André, 1981.
16. Rotroff and Oakley, 1992.
17. On the broader ecology of the Mediterranean and shortages in food supply, see later in this chapter.
18. See Veyne, 1976.
19. Schmitt-Pantel, 1992; S. Miller, 1978.
20. Wilkins, 2007.
21. Forbes and Foxhall, 1982.
22. Detienne and Vernant, 1979.
23. Scheid, 2005.
24. M. Robinson, forthcoming.
25. Robinson and Graham, 1938, on the northern Greek city of Olynthus; Hoepfner and Schwandner, 1994, on the Piraeus; Laurence, 1994, on Pompeii; Claridge, 1999, on Rome.
26. Dalby, 1993; J. Davidson, 1997; Nadeau, 2010b.
27. Claridge, 1999; Laurence, 1994.
28. Dentzer, 1982.
29. Lissarrague, 1987.
30. Wilkins, 2000; Wilkins and Hill, 2006.
31. See the following and Seaford, 2006.
32. Tchernia, 1986.
33. Purcell, 1985.
34. Bowie, 1986; Corner, 2010.
35. For comedy, see Wilkins, 2000; Olson, 2007, 256–320.
36. For tragedy, see Wilkins, 2003.
37. See Olson and Sens, 1999.
38. See also Dupont, 1977.
39. See Seaford, 2006, on Dionysus; Burkert, 1979, on Hercules.
40. See, for example, Detienne, 1972.
41. Douglas, 1966; Beer, 2010.
42. Parker, 1983, Appendix.
43. Osborne, 2006.
44. Newmyer, 2006.
45. G. Clark, 1999.
46. Wilkins and Hill, 2006, on Epicurus, Aristotle, Plato, and the Stoics.
47. Grimm, 1996.
48. Curtis, 1991; Bekker-Nielsen, 2005.

49. Jameson, 1988; Whittaker, 1988.
50. A. Davidson, 1972, 225–27; J. Davidson, 1997; Detienne and Vernant, 1979.
51. Grant, 2000; Powell, 2003; Wilkins, forthcoming.
52. Green, 1951; Grimaudo, 2008.
53. Wilkins, 2004.
54. Bertier, 1972.
55. Van der Eijk, 2000–2001.
56. Scarborough, 2010.
57. For example, Dalby, 2010.
58. Pitts, 2008; Pitts; 2005.
59. Grandjean, Hugoniot, and Lion, forthcoming.

–2–

Food Histories of the Middle Ages

Paul Freedman

Alimentation versus Cuisine

Few aspects of medieval studies have seen as much progress in recent decades as has the field of the history of cuisine. Not the most important evidence of accomplishment, but at least worth mentioning, is that a number of common myths have been effectively disposed of—that Marco Polo brought pasta to Italy from China[1] or (the most venerable fable) that spices were used to cover up the taste of spoiled meat.[2] More broadly, scholars have provided vastly more information than previously available about cookbooks, diet in relation to social class and representation, regional variation and everyday life, and material culture. This is the result of the efforts of medievalists, many of whom came to the history of cuisine through literature or social history. Beyond the achievements of individuals, progress in medieval food history is also related to shifts in the perception of cuisine and its importance and implications.

As with other periods covered in this volume, the study of food has changed as the history of cuisine ceased to be considered a mere epiphenomenon or hobby interest. Looking at medieval recipes, cookbooks, or dining was once regarded by professional historians with contempt as a type of "boudoir history," on the order of the study of past fashions, or furniture, and so regarded as fundamentally unserious. Cuisine was in the same specialized or amateur category as weapons and heraldry. Baron Jérôme Pichon, an enthusiastic nineteenth-century antiquarian, edited two of the most important medieval French cookbooks[3] as well as treatises on hunting, falconry, and heraldic devices. In the case of the Middle Ages there was a special variety of dismissiveness about a professional interest in cuisine because medieval food seemed particularly bizarre and alien—the recipes reeking of spices, banquets featuring showy birds such as peacocks and herons, or intimidating and unlikely sorts of game animals.

There are two incorrect popular ideas about medieval food that can be regarded as either contradictory or complementary. On the one hand medieval meals are supposed to have been primitive in content and style, relying on roasted animals eaten with the hands in the most unceremonious (i.e., barbarian) ways. The film *Becket* (1964) depicts the court of Henry II tearing apart meat in a style little different from portrayals of the camp of Attila the Hun. The courteous and relatively cultivated Becket shows the king some forks he has ordered from France, and they agree this is a useless if interesting fashion, for why avoid getting your hands dirty when they can be washed as easily as a fork? Needless to say these scenes are inaccurate in several ways, from the chronology of the fork's arrival to a misunderstanding of medieval manners.

The other prevalent notion of medieval cuisine is the reverse: that it was fatiguingly ceremonial and elaborate, and the dishes more or less inedible, not by reason of crudity, but because of the primacy given to appearance, spices, exoticness, and barren ostentation. The antiquarian Alfred Franklin in the late nineteenth century had his chef prepare a dish from the cookbook of Taillevent and then lamented that the medieval chef's master, the prudent and intelligent King Charles V, should have partaken of such "abominable ragoûts."[4] The author of a book written eighty years ago devoted to festive meals asserted that the dishes served at medieval banquets ranged from merely "unpalatable" to "revolting."[5] Similar reputational problems of vulgar and unappetizing luxury afflict Roman cuisine, especially in cinematic representations.

Since the 1970s, however, culinary historians have shown that medieval cuisine had complexity, subtlety, variety, and a particular aesthetic sensibility. Although medieval taste differed from that of the modern era, the Middle Ages represent a substantial culinary historical period, not to be regarded as either impoverished or absurdly elaborate.

Attention to the social importance of medieval cuisine is not the same thing as recognizing that it had a more appealing set of characteristics, but the two developments, which are of crucial importance for understanding what has happened over the past forty years, are related. To examine what medieval cuisine really was and to try to understand the often brief or telegraphic style of recipe instructions, one has to believe that the enterprise amounts to more than mere historical recreation. Cuisine had to emerge as an acknowledged field of investigation with significance for the history of everyday life (including material culture) and the history of *mentalités.*

These two tendencies, daily life and mental outlooks, which in the late twentieth century were prominently identified with the *Annales* school, have a separate but interrelated historiography as regards medieval cuisine. The *Annaliste* approach to the history of ordinary people and interest in all aspects of life in society from the start encouraged investigation into problems of food supply, production, and distribution with particular attention to diet, nutrition, and famines.[6] Odile Redon and Bruno Laurioux distinguish between research on basic food necessities, which constitute the "histoire de l'alimentation," and investigation of the cooking styles and preferences of those with sufficient affluence to have some choice in the matter, "histoire de la cuisine."[7] The first was always an eminently respectable topic; its significance was enhanced by the program of the *Annales* to give attention to the bottom 90 percent of the social hierarchy. Studies of the fragility of the food supply or the difficulty of obtaining adequate nutrition were among the most important sections of grand historical syntheses of premodern life emphasized by historians of the Middle Ages, notably Marc Bloch, as well as early modernists, Pierre Goubert, for example, and modern historians such as Eugene Weber.[8] The struggle to obtain adequate yields from crops and the background to the economic and demographic growth of the eleventh to thirteenth centuries are at the center of the work on social and economic history by Georges Duby.[9] The arrival of the Great Famine of 1315–1317 and the Black Death of 1348–1349 have often been viewed in terms of Malthusian problems of population versus food supply: that these crises were related to population growth outstripping the agricultural technological limits of the time, thus weakening health and resistance to disease. In what follows, we begin with the food consumed by the majority of medieval people and then pass on to the preferences of the more privileged, but without seeing tastes and class structure as divided in an absolute manner, any more than is the case in most other historical societies.

The Diet of Ordinary People

Considerable attention has been given to the standard of living of peasants and the lesser sorts of townspeople, and although the information certainly supports the image of medieval life as a constant and anxious struggle for adequate nutrition, the actual diet seems to have been a bit more varied and a little less threatened by circumstance than was thought in the 1960s and 1970s. In an almost luridly grim account of famines and ordinary near-starvation, Piero Camporesi emphasized the extremities to which peasants were reduced in times of dearth to try and obtain some sort of nourishment from rotten, dubious, poisonous, or unpleasant products of the darker side of the natural world. Humble black bread represents a nearly blissful condition according to the images obtained mostly from literature and chronicles.[10] Studies of material culture and of the objects and practices of everyday life (*Alltagsgeschichte*) have modified the image of medieval life as uniformly frightful. A book by Ernst Schubert synthesizes a considerable body of recent German scholarship that shows the difficulty of supplying food to an expanding population, but also the effective mobilization of resources and the diversity of products grown, caught, herded, processed, and distributed. The economy required that 80 percent of the population be involved in the production of food, but what is more characteristic of the period than scarcity as such was how different the food that we think familiar would have been. For example, medieval pigs would have seemed closer to wild boars than the pigs we have today.[11]

Christopher Dyer poses the question of basic nutrition rather clearly in an essay entitled "Did the Peasants Really Starve in Medieval England"; his answer is basically that under normal conditions they did not, although the English peasant's lot may have been better than that of his continental contemporaries.[12] Dyer has worked on diet and overall standards of living, and his findings, based on estate accounts as well as charitable establishments, tend to be more optimistic than the once-prevailing orthodoxy.[13] While it was formerly considered an established fact that peasants almost never ate meat, its presence in the diet of the rural population is now accepted.

Above all, it is through advances in archaeology that medievalists have a better idea of what was eaten and what the conditions of life were. Techniques in analyzing organic matter through stable isotopes are just starting to allow us to have a sense of what people ate and where it came from. Impressive progress has been made in archaeo-zoology (animal remains) and paleobotany (fossilized or preserved plants and pollen). Recent studies for medieval England and France reflect some of these developments.[14] Archaeology, material culture, and an anthropological approach to the service and consumption of food are interrelated, and among the examples of this melding of technical and cultural approaches is the proceedings of a conference held at Sens, France, in 2004 that encompassed both the matter and mental aspects of cuisine.[15]

Salted herring and chicken were eaten by all segments of society,[16] but clearly the food of the rich was superior in variety, freshness, and most certainly ostentation. Persons with the means to decide among many options what they wished to consume selected according to a set of culturally conditioned taste preferences. Basic aspects of what can be termed a medieval aesthetic include the widespread use of aromatic products, a liking for both sweet and sour, attention to color, an overwhelmingly protein diet (meat, game, fish), the importance of sauces, and a fondness for elaboration in both cooking methods and number of ingredients. All these tendencies are evident in the substantial evidence provided by medieval cookbooks that, by their very nature, are designed to serve those who can select what they want to eat. In a society in which basic subsistence is often a challenge for the majority of the population, cookbooks are in themselves a luxury product.

Cookbooks

It is a long way from assessments of the life of the masses to the passion for color and trompe l'oeil in cooking for aristocratic tables, or so it seemed until recently. The perceived importance of cookbooks has been enhanced by their significance for the history of daily life and the way in which they contribute to an understanding of the mental outlook of the late Middle Ages—the relation between taste and culture.

True, there had always been a certain historical interest in cookbooks as an unusual philological resource, or in medieval treatises on service at table and descriptions of particular banquets for their ceremonial aspects. Antiquarian studies of private life in the Middle Ages often included sections on the culinary tastes of the upper classes.[17] For England there is a venerable tradition of inquiry into "curious" cooking texts, notably the first printed edition of the principal medieval English cookbook, known as *The Forme of Cury* (1789), and the short works collected in Warner's *Antiquitates Culinariae* of 1791.[18] In a nineteenth-century assortment of materials on the education of children and the teaching of manners, Frederick Furnivall included a number of recipes and dietaries. He also offered the fifteenth-century "Booke of Kervynge," which gives directions on how to cut up and serve various sorts of game and fish.[19] This and other materials related to cooking and cuisine were published because of their philological, quasi-literary, and antiquarian value.

Medieval cookbooks were written, for the most part, by cooks who were court employees in the service of kings or other rulers. It is not usually specifically clear to whom they were addressed, but of course it is certain that they were intended for a professional audience of other cooks and in some cases aristocratic patrons. The authors of the French *Viandier*, the English *Forme of Cury*, or the Catalan *Libre del coch* served royal masters, and these books show the practice of grand kitchens at a particular time and place. The instructions assume enough knowledge of organizing a large kitchen so that amounts and detailed steps are usually omitted.

The cookbooks are practical manuals, therefore, but they assume that the ultimate consumer of the recipes will be someone who lives on a grand scale. Not all cookbooks, however, address only the most rarefied social space. The 400 recipes included in the book known as the *Menagier de Paris* (ca. 1390) show the tastes of a man of easy circumstances but no great rank He derives some of his recipes from the *Viandier* but offers comments, modifications, and glosses that prove this was not a mere aspirational "coffee-table book" *avant la lettre*.[20] There are other relatively modest (from a social aspect) treatises such as most of the short manuscripts that include recipes designed for the use of ecclesiastical or petty noble establishments.[21]

There are some 150 cookbook manuscripts that survive in European libraries.[22] On the one hand, this is an impressive number given the seemingly ephemeral or at least plebian nature of these works, which were mostly intended as a kind of aide-mémoire for professional cooks. On the other hand, there are more medieval manuscripts extant of one text, John Mandeville's fictitious travels (300), than of all cookbooks combined. Most of the cookbooks are from the fifteenth century although the most famous, the aforementioned *Forme of Cury* and the *Viandier* (attributed to Taillevent), were composed in the late fourteenth century. There is nothing between the short treatise of Anthimus in sixth-century Gaul and the latter part of the thirteenth century.[23]

There are a few works for which more than one manuscript exists, but every manuscript has different contents with pieces added or subtracted and different associated texts. Medieval books were not, as is usually the case now, single works between one set of covers but rather varied collections of different but nevertheless (in the compiler's mind) associated texts. Thus, medieval cookbooks tend to be bound with medical and dietary treatises, an indication of an implied intellectual coherence. The largest number of surviving cookbooks is from Germany and the Low Countries, followed by England. France and Italy have fewer such records than one might expect, but to some extent this may be related to accidents of preservation rather than the total number of cookbooks that might once have existed.[24]

Immense progress has been made in presenting these difficult texts, but the majority remain unprinted.[25] In some cases there are modern editions of previously inaccurately edited works. Constance Hieatt and Sharon Butler have carefully edited *The Forme of Cury* (first published in the eighteenth century) and its family of related cookery books.[26] Hieatt has also produced several new editions of English cookbooks that considerably advance our understanding of their contents and inter-relationship.[27] Terence Scully has provided the text of the *Viandier* based on its complex manuscript tradition.[28] Additionally, Scully has made available editions and translations of the magnificently elaborate recipes of Master Chiquart, chef for the Duke of Savoy, and of a Neapolitan cookbook, a unique fifteenth-century manuscript in the Morgan Library (New York) from the late fifteenth century.[29]

Advances in understanding Italian medieval gastronomy and editions of cookbooks have been described by Benporat, Laurioux, and others, and considerable attention has been given to the close relation as well as contrasts between medieval and Renaissance Italian culinary tastes and practices.[30] The southern Italian cookbook tradition, exemplified by Scully's 2000 edition of the Morgan Library manuscript, was influenced by Catalan texts as the kings of Naples in the latter part of the fifteenth century were either simultaneously the rulers of Aragon-Catalonia or branches of that dynasty. The influence of the Catalan *Libre de sent soví* is discernible in the Neapolitan collection that also drew on the recently discovered text of a fourteenth-century treatise, *De apereylar be de meyjar.*[31] The Neapolitan cookbook in turn seems to have had a role in the composition of the Catalan *Libre del coch* by Mestre Robert, chef to King Ferrante of Naples. The *Libre del coch* was printed in Catalan and translated into Castilian, and was probably the most influential cookbook in Renaissance Spain.[32] The two major Catalan treatises have received modern editions.[33]

In the German-speaking world, increased knowledge of cookbooks has been more continuous and less concentrated solely on recent years. The best-known German cookbook, the *Buch von guter Speise*, was the object of a scholarly edition in 1865 as well as a new edition (and English translation) in 2000.[34] Trude Ehlert has done notable work in bringing together German medieval recipes and in editing short and previously unknown or little-known manuscript texts.[35]

Medieval Cuisine and Social Distinction: Literature and Anthropology

The evidence afforded by the cookbooks shows medieval taste in cuisine and the importance of spectacle and presentation. Color, elaborate forms of service, and the hierarchical arrangement of guests were all necessary components not only of aristocratic dining but also of the customs of the merely affluent. The ceremonial of medieval banqueting has received attention as a type of performance since the pathbreaking work of Johan Huizinga. Tableaux performed at the great Burgundian court celebrations, such as the Feast of the Pheasant in 1454, show a grave blend of culinary spectacle, piety, and grandeur. At this particular event, vows to liberate conquered Constantinople were made in the name of the pheasant, a featured dish of the banquet, in the way one might swear an oath on the Bible or a sword. This is an example of life imitating art since the custom of making solemn promises on cooked birds was established by the fourteenth-century chivalric romances *Les Voeux du Paon* (a peacock) and *Le Voeu du Héron* (a heron).[36] Huizinga communicated a sense of the social hierarchical and aesthetic significance of court ceremony, pageantry, games, and vows discernible in both chronicle and literature.

Both comical and chivalric literature are revealing about the social values placed on food of different sorts. There is an immense satiric literature about peasants, and presentations of their comical lowliness included stylized beliefs about what they ate. Two themes were emphasized: the coarseness of their food and their greediness. French short comical stories (*fabliaux*), German carnival plays, and other peasant satires showed peasants eating disgusting food, or consuming grotesque quantities of food and drink with unpleasant consequences.[37] The courtly class, by contrast, was impelled by spiritual rather than the lower physical appetites. In romances the knights seem to take no interest in food, compared to their pursuit of honor and love. When they do dine, however, the ceremonial aspects are impeccable, and the meals reflect an upper-class preference for game and spices.

As with any historical period, medieval fiction requires a certain amount of scene-setting and revelation of character that is evoked by describing meals, table manners, conversation, or the dining utensils and paraphernalia, so that, for example, we learn about Lancelot and Perceval as they partake of elegant meals at the mysterious castles they visit in the romances of Chrétien de Troyes. In some cases the food itself conveys symbolic meaning; elsewhere, eating habits are indications of moral standing.[38] Culinary luxury is a sign of princely power in literary and artistic works. In the *Très Riches Heures* of the Duke of Berry, the month of January is given over to feasting. The duke is appropriately served at a lavish table with gold and silver accoutrements, and he is welcoming guests who have just dismounted from their horses. Actual eagerness for culinary sensation, as opposed to dignified performance, however, is a sign of weakness inappropriate in persons of high rank. Satires of the clergy frequently associated them with gourmandise as well as sexual license.[39]

Even more than literary studies, the discipline of anthropology has allowed cuisine to be brought to the attention of historians unaccompanied by awkward trappings of elitism or antiquarianism. Beginning in the 1970s, what people ate was perceived as important in terms of the mental as well as physical structures of everyday life and the culture of a period and place of civilization. Foodways became as significant in the opinion of historians as the more established relation between environment and subsistence. The anthropological approach to food choices has highlighted the symbolic import of religious rules, manners, and the sense of what was deemed good to eat and what was not.[40] The anthropologist Sidney Mintz showed how the taste for sugar encouraged the growth of slavery in the New World, thus linking a seemingly frivolous European fashion for sugar in drinks such as coffee, tea, and chocolate to cataclysmic historical shifts.[41] Mintz has subsequently remarked that the significance of food as a dimension of human consciousness makes it inexcusable to omit it from the study of human behavior, acts, and attitudes.[42]

In 1970, Louis Stouff's exhaustive and original work on food and provisioning in Provence bridged the artificial divide between discussions of subsistence versus dining by looking at markets and the food supply from several social perspectives.[43] But the greatest progress was made by medievalists who regarded food as a marker of social class and identity. Massimo Montanari wrote about the food of the peasantry and subsequently about food as an expression of social distinction.[44] A colloquium entitled *Manger et boire au Moyen Âge*, held at Nice, France, in 1982, was explicitly oriented around the social symbolism of dining and the manner in which the dominant classes demonstrated their superiority through the type of food they ate and the way it was served and consumed.[45] An extensive discussion of the relation between class and consumption, structured in terms of both standards of living and cultural symbolism, was set out in a doctoral thesis by Allen Grieco in 1987.[46] In Barcelona, Antoni Riera i Melis looked at the culinary tastes and opportunities of different orders of society in several essays, culminating with a comprehensive survey in 1997.[47]

These works demonstrate the difference between the diets of the rich and the poor in terms of such basic distinctions as the consumption of cereals (white wheat bread versus bread from other grains or various kinds of pottage) or the amount and variety of meat available to the wealthy. Beyond contrasts in the quality and quantity of food, determinations about what was considered prestigious or lowly depended on expense or exoticness (such as spices) but also reflected theories of nature and the chain of being, whereby the literal position relative to earth and sky gave a social coloration to foods. Thus, underground bulbs (onions, garlic) or root vegetables (turnips, carrots) were beneath fruit from trees; water birds were lower, hence less desirable, than small soaring songbirds such as larks or ortolans.[48] Whole categories of food were associated with the peasantry and so considered largely beyond the legitimate repertoire of aristocratic consumption: porridge, vegetables, and dairy products. Some movement or sophistication was possible; thus wheat porridge (frumenty) was a standard banquet item when served with venison; cheese became fashionable in the late Middle Ages, culminating in the composition of an entire treatise on cheese by Pantaleone da Confienza.[49]

Spices: An Aspect of Aristocratic Taste

Spices were the clearest indication of high social status in dining as well as perhaps the best-known trait of medieval cuisine, one that distinguishes it from modern European food habits. Disgust for the (supposedly) indiscriminate use of excessive quantities of spices characterizes the works of French culinary reformers of the seventeenth century, for example, the cookbook author known as L.S.R., and was the object of satire in Boileau's play of 1665 *Le repas ridicule*, where the nouveau riche host boasts of having all the dishes scented with nutmeg.[50] The medieval passion for spices is also sometimes exaggerated by modern writers eager to show the barbaric splendor and excessive ostentation of the Middle Ages.[51]

Constance Hieatt and Sharon Butler have tried to prove that this picture is wrong and that medieval recipes call for very little more in the way of spices than modern ones.[52] This goes a bit too far in the direction of normalizing medieval cooking. In fact, the use of spices *was* quite considerable, and there was an infatuation with sharp and piquant flavors. What recent research suggests is not so much the large quantities of spices used in recipes or served at fancy meals as three facets of their popularity: (1) the variety of spices (well over twenty in common use), (2) the fact that they were combined, creating a spectrum of flavor, and (3) their ubiquity across the menu, so they were not limited to one part of the meal. Galangal (a Thai and Indochinese condiment related to ginger), cubeb (a peppery Indian spice), and grains of paradise (a sharp reddish African spice), all now unknown to Western cuisines, were common in medieval recipes. Aromatic perfume substances such as ambergris or musk were also used in the preparation of food and special flavored wines.[53] The frequency of spices in medieval cookbooks has been demonstrated by several exhaustive tables drawn by Laurioux, which show in sum that spices appear in 75 percent of recipes, around 90 percent for those from England.[54] They were particularly notable in confections and after-dinner sweet preparations that had a medicinal and ceremonial, as well as gastronomic, distinction.[55]

Studies have also demonstrated how the culinary allure of spices was enhanced by considerations of medicine as well as the general appeal of the exotic products of Asia.[56] The prestige of the East and the seemingly alien nature of cuisine of the Middle Ages in relation to modern European or American food make it appear as if the taste of medieval Europe must have been substantially influenced by the cuisine of the Islamic (Arab and Persian) civilizations and, behind them, that of India. The use of spices is only one of a number of apparent characteristics shared by Middle Eastern and medieval European cuisine that have since passed out of use in the West: rose water and other scented effects, dried fruit in main courses, the use of lemons and almond milk.[57] In addition, the creation of the aforementioned spice combinations would seem to derive from what remain to this day Middle Eastern and Indian culinary aesthetics and practices. Modern European cuisine uses spices singly, if at all, as with saffron in modern *risotto Milanese*. Herbs can be combined (as in bouquet garni or the now-ubiquitous "herbes de Provence"), but herbs survived the eclipse of their more piquant imported Asian cousins.

The nature of external influence on European gastronomy in the Middle Ages has been controversial. Evidence against the seemingly intuitive Islamic origin of European tastes includes the Roman propensity for spices (so that European preferences in this regard antedate the expansion of the Arabs) and the difficulty of tracing particular dishes from Arab or Persian sources into European recipes. Even when such recipes refer to something as "Saracen" or give a Europeanized version of an Arab word (English *mawmenee* derived from the Arab *ma'mūniyya*), the dish is unrelated to anything actually made in North Africa or the East.[58] One can agree with van Winter's estimation that the cuisine of medieval Europe was "inspired by Arab example but never subdued by it."[59]

At any rate, whatever the degree of Arab influence, direct or indirect, recent research has made it clear that medieval cuisine was not a single set of recipes or principles but more complex and varied than could be explained with reference to a single European standard followed rigorously by chefs everywhere. Just as a simple "diffusionist" theory whereby culinary taste traveled from the Islamic Middle East into Europe is not tenable, so it is also no longer thought that all trends and standards were born in France or that the single cookbook, the *Viandier*, is the greatest authority and the source of most other texts. As with certain forms of art, such as Gothic architecture, or courtly conventions, such as heraldry, there was what can be considered an international style, but beginning with Jean-Louis Flandrin's questions about the supposed generalization of taste throughout Europe, there has grown up an appreciation of the great variety of regional inflections.[60] There were distinctions in spice preferences, so that the French vogue for grains of paradise was only feebly imitated elsewhere, while England was particularly devoted to mace as opposed to the popularity of nutmeg elsewhere. There was also a division among European regions as to cooking fat. In the later Middle Ages butter came to prominence in parts of northwestern Europe, making more complicated an earlier contrast between pork fat and olive oil.[61] From the twelfth to fifteenth centuries the characteristic cuisines of Italy, Germany, France, Spain, and Britain became more clearly distinct.[62] One can see the changes that standard dishes experienced as they traveled through medieval Europe, so that galantine, which is usually thought of as a jellied preparation, was more of a cold ragout in Italy, but in France it could mean jelly or aspic. In Germany it was a jelly but sugared, whereas the other versions tended to be sharp and spicy.[63]

Medicine

In addition to giving a sense of the complexity of medieval cuisine with regard to geography, the last decades of research have complicated the picture of medieval culinary practices in relation to medicine. Medicine and diet are always intertwined, and often, as is the case today, the pleasure taken in eating can be regarded as antithetical to good health. Greek and Islamic medicine emphasized the importance of a proper diet, but specific advice varied depending on the physical type of the patient, especially in terms of his or her humoral balance or lack of equilibrium. The four humors (phlegmatic, choleric, melancholic, and sanguine) were tendencies ("complexions") favored by individuals and were influenced by the elemental properties of food (cold vs. hot, moist vs. dry). Thus certain foods were dangerous or helpful depending on a person's temperament as well as conditions of life, age, sex, and social status (how much physical labor was performed, for example). There was undoubtedly a substantial element of Islamic medicine, especially with the reception of the *Canon* of Avicenna, but also a preexisting and elaborate European reworking of the common inheritance of Galenic and Hippocratic approaches to dietary norms. Spices were deemed effective in tempering foods such as fish and many kinds of meat that tended to be humorally too cold and moist, as most spices were, to varying degrees, hot and dry. Recent research affords a greater appreciation of the details and intricacy of medical ideas about cooking and the implications of the medieval physiology of digestion and excretion for the order of courses and progression of the meal.

There is also debate as to how seriously to take the expressed intentions of cookbooks to incorporate medical advice. Cookbooks usually included recipes for invalids or healthful restoratives, although the latter could be spectacular and seemingly beyond the bounds of mere simple, nutritious food, as with Chiquart's chicken broth simmered with precious jewels.[64] The prefaces to cookbooks often claimed that physicians had been consulted as it was put together. Some authorities on medieval cookery assert that medieval culinary practice was substantially affected, even determined, by medical opinion.[65] Others see a lesser influence, with the doctors playing a role similar to today: advising about diet, scolding even, but not directly affecting recipes.[66]

Future Lines of Research

Because it is a relatively new field of serious inquiry, the study of medieval cuisine still requires basic work in the editing of texts, including not only the many cookbook manuscripts still only lightly explored but also a considerable medical and pharmaceutical literature related to diet and health. The iconography of food has been looked at more closely for the early modern period with its artistic predilections for domestic scenes, still lifes, and illustrated social commentary than for the Middle Ages. Because food appears everywhere, its very ubiquity makes it often unnoticed. In scenes of nativities, for example, the mother after delivery is sometimes brought chicken to help her recuperate.[67]

The depiction of peasants in artistic and literary compositions has been examined with regard to festivities such as the popular genre of peasant weddings.

These show a combination of festivity and brawling characteristic of a late medieval and early modern typology summarized by the common use of the word "Bruegelian," but with particular emphasis on sausages (often with dogs running away with strings of them) and vomiting.[68] The great feasts of the waning Middle Ages have long attracted attention, but the analysis of household accounts and other evidence of more routine high-end dining is a promising and only slightly exploited field.

The methodological advances afforded by new techniques in archaeology, which allow for the analysis of organic matter, will show not only the nature of diets but also the movement of products. Traditional excavation is also uncovering evidence of trade patterns in the Viking era as well as the significance of Egyptian ports for the Roman Empire's trade in spices or its devotion to *garum* (fermented fish paste) and how that massive production and commerce were organized.

There is a need for more exploration of the symbolic import of food and its deployment to describe hierarchy and character but also, at the same time, what was eaten. Basic aspects of medieval consumption and taste are only beginning to be adequately appreciated. As progress is made in separating out food mythology from fact, more can be done with fields adjacent to the study of culinary history, especially the history of medicine, diet, and the social fashioning of medical anxieties related to food. Wine, for example, is intimately connected with both the history of gastronomy and the history of medicine, and very basic work is still needed to assess its impact in both areas.[69]

Medieval cuisine remains rather alien to contemporary tastes. Even in this era of multiple food trends and historical recreations it is hard to imagine many serious restaurants trying on a sustained level to reproduce upper-class meals of the Middle Ages. Medieval food is strange according to modern aesthetics, labor-intensive, and hard to make. Yet if such a movement, with a modest degree of authenticity, ever did achieve even limited success, it would mark a major step in the reception of this peculiar legacy.

Notes

1. Blue, 1991.
2. Riley, 1993, 1–6.
3. Taillevent, 1892; *Menagier de Paris*, 1846.
4. Franklin, 1894, as cited by Laurioux, 1997a, 74, and Laurioux, 1997b, 8–9.
5. Mead, 1931, 53, 55.
6. Flandrin and Montanari, 1999, 4.
7. Redon and Laurioux, 2003. This is a historiographical conceit and not a reflection of historical reality. With regard to the latter, Laurioux, 1997b, 12–13, labels the distinction "une fausse alternative."

8. Bloch, 1964, 1:241–54; Goubert, 1960, 25–67; Goubert, 1991, 47–52; Weber, 1976, 130–45.
9. Duby, 1962; Duby, 1973.
10. Camporesi, 1989.
11. Schubert, 2006.
12. Dyer, 1998.
13. Dyer, 1983; Dyer, 1989.
14. Alexandre-Bidon, 2005; Woolgar et al., 2006.
15. Ravoir and Dietrich, 2009.
16. Schubert, 2006, 120–25, 134–36.
17. Belgrano, 1875, 151–79; Franklin, 1894; Frati, 1900.
18. Pegge, 1780; Warner, 1791.
19. Furnivall, 1868.
20. *Menagier de Paris*, 1981.
21. So, for example, two Anglo-Norman texts edited by Hieatt and R. Jones, 1986, and another pair of English recipe collections edited by Austin, 1888.
22. For cookbook manuscripts see Laurioux, 1997a; Laurioux, 1997b.
23. Laurioux, 2005, 37–55.
24. Laurioux, 1997a, 33, 54.
25. Hieatt et al., 1992; Laurioux, 1997b, 65–69.
26. Hieatt and Butler, 1985.
27. Hieatt and R. Jones, 1986; Hieatt, 1988; Hieatt, 1996, 54–71.
28. Taillevent, 1988.
29. Chiquart, 1986; Scully, 2000.
30. Benporat, 1996; Laurioux, 1996; Flandrin and Redon, 1981.
31. Borau, 1995.
32. Scully, 2000, 25.
33. Grewe, 2004; Leimgruber, 1996.
34. Birlinger, 1865; Adamson, 2000.
35. Ehlert, 1991; Ehlert, 1996a, 135–81; Ehlert, 1999; Ehlert, 2000.
36. Huizinga, 1954, 84–93. See also Lafortune-Martel, 1984.
37. G. Jones, 1960, 78–86; R. Adams, 1986; Freedman, 1999, 147–50.
38. Guerreau-Jalabert, 1992, 561–94; Haro Cortés, 2010.
39. Santucci, 1984; Hyvernat-Pou, 1984; Planche, 1984.
40. Flandrin and Montanari, 1999, 6.
41. Mintz, 1985.
42. Quoted in an article in the *Los Angeles Times* (Scott, 1993).
43. Stouff, 1970.
44. Montanari, 1979; Montanari, 1988.
45. Menjot, 1984.
46. Grieco, 1987.
47. Riera i Melis, 1991, 9–62; Riera i Melis, 1995–1996; Riera i Melis, 1997.

48. Grieco, 1992, 308–12.
49. Naso, 1990.
50. Pinkard, 2009, 126; Delaveau, 1987, 160.
51. Laurioux, 1983, 15.
52. Hieatt and Butler, 1997, xiii.
53. Laurioux, 2005, 209–11.
54. Laurioux, 2005, 160–65, 170–71.
55. Boockmann, 1996.
56. Freedman, 2008, 76–103.
57. Peterson, 1980; Heine, 1994a.
58. Laurioux, 2005, 306–35.
59. van Winter, 2007, 85.
60. Flandrin, 1981; Flandrin, 1984.
61. Laurioux, 2005, 338, 346–48.
62. Adamson, 2002.
63. van Winter, 2007, 67–71.
64. Scully, 1992; Chiquart, 1986, 98–99.
65. Taillevent, 1988, 20–35.
66. Laurioux, 1993, 136–43; van Winter, 2007, 341–54.
67. For example, in the Catalan Gothic altarpiece depicting the life of St. John the Baptist at the parish church of Sant Llorenç de Morunys, Elizabeth receives a dish of chickens after giving birth to the future St. John. Riu, 1999.
68. Moxey, 1989, 35–66; Vandenbroeck, 1984.
69. See now Jaboulet-Vercherre, 2011.

–3–

Food among the Historians:
Early Modern Europe

Kyri W. Claflin

Writing about the history of food is not new, the "food historian" is, along with the welcome extended by academic historians to well-researched history that focuses on food. Food historians can look to predecessors in early modern Europe: Jean Bruyérin-Champier in the sixteenth century, P.J.B. Le Grand d'Aussy in the eighteenth century, and Alfred Franklin in the nineteenth century, to take only the most exemplary.[1] Still, as historians of food are aware, the acceptance of this field of study in today's universities took a long time. Indeed, researchers in other fields (for example, women's history and environmental history) have made similar observations of their time spent in the academic "wilderness" when their chosen subjects did not merit serious consideration.[2]

Although historians study change, a survey of historiographical literature shows that we usually find it hard to accept something new in our own backyard. Twentieth- and twenty-first-century historiography demonstrates that it raises considerable discord in our discipline when new fields of history try to move into the mainstream of historical practice. As historian Natalie Zemon Davis observed, "When we debate what the subjects and methods of history should be we are usually debating at the same time what the shape of the historical community should be and where we stand in it."[3] With these words in mind I look to determine this shape, to explore the major trends and themes that have engaged the early modern food-historical community, and to ascertain where food history stands in relation to history in general.

Where We Have Come From

The emergence and growth of social history, the parent field of food history, is a story that illuminates how far we have come. In 1928, Eileen Power, professor of economic and social history at the London School of Economics (LSE), published what might be the first contribution to the history of food by an academic historian. Entitled *The Goodman of Paris*, it was the first English translation of a late fourteenth-century French cookbook and household manual, *Le Ménagier de Paris*.

In 1928, social history was not completely new, but it certainly was not mainstream in Europe or the United States. It was emerging primarily in the works of economic historians of agriculture and rural society.[4]

The socioeconomic history pioneered in the early decades of the twentieth century broke with the traditional history on which the historical profession had been founded in the nineteenth-century university. Professional "scientific" history was political history as represented in official documents and in the words and deeds of great men. However, economic historians, many with established connections to the LSE, witnessed the pernicious effects on working-class families brought on by industrialization. They were inspired to examine contemporary social questions by looking at social conditions in the past, and they did so by drawing on ideas from sociology, the science of society.

Eileen Power and R. H. Tawney were leading figures at the LSE. With them, colleagues and students wrote early socioeconomic history as well as the first women's history within an academic setting.[5] In France during this same period, economic historians Marc Bloch and Lucien Febvre were similarly inspired by sociology and new German historical writing to introduce the social into their study of history.[6] Power's subject, medieval nunneries, and Bloch's, medieval agrarian society, and the research interests of their colleagues and students used sociologically inflected historical research to address concerns of the current day.[7] As European scholars' socialist or Marxist political leanings made them acutely aware of the socioeconomic inequities of industrial capitalism, studying medieval society offered insight into how a different set of social organizing principles had manifested itself in everyday life.

The founding in 1926 of the Economic History Society and the *Economic History Review* reflected the many social questions posed by British historians. Power and Tawney animated the Society and the *Review* from the start. In France, socioeconomic history was established around the journal *Annales d'histoire économique et sociale*, which Bloch and Febvre founded in 1929. Their colleagues and students later came to be called "the *Annales* school" of history. From the 1920s to the 1940s social questions abounded in economic history with a primary focus on the medieval and early modern periods. As Natalie Davis notes, both Bloch and Power "were innovators and reformers."[8] Women were numerous and influential in socioeconomic history in Britain, but as Maxine Berg writes, when their presence in the profession declined, so did the memory of their achievements.[9] In France, socioeconomic history was close to a men-only club from the start. In Germany and the United States, a handful of women scholars were writing on material culture and women's economic conditions. Women's studies and food studies have rediscovered some of their work.[10]

The inroads of social history in Britain, France, Germany, and the United States—with dedicated scholars writing in specialized journals and monographs—marked a turning point. Historical attention turned to common people and everyday life. What is notable about these beginnings is that social history has both founding mothers as well as founding fathers. Inexplicably, the early women scholars have been left out of the subsequent historiographical writing on social history and food history.[11] It is time to restore them to the story.

In subsequent decades social historians occupied an increasing number of places at history department tables. Socioeconomic historians found a more welcoming atmosphere in European universities than in the United States. The early close ties forged by Power and Bloch between the British and French economic historians exploring social topics remained strong. Tawney's *Economic History Review* regularly featured work by French historians as well as reviews of French monographs. Bloch and Febvre reciprocated in the *Annales.* The wide range of socioeconomic studies of the 1940s, 1950s, and 1960s pioneered quantitative methodology in social history. From the early decades of socioeconomic history, British historians of the early modern period studied demographics, agricultural history, commodity price fluctuations, and long-term changes in trade and markets. French historians were concerned with social structures of religion and beliefs, the world of rural France, the history of *mentalités*, circulation of commodities, and specialized local studies that allowed revelatory comparative work. Both groups looked as well at class relations, popular violence, family life, guilds, artisans, laborers, and peasants.

"Discoveries in one country, in one scholarly culture," as Bernard Bailyn notes, "quickly affected scholarship advancing in other countries."[12] The *Annales* influences were felt throughout Europe, especially when the great diversity of *Annales* historians and their work is considered. Lynn Hunt wrote in 1986, "There is no one historical journal that is more influential in the world today than the *Annales*."[13] Early German trends in sociological history, influenced by Max Weber and Werner Sombart, among others, were also a constant source of new questions for the early British and French socioeconomic historians.[14] Later, claiming to lag a bit behind French and British influences, Germans scholars began writing *Alltagsgeschichte* in the mid-1970s, which eventually encompassed "history from below," history of everyday life, anthropological history (including folklore and ethnography), popular culture, and the culture of distinct groups—for example, segments of the working class.[15]

For food historians, 1970 was a milestone with the publication of *Pour une histoire de l'alimentation*, edited by *Annaliste* Jean-Jacques Hémardinquer. For the first time, a collected volume was completely devoted to scholarly studies of food history (although the essays had been published separately over the preceding ten years in the journal *Annales*). From 1970, along with the Hémardinquer collection, studies devoted solely to the history, sociology, anthropology, or ethnography of food and culture fully constituted a new current in scholarly writing.[16] For many historians of food in everyday life, Jean-Louis Flandrin argues in his preface to *Tables d'hier, tables d'ailleurs* (1999), the dominant material concerns of the *Annalistes* led them to concentrate more on calories and nutrition than on the psychosociology of the meal. Anything that could be counted or measured figured more prominently than phenomena that required social and cultural decoding. It is a charge that can be leveled even against the Hémardinquer volume if one ignores Roland Barthes's analysis of the cultural symbolism of food choices. Indeed, from the beginning, the *Annales* historians were never a homogeneous group, and their research interests varied widely. Divergent interests in the history of food multiplied in Europe as more scholars pursued new directions, topics, and sources.

In the United States in the late 1970s, social history was still considered subversive. A critic in traditional history described social historians as making "the study of the past...a playpit for the unattended urchins of other disciplines."[17] Conventional historians branded their social historian colleagues as "topical faddists."[18] In the early 1980s, a conservative intellectual historian wrote that social history dwelled "on the least dignified aspects of [people's] history." This included such "non-rational aspects of society as...eating habits."[19] Social historians who established themselves early on made many of the same criticisms of the numerous subfields of social history emerging at the time, particularly as cultural emphasis took the place of quantitative methods. They feared that social history would turn chaotic, run out of steam, and end up "confined to pots-and-pans antiquarianism."[20] Just like other new subfields of social history, food history prompted unease about the relationship of innovation to tradition. Academic marginalization of food history was evident as recently as the 1990s.[21] Today, food, as a requirement for all humans, is finding a place in every field of history—as subject, actor, methodology, or conceptual framework.

Sociology and cultural anthropology directed historians' attention to the social and symbolic act of shared meals. The variety of distinctive choices about food and eating that all cultures make "are immensely important adornments on an inescapable necessity."[22] In the United States, the anthropological mode of history, influenced by scholars such as Mary Douglas, Clifford Geertz, and Jack Goody, sparked a turn in the late 1970s and early 1980s to incorporate the relevance of cultural codes and systems of meaning into social and economic approaches to food. In France, the interest in mentalities, defined as collective patterns of belief, had already been part of socioeconomic history for decades. The *Annales* interest in mentalities was similar to English-speaking historians' focus on the inner workings of other cultures. However, Flandrin charged that structural anthropology made little impression on "reductionist" historians focused on nutrition and "scientific" methods of quantification.[23] Flandrin took as his guide Claude Lévi-Strauss's writing on cooking and table manners and the cultural diversity of foodways. According to Flandrin two discourses of food history coexisted in the 1980s: one that insisted on the "material and biological aspects" of food and another that privileged the cultural aspects.[24] The linguistic turn of the 1980s, influenced by poststructuralist theory and literary criticism, brought about a paradigm shift in historical thinking about how individuals and communities construct meaning. The poststructuralists driving this turn were French philosophers (notably Michel Foucault), and their relativist notions made the "new" cultural history a cause célèbre. However, cultural history opened up many fresh new areas of research for food historians. Analyses of discourses and texts gave historians tools for thinking about how language shapes social realities.

As the newness wore off the purely cultural approach, William H. Sewell Jr. argued that some realities, such as "kinesthetic" or physical knowledge, cannot be grasped through discourse; these he calls "nondiscursive social realities."[25] Food historians tend to relegate material culture to a sociocultural, nondiscursive category. Many food historians understand that the social and cultural approaches to food cannot be separated from one another. Moreover, we see in recent work that social history is not inextricably bound to quantitative methods.

Although national traditions and particularities affected the timing and interpretation of new movements and turns, in general, trends in the ways historians work spread fairly rapidly from country to country. It also seems clear that whatever the specific trajectory of general historiography in individual national traditions, trends in early modern European food history have paralleled work in the broader community of historians. French historians have been less impressed than non-French scholars with the "turns" that French theorists were so prolific at introducing. Since the linguistic turn, ideas of structuralism and poststructuralism have coexisted in French historical writing. French cultural historians maintain the conviction, too, that quantification continues to be useful.[26] It is evident in much British food scholarship that socioeconomic and cultural concepts work together very well.[27]

Where We Stand Now

If relatively few American historians are working on the history of food in early modern Europe, numerous European scholars are publishing exciting research on a wide variety of aspects of food in early modern Europe. In addition to the work published in English in Europe, university publishers in the United States and Britain support translations. U.S.-based food historians actively engage with European food historians—the Internet facilitates collaborations among far-flung colleagues. There is clearly a great deal of transnationalism in terms of topical interests and areas of study.

Early modern academic food history appears in several formats: collected multiauthor volumes (overviews that are often the product of a conference), academic monographs (in-depth research), and peer-reviewed journal articles. Some exhibition catalogs in recent years have featured essays by distinguished food historians.[28] Electronic publishing for scholarly work is still in its infancy, but a few Internet-only journals are testing the market.

Collected volumes generally fall into two categories. In one, the essays follow a broad thematic concern (e.g., consumption) and the volume includes one or two chapters about food. The other consists of volumes in which all essays are about food from a variety of geographic and disciplinary perspectives, still organized under a thematic umbrella. If collected volumes are sometimes uneven, this format has the advantage of bringing together essays on a single theme while offering multiple perspectives. Few scholars have mastered the languages to work comfortably in, say, French, Spanish, German, Dutch, and Italian. Few historians have the time and resources to visit local archives in multiple countries. The diversity that is possible in collected volumes gives all food historians the possibility of thinking comparatively over larger geographic areas of Europe. Each collected volume also offers multiple models for writing food history.[29]

Monographs have taken their own criticism. Monographs tend to be narrow and analytical (eschewing *narrative* storytelling) as the authors seek to fill ever more erudite gaps in the existing literature. Nonetheless, even as committed a narrative historian as Gordon Wood acknowledges the contribution of focused historical monographs to our collective professional endeavor to know and understand more about the past.[30] Probing deeply into new areas of research is what monographs do very well.

The steady stream of scholarship now coming off the presses demonstrates that early modern historians are writing innovative food history that engages not only the food-historical literature but also historical arguments that reach beyond the food-historical community. Food history has not diverged much from the larger early modern historical community in terms of periodization, which spans the sixteenth century through the eighteenth. Early modern European historians are working on topics that include questions of identity formation and the construction of regional and national cuisines; the history of medicine, health, and the body; the role of science and technology in culinary change; luxury food production and consumption; the history of manuscripts, cookbooks, and dietetic texts, as well as the history of food texts in relation to the larger study of book history and literacy; cross-cultural exchanges and movement of new foods, both subsistence and luxury commodities (consequences of travel, armed conquests, and colonialism); influence of religious diversity on foodways and attitudes; agricultural innovation; subsistence riots and famines; and changing tastes privileging flavor over health. Perhaps in other fields, but certainly in food history, the beginning of this period can be pushed back to the fifteenth century, especially when manuscripts and printed recipe books are the subjects of study.[31]

Food and Politics

Like scholars in social history and other subfields, food historians may find that criticism sharpens our analytical questions. Critics have accused "history from below" of robbing contemporary historical writing of politics.[32] Where food is concerned, this is a question for serious reflection, as food history with the politics left out is only a part of the history of food. Food history that has focused on gender politics, the politics of consumption, the role of power in access to food, and food and the colonial experience should put to rest generalized concerns about the absence of politics. Steven L. Kaplan's works on provisioning Paris with bread are exemplary analyses of the play of forces between the social and the political in eighteenth-century France.[33] Kaplan's work inspired *Le grand marché* (2002), Reynald Abad's magisterial study on provisioning Paris with all the foods the city required in the early modern period, leaving aside bread and grain. In France, the subject of early modern urban provisioning is inseparable from the political implications for the state of whether there is plenty or dearth.[34] E. P. Thompson's work on the moral economy of the eighteenth-century English crowd has inspired a great deal of research into the politics of provisioning, crowd behavior during food riots, and changing market culture in early modern Europe.[35]

The study of food, culture, and society would be shallow indeed if it did not seek greater understanding of the nexus of food production and consumption and politics in history. Anthropologist Sidney Mintz's *Sweetness and Power: The Place of Sugar in Modern History* (1985) has influenced many historically conceived studies of commodities, luxury consumption, the process of a luxury product becoming a necessity, and colonial power and the making of world capitalism. The banquet tables of the European elite in the seventeenth and eighteenth centuries were sites where sugarwork as a plastic art signaled distinction in nearly limitless forms, from intricately carved Italian *triomphi* to François Menon's *pastillage* representations of the palace of Circe (who turned Ulysses's companions into pigs), Circe's throne, a parterre landscape with trees and ponds, and human figures.[36] Such prolific use of sugar—an expensive commodity—in forms that would never be eaten was a truly extravagant expression of state and court power.

Historical sociologist Stephen Mennell's *All Manners of Food* (1985) examines the long-term development of patterns of state power in Britain and France, and the effect of these two different models of social and political power configurations on changes in food preferences and behavioral conventions throughout society. Mennell's book, which uses Norbert Elias's theory of social development, has been immensely influential. Although Elias's *The Civilizing Process: The History of Manners* was published in Germany in 1939, it was only after its translation into French in 1973 and into English in 1978 that his theory of the social power of elites as a civilizing force in European history became widely known and applied by historians. However, criticism of Elias's assumptions as being too deterministic and ahistorical have merit.[37] Historians are suspicious of any theory that proposes a universal model.

In "On the Civilizing of Appetite," Mennell applies Elias's theory of the psychosocial process of increasing self-control to the relationship between appetite and hunger, taking the focus off of court dining and turning instead to peasants and the popular classes.[38] Mennell does not identify with structuralist ideas about food preferences, but his assumptions about peasant behavior are much the same as the *Annales* structuralist views of the early moderns as victims to forces of nature and biology that were incomprehensible to them and therefore caused constant anxiety, resulting in lack of self-control. My discomfort with Mennell's otherwise exemplary work surfaced with revisionist arguments about the "miserabilist" view of early modern life. Many first- and second-generation *Annales* scholars put medieval and early modern people, their society and culture, on a teleological trajectory. Only as humans gained greater understanding of and mastery over their environment and technology, this analysis went, were they able to overcome the "prisons" of their environmental and mental structures and become modern—that is, as we are today.[39] Until somewhat recently, historians in the United States and Europe uncritically adopted these assumptions.

In Florent Quellier's cultural history *La Table des Français* (2007) the dominant *Annales* vision of the peasantry as miserable "animals" takes a drubbing. Although not the first historian to do so, Quellier challenges the "miserabilism" that a majority of social historians have advanced about the monotonous and insufficient diets of the peasants in early modern Europe.[40] (See also Paul Freedman's chapter in this volume.) Quellier argues that peasants were not always passive victims of their environment but were often agents in the production of their own food as well as in developing their own style of cooking.[41] His argument is supported in other French studies by Madeleine Ferrières and Philippe Meyzie.[42] Writing on British food in the early modern period Joan Thirsk makes a similar argument that past histories have underestimated unquantifiable food sources as well as the ingenuity of the common people.[43]

Consumerism and Spheres Public and Private

Historians of consumption have been working for the last three decades with probate inventories and similar sources, which demonstrate that both urban and rural popular classes owned a wide range of consumer goods in the eighteenth century, including diverse collections of cooking implements and equipment. These findings support the argument that the cooking of *le menu peuple* was more varied and complex than previously imagined.[44] Laura Van Aert and Ilja Van Damme note that today "the study of consumption is without a doubt a major preoccupation of many of the social sciences."[45] Economic, social, and cultural historians' research on consumption has transformed our understanding of early modern material culture at heterogeneous levels of society in multiple regions so that the picture of daily life is richer than it used to be.

Bruno Blondé admits that consumer durables are more easily studied than the food consumed. But, he argues, durables can be used to test theoretical concepts pertaining to food culture.[46] Blondé looks at the timing and pace of the "civilizing process" through ownership of forks, table linens, and so on.[47] In this way, he tries to discern whether there is evidence for a connection between the timing of the civilizing process and the "consumer revolution."[48] With material culture studies and archaeological research, food itself is beginning to figure more prominently in consumption literature. Mintz addresses the particularities of studying food consumption: "Food is transient. We eat it, wipe our plates, lick our lips, pat our stomachs, belch demurely, experience satiation. When food is consumed—as mothers commonly tell their babies—'it's all gone.'"[49]

The food of the affluent is more likely to have left behind traces in letters, diaries, cookbooks, menus, commercial records, and art. Barbara Ketcham Wheaton's 1983 social history of the French kitchen and table turns to such sources for evidence of how the food and culinary preferences of the French aristocracy, court society, furnished models of tastes and behavior that other social groups desired to emulate. *Savoring the Past* is not a study in consumption, although Wheaton's extensive sources demonstrate the paper trail that luxury foods and high-profile dining leave. Court dining was represented in cookbooks, such as Massialot's *Le Cuisinier Royal et Bourgeois* (1691), and in periodicals, such as *Le Mercure Galant*, that circulated throughout Europe. The spread of French aristocratic dining patterns shaped food culture not only at other European courts but also among the aspirational bourgeoisie. So much aristocratic conspicuous consumption took place in public with ordinary people looking on and even occasionally being allowed to plunder the leftovers.[50]

For historians, the rich documentation of the European elite at table provided an entry into serious historical work in food history. Wheaton was one of the modern pioneers in this field. Wheaton's work still forms a basis for the orthodoxy of social emulation used by researchers to account for the distinctive developments in French culinary culture in the early modern era.[51] Interest in court and elite culture, as well as in the framework of the modalities of social power, has occupied food historians writing about forms of conspicuous consumption in the early modern era of sumptuary regulations and ongoing social and economic critique of luxury. For Ken Albala, Renaissance banquets were among the ruling elite's most public expressions of identity formation.[52] Throughout history, dining as spectacle has conveyed the perception of power.

Historians of the Enlightenment have used German political philosopher Jürgen Habermas's theory of the transformation of the public sphere to frame arguments about the sites of modern political action and consumer culture, both of which took shape outside of court society. Habermas posits that the Old Regime court spectacle analyzed by Wheaton and Albala gave way to a public sphere where the exchange of ideas and opinions among equals determined common interests and political interaction. With *The Invention of the Restaurant* (2000), Rebecca L. Spang tested the Habermas thesis in the context of Parisian food culture. The restaurant offered the "conceptual lens" to focus new questions about the public sphere.[53] Her analysis challenges the Habermasian framework of institutions of publicness. The restaurant, she argues, requires a more nuanced conception of "public" spaces. It thus reveals weaknesses in Habermas's model.[54] This prize-winning monograph appeared during a long drought of serious new food history, and its subject encouraged other historians to engage in inquiries on cultural innovation, consumerism, and the nature of the public and private spheres.

Beat Kümin focused on taverns to contextualize eating out in early modern Europe in a deeper and wider history than Spang.[55] Kümin's evidence on meal service at inns across Europe from the sixteenth century to the eighteenth supports his argument that these establishments were precursors to the Parisian modern restaurant, both in terms of the dining public's ability to order a meal from a selection of foods and as a site contributing to the development of the public sphere. Numerous scholars have been researching a variety of ways in which early modern travelers and others procured their meals outside of the home. Travel memoirs and guidebooks are replete with reports of eating out in foreign places.[56] *The World of the Tavern* (2003), edited by Kümin and Ann Tlusty, draws on the proliferation of individual studies on taverns over several decades from a variety of perspectives. The essays cover public eating in Switzerland, England, Germany, and Russia. The volume illustrates that the ability to synthesize what may seem a large body of "fractionalized and scattered"[57] work can happen only when a critical mass is reached. Echoing Gordon Wood, we can be confident that without researchers willing to do isolated work on their small areas of interest, bringing it together to make comparisons on a larger scale would not be possible.

Turning to the private domestic sphere, Mark Dawson's microhistory, *Plenty and Grase* (2009), reconstructs daily life in two large households belonging to one family in sixteenth-century England. Dawson situates his work within the long tradition of British socioeconomic historians of the twentieth century and argues that his methodology demonstrates in the particular much of what previous historians have shown in the aggregate. Household and estate account books, unusually numerous in this case, and other family documents provide his core body of source materials. Microhistory has had a mixed reception among historians primarily because it can be difficult to write convincingly of the relevance of one case study to the larger history of the era. This is perhaps the challenge for all social and cultural historians: to relate the structures of everyday life to major events and trends in history.[58]

Abad applies a microhistorical lens to get to the mysterious bottom of a familiar story, the suicide in 1671 of the prince de Condé's maître d'hôtel, François Vatel.[59] Abad, who understands Old Regime provisioning in fish (Vatel's missing "roast" course) like no one else, re-creates the details of the entire operation: the kind of fish Vatel would likely have ordered based on the season and the geographic location of the prince's chateau, Chantilly; the location of the ports from which it would have been ordered; why Vatel was obliged to supply the fish himself (a job that normally fell to a merchant on retainer); and in just what ways the chain of fish provisioning was susceptible to dysfunction. Abad demonstrates how the success of provisioning this household (like many other great households in France) and this one momentous dinner (an anomaly) was bound up in a far larger web of factors, from weather conditions, police regulations, and merchant behavior to state policies. The essay makes explicit the obstacles that stood between production and consumption in early modern Europe.

Food Production and Networks of Knowledge Transmission

Agricultural history has engaged many scholars for decades, notably economic and rural historians. Other research into early modern food production and consumption considers guilds as powerful economic, social, and political institutions of the early modern period. There were as well a host of actors outside guild communities who shaped food commerce, trade innovations, and taste preferences in early modern Europe.[60] Sylvia Thrupp, a student of Eileen Power at the LSE, published her guild study "The Grocers of London" in 1933. LSE historian Alice Clark published *Working Life of Women in the Seventeenth Century* in 1919, an archive-based work that continues to inspire research on women's work in early modern Europe.[61] Feminist historians writing from the 1970s began to explore the role of guild wives and widows and other actors, such as market women, in early modern food commerce, contributing to a more accurate picture of women's economic power in the family and in the community of public food purveyors. Merry Wiesner Wood's 1981 article, "Paltry Peddlers or Essential Merchants? Women in the Distributive Trades in Early Modern Nuremberg," argues that records show that contemporaries in sixteenth-century Nuremberg perceived the central role of butchers' and bakers' wives in the running of retail shops.[62] Danielle Van den Heuvel's 2008 article on guilds, family economy, and women in urban food markets in the early modern Dutch Republic is another of the growing number of investigations of women food retailers in the early modern period.[63] Van den Heuvel shows that opportunities for and restrictions on women in food trades varied not only from city to city but also from one food trade to another in the same city, which suggests the possibility of fruitful comparative studies in the future.

Kaplan's work on Paris bakers provides the most in-depth view of these artisans' physically debilitating occupation and their lives as bounded by their raw materials, their family and financial realities, guild regulations, and the police.[64] Kaplan's social histories of the bread and grain trades in the Old Regime set a high standard for all historians of food who research food trades, guilds, or urban provisioning. Alongside bread, meat was also called a food of "first necessity" in the eighteenth century. Sydney Watts's *Meat Matters* (2006) examines the world of Paris butchers in the eighteenth century and the paradoxical cultural view of meat as both an elite food and an "absolute necessity." Watts brings together the production of this commodity by guild members, its regulation by the authorities, the fast-changing Parisian market culture of the eighteenth century, and the social meanings of meat in early modern consumer culture. James E. Shaw has written on the politics of the food of first necessity in early modern Venice—fish, which functioned as both the best source of cheap protein for the common people and a food with ritual importance in this Catholic society—and the disastrous dissolution of the city's fishmongers' guild.[65]

Early modern European cooks, caterers, and confectioners have not left rich records about their trades and lives, or so it has seemed. A standard assumption about cooks is that because most men and women in the culinary trades and culinary employment were illiterate, there is little evidence available to historians to reconstruct their lives and work. As a result the history of cooks has traditionally been a safe harbor for *fakelorists* (i.e., writers who perpetuate false mythologies, such as the following: On coming to France to marry a prince, Catherine de Medici brought her own Italian cooks, who proceeded to invent French cuisine).[66] There are two aspects of current historical research that will likely change this approach to writing about food in history as a series of unsupported anecdotes. First, historians of the book and of reading offer new perspectives on the spread of early modern literacy. We already know that literacy rates varied widely across early modern Europe and were particularly high in Germany and the Netherlands.

Second, acceptance of the history of food in university departments encourages historians to bring rigorous historical methods to bear on many questions heretofore inadequately researched. Jennifer J. Davis's extensive archival research into Parisian culinary trade guilds makes us understand the social and cultural functions of the guilds and the cooks who belonged to them.[67] Davis delves into the working world of Paris cooks to reveal their roles in shaping consumer tastes during a period when French cuisine was known as the most innovative in Europe. Her research is the first to provide extensive documentation of the lives and working experiences of professional cooks during a century and a half of tremendous social and economic change.

All of these works make it clear that extensive archival research into social and cultural food history remains a critical tool for historians. Continued archival examination of food trades, guilds, the lives of artisans as well as professional and domestic cooks, and the gendering of food trades will bring the business of food in early modern Europe into sharper focus.

To conceptualize professionalization strictly as it is sociologically defined and temporally concentrated in the nineteenth century causes a flattening of history. Asking what it meant to be a professional cook in early modern Europe opens up new categories of analysis. Sara Pennell's chapter in volume 4 of the series *The Cultural History of Food* (2012), "Professional Cooking, Kitchens and Service Work: 'Accomplisht' Cookery," takes up the commercialization of public cooking as it was increasingly divorced from guild activity across Europe. Her sources include published cookbooks, household accounts, and biographical information on cookbook authors. "Occupational diversification" accompanied changing demographic patterns and social practices shifting from grand banquets and feasting to private dining in the domestic setting. In order to keep working, the cook needed either to seek his fortune in establishments for public eating out or to take work as a domestic. As guild strength and regulations varied considerably from one locale to another,

Pennell adopts a comparative approach to cookbooks from Germany, France, Italy, and England. Social and economic changes among the middle classes influenced not only the culinary labor market but also the commercialization of specialized skills, such as confectionary. Pennell argues that the overall trend in this period shows a shift from the cook's knowledge as secrets shared among a formally constituted community of cooks toward the perception of such specialized knowledge as a commodity in the marketplace.

The use of cookbooks as primary sources for social history, a method pioneered in the United States by Wheaton, is moving into the mainstream of food history. Until recently, most people had not considered cookbooks as a genre of literature having a history. Flandrin and his students have worked extensively with cookbooks and dietetic texts. Bruno Laurioux (working on medieval texts) and Mary and Philip Hyman have provided insightful analyses based on close reading of manuscripts and printed sources and research on publishing history.[68] Johanna Maria van Winter has written on the earliest cookbooks from the Low Countries.[69] Textual analysis from the historical perspective (as opposed to literary theory) provides social and cultural historians with tools for seeing how manuscripts and printed books themselves changed over time and for following changes in meal patterns, ingredient use, complexity of skills required, necessary kitchen equipment, and so on. Flandrin's final book, *Arranging the Meal* (2007), does just that with French cookbooks and dining patterns. *Savoring the Past* by Wheaton and other works, including Flandrin's essay "Dietary Choices and Culinary Technique, 1500–1800" (1999) and Gilly Lehmann's *The British Housewife* (2003), deftly illustrate how a wide variety of sources complement and supplement cookbooks as historical sources. Old cookbooks, either reprinted or in facsimile, with well-researched introductions, are vital to making primary-source cooking, gardening, and dietary texts readily available to researchers. This is a trend in France, Germany, the Low Countries, Britain, and Italy. As there is deeper study, via translated texts for most of us, of Arabic influences on medieval European cooking, such knowledge will enable greater awareness of the precise nature of changes in European cuisines in the early modern era.[70] Terence Scully has translated numerous texts into English, most recently the cookbooks of La Varenne and Scappi.[71] Food cultures of northern Europe have become more accessible to Anglophones because of recent translations of early modern Dutch, Danish, and German cookbooks.[72]

Dutch society wielded influence and power in early modern Europe. Dutch trade in exotic, colonial, and luxury foods is a critical part of the economic, social, and cultural history of the era. Jan de Vries has written extensively on what he calls the "industrious revolution," which has repercussions for analyses of domestic material culture, including food culture. He argues that the Dutch conception of consumerism and luxury as virtues promoting national economic development contributed to significant changes in the wider European outlook on "the New Luxury," desires for material goods that were not influenced by royal courts but were "generated by urban society."[73] Countering Elias's argument that court society generated elite tastes and these were in turn emulated by nonelites, de Vries sees the Dutch people themselves as agents of innovation in their daily lives.[74]

Science, Experimentation, and Ideologies of the Body and Identity

Malcolm Thick's contextualization of Sir Hugh Plat in his time (the late sixteenth and early seventeenth centuries) and among his circle of acquaintances and colleagues represents a welcome research trend. Food historians may recognize Plat only as the author of one or two small cookbooks, including *Delights for Ladies* (ca. 1600). As for many of his contemporaries, his interests were far more catholic than this one book suggests. Writing about "secrets," such as making sugar plate, and living a life of continual experimentation with processes of nature and science were common activities among the polymaths of Plat's era. Thick demonstrates the connections between Plat's many activities, including cooking, pharmacy, alchemy, inventions (including a pasta press machine), and new food preservation techniques. Further research like Thick's into the complexity of authors' lives and activities will give insights into the writing and publishing history of early cookbooks and the develop-ment and dissemination of both new tastes and cooking methods. Just as important, re-creating networks of actors in the food and science realms will establish further the relationship between culinary experimentation, artisanal secrets, and activities taking place in the early modern laboratories of natural philosophers. Historians of science have shown that early modern social networking occurred via laboratory experimentation and that results were shared among European (even international) participants in the early Republic of Letters.[75] Most laboratories were located in homes, and philosophical (scientific) societies met both in homes and coffeehouses, the prime sites for cross-pollination of ideas among individuals avid for the secrets of domestic medicine and alchemy, as well as desirous of recipes for exotic fare, such as sugar, chocolate, tea, and coffee, and for new techniques, such as artificial freezing (for making ice cream and chilled drinks). We need to look further into early modern sites of experimentation and knowledge production for insights into many areas, the technical innovations in food production being just one possibility.[76]

Many early European cookbooks and books of secrets feature recipes for dis-tilling cordial waters, for example, as well as descriptions and illustrations of the necessary equipment, such as the alembics pictured on the frontispiece of Hannah Woolley's *The Queen-Like Closet or Rich Cabinet* (1670), which depicts a range of a woman's household activities: distilling, hearth cooking, and baking in an open stone oven. However, not many scholars have questioned the connection between women's distilling activities and what went on in alchemical and medical laborator-ies. Elaine Leong and Sara Pennell investigate the interaction between laypersons and professionals in the early modern "medical marketplace." The connections were all the stronger in that most medicines kept in the home could be easily re-created with ordinary cooking methods and equipment.[77] Both of these historians of early modern England have fruitfully explored various facets of the social and cultural history of medical and culinary recipes, the people who collected them, and the books in which they were found.[78] Very recent publications appearing as this volume goes into production indicate that this is indeed a rapidly expanding topic of interest.

It is only a short step from medicine to food in early modern societies, and historians of food, medicine, and science are (at last) working more closely. Tom Jaine reported in *Petits Propos Culinaires* 86 (2008) on a conference at Warwick University entitled "Reading and Writing Recipe Books, 1600–1800." Disciplines other than food history were represented in greater numbers, and most of the recipes discussed were not culinary but medical. Albala's in-depth study of European dietary literature, *Eating Right in the Renaissance* (2002), draws on a broad range of primary sources. Explicating early modern theories of the humoral body reveals the conformation of the early modern mind as well. Popular histories of Renaissance food often portray the dietary choices of this era as weird, just as early modern medicine has been dismissed as barbaric. Dietetic theories unlock the logic of the early modern taste preferences. Surveying dietetic writing over three centuries and across Europe—writing history that is both temporally deep and also geographically wide—provides scope and context to see changing relationships between medicine and cooking at a time when regional and national cuisines were becoming more diverse from one another.

Jaine also noted that the seventeenth-century male penchant for collecting recipes has gone virtually without notice when in fact men compiled many collections (both medicinal and culinary). This observation opens the door to the early modern world of the virtuosi, cultivated gentlemen, natural philosophers, and collectors of rarities and oddities. Brian Cowan's *The Social Life of Coffee* (2005) is not simply another luxury-commodity biography. He looks at coffee as the lens through which he envisages the world of the virtuosi in seventeenth- and eighteenth-century England, a world peopled by John Evelyn and Sir Kenelm Digby, just to name a few of the cookbook authors who will be familiar to many food historians. Cowan situates these men in a network of natural philosophers who, among other activities, formed the Royal Society along with Samuel Pepys, Elias Ashmole, Francis Bacon, and Samuel Hartlib. Their experimental interests ranged from the strange new drink, coffee, to Denis Papin's experiments with his steam "digester," an antecedent of the pressure cooker. Changes in coffee drinking and coffeehouse regulation also provide the conceptual framework for Cowan's smart and fresh perspective on the cultural history of early modern Britain.

Emma Spary demonstrates that in Enlightenment Paris the mastery of knowledge, technique, and discourse shifted as the practice of distilling moved from home laboratory to the eighteenth-century luxury marketplace. What had been an activity of women in the domestic sphere and of guild artisans became a lucrative high-status commercial venture in the hands of what Spary calls "professional innovators."[79]

Spary joins anthropologically inflected food history with actor-network theory.[80] She argues that the identity or meaning of a prepared food or drink is not fixed. Rather, alimentary objects were "differently defined by the individual constituencies of actors" involved in production and consumption of the product.[81] Knowledge claims regarding food and the body were highly contested in the public domain: there was no single scientific model that dictated dietary choices among the eighteenth-century public.

In another approach to food and the early modern European body, Rebecca Earle's prize-winning *American Historical Review* article (2010) probes the "centrality of food to Spain's colonial endeavor" within the framework of Galen's system of the humors as the ideology that did the most to shape the Spaniards' physical and mental experience of colonization. Many histories have been written about the Columbian exchange, which sent New World foods to Europe and Old World foods to the Americas (see Jeffrey Pilcher's chapter in this book). Histories have also focused on the experience of Spanish conquest on the bodies of the conquered. Earle's book (2012), from which this article is drawn, provides a provocative and insightful analysis of the sixteenth-century ideological view of the body and of identity as shaped by diet. She writes that in the prevailing thought of early modern Spanish culture the humoral body was mutable, not fixed. Because the Spanish diet was one of the most powerful cultural practices that constructed the Spanish identity, eating New World foods threatened to erase "caste differences" between the conquerors and the Amerindians. The Galenic theory of diet and the body shaped the colonial experience in the minds of the colonists, and it played a role in emerging ideas about race.[82]

As with other ideologies and language in early modern Europe, we must guard against imposing the nineteenth-century idea of nation and nationalism for what was likely a very different perception of community.[83] In the sixteenth century, when Spaniards talk of Spanish food and Spanish bodies there was hardly a Spain, certainly not as it became in the nineteenth century. Spain was not a "structural reality": the reality was the Castilian monarchy. In his 2007 essay, "Sweet Food of Knowledge: Botany, Food, and Empire in the Early Modern Spanish Kingdoms," Fabio López-Lázaro examines "the significant role food played in the construction, administration, and 'imagining' of [the Spanish] empire."[84]

The early modern period in Europe was a time when regional food and foodways were becoming emblematic of national cuisines. That food has a role in identity, self-understanding, and group representation is undeniable. As food choices ceased to be about medical consequences, European elites were free to choose what they ate on the basis of taste, distinction, and the expression of identity.[85] Alberto Capatti and Massimo Montanari's *Italian Cuisine: A Cultural History* (2003) provides an admirable model of writing about the culinary traditions of a nation that was not a nation for most of its history. There is much to discover about the mechanisms by which regional cuisines over time formed into something larger, national cuisines, which in turn need to be interwoven with questions about the early modern understanding of identity and "nation."[86]

Conclusion: Going Forward

The winter 2011 issue of *French Historical Studies* featured a forum on "History and the Telescoping of Time." The contributors defined the "flattening" of history, or "telescoping of time," as the effect produced by the increasing amount of historical research and writing that is confined to the very recent past, especially the last century.[87] The focus on the "modern," a small slip of time, is comfortable in part because there are so many resources available in modern languages (especially English) and easily accessed via the Internet. If this is a growing trend it may result in resistance to conceptualizing questions in terms of larger themes and longer, continuous narratives.[88] I call attention to this phenomenon because I see a pressing need to teach students in food studies programs the importance not only of historical method to the broader interdisciplinary study of food but also of the contextualization of events and ideas within a larger historical framework.

Food is a powerful theme that can encourage analyses across time and regions. Collaborative research projects offer possibilities for researching food as a transhistorical and transnational object of study—especially collaborative projects that attract scholars from multiple disciplines, institutions, and countries. From the sciences as well as the social sciences and humanities, food scholars may find collaborative research projects a vehicle that will allow us to test paradigms, to develop innovative analytical tools, and to conceive of fresh, creative questions about food and the past.

The early modern period is prime territory for geographically wide projects. The nation-state of the nineteenth century does not, in fact, easily project backward two or three centuries, and what appear to be references to national characteristics in source material from that time muddy the question;[89] it is not yet clear exactly how nation and identity resolve in early modern Europe. Rethinking national identity separately from ideological nationalism requires altering our conception of how Western cultures developed. Historians Carla Hesse and Thomas Laqueur suggest the need for "histories of national identity that are not connected with the nation-state."[90] As food is so strong a marker of social and cultural identity, comparative research in early modern food history offers ideal opportunities for finding new understanding of the meaning of "nation" before modern nationalism.

Early modern fascination with mastery over nature—reflected in the many projects for describing and classifying in natural history—was separate from the power of the state. The men (and some women) pursuing such projects in the late sixteenth and seventeenth centuries created sites for polite discourse and study, such as *Wunderkammern* and museums, which influenced opinion, behavior, and identity formation outside the influence of court society. Moreover, much learned inquiry into nature involved simultaneous experimentation with foods and methods of preparation.[91] Alongside these trends, transformations in the mechanical arts and instrument making abounded across Europe in the early modern period.[92] Further research needs to explore the interconnection between culinary practices and scientific inquiries in this period. Cuisine itself could be approached as an experimental science.

A last suggestion for future research is to revisit the role of emulation in changes in tastes, styles, and preferences in French food history. Emulation theory has been effectively questioned in the past couple of decades in a significant number of works on consumption in other regions and with a variety of domestic objects. So far culinary culture has escaped similar scrutiny. New analyses of changes in tastes and styles will likely reveal a more complex and nuanced process of construction and reproduction of French culinary culture.[93]

Notes

I am grateful to Peter Scholliers, Jennifer Davis, and Priscilla Ferguson for their insights and comments in the drafting of this chapter.

1. For other examples, see Albala, 2009, 6–8.
2. See Cronon, 1992.
3. N. Z. Davis, 1988, 2.
4. Sée, 1927; Thirsk, 1955.
5. Berg, 1992; B. Smith, 1984; N. Z. Davis, 1988.
6. N. Z. Davis, 1988.
7. About the collegial relationship between Power and Bloch, see N. Z. Davis, 1988.
8. N. Z. Davis, 1988, 19.
9. Berg, 1992, 311. Berg provides an excellent historiography of women in economic history. See also Berg, 1996.
10. See, for example, N. Adams and B. Smith, 2001.
11. Another excellent essay about Eileen Power and women's contributions to historiography is B. Smith, 1984.
12. Bailyn, 1982, 12.
13. L. Hunt, 1986, 209.
14. Brodnitz, 1928.
15. Fletcher, 1988, 558–59; Eley, 1989. Eley underscores that, in practice, *Alltagsgeschichte* is very heterogeneous.
16. Flandrin and Cobbi, 1999, 11.
17. Judt, 1979, 66.
18. Stearns, 1985, 326.
19. Himmelfarb, quoted in Strauss, 1991, 138.
20. Sterns, 1985, 327, 321.
21. Ruark, 1999.
22. Mintz, 1985, 3.
23. Flandrin and Cobbi, 1999, 21.

24. Flandrin and Cobbi, 1999, 22. Jean-Claude Bonnet and Alain Girard also favored cultural approaches to cookbooks and other food-related textual sources in the 1970s.
25. Sewell, 2001, 220.
26. Chartier, 1985, 688.
27. See Weatherill, 1988; Shammas, 1993.
28. See *Livres en bouche*, 2001; Ajmar-Wollheim and Dennis, 2006.
29. The collected volumes reviewed in the writing of this essay include Peltre and Thouvenot, 1989; Margolin and Sauzet, 1982; Viallon-Schoneveld, 2004; Lambert, 1992; Fiorato and Baratto, 1999; Redon et al., 2005; Flandrin and Cobbi, 1999; Kümin and Tlusty, 2002; Berg and Clifford, 1999; Flandrin and Montanari, 1999; Tomasik and Vitullo, 2007; White, 2007; V. Burke and Gibson, 2004; U. Klein and Spary, 2010; Jenner and Wallis, 2007.
30. G. Wood, 2010, 20.
31. For example, Lambert, 1992; Van Winter, 2007.
32. Judt, 1979. Judt is making a specific point that the anthropological mode of cultural history is nonpolitical because it ignores his belief that power in society is based on class relations. I reject the implication that the politics have to be Marxist to qualify as politics.
33. For example, Kaplan, 1984; Kaplan, 1996.
34. Clement, 1999; Montenach, 2009.
35. Thompson, 1971; Bohstedt, 2010.
36. Menon, 1750, 348; see also Day, 2000; Day, 2002.
37. Brown, 2002, 24–25.
38. Mennell, 1987.
39. S. Clark, 1983, 67.
40. See Flandrin and P. Hyman, 1986, in which their close reading of many types of primary sources buttresses their argument that in some cases geography appears to have had more to do with diet than money or class. See C. Jones and Spang, 1999. Jones and Spang not only provide their own rebuttal to "miserabilism" but also include here a good historiography of works that have been chipping away at this theory. See also Watts, 2006.
41. Quellier, 2007, 40–41.
42. Ferrières, 2007; Meyzie, 2007.
43. Thirsk, 2007.
44. Roche, 2000; Pardailhé-Galabrun, 1991.
45. Van Aert and Van Damme, 2005, 139–40.
46. Blondé, 2005, 37–40.
47. Blondé, 2005, 43.
48. Blondé, 2005, 47.
49. Mintz, 1993, 262.
50. Wheaton, 1983.

51. See Pinkard, 2009.
52. Albala, 2007a.
53. Spang, 2000, 84–86.
54. Spang, 2000, 87.
55. Kümin, 2003.
56. Roche, 2003.
57. Kümin and Tlusty, 2002, 5.
58. See P. Burke, 2001, 10–11.
59. Abad, 2002.
60. Farr, 1988. Farr is especially informative about the changing conditions among pastry cooks.
61. Thirsk, 1985. Thirsk gives a good accounting of early nonacademic British women who wrote on the history of women in early modern Europe.
62. M. Wood, 1981.
63. Van Den Heuvel, 2008.
64. Kaplan, 1996.
65. Shaw, 2002.
66. A. Smith, 2001.
67. J. Davis, 2004.
68. See, for example, Flandrin, P. Hyman, and M. Hyman, 1983; P. Hyman and M. Hyman, 1992.
69. Van Winter, 2007, 211–56.
70. For example, Nasrallah, 2007.
71. Scully, 2006; Scully, 2008.
72. For example, Rose, 1989. Only a very small number of German-language cookbooks are available in English translation. There are a great many where translations would provide sources for rich comparisons across the European continent.
73. De Vries, 2008, 44.
74. De Vries, 2008, 52. Of course, a great deal of Dutch art provides visual representations of luxury foodstuffs in still life paintings and of the abundance of foodstuffs associated with Dutch urban markets. See Hochstrasser, 2007; Honig, 1998; Sullivan, 1999.
75. Findlen, 1994; Harkness, 1997.
76. For more about early modern laboratories and their settings, see Shapin, 1988; Harkness, 1997; U. Klein, 2008.
77. Leong and Pennell, 2007, 135.
78. Leong, 2005; Leong, 2008; Pennell, 1997.
79. Spary, 2010, 232.
80. Spary, 2010, 226.
81. Spary, 2010, 226–27.
82. Earle, 2012.
83. Hesse and Laqueur, 1994.

84. López-Lázaro, 2007, 8, 12.
85. Flandrin, 1989.
86. Hesse and Laqueur, 1994.
87. Smail, 2011.
88. Neuschel, 2011, 52–53.
89. Kümin, 2003, 80; Hesse and Laqueur, 1994.
90. Hesse and Laqueur, 1994, 2.
91. See, for example, Alexis of Piedmont, 1562; Sir Hugh Plat, 1602; Sir Kenelm Digby, 1677.
92. U. Klein and Spary, 2010, 1–23. See, for example, Murrell, 1617, on making his own confectionary tools.
93. See, for example, Auslander, 1996. I am grateful to Jennifer Davis for enlightening discussions on this topic.

–4–

The Many Rooms in the House:
Research on Past Foodways in Modern Europe

Peter Scholliers

In 2007 I published a survey dealing with research about Europe's foodways in the nineteenth and twentieth centuries.[1] Rather than being interested in the conclusions of this research, I wished to examine *how* scholars study food history, which offered an opportunity for testing the application and relevance of interdisciplinarity. Luckily, not only historians but also scholars who were not trained as historians investigate foodways of the past. Studying food in the modern era has indeed attracted a large number of disciplines, ranging from anthropology and sociology to communication sciences and geography. I wished to learn whether and how these approaches, methods, and insights inspired historians. My conclusions confirmed the extraordinarily thriving interest in Europe's past foodways by an ever-growing number of disciplines, the total lack of common ground of these studies, and their hesitant interest in interdisciplinary approaches.

In this chapter I want to expand this inquiry by using recent literature and asking additional questions. I am, first and foremost, interested in the way historians have dealt with the overwhelming attention from other disciplines since the early twenty-first century. Would they welcome it and explore new themes, methods, and insights, or resist and ignore the loud knock on their door? Also, I consider the question of how amateur historians (i.e., nontrained historians as well as nonacademics) set off with historical questions and debates, apply historical concepts, search for historical sources, and refer to adequate historical literature. This chapter has three sections: the first two form a chronological survey with the year 2005 as a caesura (in order not to replicate my 2007 survey and to emphasize recent developments), while the third section is a lengthy conclusion.

Separate Rooms in a Cozy Hut (1960s–1980s) and Accessible Rooms in a Welcoming House (1990s–2005)

Broadly speaking, two intellectual loci in food studies existed between 1900 and 1960: that of economic history and that of folklore.[2] The two neglected each other. Economic historians dealt with the food supply, hunger, and prices, while folklorists studied regional variations, table manners, and cooking utensils. Next to these, there was popular literature that provided entertaining food stories. In the late 1950s, historians discovered the study of everyday life. This turn came along with the popularity of *Annales* and *Alltagsgeschichte*.[3] The latter paid attention to anthropological approaches, that is, the daily (or "lived") experience of ordinary men and women, where the cultural dimension of food and drinks played a role.[4] The *Annales* methodology encompassed the study of long-term developments and structures of daily life, searching for inspiration with economists, sociologists, ethnologists, linguists, and natural scientists. Soon, the quantitative approach dominated the interest of *Annales* historians, while the ethnological sway, or the attention to material culture, vanished. This upsurge of social food historiography, with its quantitative considerations, had such a strong impact that other approaches could not ignore social history's prevailing position.[5] Most historians were rather pleased with this situation, which mirrored the more general position of social history in those days as new, critical, emancipating, and challenging. As French historian Jean-Louis Flandrin later put it, historians then viewed ethnology as "too anecdotal" and anthropology as providing general patterns with arbitrary, subjective, and ethnocentric starting points that "reach only very poor ideas."[6]

Yet socioeconomic history's supremacy was challenged discreetly when a few authors took a distinctly innovative look at food history. None of them were historians by training. Ethnologist Günter Wiegelmann published a general food history of Germany in 1967, paying attention to regional cooking and daily as well as festive food.[7] Philosopher and psychologist Jean-Paul Aron, *Annaliste* in the margins, published a book in 1973 that put the nineteenth-century Parisian diner at the center of attention, considering restaurants, menus, taste, and fancy cuisine.[8] In 1977, philosopher-historian-sociologist Theodore Zeldin devoted forty pages of a book on French nineteenth-century social history to food, considering taste, regional cuisine, cooks, and culinary writers. In 1982, anthropologist Jack Goody wrote a book with historical and comparative perspectives, asking about the lack of haute cuisine in African societies (and, by contrast, its significance in Europe). In 1985, sociologist Stephen Mennell published a book in which he compared the long-term culinary traditions of England and France, considering networks of people with their preferences and appetites. Also in 1985, anthropologist Sidney Mintz published a study on the economic, political, and cultural history of sugar. These authors had several inspirational sources but especially important was Claude Lévi-Strauss's decoding of foodways in order to reveal the underlying meanings and structures of society.

Sociologist Jean-Pierre Poulain admitted in 2002 that French food scholars had for years neglected the richness of the aforementioned anthropological, sociological, and ethnological research.[9] Jean-Louis Flandrin and Massimo Montanari emphasized the fact that initially (i.e., in the 1970s) only a few historians of antiquity were interested in cultural aspects of food.[10] Yet there were traces of changes in the late 1980s. The journal *Food and Foodways* organized roundtable discussions about Goody's and Mintz's books.[11] Moreover, some historians did see the benefits of looking over the sky-high fence. Hans-Jürgen Teuteberg, the German historian dealing with the history of housing, enterprises, and consumption, collaborated with the ethnologist Wiegelmann. They developed a partnership with a clear division of labor: Teuteberg focused on socioeconomic issues and Wiegelmann on ethnological ones.[12] In France, Flandrin, an *Annaliste* and historian of the family and mentality in the eighteenth century, was more sweeping in his view of food history. Around 1980, he pleaded for genuine integration of ethnology into the social historians' approach. He explored *new* sources (menu cards, recipe books, and culinary writing in general), used *new* methods (a form of close reading of texts), and, especially, addressed *new* topics (such as pleasure, taste, emotion, haute cuisine, and the organization of a meal).[13] He fiercely opposed the prevailing socioeconomic food historiography of the day[14] and criticized some sociologists' approach to history as too readily accepting of stereotypes.[15] In Italy, Massimo Montanari, at the outset an agricultural historian of the Renaissance, started writing about food history in the 1980s and gained a reputation with his *La fame e l'abbondanza*, published in 1993. Montanari paid great attention to careful reading of texts, considering the significance of what these sources "say" (i.e., representations and constructions).

In 1996, Flandrin and Montanari edited *Histoire de l'alimentation*, a survey of European food history from Antiquity to the present.[16] This book is acclaimed as a genuine benchmark.[17] Some believe that it shows the autonomy of cultural history with regard to anthropology and a move away from the too-general "food history" to the more focused "culinary history."[18] However, some reviewers pointed at serious weaknesses.[19] Overall, the importance of this book lies in the richness of the long-term approach, the avid cultural turn, and the variety of sources, including recipe books, letters, literature, accounts, menu cards, and statistics; yet most sources were written texts, with few objects or images. I count forty-four authors (for the French edition), among whom are only three nonhistorians.[20] The introduction's reference community includes older research by G. Schmoller, W. Abel, F. Braudel, C. Lévi-Strauss,[21] work by some *Annalistes*,[22] and the editors' own previous works, as well as current studies, but, astonishingly, no works by Goody, Mennell, Mintz, or Wiegelmann. It looks as if historians had fully incorporated the views, methods, and findings of other disciplines. Flandrin and Montanari's book did influence many researchers, but it did not introduce the cultural turn in European food historiography: the book was a decisive exponent of a broader paradigmatic change that put culture at the center of political, economic, and social historiography. Thus, around the year 2000, food history writing was particularly receptive to new trends in general historiography, perhaps more so than other fields of history.

A House in Full Expansion since 2005

By 2005, food history had specialized journals, canonical literature, regular conferences, specific teaching, media recognition, and an impact on general history writing.[23] Because of this, some historians proclaim the arrival of a *new* food history that merges material aspects with symbolic ones but *excludes* plain socioeconomic history (of trade, diet, famines, food aid, agribusiness, and the like).[24] This delineates the field of food history but hacks it loose from one of its inspirational sources. Critics go on stressing the need to incorporate other disciplines as a key element for a bright future of food studies. However, this multidisciplinary approach is precisely why some critics do not perceive food history as a distinct field with one denominator: it lacks common theoretical perspectives, approaches, aims, definitions, and methodologies, as well as secondary literature that may provide reliable, essential information.[25] Moreover, it is emphasized that scholars of past foodways (regardless of their discipline) must take account of developments in mainstream historiography, move from specific investigations to general understandings, avoid reductionism and separatism, and combine the cultural with the social, economic, and political.[26]

Still, the need for a common ground depends on what one aims at when studying past foodways. I suggest two options. First, there is food historiography that is secondary to social, political, economic, cultural, medical, intellectual, and any other history, or that is secondary to sociology, anthropology, economics, dietetics, and any other science. This implies that there is no need for common ground and that food history is subservient to other histories or sciences. Here, food history, and food studies in general, give in to the research agenda of other (sub)disciplines, hence the more or less moderate attention paid by anthropologists, sociologists, natural scientists, or social geographers to (food) history,[27] which has proved to be very gratifying.

Second, there is food historiography that spans social, political, economic, cultural, medical, intellectual, and any other history or science—that is, an umbrella approach that is solidly rooted in historical questions and debates. It is argued that food has all the features to play such a leading role, even to the extent of evoking a new world history (or chronology).[28] Common ground, then, is supplied by the historical sciences' habitual techniques: historical critique, use of historical sources, historical problems, and so on. By no means, however, is one common ground possible or wished for because of the myriad approaches in historical sciences, ranging from positivism to new historicism, from economic history to cultural history, and from emic to etic approaches.[29] This richness appears in today's food historiography on modern Europe and seems to have developed at an ever-increasing pace since 2005. The recent literature—in fact, a torrent of books, papers, and book chapters—can be systematized in five categories that each have clear common features: the commodity biography, long-term history, transnational history, history of inequality, and history of health.[30]

The commodity biography has been around for longer, and Mintz's *Sweetness and Power* is often referred to as a model. After a first wave of successful work in the 1990s (e.g., on salt, cod, tomatoes, and chocolate), it seems that the interest in commodity biographies has revived recently (e.g., beans, potatoes, cheese, milk, tea, tomatoes, and truffles).[31] In general, sociocultural approaches are preferred, aiming at incorporating production, retailing, image, use, policies, and representations. With the recent interest in culinary heritage and traditional cooking, it seems likely that commodity biographies will flourish, paying interest to so-called forgotten vegetables, fruits, or herbs.[32] Socioeconomic historians have applied a variant of the commodity biography when discovering the benefits of studying the food chain, paying particular attention to food processing and marketing. Often they focus on a single product while increasingly paying attention to cultural matters, although mostly keeping to only one link in the chain.[33] The vivid interest in the history of food retailing is part of this trend. Again, this is not a new field of study, but the focus has shifted from a primarily economic approach to the intersection of histories of business, consumption, and design. Moreover, the understanding of the effects of lengthening the food chain, with the move from markets to supermarkets, has led to interest in the psychology of sellers and buyers.[34]

A second line of interest is the exploration of leading threads in food history from prehistoric times to tomorrow.[35] The commodity biographies noted in the previous paragraph contain some examples of long-run world history,[36] but a growing number of individual authors dare to address *all* food and drink throughout time and place.[37] This seems to offer, too, a fertile field for publishing large, collective overviews,[38] as well as books in the genre of public history (sometimes linked to "historic culinary performances").[39] Today, all of these books offer the literature that some critics asked for. In general, trained historians publish this kind of work, although some amateurs, without any inhibition and having diverse or no academic training, practice the genre too. Both wish to offer large syntheses of a gigantic and complex development, hoping to bring some clarity to world history as such (although some view their contribution as an "appetizer" or an "amuse bouche").[40] Naturally, such ventures are risky, leaning toward overgeneralizations and confirming stereotypical knowledge, and, regrettably, they are often nothing more than a collection of anecdotes.[41] Moreover, they are often biased toward Eurocentrism.

A third category is dealing with the criticism of Eurocentrism, putting "Europe" or "the West" within the frame of the global exchange of foodstuffs, migrants, and ideas.[42] This category has attracted much attention for a decade, opening an eclectic field of possibilities where interdisciplinary approaches may flourish.[43] Historians Alexander Nützenadel and Frank Trentmann have published a collection that aims at counterbalancing the fragmentation of food studies by putting food definitely in a global perspective.[44] Their book pays attention to four pairs of dynamics and tensions: markets and empires, migration and identity, global and local actors, and food chains and moral geographies. These are linked to broad—both old and new—questions of socioeconomic historiography, such as the "great divergence" between the West and the rest,[45] colonialism and decolonization, hunger, identity construction, and migration. Such a global project, nevertheless, may be problematic in that the notion of globalization needs to be clearly defined. In this respect, one reviewer detects "rival and almost mutually exclusive approaches" among the authors of the volume,[46] which obviously adds to fragmentation.

Matters of identity appear within the context of transnational studies. Identity as a tool for analysis is not new, though, and prior to 2005 many researchers had looked for identities that are constructed through food. This line of research has continued.[47] However, what is new is situating food and identity within the study of ethnicity, emphasizing the encounter with "the other" (involving very diverse forms of conflict, hostility, negotiation, incorporation, and acculturation). For example, in 2006 anthropologist Thomas Wilson edited *Food, Drink and Identity in Europe*, in which food is situated within globalization studies that investigate the way peoples grow closer or drift apart.[48] This collection addresses the role of food in the construction of local, national, and international cultures. European culture is the primary focus, which offers a clear example of Eurocentrism. Yet it moves beyond simple Eurocentrism because it examines the matter of Europeanization—that is, the recent process of day-by-day adaptation to or rejection of norms and practices that are constructed as European, which leads to tension between people and institutions, between regions, and between individuals. Issues of identity construction also appear profusely in other work.[49] This interest will likely not disappear from food history writing, and particularly the interest in migrants' foodways and so-called ethnic cuisine may flourish.[50] This focus incorporates oral history, which proves to be a particularly enriching approach.[51]

One of Nützenadel and Trentmann's "pairs of dynamics and tensions" refers to "moral geographies," which addresses the history of hunger. This introduces the fourth category: inequality. This is not a new topic. By and large issues of food scarcity and hunger were left to traditional socioeconomic historians, who supplied highly significant work.[52] James Vernon, however, proposes a history of the perception of hunger in the British Empire (including India and Ireland), applying the tools and concepts of the cultural turn. He deals with social and political protests, hunger marches, policy making, statistics, political controversies, kitchen design, household education, social psychology, cooking utensils, Thatcherism, investigative journalism, workhouse diets, chemical laboratories, new words ("malnutrition," for example), and consumers' associations.[53] The thesis that politicians, the media, scientists, social critics, and the general public *construct* hunger and its amplitude and impact, and that hunger is not solely the consequence of the objectively measurable lack of food, will no doubt upset some readers. It has certainly upset some social historians as illustrated by a review by Derek Oddy, one of the leading researchers of modern British food history.[54] Oddy expresses his bewilderment with regard to the cultural approach, methods, and views, "dipping into sensational aspects of the subject without a coherent analytical approach." Overall, his critique focuses on the lack of materialistic grounds, the use of poststructuralism, and vagueness (of purpose, references, and methodology). On the paradigmatic level, and relevant to my question about interdisciplinarity, the review could have had as a title, "Who Needs the Cultural Turn?" Vernon's reply is equally sharp, mentioning Oddy's "misrepresentations and factual errors" and stressing that "I wanted to understand hunger as a cultural category, not a biological condition" in order to study "how and why the meaning of hunger changed over time."[55] This intellectual conflict is a telling example not only of diverging paradigmatic views but also of the great difficulty of crossing intellectual borders.

Vernon's book testifies to a renewed, more general interest in the history of hunger.[56] This implies attention to policy, which tightly connects food to political history writing.[57] In turn, the latter leads me to the study of living conditions during world wars, which has benefited from revived attention.[58] Here, approaches remain, in general, very traditional, although new ways are tested, focusing on consumers, retailers, black marketers, and producers as active players within the context of starvation, rationing, and ethics.[59] Research on food during periods of starvation and wars unavoidably addresses the question of food inequality between social classes. This type of research is classic in the field of food historiography; it somewhat lost its sway in the early twenty-first century but regained attention in the past couple of years, offering a mix of astoundingly traditional socioeconomic history writing with innovative cultural historiography.[60]

The problem of inequality and hunger introduces the fifth category: the history of health in relation to food. Once more, this investigation is not new,[61] but since 2005 an increasing number of researchers have dealt with it in an innovative way (i.e., a fully cultural history of dietary recommendations, laboratory investigations, vegetarianism, taboos, and illnesses). Food fraud, food scares, and food control became popular research themes most likely because these are high on today's public and political agenda.[62] In 2005, economic historian Alessandro Stanziani published a book that deals with the history of food quality in France, studying the *construction* of reputations of products, producers, and regions, using the examples of butter, meat, milk, and especially wine and questioning concepts like "pure," "natural," and "adulterated."[63] He considers changing markets, the hygiene movement, legislation and control with regard to falsification, technological innovation, and the ensuing power relations between consumers, producers, and the state. Reviewers of the book do not situate it in food history writing but stress its importance for economic theory and economic history.[64] In 2010, geographer Peter Atkins brought together his proficient research on the history of milk, which shows the relevance of state regulation, commercial interests, public health, technology, and transport, pleading for more attention to the materiality of foodstuffs. More new approaches to health and nutrition are offered in proceedings of recent conferences demonstrating the intense interest in this topic.[65] These publications take a thorough interdisciplinary scope, incorporating findings and techniques of the natural sciences (by dieticians, physicians, and chemists) and introducing new concepts like "biocultural."[66] Lots of studies have appeared with regard to particular temporal and spatial developments,[67] showing that the alliance between the social and natural sciences in the field of nutrition, medicine, and environment seems to be well on its way.

Five trends, therefore, have clearly developed since 2005. Other new trends may be added, but they are so far less marked. Attention to novels, with their abundant information about foodways, is clearly growing,[68] while the study of material culture of food (places and utensils) has certainly taken off.[69] Both connect historical sciences to literature, design, and (home) architecture, implying (to historians) the use of new sources and methods. Clearly, there are other interests, like the diffusion of taste and savoir faire (using cookbooks), the workers of the catering business (labor market, hierarchies, wages, hiring and firing, contracts), or celebrations (public and private occasions), but these are just on the verge of emergence.[70]

The question remains: What is the position of all this food history writing? If it is part of larger historical problems (the standard of living, development of etiquette, globalization process, diversification of taste, etc.), then food history may be perfectly content with a "subordinate" and assisting role as part of economic, social, political, or cultural history. However, food history may do exactly the opposite and surpass or integrate all domains, debates, and approaches, trying to achieve "total" or "integral" history, taking all possible societal changes together via food history. This, too, is justified because it may be argued that "food" has the ability of covering *all possible* developments indeed (see the preceding). So far, I see no examples of such an approach.[71] Still, there is the danger of separatism and reductionism and, hence, the danger that food history could lose track of other historical fields—that is, self-contently, food history could exclude itself from other disciplines, debates, approaches, or methodologies.[72] This must certainly be avoided.

A Solid House with a View

Today, food history inhabits a large house with many rooms, with the occasional remodeling of a new room. This house is very visible from a long distance. It is busy and noisy, and lights are on day and night. It looks solid and gleaming, and many people from all over the world pay it a visit. Its confusing atmosphere, which is caused by the many rooms with very different people, conversations, and ambiances, may worry some visitors. Not many other buildings accommodate such a varied collection of people who all wish to contribute to the writing of the history of food. Some dwellers consider food as their main (and sometimes only) concern, whereas others pose questions in which food plays a subordinate role.

The basement is divided into two large rooms. Agricultural historians occupy one room, but periodically imaginative socioeconomic historians visit this place to studying starvation, hunger, and social policy. The other basement room is occupied by ethnologists and archaeologists who study regional ways of cooking, products, and utensils in the past. They do not bother about historical problems, concepts, or literature, just as the historians in the other room do not care about ethnology or anthropology. There is no door between the two rooms, but each basement room has its own staircase leading to the ground floor. The stairs from the agricultural basement lead to a big room that used to be filled with social historians; a pallid picture of Fernand Braudel is still on the wall. Now and then, an agricultural historian climbs up. He or she may meet with sociocultural historians, geographers, sociologists, anthropologists, economists, philosophers, and even a psychologist, who all apply historical concepts, insights, sources, and methods. This room has many doors and windows that used to be wide open (some of them still are, but others have been closed, like the orthodox Marxist one). The ethnologists' basement has almost emptied out because most climbed the stairs to another large room that is filled with sociologists, anthropologists, and art historians from all over the world who study symbols, icons, objects, and communication related to food in the past and present (here is a recent picture of the venerable Claude Lévi-Strauss). There is a big, open door between this room and the social historians' room, and some social historians feel at ease in both rooms, adopting the theories, concepts, and findings of ethnology or anthropology. Other socioeconomic historians, however, cannot imagine ever entering the ethnologists' room, although they glance at what is going on in it.

Two smaller rooms on the ground floor were added not that long ago, and here is where youngsters particularly love to reside: poststructuralist historians in the one and poststructuralist ethnologists in the other room study representation, significance, exchange, and assimilation of taste and cuisine in the past and present. The door between them has been removed, and people circulate easily between these rooms. Some traditional social historians, ethnologists, sociologists, or art historians do stop over in both rooms, although they might feel very uncomfortable. These rooms are in direct contact with a room on the second floor where literary and communication scientists study the role of food in novels and films. The second floor also has a small room where natural scientists have dwelled for very long without having any contact with the other rooms; they study the history of nutrition, nutritionists, and food in relation to health. Recently, more and more people from the ground floor visit this small room, which might turn out to be far too small according to the growing interest in sociocultural matters of health, food quality, and safety. Finally, there is a tiny but cheerful room with journalists, artists, chefs, and amateurs without professional training who "do" food history without having much contact with the other people in the house. They love to publish nice coffee-table books.

All in all, a great variety of people live in this house. Some stay a short while and visit several rooms, perhaps coming back after a while, but others occupy a room for a very long time without ever leaving it. How should the rooms in this house be used? It would be wrong to run through every room and rapidly sniff its atmosphere. Also, it would be limiting to hang around in just one room. Either would lead to impressionistic and unconnected history writing. It would be far better to have a clear set of questions that are embedded in historical traditions and debates: This requires the usage of several rooms and the effort to integrate the other's wisdom in one's own research without, however, losing the basis of one's discipline. This explicitly implies that "doing" food history supposes the mastering of a discipline's approaches, methods, questionings, and traditions (be this history, ethnology, sociology, or any other). Furthermore, the dwellers and visitors in this house should make clear what the house is all about, convincing colleagues who live in other, sometimes remote houses to pay them a visit.

Food (culinary/gastronomic/taste) history has obtained great success in the past decade, and a growing number of "established" historians have turned to food history. Does this endeavor have an actual impact on general history, sociology, anthropology, or any other discipline? Should its impact increase? Despite ongoing specialization, I would plead to hang on to an interdisciplinary scope, for this is a guarantee of innovation and progress. This chapter deals with Europe. There are common traits between European food historiography and that in other regions, but to what extent? Which are the differences and similarities? Are there many contacts? This chapter deals with Europe, but which Europe? I focused on English, French, German, and some Italian and Spanish works, and I read journals with papers in English on countries with languages unknown to me. No doubt, I missed a lot of developments in northern, central, and eastern Europe. Finally, I did consider the relevance of food history for general history, but I did not consider the relevance of food history for sociology, anthropology, or other disciplines. This, however, is another chapter to be written.[73]

Notes

Many thanks to Priscilla Ferguson, Darra Goldstein, Merry White, and especially Kyri Claflin, for talks, thoughts, and comments.

1. Scholliers, 2007.
2. This section is about European history in the nineteenth and twentieth centuries, but similarities with preindustrial Europe are manifold; see Meyzie, 2010, 7–16, and Kyri Claflin's chapter in this book.
3. With regard to international influence, see, e.g., for Germany, Teuteberg, 2008, 26–29.
4. Teuteberg, 2008, 33–34.
5. Scholliers, 2007, 451.
6. Flandrin, 1999b, 19 and 22.
7. Wiegelmann, 1967 (reprinted 2006, including a postscript with comments and a comprehensive updated bibliography).
8. See Aron, 1976, the second edition of the original French. Subsequent editions appeared in 1989 and 1992. Aron wrote a contribution for the 1975 *Annales* collection, exploring food fraud in the nineteenth century, with no attention to cultural elements, though.
9. Poulain, 2002, 202.

10. Flandrin and Montanari, 1996b, 13.
11. Mintz, 1987; Goody, 1989.
12. Teuteberg, 2008, 32. H.-J. Teuteberg sees Wiegelmann as a *Türöffner* (i.e., a "door opener") for food ethnohistory.
13. Two pertinent articles: Flandrin, 1981, and Flandrin and Hyman, 1986.
14. Flandrin, 1999b, 19–22.
15. E.g., his extensive review of Goody and Mennell in Flandrin, 1987.
16. Flandrin and Montanari, 1996 (translated into Italian [1997], English [1999], and Spanish [2004]).
17. E.g., Ferguson (2005, 692) wrote that the "publication is a convenient benchmark for the coming-of-age of scholarly inquiry about food" and a "guiding book."
18. E. Spary, e.g., points at it as one of the recent books that "contribute to an increasingly rich cultural history of cuisine, tastes and recipes which stands independently of anthropology" (Spary, 2005, 769).
19. D. Gabaccia sees primarily a Eurocentric and Mediterranean bias, individual (short) essays, and myth deconstruction, but no "historical introduction to world foodways" (Gabaccia, 2001, 987).
20. The authors' geographical origins are as follows: France: 19; Italy: 15; Germany, the United States, and Spain: 2 each; the United Kingdom, Austria, Canada, and Switzerland: 1 each. The nonhistorians are the sociologist C. Fischler and geographers Y. Péhaut and J.-R. Pitte.
21. Lévi-Strauss is acknowledged via the words "le ton a été donné par C. Lévi-Strauss" (p. 13).
22. Hémardinquer, Stouff, Bernard, Boehler, Aron, Dumon, and Le Roy Ladurie are mentioned.
23. The latter is shown by de Vries, 2008 ("Food" appears in forty-six places in the book).
24. Kirkby, Luckins, and Santich, 2007, 6.
25. Ferguson, 2005, 700; Super, 2002, 175; Atkins, 2010, 4.
26. Ferguson, 2005, 699; Spary, 2005, 771; Super, 2002, 175.
27. Freidberg, 2010.
28. Montanari, 2003, 1 and 16.
29. Miller and Deutsch, 2009, 79–80 and 88.
30. P. Atkins's (2010, 4) nine dimensions are an alternative: food systems, diets, feasting and fasting, health, cooking, catering, technology, politics, and symbols. Another alternative is J. Pilcher's five themes: diffusion of food, tension between agriculture and pastoralism, class, identities, and the state (Pilcher, 2006a).
31. E.g., Albala, 2007b; Kaplan, 2008; Portincasa, 2008; Horowitz, 2006; Reader, 2009; Krieger, 2009; Atkins, 2010; Gentilcore, 2010; Rittersma, 2010.
32. Stocks, 2008. An immeasurable number of cookbooks exist that deal with traditional, authentic, genuine, historical, or grandma's recipes, ingredients, and

cooking. Moreover, this interest leads to public-history events where old food-ways are tested.

33. Sarasúa, Scholliers, and Van Molle, 2005; Bieleman, Buyst, and Segers, 2009; Belasco and Horowitz, 2009. An example of studies that deal with one food item: Godley and Williams, 2009.

34. Schroter, 2008; Barker, 2009; Alexandre et al., 2010, Teughels, 2010; Van den Eeckhout and Scholliers, 2011.

35. This approach is enthusiastically welcomed by "world historians," e.g., Y. Chen, 2010.

36. E.g., Gately, 2008.

37. E.g., Civitello, 2004; Rowley, 2006; Freedman, 2007; Pilcher, 2006a; Standage, 2009. With regard to food in one country, see, e.g., Rambourg, 2005.

38. E.g., Allen, Albala, and Nestle, 2007; Albala, 2011; Parasecoli and Scholliers, 2011.

39. E.g., Rotherham, 2009.

40. Civitello, 2004, xi.

41. E.g., Gélinet, 2008; this fluently written book jumps from one salient chapter ("Le suicide de Vatel") to another staggering theme ("La fabuleuse histoire du champagne"); hardly any notes or bibliographic references are given.

42. See Ferguson's (2005, 700) plea for the study of *movements* between times, places, people, and cultures, i.e., between markets, menus, and meals.

43. Scholliers and Grieco, 2009, with contributions by P. Atkins, D. Gentilcore, J. Contreras, M. Galli, J.-P. Williot, S. Zubaida, A. Kershen, and A. Crosby.

44. Nützenadel and Trentmann, 2008, 2. Noteworthy in terms of an interdisciplinary approach: the first footnotes of the Introduction refer to Lévi-Strauss and Goody (but both names do not reappear in the volume).

45. The term "great divergence" was coined by Pommeranz, 2000, and is widely used with regard to unequal social and, primarily, economic development between Europe and Asia (especially China and India).

46. Fernàndez-Armesto, 2008, 460.

47. Hache-Bissette and Saillard, 2007; Weinreb, 2011.

48. Wilson's book shows the social researchers' interest in past foodways: it brings together sociologists, anthropologists, literary scientists, and historians.

49. Tyrrell, Hill, and Kirkby, 2007; Franc, 2006; Warde, 2009; Montanari, 2010.

50. Cwiertka, 2005; Beyers, 2008; Panayi, 2008; Buettner, 2008; Amenda, 2009.

51. Duru, 2005.

52. Fogel, 2004.

53. Vernon, 2007.

54. Oddy, 2008.

55. Vernon, 2008.

56. Del Arco Blanco, 2010.

57. Brejon de Lavergnée, 2007; Lhuissier, 2007; Maixé-Altès, 2009; Gurney, 2009.

58. Buccheim, 2010; Mouré, 2010; K. Hunt, 2010.
59. Trentmann and Flemming, 2006; Linne, 2010; Futselaar, 2010.
60. Hyldtoft, 2007; Matalas, 2006; De Vooght, 2011.
61. Fenton, 2000.
62. Gratzer, 2005; Bernabeu-Mestre and Barona-Vilar, 2008; Steere-Williams, 2010; Van den Eeckhout and Scholliers, 2011; Geyzen, 2011; Spiekermann, 2011.
63. See also Stanziani, 2007.
64. Prestwich, 2007; Simmons, 2007.
65. Audoin-Rouzeau and Sabban, 2007; Oddy, Atkins, and Amilien, 2009; Grieco and Scholliers, 2008.
66. Moffat and Prowse, 2010.
67. Waddington, 2006; Wilson, 2008; Barona, 2008; the section "Food Regulation" in Atkins, Lummel, and Oddy, 2007, 77–128 (including chapters by V. Hierholzer, D. Oddy, P. Scholliers, and A. Stanziani); Baumann, 2008; Orland, 2010.
68. Daly and Forman, 2008; Gymnich, Lennartz, and Scheunemann, 2010.
69. Young Lee, 2005 (with contributions on Europe by D. Brantz, K. Claflin, I. McLachlan, C. Otter, and P. Young Lee); Williot, 2006; Januarius, 2008; Kenneally and Lebel, 2009; Mutch, 2010.
70. Respectively, Drouard, 2007 (on France); Dennis, 2008 (with a long-term view); Driver, 2009 (on Canada); Lavandier et al., 2005 (on French presidential receptions); Söderlind, 2010 (on the Nobel Prize banquets; see also http://nobelprize.org/nobel_prizes/award_ceremonies/banquet/menus/).
71. The series Food Culture around the World (general editor: Ken Albala) may be seen as attempting this integrated survey (with regard to Europe, this series contains volumes on the Mediterranean, Scandinavia, Belgium, Germany, France, Spain, Great Britain, and Italy).
72. Super, 2002, 175. See, too, Grignon, 2007, 6–7.
73. Food history is only moderately present in, e.g., Germov and Williams, 2008 (sociology) and Counihan and Van Esterik, 1997 (anthropology).

Sustenance, Abundance, and the Place of Food in U.S. Histories

Amy Bentley

Food is at the base of human existence and has long been a part of the historical record, but only in the last couple of decades has food been a major focus of study in the United States. While in the past historians would undoubtedly have agreed that food is at the base of civilizations (recall, for example, the old adages "An army moves on its stomach" and "Tell me what you eat; I will tell you who you are"), most would have regarded food as too trivial to be at the center of a serious field of study. Thus, the idea that food has a history worth documenting remained largely unacknowledged by most academic historians, though it lay embedded in the more established subdisciplines of history: economic, political, and, more recently, social and cultural history. Even today one is hard-pressed to find a sustained discussion of food in mainstream college and high school U.S. history textbooks. For even as food history and the broader field of food studies have gained momentum in recent years, in some traditional academic circles food history remains secondary, originally because of the deep association of food with the domestic (and thus female) sphere, and also because of its more recent alliance with the field of popular culture. This chapter examines the historiography of food in U.S. history, charting its growth and development, including the tensions regarding recognition. These tensions are not without irony, given that the conflicts over and ideas about the overwhelming American abundance of material resources, including food, have been such a driving force in U.S. history.

Food History: Origins, Antecedents, and Definitions

"Food history" in the United States overlaps and intersects with other related topics, including histories of agriculture, the environment, nutrition, health, technology, and culture. Although consumption has been the primary focus of food history, it is also an umbrella term covering agriculture, culinary history, nutrition and diet, environmental history, commodities, and technology, among others. While "food" remained on the periphery of academic historical scholarship until recently, "agriculture" was a fairly regular topic of interest for gentlemen of letters and early historians of the eighteenth and nineteenth centuries. Later, in the early to mid-twentieth century, food mainly functioned as an indistinctive backdrop through which to examine, for example, labor relations (workers in canning factories and slaughterhouses), agrarian political movements (the Grange movement), or industrialization (the rise of food-processing conglomerates).

It has become more acceptable to explore the lives of everyday people, including women and minorities. This, combined with the rise in cultural history—especially that which explores consumption in all its forms—created an atmosphere in which formerly mundane and seemingly irrelevant topics, including food, were deemed worthy of scholarly historical inquiry. In retrospect, it is surprising that it took such a long time for food-centered history to emerge. After all, not only does everyone have to eat (and ideally several times daily) to survive, but great civilizations, both ancient and modern, meticulously recorded by traditional history, have essentially risen and fallen according to rulers' abilities to feed their people.

While food history is a subdiscipline of history, it is also positioned within "food studies," food-focused interdisciplinary research grounded in the humanities and soft social sciences. Food studies has distinct and important antecedents in a number of disciplines, including anthropology and folklore, fields that have long regarded the study of food as key to understanding cultures and societies and the lives of individuals. Anthropologists including Audrey Richards, Claude Lévi-Strauss, Mary Douglas, and Marvin Harris all wrote extensively and perceptively about the place of food in diverse cultures.[1] Folklorists, including Donald Yoder, who is credited with coining the term *foodways*, approached food as material culture in its vernacular settings in the United States.[2] Amateur and professional cookbook writers and food journalists focusing on cuisine, ingredients, and cooking techniques have been vital to the development of food studies scholarship. Libraries that once refused or self-consciously maintained cookbook collections are now proudly developing and promoting them, and correspondingly receiving large numbers of researchers.[3]

While tending to be more focused on food consumption than production, food studies also owes a debt to the many biologists, food activists, nutritionists, and rural social scientists who have focused on food production. Generally more oriented toward the sciences and hard social sciences and quantitative methods, these scholars speak in terms of "food systems," chains of institutions, processes, and peoples linking the production of food with its distribution. They tend to concentrate on the relations of food production to economics, the environment, and human nutrition yet increasingly have recognized the importance of understanding food in its social, cultural, and historical contexts.

Food within Traditional U.S. Historiography

From the colonial era on, Americans have recorded the histories of their communities, but food, while tremendously important to these early communities, was not a prominent feature in the written record. Colonial leaders John Smith and William

Bradford, for example, compiled "city on a hill" records of their settlements, and others created narratives that provided providential evidence for Europeans' migration and eventual creation of successful settlements in the New World. Food was, of course, critically important to the settlers as is evident from George Percy's account of the Virginia colonists' "starving time" and the draconian measures, as recorded by William Strachey, meted out in the face of desperation, violence, and even cannibalism.[4] Similarly, William Bradford's brief mention of a Pilgrim/Native American feast of "thanksgiving" notwithstanding, overall food production and consumption were largely omitted from these early historical accounts.[5] Neither the record keepers nor the more official historians of the period focused much on documenting information about food.

Nineteenth-century Romantic-era histories, such as those of George Bancroft and Francis Parkman, gave food even less attention, even though their sweeping grand narratives presented an optimistic vision of American progress built on the economics and politics of abundance.[6] The next school of historians overlooked food as well. The early twentieth-century progressive strain in American history, led by such historians as Charles Beard, Frederick Jackson Turner, Vernon Parrington, and Arthur Schlesinger, Sr., steered away from the earlier grand romantic narratives, focusing instead on conflict.[7] Inspired by the reform impulses occurring at the time of their writing, the progressives were concerned with larger themes of class conflict, economic interpretations of the Constitution, and, in Turner's case, the ways in which Americans and their institutions were shaped by the frontier and its closing.[8]

These historians simply did not see food as central to national development, especially as compared with other topics: politics, class conflict, economics, international trade and relations, religious and intellectual movements, and scientific discoveries. While food is embedded in all of these subjects, perhaps because of its ephemeral and domestic nature (an issue discussed in detail later), or perhaps because of food's visceral sensuality and its intimate connection with bodies and bodily functions, food consumption was neglected as a topic fit for serious historical inquiry. Further, historians of this era (knowingly or not) took a "great man" approach to historical events: that men—men in nearly all cases—because of some element of their character (bravery, charisma, integrity) are the primary cause in determining a course of events. While some early histories more grounded in economics or influenced by Darwinism,[9] for example, analyzed events in broader structural terms, it would be several decades before the great-man approach was effectively challenged.

When food did appear as a subject of historical scholarship, it tended to be in the form of production (agriculture and to a lesser extent processing) rather than consumption. To illustrate in quantitative terms, a survey of the flagship U.S. history journal, the *Mississippi Valley Historical Review*, revealed that from 1914, the journal's beginning, to 1964 (when the *MVHR* became the *Journal of American History*, which remains the American history journal of record) agriculture as a topic heavily outweighed the topic of food consumption. In that fifty-year period, 32 journal articles and 115 book reviews featured agriculture and food processing, while only 2 articles and 8 book reviews focused on food and food consumption.[10] Indeed, historians were interested enough in agricultural history that it was able to sustain its own organization and professional journal. In the early twentieth century, a group of employees at the U.S. Department of Agriculture (USDA) formed the Agricultural History Society. Scholarship in the society's journal, *Agricultural History*, has until the late twentieth century tended to focus on such traditional topics as agricultural economics, crop production, and agrarian political movements.[11]

Prior to World War II, a few exceptions to the absence of food-centered studies dot the historiographical landscape. The most prominent example, Richard O. Cummings's *The American and His Food: A History of Food Habits in the United States* (1940), grew out of Cummings's training in the history of science and technology. Cummings explained that while writing a dissertation on the history of the American ice industry he "looked for a work on diet but found that the subject had been neglected by historians."[12] *The American and His Food*, a history of food and nutrition in the United States up to 1940, told a sweeping tale of colonial and early republic history mainly focused on changes in the food supply as a result of scientific and technological developments and the subsequent effects of these changes on Americans' nutrition. A reviewer of the book wondered why no one had written such a book before: "Since written history is supposed to survey everything that has concerned man, the history of food should have some place in general accounts and special studies. One might wonder why more attention has not been given to it in the past since so much of man's primary activity is directed to the securing of food, shelter, and clothing."[13] Despite the reviewer's acknowledgment of neglect and Cummings's important study, the field did not take off. Indeed, *The American and His Food* was perhaps the only academic history of food in the United States for several decades, and it served as a model for later books covering the same terrain.

After World War II: Midcentury Consensus History

In the mid-twentieth century historians began to take more notice of the role of food in American historical scholarship. The dominant zeitgeist of the period, commonly known as "consensus history," tended to focus on Americans' common attributes and experiences, what citizens might have in common rather than the class or cultural differences featured by the progressive historians of an earlier generation.[14] Influenced by Cold War anxieties, consensus historians found a natural contrast, for example, between U.S. politics and culture and that of its rival, the Soviet Union, a contrast that minimized differences among Americans themselves and accentuated American abundance and plenty. The "melting pot" metaphor popular in the early twentieth century found renewed popularity, and, combined with an emboldened postwar notion of American exceptionalism, consensus historians often struck a celebratory tone. Yet largely as a result of the two World Wars and advances in transportation and communications, scholarship in this period frequently exhibited an element of cosmopolitanism as well, an awareness of the place of the United States within a larger world.

Though food is not a central component of consensus history, two prominent consensus historians, Daniel Boorstin and David Potter, featured food in their historical analyses. Boorstin, perhaps the most prominent, if not the most popular, consensus historian of the period spent a dozen years as the librarian of Congress after having taught history at the University of Chicago for twenty-five years. His three-volume series, *The Americans* (which won major awards including the Bancroft, Parkman, and Pulitzer prizes), highlighted the importance of food as a fairly significant component of U.S. growth and development. The genius of American citizens, Boorstin argued, was their pragmatism, which was produced in part as a result of the landscape and material conditions in which they lived and was therefore not necessarily reproducible in other countries. In the second volume, for example, Boorstin used food as an example of the democratic nature of mass production as canning, shipping, and mass production of meat resulted in overall better diets for Americans.[15]

Similarly, Potter's well-known 1954 study, *People of Plenty: Economic Abundance and the American Character*, employed a material analysis of what used to be unselfconsciously called the "American character." Potter, in part writing against the progressivists, argued that the United States and its citizens have been shaped, blessed, and at times intellectually and socially hindered by inhabiting one of the most resource-rich and economically successful countries in the world. *People of Plenty* was one of the first studies to connect American abundance to several phenomena, including increased mobility, decreased emphasis on community, advertising, individualism, and the distinct nature of American democracy, including the illusion of classlessness. Careful to develop how abundance shapes individuals as well as society, Potter articulated—and saw as related—the enormous impact of abundance in both the public and private spheres. Potter argued that the long history of abundance in the United States—a product of both natural resources and technological innovation—profoundly shaped the American character and outlook. He described the country's vast natural resources, its large expanses of seemingly uninhabited land perceived as inexhaustible and available for the taking, impressive industrial and scientific advances, and (at his time) the world's highest per capita income, caloric consumption, and agricultural output. Noting that the average American consumed 3,186 kilocalories daily (or that this number of calories was theoretically available in the food supply), Potter characterized the American diet as "unquestionably the highest nutritional standard in the world."[16] World War II for Potter illuminated the idea that for those living elsewhere in the world, the promise of America was not its abstract ideals of democracy but its concrete realities, symbolized by, among other items, an abundance of food.

The 1980s: Food History Emerges

In contrast to the consensus history of the 1950s, the 1960s set in motion a period of great intellectual, social, and cultural upheaval. Spurred on by the successes of the African American civil rights movement, other marginalized groups asserted their rights to equality under the law, access to opportunity, and social acceptance in society. Further, in the 1970s many Americans assumed a post-Vietnam, post-Watergate distrust of government and of institutions in general. Baby boomers, now college-aged, experimented with creative alternatives to the social status quo, and the United States witnessed dramatic changes with regard to sexual mores, music, fashion, cultural expression, and ideology. Women and minorities asserted their right to what previously had been the purview of mainly white middle- and upper-class males, including employment opportunities, higher education, and political office. The personal had indeed become the political. These dramatic social movements helped foster a new paradigm for historical scholarship—a transformation of the notion of who and what, for example, was an acceptable topic for academic study. Whereas in earlier generations "history" meant the stories of powerful men and powerful institutions, the new social history of the 1960s and 1970s shifted the focus to the lives of ordinary people. This, combined with previously marginalized groups' assertions of distinctiveness and neglect in historical accounts, led to the possibilities of new histories yet to be written.

The French *Annales* school should also be credited for having decades earlier understood food as integral in uncovering the history of European peoples from the Middle Ages onward. World systems historians, including Fernand Braudel and Immanuel Wallerstein, employed political-economic analysis to understand food as a commodity and as vital to daily subsistence across the centuries.[17] Thus, greater awareness of the private sphere and the seemingly mundane opened the door to food as a more legitimate topic of inquiry. Robert Forster and Orest A. Ranum's 1979 *Food and Drink in History*, a book comprised of food-focused articles originally published in the journal *Annales: Economies, Sociétés, Civilisations*, contains articles with such titles as "The Family Pig of the *Ancien Régime*," and "The Art of Using Leftovers, Paris, 1850–1900." Also included in this volume was Roland Barthes's notable semiotics analysis, "Toward a Psychosociology of Contemporary Food Consumption."[18]

In addition to social transformations, the 1970s witnessed a growing environmental movement, which fostered food history via the emerging topic of environmental history. World historian Alfred Crosby's book *The Columbian Exchange: Biological and Cultural Consequences of 1492* (1972), focused on the environmental effects of sustained exchange between Eurasia and Africa (the "Old World") and the Americas (the "New World"). While Crosby focused on how the transfer of people, plants, animals, and germs worked to the planet's detriment, not benefit, two central chapters focus in detail on the plants and animals that made their way across the Atlantic Ocean from one continent to the other (going both directions, west to east and east to west), leading to dramatic changes with regard to nutrition, culture, and cuisine as well as the environment. While more recent scholarship has refined, further developed, and in some cases refuted parts of Crosby's scholarship, *The Columbian Exchange* was pathbreaking in method and argument and is still a mainstay of American food history writing.

In addition to environmentally centered attention to food history, this period assumed a more cosmopolitan attitude and aesthetic that left its mark on the still-incipient field of food studies. Inspired in part by Jackie Kennedy's attention to French haute cuisine, educated housewives bought Julia Child's *Mastering the Art of French Cooking* and engaged in what Betty Fussell describes as "competitive home cooking."[19] The boom in appreciation for and experimentation with French cuisine extended to the cuisines of other countries. In the 1970s Time-Life publishers launched a series of cookbooks, *Foods of the World*. While reviewers pointed to shortcomings and inaccuracies, the series became immensely popular among a growing affluent, educated middle class that had traveled or was at least interested in re-creating cuisines and tastes from abroad.[20] In addition, several volumes covered American regional foodways. Volumes such as *American Cooking: Creole & Acadian* (1971) and *American Cooking: The Northwest* (1970) helped Americans regain an appreciation for the indigenous foods and cultures of their country as having value and importance.[21]

Culinary historians, both amateur and professional, flexed their muscles as they cast a critical eye at the increasingly industrialized food in the United States. Culinary historian Karen Hess, with her husband, *New York Times* food critic John L. Hess, in their book *The Taste of America* (1977) blasted the "fancy" food in the United States and celebrated the "real" regional cuisines and dishes of the country. Also, a new hybrid, the historical cookbook, was gaining momentum. Part history book, part cookbook, the genre appealed to a public interested in food and dining. Betty Fussell's *Masters of American Cookery—M.F.K. Fisher, James Andrews Beard, Raymond Craig Claiborne, Julia McWilliams Child* (1983) offered a new kind of "great man" narrative of American food and dining history. Fussell's *I Hear America Cooking: The Cooks, Regions, and Recipes of American Regional Cuisine* (1984), a Book-of-the-Month Club selection, took a more folkloristic approach to American regional cuisine.[22] These books showed that there was a popular audience eager for accessible, creative histories of food.

Against the backdrop of the growing interest in things culinary, the mid- to late 1980s can be thought of as the first "wave" of substantial U.S. food history by trained historians and social scientists. Food emerged as a focus of serious attention, the result of a maturing social history movement, women's history, and feminist scholarship that was expanding in breadth and depth, combined with the so-called cultural turn in history, which employed linguistic theory to explore the importance of beliefs and assumptions and their causal role in group behavior. Several strong food-focused histories were published in the mid- to late 1980s, all of which were in part products of the current intellectual and social milieu. The authors creatively employed methodologies from various disciplines to craft rich cultural and social histories of food.

Deeply influenced by the civil rights movement and the 1960s "rediscovery" of hunger in America, in 1986 social historian Janet Poppendieck published *Breadlines Knee Deep in Wheat: Food Assistance in the Great Depression.* Poppendieck sought to tell the story of hunger in America during the Great Depression through chronicling of government assistance programs, particularly farm programs such as the Agricultural Adjustment Act (AAA), which attempted to prop up the failing agricultural system. Demonstrating the paradox of so many hungry Americans amid such agricultural (over)abundance, *Breadlines* was ultimately also a book about food as seen through the lens of 1960s radicalism. In stark contrast to the consensus historians' unifying "national character," the book vividly recounts iconic Depression moments, such as the bulldozing of tons of edible grain and the slaughtering of thousands of pigs—while one-third of the nation was without adequate food—in attempts to stabilize food prices, which had dropped so dramatically in the 1930s that it threatened to bring the food system to a collapse. Ultimately viewing these government programs as a failure, *Breadlines* ended on a pessimistic note—the government programs of an abundant nation failed to adequately feed its citizens.

Warren James Belasco's 1989 book *Appetite for Change: How the Counterculture Took On the Food Industry* came from a similar perspective. Like Poppendieck, Belasco offered a criticism of the consensus narrative of abundance. Belasco, an American studies scholar whose first book was on car culture, realized that food was an equally powerful force in twentieth-century American culture. In *Appetite for Change*, part history and part autobiography, Belasco, a product of the baby boom and participant in the counterculture about which he wrote, examines how food became an effective and compelling countercultural movement through such experiments as communes, food co-ops, vegetarian restaurants, and cookbooks. However, Belasco recounts pessimistically that ethnic food, vegetarian items, and even yogurt and herbal tea were ultimately co-opted and smoothed over by a corporate culture looking to make a buck off the new tastes, flavors, and dishes of the counterculture.

Despite some feminists' initial reluctance, the strong influence of the women's movement on academic scholarship contributed greatly to the rise and development of food history in the 1980s and 1990s. The first wave of women's history in the 1970s and 1980s mainly attempted to write women back into history, to tell the stories of women in prominent positions who were previously ignored or underappreciated—a sort of "great women in history" response to traditional history. Early feminist historians were not attracted to such domestic subjects as food and the kitchen—topics, after all, that many felt had limited women's talents and opportunities. Yet female daily involvement with food was so central to women's experience for so long that it was ultimately, and eventually, fertile ground for feminist scholars.

Independent historian and journalist Laura Shapiro, influenced by the feminist movement, originally sought to write a biography of Fannie Farmer, the prominent Bostonian who published the popular *Fannie Farmer Cookbook* (1896). Upon realizing there was not quite enough material for a full biography, Shapiro realized food was clearly the central focus. "[The story] was all about food," she remembered later, "and the food was so mysterious, so inexplicable. I looked at menu after menu, recipe after recipe, and kept thinking to myself, why? Why are they cooking this way? What appeals to them? Why are they putting four saltines around a fruit salad and tying it all up with a ribbon? And gradually I started to figure it out by putting women's lives to bear on the food in front of them."[23] The result was her 1986 book, *Perfection Salad: Women and Cooking at the Turn of the Century.* In addition to the book's recognition in the popular press, the *Journal of American History*'s review was laudatory. Commenting specifically on Shapiro's cultural analysis of food, cultural historian William Leach noted, "Shapiro's extended and brilliant homage to white sauce alone makes the book worth its price. Used to blanket and to 'subjugate' all forms of food, from chicken to alfalfa greens, white sauce epitomized the ideological thrust of germ-free blandness."[24]

That the review appeared at all in the *Journal of American History* is significant, for in a period when few books on the history of food consumption were being written, let alone reviewed by an academic journal, it indicates that such a topic had begun to be acknowledged by the gatekeepers of the profession. While *Perfection Salad* was not universally well received (dietitians felt slighted by the book's poking gentle fun at the profession), such attention to a book about food and women was notable. Other important works of food history emerged through the portal of women's history. Joan Jacobs Brumberg's 1988 book, *Fasting Girls: The History of Anorexia Nervosa*, employed cultural analysis to write a book about the power and importance of food—and the refusing of it—for young women in the Victorian era. Rima Apple's 1987 *Mothers and Medicine: A Social History of Infant Feeding, 1890–1950*, employed food, in this case artificial infant formulas and infant feeding, to understand more about women's lives and the role of technology, advertising, and the medical profession on infant feeding.[25]

Perhaps the most influential food history book of the 1980s is Sidney Mintz's 1985 *Sweetness and Power: The Place of Sugar in Modern History.* A cultural history of the production and consumption of sugar, *Sweetness and Power*, while not solely about the United States, was central to the development of U.S. food history. Mintz, an anthropologist, extensively detailed and analyzed the transatlantic production and consumption of sugar from the colonial era through the mid-twentieth century, weaving into the story economics, colonization, industrialization, cultural meanings of sugar and their alteration over time, nutrition and health, and issues of class and race. Mintz deftly and inextricably linked the Caribbean slaves who planted, harvested, and processed the sugar to the British working classes who, as the backbone of the Industrial Revolution, consumed vast quantities of that sugar as a significant portion of their daily caloric intake.

Further, Mintz made remarkable use of a wide variety of sources, including recipe books from the British Library. This fact made at least one reviewer regard the book as less legitimate for using such "trivial" domestic sources.[26] Finally, Mintz's book was unique in that it put an edible commodity squarely at the center of the work and examined it from all angles, using multiple methods and theoretical frameworks. Though it was not unheard of to write about a specific food before *Sweetness and Power*,[27] Mintz's book legitimized the practice and dozens of single-food histories have been published since, especially within the last decade.[28]

Mintz's work bore influence from the burst of multidisciplinary scholarship on the history of slavery in the United States and elsewhere. Others in this area picked up on the importance of food as well, including the folklorist Charles Joyner in his 1986 book *Down by the Riverside: A South Carolina Slave Community*. Building on slavery scholarship that sought to connect American slaves with their cultures in Africa, Joyner examined the cultural practices and religious beliefs of Carolina slaves (religion, folktales, housing, metalwork) and linked them to their antecedents in Africa. Joyner focused on foods (yams, rice, collard greens) and foodways (growing, threshing, and preparation methods) inherited from Africa, a theme geographer Judith Carney further developed in her 2001 book *Black Rice: The African Origins of Rice Cultivation in the Americas*.

Also a part of the 1980s food history scholarship was Harvey Levenstein's general history of U.S. food. While a couple of U.S. food histories had been published in the decades since Cummings's 1940 *The American and His Food*,[29] Levenstein's 1988 *Revolution at the Table: The Transformation of the American Diet* provided a needed updating and further development of the story of the American landscape of food. Levenstein, a social historian by training, surveyed the importance of food in the United States from the 1880s to the 1930s. (His companion book published in 2002, *Paradox of Plenty: A Social History of Eating in Modern America*, continued the narrative through the end of the twentieth century.) Levenstein's insightful description, combined with a wealth of alternately humorous and sobering anecdotes and its wide array of information about food in modern U.S. society, made for a stimulating glimpse into American culture. *Revolution at the Table* managed to take food in the United States seriously but was critical enough to note its ironies, including an abundance of food that led to an ethos of quantity over quality, and Americans' sometimes blind devotion to the latest scientific theory that dictated what and how to eat.

Finally, in addition to social movements and the new social history, the development of cultural studies, which employs linguistic and literary theory to analyze both historical and contemporary phenomena, was also important to 1980s food scholarship. Just as Mintz employed cookbooks and recipes as legitimate primary sources, the idea of recipes as cultural texts gained legitimacy in this first wave of food history. Postmodernist theory allowed scholars to "read" any number of objects and artifacts as texts: chairs, musical instruments, and buildings, as well as food and recipes. Cookbooks, however, especially community cookbooks, took somewhat longer to be regarded as serious historical artifacts. Attitudes gradually began to change, in part aided by literary scholar Susan Leonardi's 1989 article "Recipes for Reading: Summer Pasta, Lobster à la Riseholme, and Key Lime Pie." Exploring the changing texts and contexts of subsequent editions of the *Joy of Cooking*, Leonardi demonstrated that recipes are a highly embedded discourse and that they also have a social context. Wondering aloud if they might exhibit a "female" discourse as well, Leonardi demonstrated such an approach through her conversational style and placement of herself as a cook squarely within the pages of the article. This piece had a galvanizing effect on food studies scholarship in that it provided solid justification as well as a template for using recipes as texts. Although other articles employing recipes and cookbooks as texts had been published,[30] Leonardi's article garnered an enthusiastic and sustained reception. Anne Bower's 1997 collection of essays on women and cookbooks, *Recipes for Reading: Community Cookbooks, Stories, Histories*, was a direct acknowledgment of Leonardi's work.[31]

The Turn of the Twenty-First Century: Food History Reaches Critical Mass

In recent decades we have witnessed an emerging food "revolution" that has attempted to counter (or at least circumvent) the worst aspects of the industrialization of food and its abundance of cheap, highly processed food. Those involved in the current food revolution have worked to demonstrate the connection between good food and sustainable agricultural practices and to create better-tasting, higher-quality food for restaurants and home consumption. Scholarly and political attention to food matters has deepened as the field of food studies has developed and as popular books by Eric Schlosser, Marion Nestle, and Michael Pollan, combined with films such as Morgan Spurlock's *Supersize Me* (2004), have exposed an interested public to the questionable practices of the food industry and the government's willingness to accommodate food-industry demands.[32] Add to the mix the boom in culinary tourism, restaurants, food television, books, magazines, cooking classes, artisanal products, and the search for "authentic" cuisine of every sort—as well as rooftop gardening, locavores, and freegan dumpster diving—and the result is a surfeit of interest and anxiety about food in America.

These phenomena have produced considerable interest in food studies as an academic field. Similarly, food history in the United States reached a new critical mass in the late twentieth and early twenty-first centuries. As U.S. history in general, social and cultural history, and the histories of material culture, popular culture, ethnicity, and race increased in popularity, so did histories of non-Western countries and populations. A long and varied list of food histories emanated from all of these subfields and more: social/labor history;[33] science and technology;[34] agricultural history;[35] women's/gender history;[36] race and ethnicity;[37] and cultural history and the history of consumption in its broadest sense.[38] Several university presses began their own food series, including University of Illinois, University of California, and Columbia University. In addition to the publications of several food encyclopedias and multivolume food histories,[39] numerous food histories were written foremost with a general audience in mind, yet another further indication of food scholarship entering the realm of mainstream history (both popular and scholarly).[40]

While much of the recent food history could be regarded as part of "first-stage" scholarship, there are many works that have gone beyond this initial stage and provided interesting, complex interpretations and perspectives. This includes the complexities of organic agriculture and its effects on small farms and migrant workers,[41] the documentation of the growing sense of nationalism that emerged among the colonists through a shared sense of consumption,[42] or the exploration of a similar "language of shared goods" during the lunch counter sit-ins of the civil rights era (which was being fought over: the right to sit, be served, and drink a Coca-Cola was not trivial but highly significant).[43] Similarly, in food history within the context of gender are works that show how food has multiple meanings for women, lending complexity to the relationship between women and food.[44]

Another compelling theme of current food history scholarship centers on whether a "national" cuisine exists in the United States. While some squarely point to hot dogs and hamburgers as the national unifying dishes, others point to more complex formulas and historical incidents, combined with industrialization and recent immigration, as developing a more intricate cuisine.[45] Others are quite insistent that there has never been and cannot ever be such a thing as an "American cuisine" and insist instead that cuisine lies at the geographical level of region as opposed to nation.[46] History/cookbook hybrids have also reached a new maturity, being published with different purposes in mind: cook-friendly collections of recipes with some history, or as more of a rigorous ethnography and history of a region and cuisine, with accompanying recipes, whose main purpose is to document dying traditions.[47]

Conclusion

The constant popularity of food history for the general reader and the proliferation of amateur historians writing and publishing food histories makes for a rich and interesting mix, though not without some tension. Over the decades, culinary historians (largely nonacademic) have produced a fair amount of culinary history that has mainly gone unnoticed (or ignored) by professional historians, in part because of the seemingly irrelevant nature of the topic, but also in some part because of the (perceived or real) amateurish quality of work. This potential tension between amateur and professional standards and conventions of historical scholarship is not new, nor is it uncommon in the broader landscape of historical scholarship.

Further, debates and divides exist among academic historians themselves over standards of evidence, thoroughness of research, historical claims, and uses of theory to inform empirical data. Cultural history, for example, as well as the study of popular culture, has been received by historians with varying degrees of enthusiasm. The history profession was thrown into somewhat of a crisis as postmodernism challenged positivism and empirical methods. Historians have gradually become more comfortable experimenting with new methods and theories and have also gradually accepted as legitimate topics those previously considered too mundane, such as food, though to many the topic still smacks of amateurism.

Finally, one historian, whose area of expertise is outside of food history, wonders if there is a high cost to developing a narrow, "laser-like focus" on food, "the cost of rendering it hermetic." For example, when one is writing about women and cookbooks, she posits, it may be difficult to resist the tendency to essentialize the relationship between women and food, to see it in gendered terms without critical analysis. Employing "frameworks that cut across cultural forms," argues Kathy Peiss, "would be a more fruitful approach."[48]

For these reasons it remains to be seen whether traditional history departments in the United States will ultimately embrace food history as a totality. Given current debates concerning food safety, global environmentalism, and the effect of food production on indigenous peoples and cultures worldwide, and with Americans' renewed interest in high-quality, minimally processed food, culinary tourism, and fine dining, combined with ever-rising rates of obesity and its adverse consequences, it is clear that food history as a focus of both scholarly and popular inquiry is a topic that is here to stay.[49]

Notes

1. Richards, 1939; Lévi-Strauss, 1970; Douglas, 1972; M. Harris, 1975.
2. Yoder, 1972.
3. Barron, 2011.
4. Percy, 1907; Strachey, 1969.
5. Bradford, 1856; see also LaCombe, 2012.
6. Bancroft, 1878; Parkman, 1869.
7. Beard, 1913; Turner, 1921; Parrington, 1927; Schlesinger, 1918.
8. Boyer, 2001.
9. Fiske, 1892.
10. Examples of topics include agricultural biographies, water/irrigation, agricultural policy, politics, economics, agrarianism, farm labor, plantation (slave) labor, ranching, dairying, fishing industries, sheep (whaling, salmon, oysters), sugar, rice, corn, farm and harvesting technology, and the wine, meat-packing, and fruit industries. On the consumption side, topics include the general history of food

consumption, restaurants, rum, alcohol, tea, grocery stores, vitamins, pigs, chocolate, and cookbooks.

11. Later the Agricultural History Society, as with all historical subdisciplines, evolved with the times; Danbom, 2010. Thanks to Brian Cannon for the reference.
12. Cummings, 1940, v.
13. Boudreau, 1942, 432.
14. Boyer, 2001.
15. Boorstin, 1973.
16. Potter, 1954, 83.
17. Braudel, 1981; Wallerstein, 1974.
18. Forster and Ranum, 1973.
19. Fussell, 2000.
20. Claiborne, 1968.
21. Book titles include *American Cooking: Creole & Acadian*; *American Cooking: The Eastern Heartland*; *American Cooking: The Great West*; *American Cooking: The Melting Pot*; *American Cooking: New England*; *American Cooking: The Northwest*; *American Cooking: Southern Style*.
22. For an important folklore perspective see Camp, 1989.
23. Correspondence with Shapiro; notes in author's possession.
24. Leach, 1986, 785.
25. See also Curren, 1989.
26. Roxborough, 1986, 575. See also Bentley, 2008.
27. Salaman, 1949.
28. E.g., Coe and Coe, 1996; Edge, 2006; Fussell, 1992; Jenkins, 2000; Kurlansky, 1997; Smith, 1994.
29. Hooker, 1981; Root and De Rochemont, 1976.
30. For example, Kirshenblatt-Gimblett, 1987.
31. The material culture of food and dining are also important at this time. See Grover, 1988.
32. Schlosser, 2001; Nestle, 2002; Pollan, 2006; Spurlock, 2004.
33. Rothenberg, 2000.
34. Horowitz, 2006; Cronon, 1991; Belasco and Scranton, 2002.
35. Guthman, 2004; Stoll, 2002; Horwitz, 1998; Fitzgerald, 2003.
36. Bentley, 1998; Theophano, 2003; Parkin, 2006.
37. Cinotto, 2001; Cinotto, 2008; Diner, 2001; Gabaccia, 2000.
38. Trubek, 2008; Tower, 2004; Neustadt, 1992.
39. Smith, 2004; Katz and Weaver, 2002; Parasecoli and Scholliers, 2011.
40. Kuh, 2001; Kamp, 2006.
41. Guthman, 2004.
42. Breen, 2004.
43. Weiner, 1996.

44. Avakian, 1997; Williams-Forson, 2006.
45. Pillsbury, 1998.
46. Mintz, 1997.
47. Lauden, 2011.
48. Peiss, 2007.
49. Thanks to Brett Gary for, as ever, his keen and insightful review of this chapter.

–6–

Five Hundred Years of Fusion: Histories of Food in the Iberian World

Jeffrey M. Pilcher

In 1972 Alfred W. Crosby Jr. published *The Columbian Exchange* as the second volume in the Greenwood Press series Contributions in American Studies—after *The Rhetoric of American Politics* and before *The Presidency of Rutherford B. Hayes.* The incongruity of its placement reflected the novelty of its subject; environmental history had been recognized as a field of study only in the 1960s, and most early researchers focused narrowly on the U.S. conservation movement. Crosby sought to explain nothing less than the world historical encounter between Afro-Eurasia and the Americas as, in the words of his subtitle, *Biological and Cultural Consequences of 1492.* Although few people actually understood it at the time, his conceptualization of the exchange of plants, animals, and pathogens became a central theme in world history.[1] More than a generation later, students continue to be astonished by the thought of Irish cooking before the potato, Italian pasta and pizza without tomato sauce, or Indian and Thai cuisines unflavored by chili peppers. Crosby may never have considered himself a food historian; he published the chapters on disease as journal articles, while those on food appeared first in the book. Nevertheless, the historiography of food in the Iberian world is largely an elaboration of his original thesis. The fusion cuisines that resulted from Columbus's voyage in 1492 have shaped the populations, economies, and identities of Spanish and Portuguese speakers everywhere.

Historians interested in culinary exchanges, and cultural change more broadly, have borrowed insights from other disciplines, starting with Crosby, who adopted the perspectives of ecology and geography to ask larger questions of his sixteenth-century primary sources. Others have tightened the scale of inquiry to a microhistorical frame and used the tools of anthropology to glean from their documents the local meanings and material cultures that shaped the reception of new foods within particular societies.[2] Linguistic, botanical, and, increasingly, genetic analysis have also helped to trace the spread of foodstuffs around the globe.[3] In turn, scholars from other disciplines have been drawn to historical methods and narratives. Anthropologists Sidney Mintz and Arturo Warman used historical sources and chronologies to document the global travels of sugar and maize.[4] The historian's skill at writing for audiences beyond the academy also appealed to some social scientists. History has thus provided an interdisciplinary meeting ground where different methodological approaches have come together in new and fruitful ways.

The periodization of studies of food in the Iberian world reflects wider trends within the discipline. The modern historical profession was born in the nineteenth century of an urge to chronicle—and glorify—the political lineages of emerging nations. Latin American intellectuals generally looked to France rather than Germany or the United States, where the historical seminar first took shape, and they quickly perceived food as vital to national development. A particularly influential generation of scholars, writing in the 1930s, considered food and nutrition to be among the leading environmental determinants of national character. Acknowledging long histories of racial and cultural mixing, they adopted a Lamarckian optimism about human adaptability in place of the social Darwinist disdain for supposedly inferior peoples common in the North Atlantic world. A subsequent generation, made up of social historians, who were ascendant from the 1960s to the 1980s, retained the focus on nutrition but employed quantitative methods to study historical variations of diets within societies rather than to draw sweeping conclusions about national character. Indeed, nationalism was largely shunned in this era by Spanish- and Portuguese-speaking scholars, many of whom had fled from military dictatorships at home. Studying abroad in northern European and North American universities, they became acquainted with debates about historical standards of living and applied those methods to Latin American histories of conquest, latifundia, and slavery. The present generation, dominated by cultural historians, has embraced food with even greater vigor, while taking a more diverse approach to its study. Cultural and environmental historians have refined Crosby's thesis by exploring the social conditions that influenced the movements of foodstuffs. Other scholars have sought to understand the role of food in shaping national identities, gender roles, social hierarchies, racial categories, and globalization. Although eclectic and evolving, this group has won recognition for the study of food as a historical subdiscipline in its own right and not merely as a metaphor or data series for political or economic historians.

Fusion Cuisines, Mestizo Nations

Latin American youth responded to the "lost generation" of World War I by turning away from European models and seeking inspiration from the indigenous civilizations of the Americas. In doing so, they repudiated the positivist intellectuals of the nineteenth century, who had perceived their national histories as the tragic consequences of unfinished conquests. Fin-de-siècle Latin American leaders had believed that progress would come only by "whitening" the colored races through continued European migration, thereby completing the missionary efforts begun in the sixteenth century. By contrast, postwar nationalists sought to revalorize Native American and

African influences and to counter the theories of scientific racism that miscegenation led inevitably to degeneration. Brazilian sociologist Gilberto Freyre and Cuban ethnomusicologist Fernando Ortiz were among the first to sketch out the food histories of Latin America in their efforts to show the cultural persistence of conquered and enslaved peoples and to challenge racial explanations for underdevelopment.

From the days of Columbus's voyages, Iberian settlers and their Creole offspring distrusted American foods, which seemed so different from those of the Mediterranean. Indeed, as historian Rebecca Earle has demonstrated in an important article, food played a central role in differentiating Spaniards from Indians, not only as a matter of social status but in a corporeal sense as well. Colonists feared that their bodies would degenerate in the insalubrious New World environment, and they sought out wheat bread, wine, and meat to preserve their health.[5] Negative views of indigenous foods became part of "caste" stereotypes that governed colonial race mixture and persisted long after most Latin American nations gained independence in the 1820s. By the end of the nineteenth century, intellectuals employed the nascent science of nutrition to explain the failure of rural, often-indigenous populations to acquire modernity. In an essay called *Food and the Races* (1896), Dominican intellectual José Ramón López berated the plantain and other tubers as an impediment to development in the Caribbean. His Mexican contemporary, Francisco Bulnes, made a similar claim about the supposed deficiencies of maize compared to wheat. These positivists employed spurious nutritional calculations but correctly recognized that peasants who could support themselves with sturdy crops such as maize or plantains had little incentive to submit to the exploitation of early industrialization.[6]

The Mexican Revolution of 1910 marked the beginning of a continental shift in the perception of indigenous peoples and more generally in nationalist ideology. Andrés Molina Enríquez, in his book *The Great National Problems* (1909), championed the mixed-race mestizo as the exemplar of the Mexican nation and recognized maize "in an absolutely indubitable manner [as] the national cuisine."[7] Refuting Bulnes's claims about the superiority of wheat, Molina Enríquez blamed national problems on the unequal distribution of land, which contributed to malnutrition and impeded economic development. Even after the triumph of revolutionary armies, social reform was mired in the countryside, partly because of a long-running split between rival approaches to the "Indian problem." Manuel Gamio, an anthropologist trained by Franz Boas at Columbia, advocated a policy of "indianismo" seeking to accept Indian culture within the national life, if only through the sale of fake pre-Hispanic curios to tourists. By contrast, education minister José Vasconcelos preferred a policy of "indigenismo," which meant assimilating Indians into a racially mestizo but culturally Hispanic nation. Rivals within these two camps attached great importance to the work of anthropologists, including an unsung pioneer of food studies, Margaret Park Redfield. As the daughter of renowned sociologist Robert Park and the wife of his protégé, anthropologist Robert Redfield, she was well versed in the Chicago School of Sociology and its theories of immigrant assimilation in the United States. Moreover, she had conducted the actual fieldwork for her husband's influential village ethnography—while he held an administrative position in Mexico City—but received authorial credit only for an article on the folk foods of Tepoztlán. In this insightful essay from 1929, she attributed the origins of *mole poblano*, widely considered to be the Mexican national dish, to pre-Hispanic civilizations, an "indianista" stance curiously at odds with the "indigenista" program of assimilation suggested by the Chicago school.[8]

Likewise, in Brazil, Gilberto Freyre gave a prominent role to food in his vision of race mixture and national history. Freyre, like Gamio, had studied with Boas at Columbia, and he brought a cultural and environmental approach to his scholarship. His nationalist ideology was profoundly regional, shaped by his background in the northeastern state of Pernambuco, a center of colonial sugar culture and of Brazil's African heritage. In 1933, he synthesized the themes of patriarchy and miscegenation into his magnum opus, *The Masters and the Slaves* (translated into English in 1956). A sociological bodice ripper, the book described lurid encounters between virile Portuguese settlers and Tupi-Guarani, African, and *mulata* women. Freyre applauded the resulting race mixture and attributed Brazil's problems instead to the tropical environment and poor nutrition. The masters consumed rancid imports from Europe, and the slaves subsisted on meager rations of dried beef and cassava. Even while lamenting the inadequate diet, Freyre lovingly recounted the gastronomic contributions of each race: the slave women's *vatapa* (shrimp in palm oil), *carurú* (okra with malagueta pepper), and couscous; the indigenous *beijú* (manioc pastries), *moquem* (fish roasted on coals), black beans, and cashews; and the Portuguese livestock and convent sweets. Although later scholars have criticized Freyre for a sentimentalized view of patriarchy and slavery, he had an astonishing popular influence, helping to shape an inclusive Brazilian nationalism.[9]

The most theoretically sophisticated of early scholars of racial and culinary blending in Latin America was Fernando Ortiz, who developed the concept of transculturation, referring to the mutual influences of cultural encounters, in contrast to Chicago sociologists' notion of assimilation as a linear path toward westernization. Ortiz first laid out this theory in *Cuban Counterpoint: Tobacco and Sugar* (1940), an essay on the contrasting influence of plantation crops in Cuban history. The indigenous plant, tobacco, held particular fascination for Ortiz because of its seductive hold on the conquistadors, which reversed the usual relationships of colonial power. And whereas Havana cigars had won export markets around the world, Cuban sugar was sold only under preferential quotas to a neocolonial power, the United States. Although the counterpoint of tobacco and sugar focused on Spaniards and Indians, Ortiz later emphasized the African contributions by comparing Cuban national identity to the cooking of *ajiaco*, an African stew of starchy tubers, indigenous *ají* (chilis), and Spanish dried beef, with diverse other influences. Criticizing the ethnic nationalism of Vasconcelos, Ortiz insisted that it was the process of cooking rather than the end result that provides an appropriately inclusive national metaphor, always remaining open to new ingredients and techniques.[10]

Although writing in the Latin American tradition of the essay rather than the German American monograph, these early authors were deeply concerned with the historical project of nation building. Moreover, in countering the North Atlantic hegemony of social Darwinism, they took unconventional approaches to cultural *mestizaje* and popular nutrition, thus setting a path that was followed by a future generation of social historians.[11]

Penurious Peasants, Starving Slaves, and Aztec Cannibals

Young historians expressed the rebellious spirit of the 1960s by turning away from elite political and intellectual topics to study the past "from the bottom up." The quantitative methodologies of demographic and economic analysis provided this new social history with tools to excavate the structures of everyday life in the past. Fernand Braudel of the French *Annales* school exemplified this work with his emphasis on the Malthusian "weight of numbers" balancing food production and population levels. Debates over standards of living, which in Europe focused on the social effects of early industrialization, took on new inflections among scholars of Latin America, who explored possible links between harvest failures and peasant uprisings or between plantation rations and slave revolts. The most extreme materialists even attributed Aztec ritual sacrifice to inadequate preconquest diets. In this brief section I cannot hope to do justice to the agrarian historiography of Latin America and will discuss only a few works that focus on food and society. Moreover, although Crosby falls within this social historical tradition, the Columbian exchange was taken up most thoroughly by a later generation, and I will examine it in a subsequent section.

Economic historians have contributed greatly to our understanding of food and society, although their historical price indexes have been motivated more by questions of monetary theory and living standards than of cultural change. The early twentieth-century work of Earl J. Hamilton stands out in this field for its comprehensive analysis of the so-called price revolution in early modern Spain, the inflation resulting from massive imports of American silver. In seeking to reconstruct long-term price movements, he conducted exhaustive research in the archives of the Casa de Contratación, the trade board responsible for Spain's overseas empire, as well as in the account books of institutions such as Seville's Hospital de la Sangre. Such data are useful not only for charting living standards but also for obtaining detailed information on the foods that were actually consumed at particular times. Thus, although early modern medical texts were full of warnings about the American tomato, which resembled the deadly nightshade, Hamilton found records of tomatoes in Seville markets already from the early seventeenth century—apparently they were served in salads with cucumber.[12]

Social historians also applied the tools of demography and geography to exploring connections between land and labor in Latin America. The interdisciplinary

"Berkeley school" was particularly innovative, beginning in the 1930s with Carl O. Sauer, an early advocate of historical and anthropological approaches to human geography. In examining pre-Hispanic staples, he observed important distinctions between the maize-growing region of Mesoamerica and the tuber-propagating horticultural societies of the Caribbean and South America. In the postwar era, the Berkeley school took a demographic turn under the influence of physiologist Sherburne F. Cook and historians Lesley Byrd Simpson and Woodrow Borah, who pioneered methods for quantifying the precontact population of the Americas.[13] Their controversial claim that Mesoamerica may have had as many as twenty-five million inhabitants on the eve of the conquest seemed to support the "black legend" of Spanish atrocities by pointing to massive deaths from disease and exploitation. In the hands of other researchers, however, the high numbers often served to reinforce an opposing "white legend" that made the conquistadors look benevolent by comparison. Materialist anthropologists Marvin Harris and Eric Harner concluded extravagantly that overpopulation and food shortages had caused Aztec ritual sacrifice and cannibalism, a theory that has received very little credence within the academy.[14] Moreover, a high precontact population would suggest the corollary that those who survived the conquest had better access to food than the populations of either Europe or the Americas before 1492, a thesis elaborated on by John Super.[15] Nevertheless, a magisterial ethnohistory by Charles Gibson strongly reasserted the black legend by demonstrating, among other things, that wheat haciendas were an important vehicle for the expropriation of indigenous land and that the cruelty of Spanish rule drove countless Indians to drink.[16]

The problems of food production and urban provisioning remained a perennial concern for social historians of the Iberian world. The Berkeley school maintained its scholarly leadership as students of Cook and Borah, including Arnold Bauer and Eric Van Young, moved beyond the earlier institutional works on provisioning to examine economic fluctuations and commercial linkages in the region.[17] The *Annales* school also held great influence, most notably through the work of François Chevalier on the transfer of Spanish stock-raising traditions and the rise of the Mexican hacienda.[18] The Sorbonne in Paris meanwhile attracted a parade of Latin American doctoral students, including Enrique Florescano, who worked under Ruggiero Romano, Pierre Vilar, and Fernand Braudel to compile a price series for maize in eighteenth-century Mexico. Florescano concluded that increasingly severe food shortages caused famine and disease, which contributed to the crisis of independence.[19] Histories of prices and provisioning have grown ever more sophisticated, as economic historians continue to debate the living standards of late colonial Latin America.[20] Scholars have also looked for evidence of declining incomes in late nineteenth-century Mexico as a cause for the Revolution of 1910.[21]

Economic historians likewise turned their attention to the study of slave diets in the Americas. A controversial tone was set by Robert Fogel and Stanley Engerman's *Time on the Cross* (1974), which argued that plantations in the antebellum U.S.

South were profitable enterprises, in part because owners kept their slaves well fed and hence productive, a thesis that provoked devastating critiques of both method and evidence by Herbert Gutman.[22] In the midst of this debate, medical and demographic historian Kenneth Kiple sought to shift the focus from planter intentions to nutritional consequences. Unlike Engerman and Fogel's rosy picture of nineteenth-century North American slavery, Kiple showed eighteenth-century Caribbean sugar plantations to be rife with malnutrition. Reading historical documents of slave rations and contemporary diagnoses in light of modern medical science, he found widespread evidence of protein, vitamin, and mineral deficiencies, including pellagra, beriberi, scurvy, night blindness, and anemia.[23] Anthropologist Robert Dirks took this argument a step further, arguing that slaves experienced relief-induced agonism, a condition of aggressive behavior among semistarved people who are allowed to eat plentifully. At harvest, the peak time of plantation labor demands, extra rations of sugar, rum, and protein were often accompanied by orgiastic revels of drinking, dancing, and occasional rebellion, constituting a "Black Saturnalia."[24] Kiple and Dirks have been criticized, in turn, for biological determinism by scholars who have attributed slave revolts to conscious decisions by oppressed peoples rather than "spasmodic" response to stimuli—to borrow a term from E. P. Thompson.[25] In any event, records from the African slave trade continue to provide a valuable source of historical evidence on mestizo cuisines in the early Americas. In a recent study of slave ships, geographers Linda Newson and Susie Minchin have gleaned archival references to couscous made from maize in seventeenth-century Cartagena.[26]

Meanwhile, social histories of commodity production provided rich sources on the historical origins of the contemporary global food system. In Latin America, these works were often influenced by the perspective of dependency theory, which argued that liberal free trade served only to impoverish the export economies of Latin America. Thus, historians documented the boom-and-bust cycles of commodity production in the region—sugar, coffee, bananas—as well as the foreign firms that benefited from them.[27] Meanwhile, scholars of migration have illuminated the movements of farmworkers, whether through indigenous labor drafts or transoceanic migrations. For example, James Scobie's classic *Revolution on the Pampas* (1964) revealed that land speculation precluded the settlement of farmers in nineteenth-century Argentina; Italian migrants, known as *golondrini* (swallows) because of their annual travels between harvests in the northern and southern hemispheres, lacked permanent ties and did little to improve the land. These works explored the deep historical roots of commodity exports and of marginalized labor in creating the modern global food system.

The generation of social historians made at least two fundamental advances in the study of food in the Iberian world. The first legacy of their intensive archival research was a more accurate mapping of historical production and consumption of foodstuffs, thus providing an indispensable empirical foundation for future study.

Second, the hard numbers they compiled effectively refuted the more romantic beliefs of previous generations. Thus, anthropologist Peter Fry challenged Freyre's interpretation of Brazilian history through an essay on *feijoada*—a Rio de Janeiro favorite of rice, black beans, and offal meats. Fry argued that the acceptance of this South American "soul food" as a national dish demonstrated not racial harmony but rather the hegemonic appropriation of Afro-Brazilian symbols to uphold an unequal society.[28] Such symbolic analysis later became a basic tool for cultural historians, even as cultural and environmental analysis supported revisionist work on transatlantic exchange.

Field and Kitchen: Processes of Culinary Exchange

Recent historiography on the Columbian exchange has benefited from an important shift within the field of anthropology, beginning in the late 1980s, from an understanding of culture as the material goods and behaviors of a particular society toward a processual study of the agency, practices, and performances that create those expressions. This change within the social sciences, reflecting a poststructuralist desire to comprehend the reproduction, manipulation, and transformation of systems of power, was well suited to historians, with their emphasis on change over time and discomfort with static views of culture. Food historians looked for agency and practice in the ways that particular groups within societies perceived opportunities or threats from the arrival of new plants and animals in local ecologies. Scholars also inquired why foodstuffs and cooking methods gained acceptance in some areas but not others. Such historical investigation of environmental conditions, social practices, agents of transfer, and cultural perceptions has provided a more nuanced view of the exchange of foods within the early modern world.

The centuries after 1492 offer a unique historical laboratory on culinary exchange because of the intensity of new transoceanic introductions, but the longer history of globalization can also illuminate the analytical processes at work in the early modern era. It is important to distinguish between foods involved in long-distance trade, such as spices that could be grown only in particular environments, and stepwise exchanges between farmers who pass on new seeds and techniques to neighbors. Indeed, the haphazard diffusion of maize revealed both the speed and selectivity of cultural change. The methods of transmission, in turn, influenced the social status accorded to those crops; foods that were globalized by trade—for example, chocolate and coffee—often maintained higher status than crops that were transplanted to local fields, allowing more universal consumption. It is equally important to keep in mind the different ways that novel plants were used; some were grown purely for ornamental purposes, others as vegetables in kitchen gardens, while a few became staples in the fields. Although medical, botanical, and agricultural manuals have traditionally been the main source of information on these exchanges, archaeological and social historical research have helped to illuminate blind spots left by elite texts, particularly regarding the everyday practices of ordinary people.

The originality of Alfred Crosby's thesis lay in combining existing facts, already known to specialists, into a broad and captivating interpretation. In piecing it together, he relied on the work of botanists and historical demographers who untangled the complicated origins of global plant domestication. Researchers of the late nineteenth and earlier twentieth centuries, notably the French botanist Alphonse de Candolle and the Russian geneticist Nikolai Vavilov, corrected long-standing errors regarding the source of plants such as maize. Moreover, in the postwar era Ping-Ti Ho and William Langer conducted pioneering demographic studies of the effects of American crops on China and Europe.[29]

Like these earlier authors, Crosby viewed biological and cultural exchange largely as problems of historical demography: how the decline of Native American populations opened spaces for the spread of Old World foods, and how the arrival of productive American crops contributed to early modern population growth or at least stability in Europe, Asia, and Africa. In narrating the biological conquest of the New World, Crosby wrote in a strong, active voice of pathogens slaying multitudes and settlers harvesting wheat and grapes. Even the farm animals were dynamic: "fast, tough, lean" hogs; cattle "armed with long horns"; the horse "an aristocrat in the equestrian flesh"—all reproducing at unprecedented rates. The chapter on the diffusion of American crops in the Old World, by contrast, was written in the passive voice: crops were planted and populations rose, but without an explanation as to why, beyond the basic ecological facts of where it was possible to grow particular crops. This neglect for the intentions of Old World farmers and cooks seems all the more curious given the lengths to which the conquistadors went to transplant European foods to the colonies and their deep suspicion of American crops. Still, pioneering historians must work with available materials, and such an imbalance is hardly surprising for a Latin Americanist, well grounded in the primary sources of the conquest but reliant for Old World data on the UN Food and Agriculture Organization's *Production Yearbooks*.[30]

The work of filling in Crosby's big picture required meticulous attention to local social conditions. Economic historian Justo L. del Río Moreno, for example, has analyzed the process of acclimatization of agricultural systems from Andalucía to the Americas in the first half century after Columbus, providing a detailed mapping of both subsistence and commercial production.[31] Linguistic analysis has long been central to tracing the movement of plants—at times misleadingly, as in the Italian usage of *grano turco* (foreign grain) for maize. Yet studies of African and Asian languages have begun to provide intriguing clues about the spread of New World crops.[32] Close attention to material culture has also proved revealing; Mexican anthropologist Arturo Warman's deep familiarity with maize, particularly its ability to thrive as a pioneering plant on hillsides unsuitable for other crops, helped him to follow the plant's spread among impoverished peoples farming marginal land throughout the Mediterranean and South and Southeast Asia. Warman also pointed to a tragedy of localization, the epidemic of pellagra, a dietary deficiency disease that resulted from the global diffusion of maize without the local knowledge of alkaline treatment developed by Native American cooks.[33]

Scholars have revealed that the impact of American foods varied widely depending on local social conditions. In the Balkans, where maize became a staple in the seventeenth century, Warman attributed the plant's spread to the desire of Turkish landlords for a cheap food for peasants and livestock that would allow the sale of more valuable wheat in commercial markets. By contrast, William McNeill has interpreted the arrival of maize as the economic basis for later independence movements by Greek and Serbian peasants, who could subsist year-round in remote mountain valleys, far from Ottoman rulers.[34] James McCann has shown that maize spread slowly across Africa, gaining early acceptance only in particularly favorable niches such as among the Asante on the Gold Coast. The disruptions of the slave trade helped a novel and productive rotation of maize, cassava, and cocoyams to take root in the local ecology, thereby providing the resources for Asante warriors to conquer a vast West African empire.[35] (See also McCann's chapter in this volume.) Sucheta Mazumdar also emphasized the importance of social upheaval in a comparative study of China and India. Following Esther Boserup, she reversed Crosby's Malthusian causation by showing that population was an independent rather than dependent variable in the Columbian exchange. She observed that Chinese cooks embraced maize and other American foods already in the early seventeenth century during the famines at the end of the Ming dynasty, whereas Mughal farmers ignored the unfamiliar crops for 200 years until pressured by the commercial demands of British imperialism.[36] These ongoing debates emphasize the importance of the agency of local cooks and farmers in mediating the exchange of foods.

Crosby has also been faulted for his inattention to the agents of transfer in the Columbian exchange. In contrast to his focus on European conquistadors and merchants, more recent works have highlighted the importance of African slaves in conveying plants across the Atlantic. Geographer Judith Carney made this argument most forcefully based on striking continuities between West African methods of growing and processing rice and the historical plantations around Charleston, South Carolina. The argument for slave-based transfer, called the "black rice" thesis after the title of her prize-winning book, has been criticized by economic historians for failing to demonstrate significant numbers of West African slaves with rice-growing skills in the early Carolinas, although archival records for the early slave trade are highly fragmentary. Nevertheless, in a subsequent book coauthored with Richard Rosomoff, Carney surveyed the enormous legacy of African foodstuffs, farming practices, and cooking methods throughout the Americas. In uncovering these histories, she also worked to correct a long-standing bias in the historical memory of Europeans, who claimed credit for skilled labor performed under brutal conditions by African slaves.[37]

Transfers of cultural knowledge have likewise been central to the interpretations of other recent scholars. Paula de Vos has explored the ways emergent scientific worldviews filtered European colonial encounters with Asian and American foods.[38] Marcy Norton, meanwhile, has demonstrated that at times Europeans adopted indigenous practices, despite the conquistadors' efforts to impose their own cultural stamp on the New World. In a study of tobacco and chocolate, following Fernando Ortiz, Norton rejected both biological determinism and cultural constructivism. Spaniards began using these products not because of their addictive qualities, nor even because they had been incorporated within European medicine and taste, but rather through social acts of consumption with Native Americans that borrowed indigenous practices and technologies. Thus, she argues, Castilian nobles first added sugar to their chocolate not to make it more European but rather to substitute for perishable American flavorings.[39] Other scholars have pursued this thread both geographically and socially to explore elite consumption within Hapsburg Austria and cacao's commodification among the working classes of nineteenth-century Spain.[40]

Recent work on the Columbian exchange has therefore produced a number of important findings while also suggesting paths for future research. Empirical studies have begun to fill in the map of food production with greater detail, particularly in Africa and Asia, while also suggesting new theoretical understandings of culinary innovation. At the most basic level, new foods gained acceptance when they complemented rather than disrupted existing cooking systems and crop rotations. Contrary to trickle-down social theories, novelties also tended to appear first along the margins, both of the daily round of meals and among poor people willing to experiment under difficult circumstances. When large-scale dietary change did take place, it seemed to follow in the wake of wider social upheavals, whether the demographic collapse of the conquest, the yoke of imperialism, or the industrial transformations of contemporary times. Finally, the study of food has helped reverse the usual relations of power, showing how women, the poor, colonial subjects, immigrants, and other marginalized people can shape the tastes of a society.

Food History as Cultural History

The cultural turn of the late 1980s has sometimes been seen as a radical insurgency within the historical profession that denounced the "positivist" quantification of social history in pursuit of a more elusive subjectivity. Yet despite polemics between the two camps, cultural historians have largely carried on the project of studying history from the bottom up by using the interpretive techniques of literary criticism and cultural anthropology to comprehend mental worlds of the past. Revisionist works on the Columbian exchange by Carney and Norton, for example, illustrate the value of cultural approaches for elaborating Crosby's essentially demographic thesis. In a similar fashion, discursive analysis of cookbooks, menus, nutritional works, advertising copy, and other food-related texts has provided new insights on the historical construction of national, racial, gender, and class identities. The study of food has been particularly useful in illuminating the lives of working women, for whom cooking was a burden of daily drudgery but perhaps also a source of identity and a means of artistic expression.

Critics who dismissed cultural history in general as antiquarianism were particularly contemptuous of food history, even as some feminists considered the topic to be complicit with patriarchal oppression. Mexican historian Sonia Corcuera de Mancera spoke for many pioneers in the field when she described curious remarks about her scholarly work as a "book of recipes."[41] The book in question, *Between Gluttony and Moderation* (originally published in 1979), revealed the deep social and religious significance of food, especially the Mexican staples of maize tortillas and wheat bread. Drawing on an eclectic range of primary sources, she focused on expressions of cultural blending in Mexican food, whether among street vendors or kitchen workers, *pulque* taverns or elite banquets. Like Corcuera, many social historians in the 1980s began turning to culture in order to appreciate the nuances of class divisions within Latin American societies. Vincent Peloso explored the meanings of particular foods and not just dietary aggregates to understand the growing inequalities of Peru's nineteenth-century commercial economy. The loss of self-sufficiency among highland indigenous communities was keenly felt with the decline of traditional festival dishes such as *ocopa* (crayfish potato salad) and *pachamanca* (communal barbecue of meat and tubers), even as ceviche, *parihuela* (seafood stew), and Chinese specialties flourished in the cosmopolitan restaurants of Lima.[42]

Spurred on by these examples, cultural historians revisited the early twentieth-century focus on culinary nationalism, taking a critical eye to the way that foods have helped naturalize boundaries between citizens and foreigners. These studies built on the anthropological insights of Benedict Anderson, who showed nations to be "imagined communities" constructed by modern cultural industries, as well as Arjun Appadurai's essay on the circulation of recipes among middle-class Anglophone cookbook writers in postcolonial India.[43] I examined similar exchanges of regional cuisines in nineteenth-century Mexico in my book *¡Que vivan los tamales!* Unlike in India, ethnic and class divisions such as that between corn tortillas and wheat bread frustrated culinary nationalism for a century after independence. Only with the end of revolutionary reform in the mid-twentieth century did the middle classes accept maize dishes as the basis for a national cuisine.[44] Sarah Bak-Geller Corona has recently emphasized the global construction of the Mexican national cuisine, especially by French publishing houses, while José Luis Juárez López has revised the chronology through a study of culinary discourse tracing in great detail the conflicted roots of nationalism in the late nineteenth and early twentieth centuries.[45] Meanwhile, Steffan Ayora-Díaz has examined the rise of culinary nationalism in separatist regions, showing how Yucatecans sought to forge an autonomous gastronomic culture, only to see their project subsumed within a hegemonic national culture.[46] A similarly ambivalent culinary identity emerged in Puerto Rico, according to Cruz Miguel Ortíz Cuadra. In passing from Spanish colony to North American dependency, residents made the nutritional transition from rice and beans to Burger King without valorizing Creole traditions.[47] Yet official attempts to instill culinary patriotism had limits, as Paulo Drinot has shown in an examination of public dining halls in 1930s Peru, which served as a xenophobic populist measure intended to break the working classes' dependency on Chinese restaurants, known as *chifas*.[48]

Such national studies have had unquestioned value in showing the ideological uses of food, but there are important limitations on nation-centered analysis in a global food system. Scholars have increasingly turned to transnational histories of commodity chains connecting production and consumption, an approach pioneered by the rural sociologist William Friedland and world systems theorist Immanuel Wallerstein.[49] Mintz's renowned history of sugar was an important early work, although it focused largely on the Anglophone world. Stuart Schwartz's edited volume, *Tropical Babylons*, provided a comparative perspective on the origins of plantation production in Spain, the Canaries, the Caribbean, and Brazil, as well as on early sugar markets in continental Europe.[50] Steven Topik has likewise studied coffee, showing how consumers in the developing world have benefited from low-paid labor, whether on large slave plantations in Brazil or precarious freeholdings in Central America.[51]

Environmental historians, like economic historians, have contributed to this transnational field of study. Sterling Evans examined the meshing of multiple commodity chains through a study that connected wheat grown by family farmers on the plains of North America with henequen binding twine produced on Yucatecan plantations.[52] Meanwhile, John Soluri demonstrated the consequence of U.S. demand for a single variety of banana, the Gros Michel, created in large part by Chiquita advertising based on images of Carmen Miranda. The rampant spread of Panama disease among the monoculture plantations of Honduras, in turn, diverted vast tracts of land from the subsistence needs of local peasants.[53] My own work on Mexican meat supplies has likewise emphasized the importance of consumer tastes, in this case, the Hispanic preference for freshly slaughtered meat, in rejecting the refrigerated technology of Chicago packinghouses.[54]

The movements of peoples and of ideas have been just as important as the movement of commodities in the globalization of food. Historians of food have emphasized the role of proletarian migrations, most notably, Italians and Chinese, in reshaping the cuisines of South America around the turn of the twentieth century.[55] Patricia Vega Jiménez has attributed the Costa Rican national dish of rice and beans called *gallo pinto* (spotted rooster) to another group of migrant railroad workers, Afro-Caribbeans.[56] Entrepreneurs as well as laborers traveled during this period, and the industrialization of food in Latin America was promoted largely by immigrants.[57] Diasporic history can also help to understand the movement of ideas about food; for example, a research group at the University of Córdoba led by Antonio Garrido Aranda has explored fasting behaviors within the Spanish empire as a study of religious transculturation and the limits of European church authorities in the Americas.[58] In a book called *Planet Taco*, I show how the idea of Mexican food has been transported around the world in the postwar era, largely by North Americans who discovered tacos and burritos in the Southwest and thereby globalized U.S. stereotypes of Mexican food.[59]

More traditional political and institutional histories of food have likewise been influenced by the cultural turn. A research project on the history of Mexican wheat prices, undertaken by the Center for Advanced Studies in Social Anthropology (Centro de Investigaciones y Estudios Superiores en Antropología Social, or CIESAS) and following the example of Enrique Florescano, culminated in a broader history of the colonial bread industry by Virginia García Acosta, who showed how bakeries reproduced and reinforced the hierarchical system of castes in the different grades, ranging from pure, white French bread produced for the viceroy to coarse, dark *pambazos* intended for the mestizo underclass.[60] Enrique Ochoa also added cultural analysis to his study of twentieth-century Mexican food politics by considering how welfare agencies and parastatal food-processing industries sought to promote modernity among the working classes through the distribution of wheat, dehydrated milk from the United States, and even animal crackers, thus preserving the legacy of Francisco Bulnes under a purported revolutionary regime.[61] Although these studies examined policy and culture separately, the potential for a cultural history of food politics was demonstrated in a recent essay on beef, populism, and Juan Perón. Historian Natalia Milanesio showed how the Peronista government played on masculine associations in Argentine popular culture in creating an entitlement to beef for his working-class constituents, known as *descamisados* (shirtless ones), at the expense of British exports. The populist policies backfired, however, when droughts devastated the livestock industry around 1950. Dietitians put a brave face on the catastrophe by emphasizing the dangers of excessive beef consumption and calling for more fish and vegetables. The government even promoted traditional alternatives such as artisanal cold cuts and preserved sweets, but the shortage of beef, along with death of Eva Perón, dealt a mortal blow to the regime.[62]

In addition to politics, cultural historians of food have also begun to study the social historical trinity of race, class, and gender. Rebecca Earle's research on conquistador anxiety about the quality of American diets and access to European foods has contributed to new understandings of race as a fluid concept taking shape under New World social and environmental conditions.[63] In a similar fashion, Teresa de Castro has shown how the Spanish conquest of Grenada, also in 1492, helped to create a Morisco culinary identity among Muslims who converted to remain in Andalucía.[64] Class identities were also tightly woven into the consumption of appropriate foods, as Carmen Sarasúa has demonstrated through the study of a nineteenth-century Spanish provincial noble family's bankruptcy case. Despite crushing debts, they maintained their social rank to the end by consuming multiple forms of meat daily, regardless of the Catholic fast, as well as plentiful vegetables and chocolate. Class privilege in La

Mancha meant eating more rather than different foods from neighboring peasants, thus preserving backward-looking regional traditions instead of pursuing the latest fashions from cosmopolitan cities.[65] The construction of class identity was also central to two outstanding dissertations on food and gender in twentieth-century Latin America. Rebekah Pite examined the work of Doña Petrona Carrizo de Gandulfo, Argentina's most influential cookbook author, who helped immigrant and working-class women to achieve social mobility, but without questioning standards of domesticity. Sandra Aguilar-Rodríguez meanwhile analyzed the ways that new foods and cooking appliances came to represent modernity in the lives of middle- and working-class women in Mexico. Both authors gave careful attention to the relations between gender and class in times of rapid social change.[66]

Mexican historian Eric Van Young once called on cultural historians to colonize other fields of study,[67] and because food intersects with so many aspects of human life, from the material to the spiritual, it offers rich sources for this endeavor. Indeed, historians of food in the Iberian world have applied their critical discursive and symbolic analysis to diverse political, economic, and social topics. Yet unlike many others within the broad rubric of the new cultural history, they have focused more on social historical concerns than on French poststructuralist philosophy, apart from the odd reference to Michel Foucault's "biopower." The materiality of the subject may have helped to keep food histories grounded in the soil and the kitchen, although a similar physicality did not restrain historians of sexuality. Then again, many pioneers in the field began as quantitative social historians, and their examples have continued to guide younger practitioners. The best historical synthesis of food in Latin America, by Berkeley school stalwart Arnold Bauer, combines a sweeping perspective on material culture and household economy with an insightful study of the changing nature of consumer culture and identity within the region.[68]

Conclusion

Food studies has always been an interdisciplinary field, reflecting the multiple ways that food nourishes human societies. Anthropologists, geographers, sociologists, and nutritionists, to name only a few, have provided insights on this fundamental academic endeavor. The tools that historians have contributed include the innovative use of primary sources, a sensitivity to multiple chronologies, and an openness to the languages and methodologies of diverse social sciences. Equally important has been the historian's tradition of writing narratives that are accessible to a wide, educated readership, and food has likewise generated wider public interest. The work of Alfred Crosby exemplified this democratic impulse within the historical profession; there are few scholars of the Iberian world, certainly in the United States, who have had greater public influence. His innovative conceptualization of biological and cultural change, although modified in important ways, remains a fundamental tool for understanding the past among students at all levels, from elementary to graduate school.

Despite the important intellectual advances summarized in this essay, we have only begun to understand the connections between food and society, leaving much important research for future scholars. Whereas Crosby identified a few basic cultural and demographic trends, we still have much to learn both empirically and theoretically about the complex mosaic of culinary and racial blending in Latin America. While scholars have begun to move past the Native American–European dichotomy that predominated in the field for more than a century to consider African contributions to eating in the Americas, other ethnic groups such as Asians and Arabs remain little studied. Comparative history is likewise little practiced within the Iberian world, despite rich potential case studies. Innovative new fields and topics, including the nutritional transition, performance studies, and sensory history, likewise have much to offer historians of food in Latin America. Perhaps most interesting of all have been the complicated ways that foods have contributed to the maintenance and transformation of hierarchies. Although images of race, nation, and progress are often shaped by hegemonic elites, popular dishes such as *ajiaco*, *feijoada*, *gallo pinto*, and tacos offer compelling evidence of history being made from the bottom up.

Notes

1. On the early reception and subsequent influence of Crosby, see Earle, forthcoming.
2. Vega Jiménez, 2004.
3. Staller et al., 2006.
4. Mintz, 1985; Warman, 2003.
5. Earle, 2010.
6. Derby, 1998; Pilcher, 1996.
7. Molina Enríquez, 1978, 279.
8. Park Redfield, 1929.
9. Freyre, 1956.
10. Ortiz, 1993; Rojas, 2005.
11. Following in these traditions were nonprofessional historical compilations such as da Camara Cascudo, 1967; de Carcer y Disdier, 1953.
12. E. Hamilton, 1934. On the tomato, see E. Hamilton, 1976, 859; A. Davidson, 1992.
13. Cook and Borah, 1960; Cook and Borah, 1963.
14. M. Harris, 1985; Harner, 1977; Sahlins, 1978; Coe, 1994.
15. Cook and Borah, 1979; Super, 1988.
16. Gibson, 1964; W. Taylor, 1979.
17. Bauer, 1975; Van Young, 1981.

18. Chevalier, 1970.
19. Florescano, 1969.
20. Castillero-Calvo, 1987; Johnson and Tandeter, 1990; Quiroz, 2005; Williamson, 2009.
21. Coatsworth, 1976; Cross, 1978.
22. Fogel and Engerman, 1974; Gutman, 1975.
23. Kiple, 1984.
24. Dirks, 1987.
25. Thompson, 1971.
26. Newson and Minchin, 2007.
27. S. Stein and B. Stein, 1970; Schwartz, 1985; Gudmundson, 1995.
28. Fry, 1977.
29. Ho, 1955; Langer, 1963.
30. Crosby, 1972, 77, 80, 87.
31. del Río Moreno, 1991.
32. McCann, 2005.
33. Warman, 2003, 14–18, 40–42, 104–11, 132–50.
34. Warman, 2003, 108; McNeill, 1991.
35. McCann, 2005, 42–49.
36. Mazumdar, 1999.
37. Carney, 2001; Carney and Rosomoff, 2009. See also the exchange in the *American Historical Review*, February 2010.
38. de Vos, 2006.
39. Norton, 2008.
40. Lindorfer, 2009; Fattacciu, 2009.
41. Corcuera de Mancera, 1991, 7.
42. Peloso, 1985.
43. B. Anderson, 1991; Appadurai, 1988.
44. Pilcher, 1998.
45. Bak-Geller Corona, 2009; Juárez López, 2008.
46. Ayora-Díaz, 2010.
47. Ortíz Cuadra, 2006.
48. Drinot, 2005.
49. For a summary of this literature, see S. Hamilton, 2009.
50. Mintz, 1985; Schwartz, 2004.
51. Topik, 1998.
52. Evans, 2007.
53. Soluri, 2005.
54. Pilcher, 2004; Pilcher, 2006b.
55. See, for example, Corti, 1997; Remedi, 1998; Camargo da Heck, 1998; Balbi, 1999; Arcondo, 2002.
56. Vega Jiménez, 2012.

57. Weis, 2008.
58. Grupo Interdisciplinario de Cultura Alimentaria Andalucía-América, 1996.
59. Pilcher, 2012.
60. García Acosta, 1988; García Acosta, 1989, 158–59. See also León García, 2002; Super, 1996.
61. Ochoa, 2000.
62. Milanesio, 2010.
63. Earle, 2010, 688–90.
64. de Castro, 2002.
65. Sarasúa, 2001.
66. Pite, 2007; Aguilar-Rodríguez, 2008.
67. Van Young, 1999, 213–14.
68. Bauer, 2001.

Part II. The Middle East

7

Food Studies in Ottoman-Turkish Historiography

Özge Samancı

Food is vital to human life, and the act of eating embodies many symbolic meanings. However, as is true for other areas of the world, food has only recently become the subject of scholarly research in Ottoman-Turkish historiography. Since the 1950s studies in Ottoman economic and monetary history have touched on the subject of food within the limits of the provisioning system of foodstuffs in the Ottoman Empire, but the new focus on Ottoman food history and culture only started in the 1980s. Some of these studies are popular works written by amateurs—that is, nonprofessional historians—in attempts to describe the past of Turkish cuisine. Other studies are devoted to the identification and transliteration (from Arabic script to the Latin alphabet) of old cooking manuscripts, cookbooks, and archival documents relating to the Ottoman elite food culture, especially in the capital city of Istanbul. Since the late 1990s food has become increasingly popular as the subject of both academic and popular history. Ottoman food culture, which represents a very broad subject in terms of time and space, is a trendy subject in Turkey at present.

This chapter introduces the primary historical approaches to food studies in Ottoman-Turkish historiography, including a review of the different methods and sources used. I aim to give a representative sample, not an exhaustive inventory, of the important works in food history in Ottoman-Turkish studies. The chapter is organized according to four main approaches to food studies. First, there is Ottoman economic and monetary history that concerns questions of food supply. Second, popular writing and folklore studies have played a role in food-related research. Third, the study of old cooking manuscripts and archival documents that are part of Turkish literature studies (Turcology) has influenced food history. Last, the chapter evaluates the writing of food history by both nonprofessional and professional historians in the past decade.

Food in Ottoman Economic History

Ottoman economic history began to emphasize food-related subjects, directly or indirectly, during the 1950s. The *Annales* school, well known in European historiography at that time, influenced approaches and topics taken up by Ottoman economic historians.[1] Economic history was an important factor promoting the study of the food history of the Ottoman Empire (1299–1923). Ottoman economic historians focused their attention on food production and food supply systems, especially in order to explain problems concerning food prices. Assuring a steady food supply was one of the biggest problems of preindustrial societies, and the Ottoman capital was no different. Every Ottoman government considered its first task to be feeding its subjects, particularly those living in Istanbul. Consequently, the provisioning system of the Ottoman capital city, Istanbul, has been studied extensively.

The first interest of economic historians was the supply of staple foods, such as wheat, to the densely populated capital. The main sources used were Ottoman archival documents relating to the treasury and tax registers. Lütfü Güçer was the first to write about the system of supply of cereals to mid-eighteenth-century Istanbul.[2] In his 1949–1950 article, Güçer explored the production of cereals in the Ottoman Empire, different taxes on cereals, and the state politics of cereal supply. Alexandrescu-Dersca Bulgaru and Maria Matilda published their study on the subject in 1957. In 1984, Tevfik Güran studied the new establishment that the Ottoman government put in place at the end of the eighteenth century in order to organize the grain supply of Istanbul.[3] Provisioning continued to be the focus of research in the following decades,[4] including two works published in 2001 and 2008 on the cereal supply to Istanbul, which included information about the production of wheat flour, the use of wheat flour in baking, and the types of bread and other kinds of pastry produced in the city's markets from the seventeenth to the mid-nineteenth centuries.[5]

The cultivation of rice in the Ottoman lands since the early days of the empire has attracted attention since 1978 with studies that underscore the importance of rice in provisioning the palace and the hospices.[6] The Ottoman government itself organized and supervised the meat supply to Istanbul and to the palace, and through the centuries the system of meat provisioning (principally sheep) underwent significant changes that have been studied in depth.[7] The importance given to the production, as well as supply, of wheat, mutton, and rice emphasizes their place among the basic foodstuffs in Ottoman cuisine.

In 1962, French historian Robert Mantran, using the methods of the *Annales* historians, authored one of the earliest studies in Ottoman social and economic history. While depicting social and economic life in Istanbul during the second half of the seventeenth century, Mantran devoted one chapter to the problems of provisioning Istanbul, which included detailed descriptions of the different foodstuffs available in Istanbul markets at that time. Suraiya Faroqhi's 1984 *Towns and Townsmen of Ottoman Anatolia* is an important work in Ottoman socioeconomic history that features information on and analysis of social and economic life in Anatolian cities in the sixteenth and seventeenth centuries, including food production, trade and markets in food, and the organization of butchers and the Istanbul meat trade. While these works of socioeconomic history provide useful information about the food production system and the network of food trade in the Ottoman Empire in the early modern era, they do not contain data about the food consumption patterns of the general population.

Economic historian Ömer Lütfi Barkan was the first to show a serious interest in food, using Ottoman palace kitchen registers as source material. Barkan published a series of palace kitchen registers that have become valuable primary sources in Ottoman food history research.[8] His studies were also important for food historians because they demonstrated that Ottoman archival sources contain a large amount of evidence concerning food and drink. Barkan also studied documents from Ottoman pious foundations (*vakfiye*) to calculate food prices in sixteenth-century Istanbul and Edirne.[9] The registers of market prices (*narh defterleri*) introduced in the works of Mübahat Kütükoğlu are another important Ottoman food history resource as they detail the kind of foodstuffs available in Istanbul markets.[10]

The food production and supply system in the Ottoman Empire continues to be a topic of great interest in economic history. For example, in 2004, Ottoman economic historian Arif Bilgin studied the food supply system of the Ottoman palace kitchens in the classical era (from the mid-fifteenth to mid-seventeenth centuries). Bilgin provides information about the culinary consumption patterns of the Ottoman elite in the classical period including the kinds of foodstuffs used in cooking and some types of dishes. This was the first detailed study devoted to palace kitchen organization, known as *Matbah-ı Âmire Emâneti*, and it has been a vital resource for Ottoman food historians who have taken a sociocultural approach to food research after 2000.[11]

Turkish Cuisine as Cultural Heritage

The first attempt at popular writing about Ottoman cuisine appeared in a 1948 book written by Süheyl Ünver, a historian of medicine. Ünver's *Fifty Turkish Dishes in History* consisted of the recipes found in an eighteenth-century Ottoman culinary manuscript. Using the palace kitchen records that Barkan had transliterated, Ünver published a second popular book about Ottoman palace cuisine during the reign of Sultan Mehmet II in the fifteenth century.[12] His books encouraged further studies, both popular and academic, about Ottoman cuisine in the following decades.

Folklore studies became important after the foundation of the Turkish Republic in 1923, as part of the search for the ancient roots of Turkish culture. Apart from a few studies about local foods of Anatolia,[13] ancient Turkish culinary culture was not a significant part of folkloric studies until the 1980s. The need to break away from the past in order to construct the new republic may be one of the reasons for the lack of interest in Ottoman culinary culture.[14] A nonprofessional historian, Burhan Oğuz, contributed to the history of Turkish cuisine with his 1976 work on the food consumption patterns of the Anatolian people. His book, part of a series of eight volumes on the origins of the culture of Turkish peoples, was an early source of encyclopedic information about the history of food ingredients, beverages, cooking techniques, and table manners in Anatolia from the ancient past to the twentieth century. The series is an attempt to reconstruct Turkish culture from the earliest civilizations of Anatolia, which must be situated within the aspirations of constructing a long-standing Turkish history. In 1978, historian Bahaettin Ögel looked into the ancient roots of Turkish cuisine and traced the culinary habits of Turkish peoples throughout their long history from the time when they lived in Central Asia.

From the 1980s, folklore studies included a new emphasis on culinary culture that was largely motivated by the beginning of tourism in Turkey. There was public interest in building a national Turkish cuisine, which supported efforts to organize food symposia both by the Turkish state and by amateur researchers.[15] The National Folklore Research Foundation (Milli Folklor Araştırma Dairesi [MIFAD]) organized two symposia, "Turkish Cuisine" in 1981 and "Traditional Turkish Desserts" in 1984.[16] The goal was to draw attention to the richness of Turkish cuisine, discover its ancient roots, and make this information known abroad. The symposia included papers with diverse topics and approaches. The food culture of Turkish people in Central Asia and the Seljuk and Ottoman cuisines were the focus in the historical research presented.[17] The papers at both symposia included new topics in the study of Turkish culinary culture such as mealtimes, food variety, formation and development of meal patterns, and the relationship between food and medicine. Unfortunately, the authors did not provide references in their studies that would have been useful to other researchers. However, these symposia were important events because, for the first time, the very ancient past of Turkish cuisine was seen on a historical continuum from the origins of Turkish people in Central Asia to Anatolia during the Seljuk and Ottoman eras. Importantly, this larger framework of the historical past of Turkish cuisine subsequently inspired further studies in Ottoman food history research.

Symposia about food culture were organized in the following years at the initiative of an amateur researcher, Feyzi Halıcı, with the support of the Turkish minister of culture. The purpose of five international food congresses that took place from 1985 to 1994 was to encourage research on Turkish food culture as well as to increase knowledge of Turkish cuisine outside of the country.[18] These congresses welcomed food journalists, food writers, amateur historians, folklore researchers, literary scholars, and academicians from Turkey. In addition, renowned food researchers and writers from Europe and abroad, including Charles Perry, David Waines, Andrew Dalby, Darra Goldstein, Claudia Roden, and Sami Zubaida, participated in the symposia with their various areas of specialization in food history and culture. Some of the new topics explored were festive meals, culinary interactions between different countries, cuisines in old Ottoman territories, and the origins of specific dishes, like baklava. The papers also drew attention to primary sources for Ottoman cuisine such as cooking manuscripts, dictionaries, travelers' accounts, and poetry. Food studies in Turkey was influenced by these symposia to embrace cooking manuscripts and cookbooks as important primary sources in the study of Ottoman food culture.

Discovering Sources of Ottoman Cuisine

Turkish literary scholars were pioneers in the search for primary sources in food history, such as culinary manuscripts, printed cookbooks, and other specific texts related to culinary culture. Ottoman primary sources were written in Arabic script, which few people read today, and therefore had to be transliterated from Arabic to the Latin alphabet, which has been used in Turkey since 1928. An eighteenth-century Ottoman cookery manuscript was transliterated in 1985 by Nejat Sefercioğlu, a researcher of Turkish literature. This manuscript of 129 recipes was the first Ottoman cookbook transcribed into modern Turkish. Orhan Şaik Gökyay published an article in 1985 that relied on a seventeenth-century Ottoman diary that contained evidence about the eating and drinking activities among the Ottoman upper classes. In 1985, Turgut Kut, a nonprofessional historian, completed a comprehensive bibliographical study, *A Critical Bibliography of Cookery Books*, listing all cookbooks of the Ottoman Empire published in Ottoman Turkish from 1844 to 1927. In addition, the bibliography included cookery manuscripts written before the nineteenth century and cookbooks published in Istanbul in Armenian since 1871.[19] This valuable reference work lists different editions of the original cookbooks as well as their tables of contents, and it remains an important secondary source in Ottoman-Turkish food studies.

Günay Kut, another prominent name in Turkish literature studies, published the transliteration of a cooking manuscript from the early nineteenth century.[20] This small manuscript contains fifty recipes for halva and other kinds of desserts. Kut also published an article about the earliest cooking manuscript known in the Ottoman world, which was written by an Ottoman physician, Shirvani, in the fifteenth century.[21] Originally, this manuscript was the translation of a medieval Arab cookbook written in the thirteenth century by Muhammad Ibn al-Kareem al-Baghdadi; however, the Ottoman author, Shirvani, added eighty recipes that were not in the Arabic version. (See Nawal Nasrallah's chapter in this volume.) Ottoman historian Stéphane Yerasimos wrote about the manuscript in 2001, and it was finally transliterated into modern Turkish in 2005 by Mustafa Argunşah and Müjgan Çakır. Günay Kut went on to study an Ottoman text that included descriptions of the banquets (with lists of the dishes served) given during the sixteenth-century circumcision feasts of the sons of Sultan Suleiman the Magnificent.[22] The transliteration of this Ottoman text was published later (in 1997) by Semih Tezcan.[23] Kut's research in Ottoman primary sources on food and cuisine in the following years led to more essays that have been valuable resources for food historians. In 1996, she contributed an essay to a book about Turkish culinary culture, embracing different topics concerning ancient

Turkish culture, such as its origins, religious feasts, celebratory foods, sociability around food, coffee, food in Ottoman charities, and table manners. It includes a detailed bibliography of manuscripts and documents relating to food, medicine, and table manners that is valuable in Ottoman food research. Her latest study concerns Ottoman festivals, parades, and entertainments organized alongside important banquets, using Ottoman texts relating to the imperial festivals (called *surname*) of the circumcision feasts in 1582, 1675, 1720, and 1834.[24]

The transliteration of the Ottoman cookbooks continued in the 1990s. The first printed Ottoman cookbook in 1844, *Refuge of Cooks* (*Melceü't-Tabbahin*), was republished with annotations in 1997.[25] Another cookbook, *The Chef* (*Aşçıbaşı*) (1900), was transliterated and republished in 1998.[26] A book on Ottoman confectionary, *Pastry Chef* (*Tatlıcıbaşı*) (1926), was transliterated in 2002.[27] There remain numerous cookbooks in the archives that have not yet been transliterated into modern Turkish.

In the past few years there has been a growing interest in Armenian cookbooks written in Turkish using the Armenian alphabet. The reason for this is a new interest in comparative approaches to Turkish food history largely aimed at discovering the underlying multicultural and multiethnic aspects of Ottoman cuisine. So far, two cookbooks published during the first decades of the twentieth century have been translated: a 1914 cookbook written by the chef of the American College in Merzifon, *The Book of the Chef* (*Aşçının Kitabı*),[28] and an anonymous 1926 cookbook, *The Perfect Cookery Book* (*Mükemmel Yemek Kitabı*).[29] Turkish sociologist Zafer Yenal wrote in his prefaces to these books that the translations will provide the opportunity in future studies to compare and contrast the content of the Ottoman cookbooks written in Turkish with those in Armenian.[30] All of the studies mentioned in the preceding constitute sources that have been used by academic and popular food historians who have taken a sociocultural approach to food history, a movement that accelerated rapidly after 2000.

Food History Writing since 2000

Ottoman culinary culture is a very popular subject at present for the general press, cookbook writers, chefs, and both nonprofessional and professional food historians. Since 2000, Ottoman cuisine has gained recognition as the ancestor of contemporary Turkish cuisine, especially in the international arena. Approximately twenty-five publications, both academic and popular, have appeared on the subject of the history of Turkish cuisine that put emphasis on Ottoman culinary influences. While some of these studies introduced new perspectives to the subject, others reinterpreted existing information.

Prior to 2000, only one book that showed interest in the past of Turkish food culture, *Timeless Tastes* (1996), had a remarkable popularity.[31] Sponsored by the

Vehbi Koç Foundation, an important private cultural foundation,[32] *Timeless Tastes* contained essays and articles about the ancient Turkish culinary culture along with traditional Turkish recipes. One of the earliest works on Turkish culinary culture, this book was eagerly welcomed and was also published in English, French, and German. In 1999, the celebration of the 700th anniversary of the founding of the Ottoman state provided an occasion for additional publications on Ottoman cuisine. *Hünkar Begendi 700 Years of Culinary Culture* (2000) was sponsored by the Turkish Ministry of Culture and Tourism. This collection of articles with Ottoman recipes also includes the bibliography of Turkish cookbooks published by Turgut Kut in 1985.[33] The food columnist and gourmet Tuğrul Şavkay published *Ottoman Cuisine* in 1999; it contains adaptations of old recipes with introductory articles about the evolution of Turkish cuisine from its Central Asian origins to contemporary times.

Among the popular general-interest books published since the year 2000, some are detailed studies that have contributed a great deal to the study of Ottoman culinary culture. For example, Marianna Yerasimos, in her book *500 Years of Ottoman Cuisine* (2002), used previously unexplored sources to trace the evolution of dishes in the Ottoman elite cuisine from the fifteenth century to the end of the nineteenth century.[34] The first part of the book is devoted to general characteristics of Ottoman cuisine and the principal types of Ottoman dishes, emphasizing methods of preparation of dishes and use of ingredients in different epochs. The second part is devoted to the adaptation of old recipes from ancient cookbooks and manuscripts. The culinary culture of Istanbul was explored by Sula Bozis in her work titled *Taste of Istanbul: Culinary Culture of Istanbul's Greeks* (2000), which gives a general panorama of the city's culinary culture while emphasizing the influence of the Greek Orthodox community. Her conclusion underlines the multiethnic and multicultural aspect of Ottoman culinary culture.

Apart from Ottoman cuisine, a series of books about the cultural history of basic food items used in Turkish cooking was published between 1997 and 2007 by a food writer, Artun Ünsal, who is an academician in political science. The series featured histories of bread, olive oil, yogurt, and cheese in Anatolia from the Neolithic era to contemporary times.[35] The author explored each food item in the historical context and also included folkloric information. Ünsal's popular writing style has drawn attention from food historians interested in working on commodity biographies in Turkish culinary culture. Among the popular works in Turkish food culture is the journal *Food and Culture* (*Yemek ve Kültür*), which began publication in 2005. Sponsored by the Istanbul restaurant *Çiya*,[36] the journal is devoted to the interdisciplinary study of food culture, including food in literature, food in folklore, food history, and the archaeology of food. It has featured translations of articles written by international scholars as well as new articles on the history of Turkish food culture.[37]

Sociocultural studies that combine anthropological and historical approaches have sought to understand and interpret the ancient culinary consumption patterns in Ottoman history. Generally speaking, such studies are relatively new; historians began to take the sociocultural approach to food history only around 2000. However, there were earlier scholars at the forefront of this trend. Prior to 2000, French scholars studied the consumption of coffee and Ottoman coffeehouses.[38] François Georgeon studied the culture of coffee and coffeehouses in Istanbul. His article about the consumption of alcohol in nineteenth-century Istanbul also reflects a sociocultural historical approach to Ottoman history.[39] The author explains that alcohol consumption was an issue of identity and boundaries between different religious groups in the Ottoman Empire. Muslims were forbidden to consume alcohol; it was not forbidden to Christians and Jews. But during the nineteenth century, since the reign of Sultan Mahmut II (r. 1808–1839) the consumption of alcohol (*rakı*) started to be legitimized among the Ottoman Muslim elite and became a sign of modernity. Anna Matthaiou's work on the culinary culture of the Greeks under the domination of the Ottoman Empire and the article "Ottoman Cuisine" in the *Encyclopedia of Islam* (1991) written by the historian Halil İnalcık are two additional early examples of food history research that reflect a sociocultural approach.[40]

İnalcık's article was influential for subsequent studies in Ottoman food historiography as the author paid attention to three key topics: the symbolic meaning of food in the Ottoman palace, the organization of the palace cuisines, and the Ottoman charity foundations that distributed food to the common people. Matthaiou's work analyzes the food consumption patterns of the Greek community in rural and urban areas in the Ottoman Empire from the mid-fifteenth to the early nineteenth centuries based mainly on historical studies on the Ottoman tax system, market regulation, provisioning systems in urban areas, and liturgical texts (*typikon*), which contain instructions about the order of the various Eastern Orthodox Christian church services and ceremonies. Her topics ranged from food items available in the Ottoman markets, market regulations imposed by the state, and the food system in both urban and rural areas. She questioned the ideological and mental basis of the culinary consumption patterns through the analysis of the representation of food in normative texts, such as religious and medicinal ones. Her study of the influence of religious rules on food consumption patterns of the Christian Orthodox population during Lent in the Ottoman Empire is an example of her sociocultural approach to food history.

In 1996, a symposium arranged at Boğaziçi University in Istanbul on food, drinks, and sociability in the Ottoman Empire signaled the rise of interest in Ottoman food history studies among historians. It was organized by the historian Suraiya Faroqhi, who has contributed to Ottoman historiography with numerous studies about economic and social life in the Ottoman Empire during the early modern period. For example, Faroqhi's 1995 book about daily life and culture in the Ottoman Empire includes an introductory chapter about the various types of food items and beverages that constitute the basis of Ottoman cuisine.[41]

The main focus of the articles in the symposium proceedings concerns Ottoman palace culinary culture with attention to sociocultural questions such as the change in elite tastes over time,[42] the status of food as a marker of social identity, and the adoption of new consumption patterns by the Ottoman elite.[43] Reindl-Kiel's article discusses the official meals arranged in the Topkapı palace in the seventeenth century during the meetings of the imperial council. The author analyzes the status of food presented on the table and underlines the difference in food served to the members of the sultan's council.[44] Some of the papers presented at the Boğaziçi symposium mark the beginning of interest in material culture studies of food and shelter in the Ottoman Empire.[45]

The consumption patterns of the Ottoman elite were the focus of another collected volume that included an article by Tülay Artan,[46] inspired by the theoretical perspectives of Jack Goody and Stephen Mennell; the article examined the cultural status of different food items (staples versus luxuries and delicacies) consumed by the members of the Ottoman dynasty in the eighteenth century. Artan concluded that Ottoman court cuisine started to diverge qualitatively from the cuisine of the common people during the eighteenth century. Archival records, including the expenses for the Ottoman palace cuisines (imperial kitchen registers), comprised the essential sources used in her study.

The food culture of the Ottoman palace has been a continuing interest among Ottoman historians. Two 2001 studies reviewed the existing literature on Ottoman culinary culture. Stéphane Yerasimos, in his work on Ottoman palace cuisine in the fifteenth and sixteenth centuries, brought together information from previous studies (including the fifteenth-century Ottoman palace kitchen registers studied by Barkan and the registers of market prices studied by Kütükoğlu) with the cooking manuscript of Shirvani in order to compare the manuscript recipes with evidence in the imperial kitchen accounts. He proposed new topics such as the food of the common people and the status of some food items (e.g., offal, fish, desserts) in Ottoman culinary culture. This work also concerns interpretations about the culinary preferences of the Ottoman sultans and the food distributed in Ottoman charity institutions, which is part of the Ottoman palace tradition.[47] Gerry Oberling and Grace Martin Smith prepared a book for the Turkish Ministry of Culture that aims to portray the evolution of Ottoman palace culinary culture from the fifteenth to the end of the nineteenth century using travelers' accounts and secondary literature.[48]

Arif Bilgin's detailed study of the system and organization of the Ottoman palace kitchens during the classical period (1450–1650) is based on a large number of archival documents and is a rich source of information about the organization of the kitchens, the work of palace cooks, and the foodstuffs used in cuisine.[49] Ottoman elite food culture during the nineteenth century was the topic of my 2009 doctoral dissertation, which encompasses the culinary consumption patterns of the Ottoman elite, focusing on continuing patterns and behaviors as well as changes from previous centuries to the end of the empire. The central topic I explore is the transformation of Ottoman elite food culture in the nineteenth century that accompanied the increasing influence of European culture. The adaptation of Western table manners and some Western culinary techniques, as well as of the French banqueting style, into Ottoman elite food culture are main topics in my research.[50] Important sources for this work included palace kitchens' expenditure registers, the cookbooks of the period, travelers' accounts, and memoirs that document the use of staple and luxury food items, culinary techniques, and table manners.[51] Subsequently, my article about the vegetable patrimony of Ottoman culinary culture illustrates the variety of vegetables and herbs used in Ottoman palace cuisine from the fifteenth to the end of the nineteenth century.[52] My 2008 edited volume with Arif Bilgin, about the history of Turkish culinary culture, published with the support of the Turkish Ministry of Culture and Tourism, includes twenty articles by experts on the different historical periods of the Ottoman Empire, including the Central Asian and Seljuk origins of Ottoman cuisine. The authors take a cultural approach to a range of topics, including the histories of tea and olive oil, the cuisine of the Greek community in the Ottoman period, and the relationship between classical Ottoman medicine and cuisine.[53]

Amy Singer, a specialist in the history of Ottoman charity foundations (*imarets*), edited a volume that includes innovative studies based on new kinds of primary sources for Ottoman food history: texts about the early period of the Sufi order, fifteenth- and sixteenth-century Ottoman court records that concern a fermented drink called *boza*, Armenian poems of the sixteenth century, records of Ottoman public kitchens (*imaret*), writings of Ottoman chroniclers, iconography (e.g., Ottoman miniatures, Orientalist paintings), and material culture evidence such as ceramics and tableware. New research topics in the book include sixteenth-century Anatolian Armenian food and feasts, a survey of the menus and clients in Ottoman charity foundations in different cities, and the ceremonies and rituals of the imperial hunt and its accompanying feasts.[54]

In addition to the research of historians, some anthropological studies of Turkish food culture have contributed to ongoing research in food history. Marie Hélène Sauner, in her work "Les Traditions culinaires de la Méditerranée: modèles, emprunts, permanences" (2001), emphasizes the particular role given to the culinary domain at the heart of the political entity set up by the Ottoman Empire. Hélène Desmet-Grégoire has studied the variety of nonalcoholic beverages in Turkish culture using an ethnological approach from a historical perspective.[55]

Research on the history of Ottoman medicine has contributed greatly to food history in Turkey. Medical manuscripts include the recipes for the dishes and the qualities of the food according to the theory of humors; they enhance our understanding of the composition of Ottoman cuisine prior to the nineteenth century. Nil Sarı's article "Food as Medicine," published in *Turkish Cuisine* in 2008, emphasizes the central role of foods and humoral theory in Ottoman medicine. Sari supplies examples of ways in which ailments were treated with foods and beverages. Nuran Yıldırım's article in the same volume examines the relationship between health and eating patterns in Ottoman society. Using four medical manuscripts, the author examines the special diets prescribed to cure sicknesses with recipes for soups, main dishes, and sweets.[56] Again, the identification and transliteration of Ottoman medical manuscripts that has been facilitated by Turkish literary scholars like Zafer Önler, who published the transliteration of a fifteenth-century medical manuscript in 1990,[57] has been invaluable to food historians.

Conclusion

The sociocultural approach to food has contributed a great deal to Ottoman-Turkish historiography. Most of these works aim to discover the similarities and changes in food consumption patterns, including beverages, cooking techniques, and table manners, over a long period of history. Elite cuisine, which developed in the Ottoman palace and in Istanbul over the centuries, constitutes the subject in most of these studies. Now, the cuisines in the vast territories of the Ottoman Empire, the differences between regional cuisines, and the cuisine of the common people, as well as the culinary practices in different religious and ethnic communities, deserve further study. The culinary culture in Anatolia before the establishment of the Ottoman state during the Byzantine and Seljuk eras, the early period in the Ottoman Empire (thirteenth and fourteenth centuries), and the republican era since 1923 are also neglected periods in food historiography.

Although there are a variety of sources that can be used in studying Ottoman culinary culture, we can say that most of the historical studies done so far are based on one kind of source—for example, the Ottoman palace kitchen records. However, the use of different types of sources for the same research may provide more detailed information and new insights. As I have shown, Ottoman archives contain many different kinds of records that can be exploited in food history research. Apart from the large number of documents about the Ottoman palace kitchen expenditures (from the fifteenth century to the end of the empire), there are also tax registers that may give information about agricultural production and food-related trade activities; court records (*kadı sicilleri*), which include market prices; and inheritance inventories (*tereke*), which list materials like tableware, cutlery, kitchenware, and some food items (e.g., jams and cereals).

This chapter has also shown that chroniclers' writings, literary sources like poems, travelers' accounts, memoirs, and cookbooks, as well as medical manuscripts and iconography, constitute other kinds of primary sources that are useful in research on Ottoman food history. Both Ottoman and European newspapers and magazines could facilitate research in late Ottoman food history studies of the nineteenth and early twentieth centuries. Just one example of this is that European newspapers such as *The Times* and *L'Illustration* include the menus of banquets given by the Ottoman palace.[58] Objects like tableware, porcelain, and cutlery, which are exhibited in museums and in Ottoman palaces, facilitate research into material culture. Oral history, which is a new method used in social science studies in Turkey, may contribute to food history research in the future. Changing food consumption and production patterns in Turkey since the 1930s—that is, the early years of the republic—could be studied through oral history projects. Ottoman food history would also benefit from further study using sociocultural historical approaches inspired by anthropology and sociology. As many fresh topics—such as meal hierarchies, the relationship between food and gender, and the analysis of the culinary habits of different religious communities—remain to be examined, Ottoman food history is a promising research area for scholars, both for historians and for other social scientists.

Notes

1. According to Erdem Sönmez, the influence of the *Annales* school on Ottoman historiography is discernable since the works of Fuad Köprülü in the 1930s. Approaches embraced by the *Annales* school are found first in studies realized by Ottoman historians like Ömer Lütfü Barkan, Mustafa Akdağ, and Halil İnalcık. Sönmez, 2010, 131.
2. Güçer, 1949–1950; Güçer,1964.
3. Güran, 1984–1985; Murphey, 1988, 217–63.
4. Özveren, 2003, 223–49; O. Yıldırım, 2003, 251–71.
5. Aynural, 2001; Demirtaş, 2008.
6. Beldiceanu and Beldiceanu-Steinherr, 1978, 9–28; İnalcık, 1982.
7. Greenwood, 1988; Uzun, 2006.
8. Barkan, 1962–1963; Barkan, 1979.
9. Faroqhi and Neumann, 2003, 10–11; Barkan, 1964; Barkan, 1971.
10. Kütükoğlu, 1978, 1–85; Kütükoğlu, 1983.
11. Bilgin, 2004.
12. Ünver, 1948; Ünver, 1952.
13. Koşay, 1935; Koşay and Ülkücan, 1961.
14. Sauner-Nebioğlu, 1995, 61.
15. Sauner-Nebioğlu, 1995, 67.
16. Türk Mutfağı Sempozyumu Bildirileri, 1982; Geleneksel Türk Tatlıları Sempozyumu Bildirileri, 1984.
17. Köymen, 1982; Genç, 1982; Ünver, 1982.
18. First International Food Congress, 1988; Second International Food Congress, 1989; Third International Food Congress, 1991; Fourth International Food Congress, 1993; Fifth International Food Congress Turkey, 1999.
19. T. Kut, 1985; T. Kut, 1990.
20. G. Kut, 1986.
21. G. Kut, 1988.
22. G. Kut, 1987.

23. Tezcan, 1997; Tezcan, 1998.
24. G. Kut, 2008.
25. Mehmet Kamil, 1844. An Ottoman cookbook published in England in 1864 by Türabi Efendi (*Turkish Cookery Book*) was republished with the same edition.
26. Işın, 1998.
27. Hadiye Fahriye, 2002.
28. Piranyan, 2008.
29. Vağinag Pürad, 2010.
30. Piranyan, 2008, 7–13; Vağinag Pürad, 2010, 7–12.
31. Pekin and Sümer, 1996.
32. The foundation established Turkey's first private museum, the Sadberk Hanım Museum in 1980, followed by the Koç High School in 1988 and Koç University in 1993. The foundation further extended its activities in the field of culture with the establishment of the Vehbi Koç and Ankara Research Center (VEKAM) in 1994, the Suna-İnan Kıraç Research Institute on Mediterranean Civilizations (AKMED) in 1996, the Kaleiçi Museum in Antalya's old city quarter in 2000, and, under the aegis of Koç University, the Research Center for Anatolian Civilizations (RCAC) in 2005.
33. Çevik, 2000.
34. M. Yerasimos, 2002; M. Yerasimos, 2005.
35. Ünsal, 1997; Ünsal, 2003a; Ünsal, 2003b; Ünsal, 2007.
36. The owner of this restaurant, Musa Dagdeviren, is a renowned chef who does research on the traditional recipes of Anatolia.
37. For example, Samanci, 2006; M. Yerasimos, 2009.
38. *Le café en Méditerranée*, 1980; Desmet-Grégoire and Georgeon, 1997.
39. Georgeon, 2002, 7–30.
40. Matthaiou, 1997; İnalcık, 1991.
41. Faroqhi, 1995. The Turkish translation of the book was published in 1997 and the English one in 2000.
42. Neumann, 2003.
43. Samancı, 2003. The article, which concerns the food items used in the Ottoman palace cuisines, also underlines the introduction of new vegetables native to America, such as tomatoes and potatoes. The beginning of the adaptation of new table manners in the European style by the Ottoman elite constitutes another important topic.
44. Reindl-Kiel, 2003.
45. Faroqhi and Neumann, 2003.
46. Artan, 2000.
47. S. Yerasimos, 2001; S. Yerasimos, 2002.
48. Oberling and Smith, 2001.
49. Bilgin, 2004.

50. Samancı, 1998; Samancı, 2011, 111–42.
51. Samancı, 2009.
52. Samancı, 2006b.
53. Bilgin and Samancı, 2008.
54. Singer, 2011b; Goshgarian, 2011; Singer, 2011a; Artan, 2011.
55. Desmet-Grégoire, 2002.
56. N. Yıldırım, 2008.
57. Önler, 1990; Önler, 1999.
58. Demirel, 2007. She used some of the menus published in Ottoman journals (*Ikdam, Tanin*) and in European ones (*Le Temps, L'Illustration, The Times*) in her book about Ottoman diplomatic relations, in which banquets organized by the Ottoman palace were an important part of the Ottoman protocol.

8

"Bread from Heaven, Bread from the Earth": Recent Trends in Jewish Food History Writing

Jonathan Brumberg-Kraus

Over the last thirty years, Jewish studies scholars have turned increasing attention to food and meals in Jewish culture. These studies fall more or less into two different camps: (1) text-centered studies that focus on the authors' idealized, often prescriptive construction of the meaning of food and Jewish meals, such as biblical and postbiblical dietary rules, the Passover Seder, or food in Jewish mysticism—"bread from heaven"—and (2) studies of the "performance" of Jewish meals, particularly in the modern period, which often focus on regional variations, acculturation, and assimilation—"bread from the earth."[1] This breakdown represents a more general methodological split that often divides Jewish studies departments into two camps, the text scholars and the sociologists. However, there is a growing effort to bridge that gap, particularly in the most recent studies of Jewish food and meals.[2] The major insight of all of these studies is the persistent connection between eating and Jewish identity in all its various manifestations. Jews are what they eat.

While recent Jewish food scholarship frequently draws on anthropological, sociological, and cultural historical studies of food,[3] Jewish food scholars' conversations with general food studies have been somewhat one-sided. Several factors account for this. First, a disproportionate number of Jewish food scholars (compared to other food historians) have backgrounds in the modern academic study of religion or rabbinical training, which affects the focus and agenda of Jewish food history. At the Oxford Symposium on Food and Cookery, my background in religious studies makes me an anomaly. There are usually only about two or three of us, and our disciplinary perspective seems foreign to many historians and social scientists of food cultures. While many other food historians, especially those concerned with modern food history, base much of their analyses on quantifiable data such as food prices, consumed quantities, and social policies, Jewish food historians place a lot more weight on earlier food traditions from the Bible and rabbinic literature. We typically distinguish between what classic Jewish literary traditions *want* Jews to do with food and what Jews *actually do* with food, which complicates much of the discussion of identity construction in Jewish food history writing. Since biblical and Talmudic food traditions are propagated by a scholastic elite, class and gender distinctions between rabbinic Torah scholars and "the Jewish masses," and between female and male Jews, further complicate the question of identity construction. Our disciplinary training often draws many of us to literary theory in order to communicate more precisely about the relationship between the idealizing, often prescriptive texts of Jewish tradition and the historical reality behind them. We are concerned about the dangers of taking texts at face value when trying to reconstruct Jewish history, whether we are dealing with the Mishnah, the third-century compilation of early rabbinic legal traditions, or late twentieth-century American-Jewish cookbooks.

The blurring of lines between etic and emic descriptions of Jewish foodways is also characteristic in Jewish food history writing. Jewish food studies themselves play a role in the modern construction of Jewish identity, and many scholars of Jewish food history have an implicit agenda regarding "Jewish identity" that is intended for the consumption of the modern Jewish audience. This self-referential function might unintentionally isolate Jewish from other food history writing. The text-centered and performance-centered approaches to Jewish food history that might strike other food historians as odd reflect competing strategic positions on the pressing internal question: "Who is a Jew?" What decisively determines who is a Jew: inherited normative traditions—"Judaism"—or whatever Jews do and feel subjectively—"Jewishness"? As a result of the differences between Jewish food historians and those in other specialties, advances in the history and culture of Jewish meals have not been well represented in recent important general cultural histories of food.[4] One goal of this chapter is to encourage a more reciprocal dialogue between the subdisciplines of Jewish studies and food history.

"You Are What You Eat" in Jewish Food History

Jewish food histories share with other food studies their frequent appeal to the famous dictum "you are what you eat" to make the point that food and social identity are connected. This saying derives from the much-repeated aphorism in Brillat-Savarin's *The Physiology of Taste*: "Tell me what you eat, and I shall tell you what you are."[5] But interpretations of "you are what you eat" in Jewish food histories take on a particularly Jewish flavor. For my analysis, I have chosen seven of the studies listed in my bibliographical note,[6] not only because they represent typical approaches to Jewish eating and identity, but also because the authors refer explicitly or implicitly to the saying "you are what you eat" to frame their arguments. First is Diner's comparative study *Hungering for America: Italian, Irish, and Jewish Foodways in the Age of Migration* (2001); the second, Kraemer's *Jewish Eating and Identity through the Ages* (2009); two books on medieval Jewish food texts and rituals in Spain and Germany, respectively: Hecker's *Mystical Bodies, Mystical Meals* (2005) and Marcus's *Rituals of Childhood* (1996); Rosenblum's *Food and Identity in Early Rabbinic Judaism* (2010); Roth's article "Toward a Kashrut Nation in American Jewish Cookbooks, 1990–2000" (2010); and Gil Marks's *Encyclopedia of Jewish*

Food (2010). The last book, though not organized as a history, nevertheless adopts a historical perspective in most of its entries. It is now, as well, the "go to" resource for Jewish food lore. I do not discuss them in chronological order but rather as examples of typical interpretations of "you are what you eat" in modern Jewish food histories. A comparison of how these works interpret the trope "you are what you eat" provides a good guide to the different ways Jewish food scholars address the relationship between food and Jewish identity construction. Are they text centered or performance centered, or some hybrid of the two basic approaches? Do the studies argue that Jews are "Jews" because they eat what the sacred Jewish texts and authorities say they should or should not eat, or that Jews are "Jews" because of what they actually eat?

Before I start my survey of Jewish food histories' interpretations of "you are what you eat," I will sketch out the typical periodization of Jewish history that they all assume. The scheme itself implicitly defines some periods of Jewish history as text centered and others as shaped primarily by historical circumstances, largely uninfluenced by Jewish texts.

Jewish History Is an Expression of Jewish Identity

Jewish food histories, whether broad sweeps from Israelite origins to the present or focused on one period, assume, roughly, five eras: (1) the biblical period, (2) the rabbinic or Talmudic period, (3) the medieval period, (4) the modern period, and (5) the contemporary period.[7]

This periodization oscillates between stressing, on the one hand, external non-Jewish history and cultures on Jews and Judaism (e.g., the medieval and modern periods) and, on the other, internal, autonomous Jewish institutions and cultures (e.g., the biblical and rabbinic periods) as most influential in shaping Jewish history and adapting non-Jewish cultures to their needs.[8] The different emphases on external and internal influences closely correlate with performance-centered and text-centered approaches. Moreover, this scheme suggests that Jewish sacred texts—the Bible and rabbinic literature—were the formative influences in the early foundational periods. As we move closer to the present, more general social processes (e.g., modernity) and interaction with non-Jewish cultures (e.g., medieval Christian and Muslim societies in northern Europe, Spain, and North Africa; modern secular North America and Eastern and Western Europe) are assumed to be more influential.

The Jewish food histories I have selected tend to focus on two particular formative periods, the rabbinic period and the modern period. In the former, the Jewish food rules and rituals as we know them today were established.[9] In the latter, moving from the Eastern European to the American Jewish immigrant experience, the stereotypical Jewish foodways of lox and bagels, delicatessens, and the modern kosher industry were established.[10] Food traditions of the biblical and medieval periods have received somewhat less attention in Jewish studies, often used only as "background" for subsequent formative rabbinic and modern interpretations or rejections of them. Studies of medieval Jewish food traditions frequently focus on their religious dimensions: the myths, rituals, and spiritual experiences associated with eating, as well as interaction with the surrounding Christian and Muslim religious traditions.[11] Even fewer studies of food traditions are associated with the most important historical events in modern Jewish consciousness, the Holocaust and the establishment of the state of Israel.[12] Postrabbinic Jewish food histories tend to be shaped more by a geographic scheme, such as in Cooper's chapters devoted to the "food of the Sephardim"[13] and the "food of Central and Eastern European Jews."[14] Jewish food histories covering Ashkenazic or Sephardic cuisines often stress the significant cultural contact between Jews and non-Jews that is reflected in shared or similar dishes. They also tend to reflect the culinary nostalgia of the Ashkenazic majority of Jews in North America whose families came from Eastern Europe, and their more recent fascination with the exotic "ethnic" cuisines of Sephardic, Middle Eastern, and other non-Ashkenazic Jews across the globe—their own Jewish "Others." I will come back to this point.

"You Are What You Eat" in and out of Jewish Texts

Since "you are what you eat" is fundamentally a statement of identity, every variation of it deployed in Jewish food histories carries the burden of modern Jewish identity politics characteristic of modern Jewish history writing. What it comes down to in my view is this question: What role, if any, do Jewish texts play in the eating behaviors that Jews actually perform? For text-centered Jewish food historians (as I am), if the eating practices of Jews are significantly informed by Jewish texts, that makes them Jewish. For performance-centered Jewish food historians, what makes foodways Jewish is that Jews perform them, regardless of whether Jewish texts inform their behavior.

These differences between Jewish food history writers are apparent in how they ascribe "you are what you eat"—for example, to texts or to their performers—and how metaphorically they take the saying. First, some attribute it to the implicit meaning of the behaviors they observe and describe what Jews are doing when they eat. This is typical of the performance-centered approach. Second, scholars may ascribe it to the point of view of the Jewish texts they are interpreting. In other words, the text is saying Jews are in some way what they eat or should eat. This text-centered approach often calls attention to the prescriptive dimension of the food text. For example, I can argue that the biblical texts of Genesis and Leviticus themselves claim that ancient Israelites were or should be what they ate. Notably, in Genesis 4:22: "And the Lord God said, 'Now that the man *has become like one of us, knowing good and bad*, what if he should stretch out his hand and take also from the tree of life and eat, and live forever!'" and Leviticus 20:24–26: "I the Lord am your God who *has set you apart* from other peoples. So you *shall set apart* the clean beast from the unclean, the unclean bird from the clean, . . . You shall be holy to Me, for I the Lord am holy, and *I have set you apart* from other people to be Mine." The Bible says that *what* we eat (the fruit of the tree of knowledge of good and bad), *might* eat (the fruit of the tree of life), and *ought to* eat set us apart and make us like God. Anthropologists like Mary Douglas and Jean Soler have made much of this but in their Durkheimian way have identified "God" with the Israelite people themselves. Hence, Jewish food historians referring to Douglas and Soler usually assume that "you are what you eat" means that Jews distinguish between fit and unfit foods to distinguish themselves from non-Jews. However, as Douglas and Soler maintain that the biblical texts say that this is the reason for Jewish dietary rules, theirs is a text-centered interpretation. Simply because the Bible prescribes these laws and their rationales does not mean that Jews necessarily follow them, or, if they do, they may not follow them for the reasons the Bible says.

Third, some Jewish food scholars stress the gap between what the texts say that Jews should eat and what their target audience of Jews actually eat. This text-centered approach often calls attention to "Who says?" and "To whom?"—that is, the class and gender of the promulgators of the texts and their audience.

Fourth, most expand the idea that Jews are not only what they eat but also "*how, when,* and *with whom* they eat it."[15] Thus, few contemporary Jewish food historians simply identify what Jews eat with the Jewish dietary laws. The Jewish dietary laws—kashrut—prescribe what Jews ought to eat, but not all, or even most, Jews keep kosher. Moreover, Jewish kosher laws are not the only Jewish food prescriptions. There are rules of Jewish food ethics and etiquette, blessings and other rituals that one should perform at the table, and foods and drinks for different holidays on the Jewish calendar that have little to do with the kashrut. There are as well food prescriptions concerned with the biblical sacrifices that no one was expected to perform, at least not literally, after the destruction of the Temple. As a result, the idea emerged that talking about anachronistic biblical food prescriptions was equivalent to performing them and that just speaking about food prescriptions theoretically could be an expression of Jewish identity: "you are what you theoretically should have eaten" or "you are what you ought to imagine yourself eating."

Finally, the verb "eat" in "you are what you eat" becomes a metaphor for a variety of food-related activities: talking about food, preparing food, remembering meals, visualizing imaginary meals, studying Jewish texts (sometimes but not necessarily about food), and buying Jewish cookbooks. But since most of these metaphors for eating originate from Jewish texts (including the practical rules of kashrut), even performance-centered Jewish food studies necessarily have Jewish texts in the background, not only the Bible and rabbinic literature, but also memoirs, recipe books, fiction, and ritual manuals like the Passover Haggadah. This brings us full circle since what makes these texts "Jewish" in the performance-centered approach is that Jews composed them. Composing texts is just another type of performance, like eating.

Hasia Diner, *Hungering for America* (2001)

Hasia Diner's comparative study of Italian, Irish, and Jewish foodways in the nineteenth- and twentieth-century "age of migration" in America represents a performance-centered approach. She uses "you are what you eat" to describe what it means when Jews (like other ethnic groups) actually perform something: eating with one another. She stresses the cross-cultural way that food typically marks every human group's identity: "Food, like sex, intensifies group identity.... 'Tell me what you eat, and I shall tell you what you are,' rephrased in common American parlance as 'you are what you eat,' works.... The notion of a common table connecting people exists in many cultures as an embodiment of communal trust. We might define a community as a group of people who eat with each other."[16] Diner notes that American Jewish foodways were not that different from other immigrant groups' strategies of acculturation, with the one important exception of their inherited prescriptive traditions of kashrut. Consequently, social conflicts, "kosher wars," broke out among American Jewish immigrants because their "cherished American ideas about individual choice, personal preference, and limitless opportunities ... clashed with the underlying rationale of *kashrut*," which was to separate Jews from the people around them.[17] In modern America, Jewish identity was not simply prescribed by texts and authorities from the top down; it was more importantly a collective process of social negotiations with a new set of sociohistorical circumstances.

David Kraemer, *Jewish Eating and Identity through the Ages* (2009)

David Kraemer's interpretation of "you are what you eat" may seem to take a position similar to Diner's; however, his primary interest is how classic Jewish, especially rabbinic texts, prescribe or otherwise determine certain social negotiations as "Jewish." Kraemer writes, "While it is true if you 'tell me what you eat ... I will tell you what you are,' food choices are only one of several factors relating to eating that communicate volumes concerning a people's identity. As important as *what* they eat are *how*, *when*, and *with whom* they eat it." When combinations of these choices happen frequently enough to establish a pattern, this "will display the identity of the eater to the discerning eyes of the interpreter who interprets carefully." So it is "always ... possible to identify something in the eating practices of Jews in a given place and period that distinguishes them from their neighbors—and from Jews in other places and periods as well. When we ... identify such distinctive practices, we will be able to interpret them as signs of current Jewish identity."[18]

Where are these distinctive patterns? In "the *literary* record of laws and other kinds of legal discourse," that is to say, in Jewish *texts*.[19] Kraemer acknowledges problems with this approach. For example, prescriptive texts represent the views only of an elite minority of Jews. And he mentions other sources, such as "archaeology, history, legends, memoirs, polemical literature, material culture and so forth."[20] Nevertheless, most of his arguments are based on biblical, rabbinic, medieval, and modern Jewish literary legal sources (halakhah).[21] Faithful to the ideology of Conservative Judaism of the Jewish Theological Seminary where he is professor of Talmud and library director, Kraemer stresses that Jewish patterns of eating are not fixed but continue to evolve historically. His criteria for noteworthy historical developments in Jewish eating are that (1) a development was a new and important change in Jewish eating, and (2) it was a practice that persisted for centuries. Fitting these criteria are the biblical laws of permitted and prohibited animals, the "founding and development of the meat-dairy prohibition" from its rabbinic origins through its postrabbinic evolution, "transgressive" Jewish eating, and contemporary "kashrut wars" representing intra-Jewish controversies, such as inspection for bugs in lettuce and fruits.[22] He frames these criteria in discussions of classic Jewish biblical, rabbinic, and postrabbinic legal sources and prescriptions about what, when, and with whom one can eat.

Most telling is Kraemer's interpretation of why modern Jews habitually eat *treyf* (nonkosher) food from Chinese restaurants, a prime example of transgressive eating.[23] He claims that many New York Jews consider Chinese food "safe *treyf*" because the prohibited pork and seafood in it are chopped so small that they are no longer discernable. These Jews are really "making a kind of halakhic decision....They are choosing to rebel in Jewish terms, and thus are in significant respects, not rebelling at all." Kraemer views loopholes in earlier Jewish legal discussions, such as permission to eat prohibited foods to save a life, as precedents for modern Jewish transgressive eating. He concludes paradoxically, "In modest or significant ways, transgressive eating was always a part of Jewish tradition."[24] For Kraemer, "you are what you eat" means that you are how you *interpret* what you eat, *through the lenses of normative prescriptive Jewish literary traditions*, at different times in different historical circumstances.

"You Are the *Texts* That You Eat" in Medieval Jewish Food Studies

Joel Hecker's and Ivan Marcus's studies of medieval Jewish food texts and rituals respectively represent text-centered and performance-centered approaches. In another sense both are text centered, for they describe practices that take "what you eat" as a metaphor for sacred Jewish *texts*. Jews, idealized as male rabbinic scholars, are those who "eat Torah."

In *Mystical Bodies, Mystical Meals: Eating and Embodiment in Medieval Kabbalah* (2005), Hecker ascribes "you are what you eat" to Rabbi Joseph Gikatilla's perspective in *The Gates of Light*, written in the late thirteenth century, and so represents a text-centered approach but in an unusual way. He says, "Gikatilla...reverses the familiar maxim, 'You are what you eat,' yielding instead 'You are that which eats you,'" to explain the mythic construction of identity in thirteenth- and fourteenth-century Jewish kabbalistic texts about eating.[25] In the kabbalistic myth of reincarnation, animals are "metaphysically transformed" into the identity of those who consume them. Hence only Jewish male scholars well versed in Torah, that is, kabbalah, should be permitted to eat meat.[26] Consequently, an ignoramus, one who is not versed in the secrets of Torah, should not eat meat, because, being a beast himself, he cannot raise the soul of the animal he eats.[27] Here, Jewish texts suggest that eating by diners qualified with the right "Jewish knowledge"—in this case kabbalistic Torah about reincarnation—has a spiritual function, to elevate the souls of both the diner and his dinner.

While edible texts play a central role in the practices Marcus interprets in *Rituals of Childhood* (1996), his is essentially a performance-centered analysis of the Jewish eating ritual intended to initiate Jewish boys into the study of Torah in medieval Germany (Ashkenaz). As Marcus describes the practice,

> The child is seated on the teacher's lap, [and] the teacher shows him the writing tablet, honey cake, and egg on which the Hebrew alphabet or biblical verses have been written. The two of them recite the texts, and the child licks honey off the tablet and eats the inscribed cakes and eggs.
>
> These gestures are a bold illustration of symbolic inversion. The child enters the Torah (*nikhnas la-torah*) by means of the Torah entering the child in the form of the special foods on which the verses of the Torah have been written.[28]

Here Marcus, too, suggests Jewish eating rituals "invert" the symbolic meaning of the ingestion of "Jewish" food. The Jewish boy goes into the Torah text that has gone into him. Why would eating the Torah carry this meaning in medieval Germany? In Marcus's Geertzian "thick description" of the cultural context of this eating rite of passage, contemporary Christian Eucharistic practices, which emphasized ingesting Christ to mark distinctive Christian identities, gave the ingestion of Torah, the quintessential marker of Jewish rabbinic identity, its symbolic power.[29] Marcus calls this "pre-modern or inward acculturation" in contrast to "modern or outward acculturation." The latter "refers to the blurring of individual and communal traditional Jewish identities and of the religious and cultural boundaries between Jews and modern society."[30] But in premodern, inward acculturation, when "Jews who did not assimilate or convert to the majority culture retained an unequivocal Jewish identity...the writings of the articulate few or the customs of the ordinary many sometimes expressed elements of their Jewish religious cultural identity by internalizing and transforming various genres, motifs, terms, institutions, or rituals of the majority culture in a polemical, parodic, or neutralized manner."[31]

The "writings of...articulate" and "the customs of...ordinary" medieval Jews asserted that they were the people who ate the body of Torah, in contradistinction to the Christian majority, those who ate the body of Christ. The rabbinic cultural ideal for Jewish males was to embody Torah. Hence, when various kabbalistic eating rituals and the Ashkenazic initiation rite use spoken words, gestures, and inscriptions to equate Torah with food, they are "ritualizations" of the metaphor that "Torah is food." Marcus, following anthropologist James Fernandez, defines "the ritualization of metaphors" as "a cultural mechanism in which individuals take a metaphorical statement about themselves to be fundamentally true."[32] In this sense, medieval Jews are the *metaphors* they eat. Jewish "root metaphors," which are "ultimately derived from late biblical religion[, and] illustrate the tendency...*to act out textual metaphors ritually.*"[33] The imaginative language of the inherited Jewish texts and myths (and their rabbinic interpreters) conveys Jewish cultural identity in premodern medieval Jewish inward acculturation. In this way, both Hecker and Marcus have contributed the important insight that text-based myths and their ritual performances shape how Jews understand that they are what they eat.

Like other proponents of similar text-oriented approaches to Jewish food, Hecker and Marcus were trained and/or taught in seminaries or religious studies programs, and they are conversant with the academic discipline of the comparative study of religions. Their attention to the interplay of idealized textual and mythic constructions of "Jewish eating" and ritual performances of Jewish social identity is quite consistent with those approaches.

Jordan Rosenblum, *Food and Identity in Early Rabbinic Judaism* (2010)

Likewise, Jordan Rosenblum's *Food and Identity in Early Rabbinic Judaism* is particularly sensitive to the complex relationship between texts, myths, rituals, and the social construction of identity in Jewish eating practices. Rosenblum uses "you are what you eat" to problematize both eating and identity. He suggests we need a more sophisticated understanding of eating, or, better, of texts prescribing certain ways of eating, and the creation of Jewish social identities. For Rosenblum, identity is "a category of practice." You are what you perform. But texts, too, perform things, insofar as they have a rhetorical purpose. When early rabbinic "texts prescribe the consumption of or abstention from certain foods...the texts themselves do not establish a distinct identity. In contrast, the prescriptions contained in a text are part of a[n]...attempt to regulate practices, and those practices contextualize and establish the participant's identity for those people writing that text." The *Tanna'im*, the early rabbinic authorities of the first through third centuries C.E. who composed and preserved the eating traditions Rosenblum discusses, were an elite scholastic class who wanted ordinary nonrabbinic Jews to adopt their practices. For Rosenblum, "the oft-stated principle 'you are what you eat' is . . . a statement about identity insofar as it refers to the practice of eating as constituting an individual's identity." He "argue[s] throughout this study that culinary and commensally-constructed tannaitic identity is *always* about practice. Identity is not a passive experience. Like the act of eating, it is an active social practice."[34] Rosenblum does not restrict active social practices to eating per se but extends them to all "culturally significant activities surrounding the preparation and ingestion of food that allows diners to make an identity statement by the manner in which they partake of their dinner." Even talking (or writing) about food belongs to the performed activities that he subsumes under the rubric "edible identity."[35]

Rosenblum means that early rabbinic food texts are like dramatic scripts that tell or imply a certain story and assign people certain roles in that story. Importantly, all roles are not equal. There are clearly stars or leading roles, supporting actors, supporting actresses, and bit parts inscribed in these scripts. The leading roles belong to "Jewish rabbinic males," and non-Jews, nonrabbis, and females have supporting roles to play in the "preparation and ingestion of food that allows" the stars "to make an identity statement by the manner in which they partake of their dinner."[36] Rosenblum identifies what he calls "the chef/sous-chef principle" as a strategy employed in rabbinic prescriptions about who could prepare their food, still allowing them their privileged "Jewish male rabbinic identity," but without requiring Jewish male rabbis to be involved in every stage of their food preparation.[37] Under the "chef/sous-chef principle," the wife of a rabbi could be entrusted to prepare foods according to rabbinic standards even if doing so did not identify her as a Jewish rabbinic male. The most important foods of the Mediterranean diet, bread, wine, and olive oil, could be prepared at least in part by Gentiles, provided that at crucial junctures they were under the supervision of Jewish rabbinic males. An *'am ha-aretz,* a Jew who does not observe the rabbinic rules of purity and tithing (a nonrabbinic Jew by definition), or the wife of an *'am ha-aretz* may cook for a rabbinic Jew under his supervision (or his wife's), but not vice versa.[38] These food prescriptions also underline the fact that the rabbis were not against social interaction between Jews and Gentiles and rabbinic and nonrabbinic Jews across the boundaries they established. Rather, negotiating social interaction across these boundaries became occasions to perform Jewish rabbinic male identity or for supporting actors to maintain Jewish rabbinic males in their starring roles. In other words, what made food "Jewish" was not so much where it came from but rather whether or not a rabbinic Jew controlled its preparation at a crucial juncture. As Diner and other Jewish food historians of the modern period point out, this power to control was transferred to Jewish women as they increasingly played more significant roles in choosing and preparing food for their households.[39]

Another important "edible identity" strategy to which Rosenblum calls attention is the Tannaitic texts' construction of certain foods as "metonymic and embodying" Jewish rabbinic male identity or rival group identities. Quoting anthropologist Emiko Ohnuki-Tierney,[40] Rosenblum writes, "'The beauty and purity of *we* are *embodied doubly in the body of the people and the food that represents them,* and conversely, the undesirable quality of the other are embodied in *their* foods and their foodway [sic].' In short, you are what you eat."[41] Rosenblum discusses "manna, the Passover, and *kashrut* practices in general" as rabbinic metonyms for Jews and "the abominable pig" for Gentiles.[42] The Tannaitic sources construct Gentiles as "pig-eaters" and Jews as "manna-eaters," "Passover-eaters" (or "*matzah*-eaters"), and "pig-avoiders." Thus, even foods that cannot actually be eaten because they are legendary (manna, the bread from heaven in the biblical exodus story) or no longer available (the original Passover lamb in Egypt or the Passover offering after the destruction of the Temple in 70 C.E.) retain their mythic power as symbols of quintessentially "Jewish" identity. Rabbinic sources talk about manna theoretically "to translate that mythical entity into the reality of one's cultural milieu. Despite the fact that manna had long since disappeared from the Israelite menu, the Tannaim (at least metaphorically) still drew on the practice of eating it in their construction of Jewish identity."[43] When rabbinic interpreters in their theoretical discussions and prescribed table talk associate the metonymic foods, such as Jewish bread or kosher meat, with Torah, Torah, too, acquires a metonymic quality. Early rabbinic males are "Torah eaters." As we have already seen, late medieval Spanish kabbalists and Jews of Ashkenaz make quite explicit the idea of Torah as the uniquely Jewish metonymic food in their "ritualized metaphors" of eating Torah.

"Secular Bibles": Laurence Roth on Jewish Cookbooks and Gil Marks's *Encyclopedia of Jewish Food* (2010)

My last two examples of variations on the saying "you are what you eat" come from two recent studies of modern Jewish foodways in which the authority of the Torah of the rabbinic and medieval Jewish sources has become quite attenuated. There is a "new Torah" that many Jews consume to express their Jewish identity: Jewish cookbooks. First, Laurence Roth in "Toward a Kashrut Nation" (2010) calls modern Jewish cookbooks "secular Bibles" and uses "you are what you eat" to summarize the peculiar role kashrut plays as a Jewish cultural identifier, even if it is not observed in actual eating practice.[44] Roth describes kashrut as a marketable brand name inscribed in Jewish cookbooks, rather than prescribed practices that the authors intend to be followed.[45] Roth concludes in his essay that the "kashrut nation" brand "reminds us that in America's current food-obsessed mood the notion that 'we are what we eat' is so hackneyed that it too has become unchallenged common sense. Perhaps, then, the most compelling fantasy retailed in American Jewish cookbooks today is not that there is a Jewish cuisine, but that such a profitable idea was ever in doubt."[46] In his somewhat cynical take, Roth makes kashrut more or less analogous to imaginary or no-longer-eaten Jewish metonymic foods, such as manna or the Passover offering. The rhetorical function of kashrut, rather than its actual practice, reflects and speaks to the tensions of modern Jewish identity: "Removed from material practice and placed in a rhetorical practice, kashrut is a powerful tool with which to allay anxiety about biological or cultural continuity and to forge connections between readers with similar interests and tastes, readers who may live at both far and close distances from each other." In the 1990s, kashrut's rhetorical function in cookbooks mirrors Jewish "obsessions about history and memory... conflicts about diasporic and homeland identities[;]...Jewish continuity and authenticity; the resurgence in America of a conservative religiosity and of a desire among American Jews to reconnect with 'traditional' Jewish practices; and the proliferation of gastronomically diverse as well as international cookery stories within the American cookbook genre."[47] The nationalization and internationalization of Jewish cuisine in modern Jewish cookbooks, which now include Jewish dishes from around the world, especially Sephardic and Middle Eastern Jewish foods (as opposed to Eastern European foods, the default Jewish cuisine for many American Jews), are significant developments analogous to the development and expression of the idea of an Indian national cuisine discussed by Appadurai.[48] In both modern Indian and Jewish cookbooks, "Jewish" and "Indian" are literary constructs of nationhood, of "social and cultural bonds" necessitated by "conflicts about diasporic and homeland identities."[49] In any case, Roth takes "eat" metaphorically in "you are what you eat." It is synonymous with economic consumption. Buying the kosher-branded Jewish cookbooks is a way to perform contemporary Jewish identity.

In his *Encyclopedia of Jewish Food* (2010), Gil Marks cites a different quotation from Brillat-Savarin—"The destiny of nations depends upon what and how they eat"—to put a more prescriptive, collective national emphasis on the idea that you are what you eat. Then he exhorts his readers that "by our food, we declare and affirm who we are and who we want to be."[50] If contemporary Jewish cookbooks are today's Jewish "secular Bibles," then Marks's *Encyclopedia* is a sort of secular *Shulhan Arukh* in which he has codified and glossed the Jewish canon of recipes contained in them.[51] But, for Marks, accurate historical information about traditional Jewish recipes, not the rhetoric of kashrut, brands his book as "Jewish." Hence the *Encyclopedia*'s flyleaf evokes Marks's authority as a "chef, rabbi, writer, historian, and expert on Jewish cooking" to attest to the Jewish authenticity of its contents.[52] Marks addresses the anxieties about Jewish cultural continuity that Roth discusses when he says in his introduction, "The collection of information and traditional recipes in *Encyclopedia of Jewish Food*—the influential and integral parts of ancient and modern Jewish history and culture—tells the story of the past twenty-five years of *Clal Yisrael*. In addition to testifying to the past and present, a community's food also influences that what it will become."[53] Jewish food tells a story; it is our past, present, and especially our future—our national destiny.

Conclusions

Let me conclude this survey with four observations. First, for those Jewish food historians interested in texts and the *mythic* constructions of Jewish identity ("bread from heaven"), Torah is a metonymic Jewish food. Especially in rabbinic and medieval Jewish food texts, Jews are explicitly or implicitly constructed as "Torah eaters." Granted, Torah can mean different things to different Jews at different times, for example, halakhah, namely kashrut, which can be "consumed" literally or as an economic commodity; "the Jewish story," Haggadah or personal memoirs consumed in "feasts of history";[54] or a "secular Bible," modern Jewish recipe books. By employing demonstrative table talk, language, and gestures, Jews attribute the name, verses, or qualities of Torah to certain foods and make them metonymic in ritualized metaphors.

Second, for Jewish food historians more interested in realistically describing modern American Jewish foodways, kashrut can have a secular function as a consumable marker of identity in the sense that it is marketable.[55] But as a consumable Jewish identity marker, it is possible to consider kashrut in competition with other Jewish identity markers. A published collection of recipes gathered from Jewish Holocaust survivors is in good company with other Jewish cookbooks mark(et)ed as "Jewish," not so much by kashrut (indeed, many of the recipes published in the Terezin cookbook are not kosher), but by their association with Jewish victims and survivors of the Holocaust and other traumatic experiences of Jewish history.[56] Kashrut itself has also been reenvisioned recently as "sustainable Jewish eating," "eco-kashrut," "ethical kashrut," or even vegetarianism. Contemporary environmentalism, the sustainable foodie-ism of the Slow Food movement, and outrage about the ethical abuses against workers and animals at one of the largest kosher meat-processing plants in America (Postville, Iowa) have influenced contemporary redefinitions of kashrut.[57] Members of this "new Jewish food movement" perform their identity by reading and talking about Michael Pollan's *Omnivore's Dilemma* (2006) and other publications,[58] contributing to and reading Jewish food blogs like *The Jew and the Carrot*, participating in local, sometimes synagogue-sponsored community supported agriculture (CSA) farms, and buying kosher meat from small, sustainable, organic kosher meat distributors like Kol Foods and Grow and Behold, or purchasing nonkosher meat at farmers' markets, or even avoiding meat altogether.

Third, the rabbinic and medieval texts idealizing Jewish rabbinic male identity as Jewish identity per se have increasingly lost their authority and relevance for many Jews as modern Jewish edible identities have been feminized. "Kitchen Judaism," considered nostalgically as the domain of our idealized Jewish foremothers, has become a new stage for the performance of Jewish food identity.[59] As the Jewish rabbinic male chef calling the shots has receded from the stage of history, the sous-chef (often constructed as female) who buys, cooks, serves, and transmits recipes of Jewish food, has become the "star" of the performances of Jewish edible identities. The Jewish food we consume is female. Jewish food is what our grandmothers and mothers cooked. Jewish food is our immigrant grandmother's negotiations with kashrut—that is, what she chose to adopt and reject from among her abundant new American options, and her choice as to when to cook Jewish or go out for Chinese or Italian. Jewish women and their stories are enshrined in the secular Bibles of Jewish cuisine, modern Jewish recipe books. So even Jewish males or non-Jewish members of the household play "female roles" when they cook and eat Jewish. So just as Bynum's Christian women mystics' characteristic roles of feeding and nourishing others—that is, their socially constructed femininity—became the symbol of Christian humanity, so feminized Jewish food has become a symbol for modern Jewish identity.

Finally, the religious studies approaches of interpreters of Jewish food history have added a distinctive flavor to their interpretations, making them different from all other ethnic and regional food histories. One can sense it especially in the power that many of these studies attribute to the formative role of less or nonmaterial phenomena like texts, myths, symbolic interpretation of rituals, and eating experiences. Granted, I may have given short shrift to the Jewish food historians more concerned with material culture, especially archaeologists.[60] The main contributions of archaeological studies of food in the biblical and rabbinic periods highlight the distinction between what ancient Jewish texts prescribed and what Jews and their neighbors actually ate. For example, archaeology provides evidence for changes in the cultural significance of Jewish prohibitions of pork. In biblical Israel, the pork prohibition did not really differentiate Israelites from their neighbors, who did not eat that much pork. Only in the Romanized Mediterranean world, when pork consumption was so ubiquitous that "pig was meat," did Jewish abhorrence of eating pork become a significant cultural marker distinguishing Jews from non-Jews.[61] Archaeological evidence also shows that Jews hardly differed from their neighbors in the technologies of their cultivation, preparation, and consumption of the three principal nonmeat staples of the Mediterranean: bread, olive oil, and wine.[62] Hence, more weight has to be given to the nuanced details, to the different explicit interpretations of these otherwise similar activities to locate how (if at all) eating differentiated Jews from non-Jews. The religious studies programs where many Jewish food historians were trained tend to promote a "worldview" approach that views human cultures as systems of myths, rituals, experiences, ethics, social institutions, and doctrines.[63] We are predisposed to look for the *meaning* of Jewish food practices within such systems and to stress textual analysis as an important way to understand these idealized constructions of Jewish eating and identity. Finally, for some of us personally committed to a Jewish life and Jewish continuity, a religious interest in spirituality for its own sake motivates or otherwise colors our Jewish food studies. There is no real dichotomy, then, between "bread from heaven" and "bread from the earth" in these holistic, systemic, worldview approaches to Jewish food history, if one sees them both as rooted and integrated in the same evolving set of Jewish national myths.

Notes

I thank Jordan Rosenblum for discussing this chapter with me and providing me with bibliographical suggestions and help with formulating my thoughts, as well as my other colleagues in the Society of Biblical Literature (SBL) Seminar on Meals in the Greco-Roman World, my student research assistant Sophie Vener, my lunch companions in the Wheaton College Faculty Dining Room, and conversation partners at the Oxford Symposium on Food and Cookery, without whom the ideas expressed here would never have come to fruition.

1. "Bread from heaven" alludes to the biblical accounts of the miracle of manna, e.g., Exodus 16:4: "The Lord said to Moses, 'I am going to rain bread from heaven for you.'" "Bread from the earth" is from the Jewish blessing *Ha-motzi* over bread: "Blessed are You Lord our God...who brings forth bread from the earth."

2. Of the twenty or so recent books or scholars whose contributions to Jewish food history I have found particularly useful, I would roughly categorize them as follows:

TEXT-CENTERED: Bokser, 1984; Tabory, 1996; Hecker, 2005; Kraemer, 2009; Rosenblum, 2010; Vais, 2010; Freidenreich, 2011, and most of Susan Weingarten's articles on food from the Talmudic period.

PERFORMANCE-CENTERED: J. Cooper, 1993; Joselit, 1994; Gitlitz and Davidson, 1999; Roden, 1996; Diner, 2001; Deutsch, 2008; Fishkoff, 2010; G. Marks, 2010; Ruth Abusch-Magder's work on Jewish women and food in Germany and America (e.g., 2002); and Lara Rabinovitch's forthcoming dissertation on Romanian Jewish delis in New York City and Montreal. They are practice centered and pay particular attention to material evidence.

ANTHOLOGIES OF JEWISH FOOD STUDIES: In Brenner and van Henten's collection of essays *"Food and Drink in the Biblical Worlds"* (1999), most are text centered. In the *"Gender, Food, and Survival"* volume of *Nashim* (Joseph, 2002), most of the articles are performance centered. In *Food and Judaism* (Greenspoon et al., 2004), there's an even balance between text-centered and performance-centered contributions. Most of the essays in the *Koscher & Co.: über Essen und Religion* exhibit book from the Jewish Museum in Berlin focus on material culture (Friedlander and Kugelmann, 2009); likewise, food-related essays by Joselit and Kirshenblatt-Gimblett for the *Getting Comfortable in New York* exhibit book of the Jewish Museum of New York (Joselit et al., 1990). Not surprisingly, studies of biblical, rabbinic, and medieval Jewish food practices are almost all text centered, while those focusing on modern American Jewish immigrant and Jewish women's food practices are mostly performance and material culture centered.

INTEGRATED STUDIES: Two books, Marcus, 1996, and Kogman-Appel, 2006, influenced by Bynum, 1991, make a point of integrating documentary sources with material culture, especially medieval art, in their analysis of medieval Jewish eating rituals.

REVIEW ESSAYS: Two recent review essays on topics in Jewish food history—Brumberg-Kraus, 2005, on ancient meals in Jewish studies scholarship, and Roth, 2010, on contemporary Jewish cookbooks—reflect primarily text-centered approaches.

TRANSLATIONS: English translations of the classic Jewish sources like the Bible and Talmud make them easily accessible. And there are many primary sources for modern Jewish food history in English or other modern European languages. However, now two Hebrew primary sources specifically focused on Jewish eating traditions are available in English, Rabbenu Bahya ben Asher's fourteenth-century mystical manual of eating, *Shulhan Shel Arba* [*Table of Four*] (Bahya ben Asher Hlava, 2010), and the seventeenth-century *Peri Ez Hadar: Fruit of the Tree of Splendor* (Krassen, 1992), the source for modern Tu Bishvat seders. Both prescribe rituals where certain food texts from the Bible and rabbinic literature are to be recited or discussed while eating. They are particularly useful resources for nonhalakhic, aggadic, that is, *mythic* Jewish eating traditions, both because they anthologize less familiar biblical and rabbinic food texts and because they interpret and apply these texts in their own imaginative kabbalistic way. There is more to classic Jewish views about food than the laws of kashrut.

3. Douglas, 1972; Douglas, 1966; Goody, 1982; Geertz, 1973; Geertz, 1983; Bourdieu, 1984; Bynum, 1987; Bynum, 1991; Rozin, 1991; Rozin and Haidt, 1997; Ohnuki-Tierney, 1993; Counihan and van Esterik, 1997; Smart, 2000; Appadurai, 1988; Montanari, 1994; Society of Biblical Literature (SBL) Seminar on Meals in the Greco-Roman World (Harland, 2010).
4. Flandrin and Montanari, 1999; Montanari, 1994; Freedman, 2007.
5. Brillat-Savarin, 1999, 1.
6. See note 2.
7. This formulation comes from the curriculum of the Reconstructionist Rabbinical College, where I received my ordination, but it's pretty standard, with some variations on modern and contemporary periods.
8. Yitzhak Baer (1968), one of the most important Jewish historians of the twentieth century, argues that this indeed is *the* fundamental issue in modern Jewish historiography.
9. E.g., Bokser, 1984; Kraemer, 2007; Rosenblum, 2010; Tabory, 1995; Vais, 2010; and Weingarten's articles.
10. E.g., Deutsch, 2008; Diner, 2001; Fishkoff, 2010; Joselit, 1994; Abusch-Magder, 2002; and Rabinovitch's forthcoming dissertation on Romanian delicatessens in North America.
11. E.g., Brumberg-Kraus, 1999a; Brumberg-Kraus, 1999b; Brumberg-Kraus, 2001; Freidenreich, 2011; Hecker, 2005; Kogman-Appel, 2006; Marcus, 1996.
12. DeSilva, 1996; Ferst, 2011; Raviv, 2003; and Dafna Hirsch's major research project on hummus in Israeli culture and national identity (in progress).
13. Jews who were living in the Iberian Peninsula, or who resettled in the Balkans, North Africa, and the Middle East, after the expulsions of the 1490s.

14. Cooper, 1993.
15. Kraemer, 2009, 2.
16. Diner, 2001, 4.
17. Diner, 2001, 224, 224–25.
18. Kraemer, 2009, 2, 3.
19. Kraemer, 2009, 6 (my emphasis).
20. Kraemer, 2009, 7–8.
21. Comparing Kraemer's book to Rosenblum, 2010, Jacob Neusner, a leading scholar of rabbinic literature, contrasts (and prefers) Kraemer's "documentary"-based study of the evolution of Jewish food laws to Rosenblum's "anthropological exegesis" of these same sources.
22. Kraemer, 2009, 4–5.
23. Kraemer, 2009, 4, 143–45.
24. Kraemer, 2009, 145.
25. Hecker, 2005, 95–96.
26. Hecker, 2005, 96, referring to Rabbi Joseph Gikatilla's interpretation in *Sha'arei Orah*, 2:11–12 of the Talmudic passage b. Pesahim 49b: "It is forbidden for an ignoramus (*am ha-aretz*) to eat meat....Anyone who is engaged with the Torah is permitted to eat meat and anyone who is not engaged in Torah is forbidden to eat meat." For a detailed study of the transformation of this tradition over time, see Brumberg-Kraus, 1999a.
27. Hecker, 2005, 97.
28. Marcus, 1996, 77–78.
29. Geertz's cultural anthropological studies (1973) and Bynum's study of medieval Eucharistic and women's spirituality (1987) feature prominently in his bibliography and arguments throughout the book.
30. Marcus, 1996, 11.
31. Marcus, 1996, 11–12.
32. Marcus, 1996, 6.
33. Marcus, 1996, 6. He sees this as a tendency of medieval Ashkenazic Jewry. I see it also in the kabbalists of Spain and in most traditional Jewish food rituals, like Sabbath meals and Passover and Tu Bishvat seders in general. See Brumberg-Kraus, 2001 and 2010.
34. Rosenblum, 2010, 6.
35. Rosenblum, 2010, 7, 7–8, 186.
36. Rosenblum, 2010, 7.
37. Rosenblum, 2010, 186–87.
38. Rosenblum, 2010, 148. In the Tannaitic sources he cites, the distinction is between a *haber* and an *'am ha-aretz*. Who exactly the *haberim* are is a controversial subject in Jewish studies, so Rosenblum (2010, 147), citing Jaffee (2006, 160), is appropriately precise in qualifying his use of these Tannaitic traditions. This demonstrates the author's knowledge of modern critical study of rabbinic texts. He acknowledges the problems with using them to derive history and

argues how to surmount them. In contrast, Cooper (1993) does not seem conversant with the recent historical-critical textual study of biblical and especially Talmudic literature (e.g., Neusner, 1979) and takes too much of what they say at face value. Hence many Jewish studies scholars interested in Jewish food history are rather lukewarm about his book.

39. E.g., Diner, Abusch-Magder, Joselit, Joseph, and Roth.

40. Ohnuki-Tierney, 1993, 131.

41. Rosenblum, 2010, 46.

42. Rosenblum, 2010, 47, 48, alluding to a chapter title in M. Harris, 1998, 67–87. For this phenomenon in the medieval European context, see Fabre-Vassas, 1997.

43. Rosenblum, 2010, 59. Contrast this to Cooper, 1993, 15. He treats the imaginary Jewish food manna in a theoretically less sophisticated way, simply classifying it as a "Biblical food." He offers some analogies to real things, like plant lice secretions or lichens said to be eaten in the Middle East, and then rejects them.

44. Roth, 2010, 88.

45. Except the Lubavitch Hasidic authors and publishers of the first of the five cookbooks he focuses on, Esther Blau et al., 1990. The other four are C. Marks, 1992; G. Marks, 1996; Roden, 1996; Levy, 2000.

46. Roth, 2010, 90–91.

47. Roth, 2010, 87.

48. Appadurai, 1988, to whom Roth (2010, 66, 75) refers.

49. Roth, 2010, 75, 87.

50. G. Marks, 2010, xi.

51. The *Shulhan Arukh* ("The Set Table"), composed by Rabbi Joseph Caro in 1563, is the standard authoritative codification of Jewish law.

52. Roth, 2010, 80–83, on G. Marks's cookbook (1996), is apropos here, too.

53. G. Marks, 2010, xi. Clal Yisrael is a Jewish insider term connoting a unified Jewish people, despite their demographic and ideological diversity.

54. The term is from Raphael, 1993.

55. Roth, 2010; Fishkoff, 2010.

56. Hersh, 2011, as reported in Fabricant, 2011. DeSilva, 1996, is an edition of recipes found in a manuscript hidden by Jewish inmates of the Theresienstadt concentration camp. Jewish women in the camp remembered and transcribed the recipes they used to cook before they were imprisoned, as a form of spiritual resistance against the material deprivation and dehumanization they suffered in the camp. It is not really meant to be used as a cookbook per se. That is not the case with the recipes in a *Drizzle of Honey* (Gitlitz and Davidson, 1999), in part reconstructed from transcripts of testimony forced from victims of the Spanish Inquisition.

57. See Fishkoff, 2010.

58. Pollan, 2007; Pollan, 2008.

59. "Kitchen Judaism" is Joselit's term (1994, 171).
60. E.g., Meyers, 2002; Joselit et al., 1990; Friedlander and Kugelmann, 2009.
61. Kraemer, 2009, 18–19, 32–33, and the sources he cites.
62. Rosenblum, 2010, 17–33, and the sources he cites.
63. E.g., Smart, 2000; Geertz, 1973; Geertz, 1983.

–9–

The Historiography of Arab Cuisine:
Issues and Perspectives

Nawal Nasrallah

Arab culinary studies have witnessed a remarkable lift in the past three decades. Recent publications in the field are more often of high quality than not, and promising research now seems characteristic. Consequently, the historiography of this aspect of Arab culture not only has been revived but has also begun to reach mainstream publications. Still, in light of the long culinary traditions the Arabs established and the significant role the cuisine has historically played, especially during the golden medieval era, the body of work dedicated to the study of its history is still sporadic and relatively small. As this chapter shows, much of the research energy was expectedly geared toward themes and issues concerning the medieval Abbasid era between the mid-eighth and thirteenth centuries when Arab cuisine and the relevant data were at their richest. Growing interest in Arab social cultures has also directed increasing attention to modern and contemporary cuisines in the region. Ultimately, serious considerations of Arab societies that include various aspects of their cultures, not just politics or religion, will contribute to a more balanced view of the Arab world.

Definition of the Arab World

The Arab world by definition designates the Arabic-speaking countries, which today cover a stretch of land that straddles two continents, western Asia and North Africa. About 358 million people live in this region, mostly Muslim Arabs, with religious and ethnic minorities of Christians, Jews, Kurds, and Amazighs, among others. Before the advent of Islam at the beginning of the seventh century, the Arabs lived mainly in the Arabian Peninsula, but also in Iraq, when the Lakhmid tribe settled around the city of Hira in the late third century C.E. Around the sixth century C.E., the Arab Ghassanid tribe settled in the Levant. The former sided with the Sassanid Persia against the Byzantines, and the latter with the Byzantines against the Persians. After the spread of Islam in the seventh century, flourishing Arab dynasties came to power, dominating the Old World from North Africa and the Iberian Peninsula to China— the Umayyads in Damascus and later in Andalusia, and the Abbasids in Baghdad.

In the early years of the sixteenth century, Arabs in Andalusia were forced to either convert to Christianity or be expelled from Spain. For much of the four centuries before World War I, most of the Arab world came under the dominance of the Ottoman Empire; after that, the region was under varying degrees of European control. Foreign rule in the Arab region continued up to the middle of the twentieth century; in various countries, this spurred nationalistic uprisings that led to their independence.

Arab Cuisine Comes to the Foreground

Arab food research got an impressively early head start and a promising one indeed. The Syrian scholar Habeeb Zayyat (1871–1954) started publishing a series of interesting, well-documented culinary articles in the Lebanese journal *Al-Khizana al-Sharqiyya* in the early 1930s, which continued until a few years before his death. He wrote about Damascene apricots, rice bread, coconut oil, and *khubz al-abazeer* (cookies with seed spices), which he claims the Crusaders learned from the Arabs and called *pain d'épices*. An article he wrote on *al-hisba* (market inspection) uses the records of the market inspectors, which provide valuable data on medieval food and crafts and trades in urban marketplaces.

In 1937, Zayyat edited and published the fifteenth-century *Kitab al-Tibakha* (Cookbook) attributed to the Damascene scholar Ibn al-Mubarrid (d. 1503).[1] He found the manuscript by chance hidden in a pile of paper rubbish. Its five and a half pages contain forty-four recipes briefly described and arranged alphabetically. In his brief introduction he also tells of an exciting discovery he made at the Bodleian Library at Oxford University: a cookbook manuscript complete with a title and author's name. It was *Kitab al-Tabeekh* by Ibn Sayyar al-Warraq, which he believed had been written during the Abbasid period.[2] Despite his interest in this manuscript, it was only after a decade that he revisited it in his 1947 article "Fann al-Tabkh wa Islah al-At'ima fi 'l-Islam" (The art of cooking and the concept of remedying foods in Islam). In this article he establishes its merit as an important document that reveals a sophisticated medieval cuisine as well as linguistic wealth that was part of the cultural language developed after the advent of Islam in the seventh century. He recommends the book as worthy of publication, and, hoping to excite some interest in it, he concludes his article with the book's own introduction and a list of its 132 chapters. However, decades passed before this manuscript was edited (more on this in the following).

Now to another region in the Arab world, Iraq. While visiting the library of Aya Sophia Mosque in Istanbul in the 1930s, the Iraqi scholar Daoud Chelebi of Mosul discovered the manuscript of a medieval Arabic cookery book, which he edited and published in Mosul in 1934. Entitled *Kitab al-Tabeekh* (Cookbook) the manuscript states it was copied in 1226 by the author himself, Muhammad bin al-Hasan bin al-Kareem al-Katib al-Baghdadi. Its collection of 158 recipes arranged in ten chapters essentially reflects the personal taste and preferences of the writer himself, as he clarifies in his introduction.

This manuscript immediately attracted the attention of the British Orientalist A. J. Arberry (1905–1969), and within a few years an English translation of it was published as "A Baghdad Cookery-Book" in *Islamic Culture* (1939).[3] In his preface, Arberry complemented al-Baghdadi's recipes with culinary poems dealing with some of the dishes mentioned in al-Baghdadi's manuscript. The poems occur in an episode in *Muruj al-Dhahab* (Meadows of gold) written by the Abbasid historian al-Mas'udi (d. 957). It is a lengthy anecdote about the banquet of the Abbasid Caliph al-Mustakfi (d. 946) during which his boon companions recited ten gastronomic poems on the most popular dishes known at the time. Besides the revelation that al-Baghdadi's recipes were testimony to the authenticity of the recurrent allusions to foods and dishes in Arabic medieval histories and literature, Arberry's artistic renderings of the culinary poems may be viewed as the equivalents of the luscious food photography in today's cookbooks. Arberry's version certainly had the ingredients for an appealing cookbook, and this explains the successful circulation of his translation for decades. Interestingly, in a footnote to this translation, Arberry alludes to the same cookbook manuscript Zayyat described in the articles mentioned earlier, namely, *Kitab al-Tabeekh* by Ibn Sayyar al-Warraq. Arberry promises a study of the manuscript in a forthcoming paper,[4] but this did not happen.

In 1948, the eminent French historian, Orientalist, and Islamist Maxime Rodinson (1915–2004) published a remarkable study of the history of the Arab cuisine, "Recherches sur les documents arabes relatifs à la cuisine" ("Studies in Arabic Manuscripts Relating to Cookery").[5] In its first part, "Arab Culinary Literature," Rodinson undertakes an extensive survey of most of the major sources related to Arab food and cookery, which were predominantly medieval, arguing that the culture of writing about food developed mainly during the Abbasid era. He argues that this was "due to the development of an elite leading a life of unparalleled luxury, united by a common understanding of social norms."[6] His discussion includes medieval cookbooks known to him, either directly or indirectly. He also lists cookbooks written in the nineteenth and early twentieth centuries chronologically. As an example, Rodinson briefly analyzes the Lebanese *Ustadh al-Tabbakheen* (Master of cooks) by Khalil Sarkis, first published in 1885. Other genres he covers are history books, such as al-Mas'udi's tenth-century *Muruj al-Dhahab* (Meadows of gold), and the bio-bibliography *Fihrist* by Ibn al-Nadeen (d. 988) with its list of contemporary ninth- and early tenth-century cookbooks, none of which exist today. The cookbooks were written by literary men, physicians, princes, astronomers, and the like. The anecdotes that had come down to us in such books, Rodinson observes, show that the cookbook writers were "on par with caliphs, participating in every way in the brilliant court life of Baghdad."[7]

In addition to these sources, Rodinson mentions doctors' dietetic treatises, which he recognizes as being based on Greco-Roman dietary literature. Some of these were translated from Arabic into Latin, such as *Kitab al-Aghdhiya* (Book of foods) by the Egyptian Jewish physician Ishaq bin Sulayman al-Isra'ili (d. 932), which was translated by Constantine the African at the end of the eleventh century and used as a dietetic text at the school of Salerno throughout the Middle Ages. Rodinson recommends that the subject of medieval dietetic theories would be worthy of detailed studies because it had a positive influence on the food consumed.

Other genres Rodinson mentions are dictionaries, such as *Al-Mukhassass* by Ibn Sidah (d. 1066) with its wealth of food-related linguistic information; food poetry, such as that by Ibn al-Rumi (d. 896); belles lettres, such as those by al-Tha'alibi (d. 1038) and al-Jahiz (d. 869); literary anthologies, including *Al-'Iqd al-Fareed* (The unique necklace) by Ibn 'Abd Rabbihi (d. 940); pamphlets on table etiquette; and even an obscure fifteenth-century Egyptian social allegory, *Kitab al-Harb al-Ma'shuq bayna Lahm al-Dhan wa Hawadhir al-Suq* (Book of the delectable war between mutton and the refreshments of the marketplace), published with an introduction and a partial translation by Joshua Finkel in 1908.[8]

Rodinson concludes that even from his brief sketch, one can realize how rich and varied these food-related genres are but laments that only a few of these sources have been published, while other works, full of information, have not been seriously studied. He might sound a little clichéd in ending the section with the pronouncement that there was so much to be done, but this was far from an exaggeration.

Rodinson's attraction to studying Arab cuisine stemmed primarily from his belief that food offers a wealth of philological information that can elucidate otherwise obscure definitions and enrich the Arabic language with new terms and usages. Also, from the sociological perspective, he writes that the history of food and cookery in itself is interesting, but it had not yet received the attention it deserved. The remainder of his study attests to his genuine interest and commitment to the issues he raises. The focus of the second part, for instance, is on a thirteenth-century Aleppan manuscript of a cookbook in which he is particularly interested given its apparent popularity—it was repeatedly copied—and the impressive number of recipes it contains. This text is *Kitab al-Wusla ila 'l-Habeeb fi Wasf al-Tayyibat wa 'l-Teeb*, which he translates as "Book of the bonds of friendship or a description of good dishes and perfumes."[9] His textual analysis points to the possibility that it was written by the famous historian Ibn al-'Adeem (d. 1263). Rodinson lists all the recipes in the book, generously annotates them, and translates the author's introduction. His initial plan had been to publish a critical edition and translation of the entire work, but he was prevented from doing so by World War II, which made important copies in Cairo and Damascus inaccessible to him.

In the last part of his study, "The Principal Characteristics of Arab Court Cookery," Rodinson identifies the salient features of the medieval cookbooks he is familiar with. He points out three factors that helped enrich and refine the cuisine: local traditions, ancient inherited techniques, and adopted exotic elements. Of course, he realizes that a full analysis would require a detailed technical study of carefully prepared editions of cookbook manuscripts like *Al-Wusla*, as well as knowledge of Middle Eastern foodstuffs. Rodinson promised to tackle such issues in a future publication, but unfortunately his promise never materialized. Instead, he wrote three short articles touching on one specific issue, equally interesting and pioneering, the influence of medieval Arab cuisine on Europe. The articles covered subjects such as Arabic dish names in medieval Italian cookbooks and the spice trade between the Middle East and the West.[10]

By way of summary, it is evident that by the end of the first half of the twentieth century, a number of scholars in both the Arab World as well as the West were well aware of the richness of the Arab cuisine and its relevance to world culinary history. However, little materialized of their promises and recommendations on where and how to pursue the field of its study until much later. Despite the excitement expressed by Zayyat, Arberry, and Rodinson about al-Warraq's tenth-century cookbook, no edited version was published until 1987,[11] and it was translated into English (the only foreign language).[12] The manuscript Rodinson was most interested in, the Aleppan *Al-Wusla ila 'l-Habeeb*, was not edited and published until 1986.[13] It is still available only in Arabic. Of the other cookbooks Rodinson mentioned, *Kanz al-Fawa'id fi Tanwi' al-Mawa'd* (The myriad benefits of variety at the table), written sometime in the fourteenth century in Egypt, was edited and published in 1993[14] and is still waiting to be translated into other languages.[15] The thirteenth-century *Fidhalat al-Khiwan fi Tayyibat al-Ta'am wa 'l-Alwan* (The best of foods and dishes offered at the table), which Rodinson rightly guessed to be of Andalusian origin, was edited and published in 1981.[16] As for the fourteenth-century *Kitab Wasf al-At'ima al-Mu'tada* (Description of everyday foods), which is an augmented version of al-Baghdadi's thirteenth-century cookbook, an English translation directly based on two manuscript versions was published in 2001.[17] The original manuscript has not yet been edited in Arabic. Ibn al-Mubarrid's fifteenth-century *Kitab al-Tibakha*, which Zayyat edited and published in *Al-Mashriq*, appeared in English translation in 1985.[18] A thirteenth-century Andalusian cookbook came to researchers' attention in the 1960s. It was edited in Arabic and translated into Spanish by Huici Miranda, who gave it the title *Kitab al-Tabeekh fi 'l-Maghrib wa 'l-Andalus fi 'Asr al-Muwahhidin*, generally referred to in English as *Anonymous Thirteenth-Century Andalusian Cookbook*.[19] (For more on these two cookbooks, see the section "Andalusia in Food History.")

Thus, Arberry's English translation of al-Baghdadi's cookbook in 1939 was the first ever attempted and was the only Arabic cookbook Anglophone researchers had access to for almost five decades. Although a remarkable achievement in itself, that translation also proved misleading as researchers of the medieval Arab cuisine were basing their assessments of an entire region on a solitary collection of recipes, which the author clearly states represented his personal preferences.

Rodinson's bafflement in the 1940s at the scarcity of editorial work, publications, translations, and research in the field is well justified: the abundance of cookbooks and literary sources with extended references to food could have facilitated and enriched our perception of the Arabs' culinary history. Equally puzzling is that long after Rodinson little has been done. A case in point is Rodinson's seminal research itself, which remained unavailable in English until 2001, when *Medieval Arab Cookery* was published by Prospect Books, the publishing house established by Oxford Symposium founder Alan Davidson.[20] In her foreword to this book, Claudia Roden writes that she had suggested in a paper for the 1981 Oxford Symposium on Food and Cookery that Rodinson's essay needed to be translated into English.[21] Roden herself drew on the French original in the introduction to her book *Middle Eastern Food* (1968).

It is unfortunate that most of the medieval Arabic culinary sources, both books and manuscripts, remain an asset only to food historians with Arabic language skills. In a few cases manuscripts have been published in facsimile because of their scholarly importance. A case in point is *Kitab al-Aghdhiya* (The book of foods) by the Jewish Egyptian physician Ishaq bin Sulayman al-Isra'ili (d. 932), a critical book in the field of food and dietetics.[22] However, even with knowledge of Arabic the search for information in medieval Arabic books, including edited ones, can be quite daunting since many lack adequate indexes. In this age of digitization, this hurdle has been somewhat relieved with the online availability of searchable scanned editions of some of the important medieval Arabic literary works, histories, and encyclopedias.[23]

The scarcity of resources in translation in the field has been alleviated somewhat by the existence of food information in secondary sources in the English language. For example, *The Renaissance of Islam*, translated from German in 1937, has chapters on standards of living, festivals, and land products.[24] Neither should we overlook Edward Lane's study of Arab society in his *Account of the Manners and Customs of the Modern Egyptians* (1860),[25] which covers topics like the use of tobacco, coffee, hemp, opium, periodic public and religious festivals, private festivities, and household expenditures; or the extensive notes to his English translation of the *Thousand and One Nights* (1840), valued for their occasional anthropological insight into medieval and premodern Arab history. The food-related notes were republished in a chapter in *Arabian Society in the Middle Ages* (1883), entitled "Feasting and Merry-Making."[26]

Compounding the small volume of work in Arabic food historiography is the fact that food studies in the Arab world itself are rare. More often than not food would constitute a chapter tucked in a history book, such as the one dealing with the life of commoners in eleventh-century Baghdad.[27] I know of few instances in which an entire book is devoted to the history of food in a given period, such as the small 1957 volume covering the period from the twelfth to the fifteenth centuries in Egypt and Syria, entitled *Al-Matbakh al-Sultani Zaman al-Ayyubeen wa 'l-Mamaleek* (The royal kitchen during the time of the Ayyubids and Mamluks). It is a useful documented source for culinary information by the Egyptian historian Nabeel 'Abd al-'Azeez. A much later monograph, *Al-Wusla ila 'l-Habbeb*, is an impressively detailed and well-documented study by the Syrian scholar Sulayma Mahjoub of the history of Arab food from pre-Islamic to medieval times. This work was published in 1986 as the first of two volumes. The second volume deals with the edited text of Ibn al-'Adeem's thirteenth-century cookbook, mentioned earlier, done by Mahjoub in collaboration with Durriyya al-Khateeb. We may add to these studies the unique ethnographic historical exploration of the street cries of Damascene food vendors, *Tareef al-Nida' fi Dimashq al-Fayha'* (Witty cries of Damascene food vendors), published in 1998,[28] and *Baghdadiyyat* by the Iraqi folklorist 'Aziz al-Hijjiyya, published in seven volumes between 1967 and 1999. This last work is a lively portrayal of social and cultural life in Baghdad in the nineteenth and early twentieth centuries that abounds with food references. *Mujtama' Alf Layla wa Layla* (Society of the *Arabian Nights*) by the Iraqi scholar Muhsin al-Musawi, published in 2000, analyzes in some of its chapters the social life represented in the *Arabian Nights* stories through the lens of food allusions, the symbolic significance of the dishes, their names, and the role they sometimes play as class, ethnic, or religious identifiers.

The limited amount of Arabic culinary material available in languages other than Arabic has so far been a serious hurdle in Arab food studies. Of course, learning languages is a valuable part of any food historian's training. According to Clifford Wright in his *A Mediterranean Feast* (1999), "One of the limiting factors in serious culinary history is that historians must be conversant with if not expert in a variety of practical and academic disciplines beyond cooking and history such as knowledge of various languages."[29] With this in mind, let us see how the Western food historians have fared in the study of Arab cuisine.

Rise of Arab Food Studies in the West

With the exception of a few publications, there was no significant scholarship on Arab cuisine in the West before the 1980s. The pioneering general food histories were largely done by nonacademics, and the character of the Arab cuisine was still hard to grasp. For instance, in *Cooks, Gluttons, and Gourmets: A History of Cookery* by Betty Wason (1962), Arab cuisine, with its famous Abbasid gourmets and gluttons, was entirely absent. Reay Tannahill, another pioneering food historian with no academic training, includes a short chapter "The Arab World" in her *Food in History* (1973). The story she tells of Arab cuisine is a lively one, albeit vague in details, and at times it is bogged down by stereotypical generalizations such as the Arabs' "instant" adoption of the conquered Persians' culture: when they defeated Persia, they "unhesitatingly abandoned their tents, camels, barley, and dates in favor of instant civilization."[30] However, Arberry's translation of al-Baghdadi's cookbook proved valuable to Tannahill's account because she based her culinary narrative exclusively on this source in illustrating the cuisine itself with recipes and gastronomic poetry.

Two works are central to a better understanding of Arab cuisine in Anglophone culture: Claudia Roden's *Middle Eastern Food* (1968) and the historian Muhammad

M. Ahsan's *Social Life under the Abbasids* (1979). Roden's introduction is a detailed account of the historical background of the cuisine and the cultural forces that influenced its formation. Its significance in food history lies in the fact that Roden was the first to introduce authentic Arab cuisine to mainstream Western readership. Her book remained the cornerstone for accurate knowledge about Arab cuisine for a long while.

When Ahsan's book appeared, it filled a lacuna of information on medieval Arab food in the English language. His sources are extensive, and his chapter on food is the first to offer such an abundance of culinary details. He fully documents meat and dishes cooked with it, bread, vegetables, dairy products, sweets, food prices, and a host of similar issues. Not only is his documentation valuable, but his observations also contained many insights. For example, his account of fish consumption in Baghdad shows river fish as an important item of food, and many kinds are named. This certainly renders unacceptable, for instance, the unfounded notion expressed as late as 2007 that the scarcity of fish recipes in al-Baghdadi's thirteenth-century cookbook is not unusual "given the context of Baghdad, a city located hundreds of miles inland from the Persian Gulf."[31]

The Growth of Food Studies

Recognition of the contribution of Arab cuisine to world culture has been disperse and individualistic in nature, but toward the end of the twentieth century, Arab cuisine started to make some noise. In this respect, anthropologist Jack Goody's *Cooking, Cuisine and Class: A Study in Comparative Sociology* (1982) marks the first attempt to incorporate Arab cuisine into a wider scholarly inquiry into food history and culture. In addressing the question why a differentiated high cuisine did not evolve in Africa, Goody surveys medieval Arab culinary practices and contends that differences in food preparations and consumption between high- and low-class people are closely related to inherent differences in socioeconomic classes. What separates the rich court cuisine from poor peasant staples is that the first is accompanied by elaborate table manners and rituals like washing the hands before meals, using utensils, serving food in courses, and the like. Goody contrasts the luxuriousness of Arab medieval cuisine with the Bedouin past before the establishment of the Abbasid Caliphate and further compares it to the voluntary poverty of the Sufis and ascetics to show the nature of the shift in medieval Arab social culture. The cookbooks the Abbasid Arabs wrote, Goody correctly concludes, are a natural outcome of a sophisticated society that produced an elaborate cuisine.

As the rise of medieval Arab food studies continued with the publication of a number of edited, and in some cases translated, cooking manuals and books (as we have seen earlier), as well as a few significant academic studies, a serious phase in the study of Arab cuisine started to dawn. In his pivotal *A Mediterranean Feast*

(1999), Wright explains that his vision in writing the book was inspired by the work of Fernand Braudel; he meant it to be a "total history" by weaving history and gastronomy into the book's structure.[32] He emphasizes the role of Arab Islamic civilization in the formation of Mediterranean cuisine and cites the agricultural revolution it brought about. He builds on historian Andrew Watson's 1983 study of Arab agricultural innovations in the early Islamic period and the diffusion of farming techniques and crops, like citrus fruits, sugarcane, eggplant, spinach, and watermelon. Wright argues against the popular opinion, even among some scholars, that "Arabs conquered by the sword and brought only ruination," and he blames such claims on tensions between Islam and Christianity, in the past and even in the present. For example, the role Arabs played in the building of the irrigation systems in medieval North Africa and Spain, Wright maintains, was overlooked by the late nineteenth- and even twentieth-century European archaeologists and scholars, who attributed it to the Romans.[33]

Wright also touches on the issue of Arab influence on European cuisine, which is still a matter of debate. He refutes the belief that the Crusaders were responsible for introducing new foods to medieval European cuisine and disagrees with C. Anne Wilson's unsubstantiated thesis that the "crusaders had considerable impact on diet of western Europe." Wilson's 1981 article, "The Saracen Connection: Arab Cuisine and the Medieval West," assumes that the new foods of Europe were experienced during medieval times while the Franks occupied Arab border cities like Jerusalem (1099–1187), Tripoli (1109–1286), and Acre (1189–1291). Her argument is based on the assumption that when the Franks were not actively fighting, they lived in harmony with Muslims and had the means to indulge in Saracens' luxurious foods and learn how to cook them.[34]

Similarities between medieval Western and Arab Muslim dishes existed, and the similarity went beyond dishes to include practices such as Arab cuisine's many sweet-and-sour stews; the practice of sweetening savory dishes with sugar; the liberal use of sugar in desserts; the use of combinations of spices such as cinnamon, ginger, cumin, coriander, and cardamom; and the techniques of coloring dishes with saffron, enriching sauces with almond milk, and scenting foods with rose water. In the earliest European cookbook, *Liber de coquina*, written in Latin in the thirteenth century, and in the fourteenth-century Italian cookbook *Libro della cocina*, there are recipes for dishes with Arabic names that are identical to the medieval Arab recipes, such as *romania* (meat stew soured with pomegranate juice), *somacchia* (stew soured with sumac), *lomonia* (stew soured with lemon), and *mamonia* (sweet rice porridge). As I have already mentioned, Rodinson was the first to draw attention to these dishes. Just how this apparent fusion of cuisines happened is still not clear, whether it was through the Crusaders' contact with the Middle East or through the presence of the Arabs in Andalusia for 800 years.[35]

Another intriguing cultural gap is the lack of research on the lasting impact of Arab immigrants' cuisine on the cooking of the Americas. This question is particularly interesting because of the varieties of dishes the immigrants brought with them and the kind of cuisines they adapted using New World ingredients, all of which makes the culinary history of the region complex and intriguing. *Arab/American: Landscape, Culture, and Cuisine in Two Great Deserts* (2008) by the Arab American ethnobotanist Gary Nabhan supplements the history of New World cuisines and provides valuable details and discussions relevant to Mexico and the American Southwest. In his chapter "The Culinary Influences of Arabia and al-Andalus in the U.S. Southwest and Mexico," Nabhan explains how, for example, typically Middle Eastern dishes like the yogurt drink, stuffed grape leaves, and hummus made their way to desolate places like the Chihuahuan Desert. He says he has "tasted, seen, and heard of traditional Middle Eastern restaurants" in places like El Paso, Mexicali, and borderlands of the United States and Mexico. His initial assumption was that they were established by Lebanese and Syrian refugees who came to America a century ago to escape being drafted into the Ottoman army before World War I. "To be sure," he explains, "that is exactly when Lebanese silk production collapsed, a locust plague occurred, and mass migrations of Middle Easterners began to peak in both the United States and Mexico."[36] This migration was assisted by American Protestant organizations, who helped refugees board ships bound for Boston and New York. Nabhan further explains that many attempted to come on their own, buying inexpensive tickets for ships coming to "America," which for them meant the United States. Instead, they found themselves landing in the ports of Mexico (Veracruz and Merida) or Brazil.

What Nabhan actually discovered was an even much earlier "darker wave" of Arab migration, which "seldom gets aired"[37] but, nonetheless, influenced the cultures and cuisines of Mexico and the U.S. Southwest. This migration began immediately following the expulsion of the Muslims and Jews from Andalusia in 1492 and continued for a century. During this time, the Spanish Inquisition forced tens of thousands of Jews and Muslims to convert to Catholicism, leave the Iberian Peninsula, or be killed. Many Sephardic Jews and "Moorish" Muslims fled to the Maghrib (North Africa), but many others migrated to the Americas.

The combination of the cuisine of Arab immigrants and the indigenous food culture formed a unique American cuisine. Nabhan writes that this is particularly evident in the Mexican spice mixtures prepared for various types of mole (sauce). He is convinced that the moles, traditionally looked at as part of the Mexican culinary heritage, cannot be viewed as a purely Mesoamerican invention. He argues that "they were probably the first sophisticated examples of Mediterranean/Mesoamerican fusion cuisine."[38] In her article "The Mexican Kitchen's Islamic Connection" (2004), food historian Rachel Lauden elaborates on the evolution of this Mexican sauce and concludes that both the Indian curry and the mole can be viewed as two vestiges of medieval Islam.

Another, sometimes even less acknowledged influence of the Abbasid culinary heritage is the role that Arab cuisine played in the formation of Ottoman cooking.

Contradicting the traditionally held belief that the Arab world under Ottoman rule was in a state of stagnation, new research in the social sciences shows that major Arab cities remained vibrant trade centers, especially for spices and, later, for coffee.[39] Food historian Marianna Yerasimos drew attention to Arab influences on Ottoman food culture in her *500 Years of Ottoman Cuisine*, originally published in Turkish in 2002 (an English translation was published in 2005).[40] From Yerasimos we learn that the oldest cookbook written in Ottoman Turkish was in fact a fifteenth-century translation of al-Baghdadi's thirteenth-century Arabic cookbook *Kitab al-Tabeekh*. It was executed by the renowned Turkish physician Muhammed bin Mahmud Shirvani (d. 1450), who served Sultan Murad II (d. 1451). Shirvani added some information on health and seventy-seven recipes to the translation and called it *Kitabu't-tabih* (Cookbook).[41] (See Özge Samancı's chapter in this volume.) This manuscript was brought to the attention of interested scholars only in 1984, and certainly more work is needed here to show the extent of cultural interaction between Arab and Turkish cuisines.[42]

The genesis of medieval Arab cuisine has also been problematic for scholars. The traditional view attributes the Abbasids' brilliant achievements in food and dining to the Persians, who occupied Iraq before the Arabs defeated them there in 636 C.E. and founded their caliphate, the center of which was Baghdad. This dismissive view of the Abbasids' culinary culture has been recycled in numerous discussions of Abbasid cuisine despite the paucity of evidence on the characteristics of ancient Persian cuisine, such as cookbooks. What we know of the Achamenean Persian (550–330 B.C.E.) gastronomic achievement is mostly drawn from hints in Greek sources, which suggest luxurious and elaborate dishes and delicacies. According to Herodotus, the Persians served a great number of side dishes, one after the other.[43] From the later Persian Sassanian dynasty (226–636 C.E.) the only document available is the fourth-century *Book of King Khosrau and His Page*, in which there is a passage where the knighted page was tested by the king on culinary matters.[44]

Fortunately, archaeological findings in Iraq offered clues to the origin of the Abbasid cuisine, pointing to roots even more ancient than the Achamenean and Sassanian presence in the region. In the early 1980s a French translation of a collection of ancient Mesopotamian culinary recipes was published. The recipes were originally written on three clay tablets in Akkadian cuneiform script, the oldest recipes ever discovered. They briefly describe how to make twenty-five stews and several bird pies, with one of them given in some detail. The decipherer of these tablets, French Assyriologist Jean Bottéro, estimates that these recipes were written in Babylon, in central southeastern Mesopotamia, around 1700 B.C.E. In his study of this ancient find, Bottéro argues that he sees close affinities between the Babylonian and Arab cuisines.[45]

Further investigation by David Waines, a leading scholar in medieval Arab Islamic culture, also supports the argument for a "family resemblance" between the two cuisines in the styles and textures of the recipes, combinations of ingredients, and use of condiments and spices. He finds in al-Warraq's tenth-century cookbook, for instance, "a tradition which, if not unbroken, at least originated in Mesopotamia, was inherited by the Persian Sassanians who then passed it on, with their own contributions, to be 'resurrected' within the Muslim culture of Abbasid Baghdad." In his view, "the Mesopotamian origins of the Arabic high culinary tradition could not be clearer."[46] To these factors we may also add the key role played by the indigenous inhabitants of Iraq during the medieval era in developing the Abbasid cuisine. They were the direct inheritors of the ancient sophisticated Mesopotamian cuisine as revealed in the excavated culinary tablets. Collectively called the Nabateans of Iraq, they were a mix of Chaldeans, Syriacs, and Arameans. Their role is more often than not forgotten or neglected because they were politically ineffective and had a low standing socially and economically, surviving mostly as rural farmers. The lack of acknowledgment of the key role they played in contributing to the agriculture and cuisine led to the rise of some medieval Mesopotamian nationalistic voices. The most relevant here, and the earliest, was the tenth-century *Al-Filaha al-Nabatiyya* (Farming practices of the Nabateans) by the Chaldean historian and agriculturalist Abu Bakr Ibn Wahshiyya. In the introduction, he bemoans the unjust disregard his fellow Nabateans have fallen into ever since they lost their political power. He says that the occupiers, the Sassanians, reaped the fruits of their knowledge, which they had been accumulating over thousands of years, and called it their own. It is to be noted that this interesting document is available only in Arabic and was not edited until 1995.

The history of the pre-Islamic Arabs, including knowledge of their material life, is still frustratingly obscure. Most of what is known was handed down orally, largely though poetry, and was documented much later in writing from the eighth to tenth centuries C.E. The Arabs were commonly described as simple and austere people due to their harsh, dry physical environment. However, the ninth-century Abbasid writer al-Jahiz offers a valuable insight into the foods of the pre-Islamic Arabs in his book *Al-Bukhala'* (Of misers). He asserts that they knew luxury in places where the land was more productive and means more abundant such as in oases and coastal stretches of the peninsula. He based his statements on their poetry and anecdotes. They knew fine white flour, fruits, roasted meat, and stew. They knew *muraqqaq* (fine, thin sheets of bread), *sinab* (dipping sauce made with mustard and raisins), and strained honey, as well as *siritrat* (dessert of honey, butter, and wheat starch), more commonly known by its Persian name *faludhaq*. Of their other foods, *thareed* (bread sopped in broth) was the master of dishes. He adds that they made *hays* (date sweetmeat), valued bread, and preferred meat to dates.[47] Incidentally, an account by Herodotus (fifth century B.C.E.) on the products of the Arabs mentions frankincense, myrrh, cassia, cinnamon, gum mastic, and other spices. From the land of Arabia, he says, "there blows a scent of them most marvelously sweet."[48]

In her book *Medieval Cuisine of the Islamic World: A Concise History with 175 Recipes* (2007), Lilia Zaouali offers a brief account of the forces that played a part in the formation of the ancient Arab culinary heritage. Zaouali is to be commended for venturing into this complex issue. She argues that "the regions conquered by Islam— Berber, Coptic, Arab, and so on—were … profoundly influenced by Greco-Roman culture in the west, and by both Persian and Greco-Roman culture in the east" and that only the Arabian Peninsula, which is the original territory of Islam, managed to escape foreign occupation.[49] Her conclusion, however, is weakened by the assumption that the occupied of necessity surrendered to the occupier's culture, which historically has not often been the case in that region.

Andalusia in Food History

After the Spanish Inquisition in the late fifteenth and sixteenth centuries, Arab culinary practices in Spain, whether Muslim or Jewish, had to be enjoyed in secret. Such circumstances hindered the circulation of a vibrant cuisine and may partially explain why only two cookbooks from that time survived from the entire medieval Arab Western region. These two cookbooks were made available in edited format relatively recently. In 1965, an Arabic edition of a thirteenth-century anonymous and untitled manuscript was published with a Spanish translation by Huisi Miranda, who gave it the title *Kitab al-Tabeekh fi 'l-Maghrib wa 'l-Andalus fi 'Asr al-Muwahhideen* (Cookbook of al-Maghrib and Andalusia in the era of Almohads), called, for brevity, *Anonymous Thirteenth-Century Andalusian Cookbook*. It contains about 500 recipes. Miranda's Spanish interpretations were met with criticism, but it should be remembered that he "was working privately in the 1960s within the constraints of Franco's dictatorship."[50] Though I am in no position to examine the quality of the Spanish rendition, some of the shortcomings may be due to the fact that he worked on a single manuscript, the only one available at the time, which had many lacunae and some folios missing from both ends. In effect, what Miranda published was not an edited text as much as a copy in print form. In 1987, Charles Perry completed an English translation.[51] It remains the only one to be consulted by Anglophones despite its weaknesses, which largely stem from the condition of the original text itself and some literal/dictionary renderings on the part of the translator.

A new scholarly Arabic edition of the *Anonymous Thirteenth-Century Andalusian Cookbook* was published in Morocco in 2003; for it, the editor, 'Abdul Ghani Abu 'l-'Azm, used a different manuscript that he himself had discovered. It is a much better text than the one Miranda used, and it even had a title, *Anwa' al-Saydala fi Alwan al-At'ima* (Varieties of dishes and their nutritious benefits). In 1981, another thirteenth-century Andalusian cookbook was edited. This one, entitled *Fidhalat al-Khiwan fi Tayyibat al-Ta'am wa 'l-Alwan* (The best of foods and dishes offered at the table), had been written by Ibn Razeen al-Tujibi.[52] These two books have not yet been translated into English.

Research on the medieval Andalusian cuisine does not compare with that done on the eastern region of the Islamic world. Expiración Garcia Sánchez states in her article "Dietetic Aspects of Food in al-Andalus," written in the 1980s, that the primary reason that the subject of food in Andalusia was practically unknown until a few decades prior to her research was the scarcity of sources. However, as an emerging field in the study of food history, Garcia Sánchez believes that the Andalusian cuisine has considerable growth potential. In this article, she chooses the analytical dietetic approach by exploring the dietetic theories prevalent at the time and the "nutritional sources" found in what she categorizes as scientific sources (which include medical-dietetic works, literary texts, and culinary manuals) as well as popular sources (which include agricultural treatises and calendars, and works associated with market inspectors, *al-hisba*). She concludes that the popular Andalusian diet was "more varied, plentiful and balanced than the diet of the Christian population of the Iberian peninsula."[53]

More recently, there have been a number of studies of the Andalusian cuisine, such as those of the Spanish scholar Manuela Marin. Her "Pots and Fire: The Cooking Processes in the Cookbooks of al-Andalus and the Maghrib," written in the 1990s, is a study of culinary techniques and procedures as documented in the two extant cookbooks.[54] However, Marin has some cautionary remarks on using cookbooks as sources especially when the purpose is to evaluate consumption patterns of specific foods. The problem with medieval cookbooks is that they were written for urban society and thereby have a limited representational value. Moreover, there is always the possibility that a given recipe was copied from another cookbook belonging to another region. In another 1990s article, "Beyond Taste: The Complements of Color and Smell in the Medieval Arab Culinary Tradition," Marin depicts the aesthetics of food preparations in the middle ages, east and west, as shown in the different manner the dishes were flavored and presented, to dazzle the diners' senses of smell and sight.[55]

The Perry/Waines Phenomenon

The history of Arab cuisine has experienced a clear turning point in the last two decades of the twentieth century with the emergence of two food scholars, journalist and food writer Charles Perry and professor of Islamic studies David Waines, whose many contributions to the field have deepened its popularity as well as its academic credentials. With typical journalistic curiosity, Perry probes into subjects like the genesis and etymology of foodstuffs and dishes, being assisted by no less than 200 dictionaries and grammars.[56] He touches on subjects like "What to Order in Ninth-Century Baghdad" and "A Thousand and One Fritters: The Food of the Arabian Nights." Most of his essays have been the product of his participation over the years in the Oxford Symposium on Food and Cookery, held annually in Oxford, England. He has translated several medieval cookbooks into English.[57] In *Kitab Wasf al-At'ima al-Mu'tada* (Description of everyday foods), he even experimented with working directly from manuscripts of unedited material.[58] His work has helped fill a gap in the number of medieval cookbooks in English translation, but one would wish that his commendable enthusiasm were equally matched with knowledge of the nuances of the Arabic language and expertise in navigating manuscripts. Nevertheless, his writings have helped popularize medieval Arab cuisine, and in that they match what Roden did for Middle Eastern cuisine in the 1960s.

David Waines's contributions, some in collaboration with the Spanish scholar Manuela Marin, are of a different caliber as they largely address a more academically oriented audience. The main concern of most of his food studies is the interaction between culinary practices and Galenic dietetic humoral theories dominant in the Middle Ages. Dietetics was a critical issue during the medieval era in Islam as it influenced the way Islamic culture looked at food.[59] In "Dietetics in Medieval Islamic Culture" (1999), Waines goes beyond the ancient Greek medico-dietetic traditions to include the indigenous Middle Eastern culinary traditions that can be traced textually to ancient times.[60] "*Muzawwar*: Counterfeit Fare for Fasts and Fevers" (2002) is about vegetarian dishes, which were called *muzawwarat* ("simulated"), because they do not include meat. They were originally consumed by Christians during Lent but started to be touted by medieval physicians as healthy light foods for invalids.[61]

Waines and Marin discuss the interaction between food customs and society in "Foodways and the Socialization of the Individual" (1998), to illustrate how all food activities can create a "social dynamic central to its understanding of Islamic societies."[62] Waines's "Cereals, Bread and Society: An Essay on the Staff of Life in Medieval Iraq" (1987) adopts Goody's theory of "differentiated food" and examines a single commodity, bread, and how it functioned as a social denominator in urban and nonurban societies. Waines's cookbook, *In a Caliph's Kitchen* (1989), is a practical guide for those who wish to re-create the medieval Abbasid dishes as it provides the original recipes along with modern versions, supplemented with an extensive introduction and food photography. It was a first in the modern portrayal of medieval Arab cuisine. Another first was an entire chapter, "Tales of Food and Hospitality," in *The Odyssey of Ibn Battuta: Uncommon Tales of a Medieval Adventurer* (2010), where Waines traces the steps of this globe-trotter, collecting and commenting on the scattered data on food, dishes, hospitality, rituals, and so on.

The Road to Maturation

The slow and seemingly isolated growth of Arab food historiography has produced a sizable and varied body of scholarship that is making its way to multiple readerships. Food is increasingly seen as a cultural marker with wide implications and is consequently making its way out of the confines of the kitchen and into main street culture. One sign of such maturation is the publication of a volume on the Middle East in the Greenwood Press series Food Culture Around the World in 2004, which is oriented toward "a wider audience of students, general readers, and foodies alike."[63] On the scholarly level, the publication of *Patterns of Everyday Life* (in the Formation of the Classical Islamic World series) in 2002 is an important indicator of the positive direction food studies has been taking due to scholars' developing interest in food preparation and consumption as a serious subject of inquiry. This is revealed in the book's collection of previously published distinguished studies in the field of material life of Arab Islamic societies from the seventh through the tenth centuries. The book approaches the subject of food and drink by examining the "inter-related textual traditions of cooking, medicine and agronomy," which, according to Waines, has been happening only recently. He recommends that "many more studies of this kind, carefully integrated into a historical framework, are required before a history of food properly speaking can be attempted."[64]

Wider cross-cultural recognition of culinary activities as central to understanding societies has extended to the production of cookbooks and food studies relevant to specific countries in the modern Arab World. Such recognition is expressed by the editors of *A Taste of Thyme: Culinary Cultures of the Middle East* (1994), Sami Zubaida and Richard Tapper, who write that "the previous relegation of this field— studies of social and cultural aspects of food—to the margins of history and social science is now being reversed."[65] In this sense food becomes a key tool in decoding cultural values even when it is a subject dealt with in other forms of culture such as literature. In fact, *A Taste of Thyme* concludes with a paper that explores modern Arabic literature in terms of food. In "Food as a Semiotic Code in Arabic," Sabry Hafez explains that his method is not anthropologically oriented but is rather "a revealing literary strategy capable of generating multiplicity of meaning within the text."[66]

A Taste of Thyme is a collection of articles that mostly deals with modern issues and is based on the proceedings of a conference held in 1992.[67] One of the studies is Tony Allan's "Food Production in the Middle East," which is a sober look at the status quo of agriculture in the Arab region. Contrary to the key role played by the "green revolution" in medieval times in cultivating plants and domesticating animals in the eastern region, and its spread westwards, today the region is becoming one of the world's major food importers due to the rapid increase in population. Diminishing water resources are becoming a major factor in the agricultural options of the countries.[68]

Food resources and providing for national communities are emerging as serious issues in need of scrutiny, not only because of explosive population growth in the region, but also because of a constant development of national consciousness in the countries of these regions. In "National, Communal and Global Dimensions in Middle Eastern Food Cultures," Zubaida speaks of the Middle East in terms of "nation-states" whose borders were arbitrarily drawn after the fall of the Ottoman Empire. Within them, regional and communal differences did exist, but over time, they have acquired "some homogeneity and coherence" that have resulted in the emergence of pride in national cuisines.[69] According to Zubaida, the approach of the nationalist cuisine is essentially based on history, yet bordering on the mythical, characterized by the "subtle and not so subtle utilization of the pre-Islamic past to construct the country histories," such as Pharaonic Egypt, Babylonian Iraq, and so on.[70]

Similarly, Peter Heine in "The Revival of Traditional Cooking in Modern Arab Cookbooks" explores how Arab cookbooks have changed in many ways during the past forty years or so. Most cookbooks started to address working women and were geared more toward international European cuisines. Heine perceives a shift after the 1980s toward a tendency that he dubs "revivalistic," which focuses more on the traditional aspects of the cuisine of a given Arab country due to the resurgence of Arab nationalism.

Arab culinary history has also departed from the limits of national consciousness and connected with the demands of a common global culture that emphasizes better and higher standards of living for all members of the community, but especially women. For instance, one ethnographic study in *A Taste of Thyme*, "Food and Gender in the Yemeni Community," by Ianthe Maclagan, examines food in terms of gender relations. It is a field study of a town in Yemen where food is the focus of tension and conflict between men and women. In such communities, for instance, women can use food as means of protest because men are totally dependent on them to prepare the food. Domestically, food gives women the kind of leverage that is denied them in the political and social domains.

The role food plays in decoding culture is again picked up in Geert Jan van Gelder, *God's Banquet: Food in Classical Arabic Literature* (2000). The book approaches food in ways similar to those in Hafez's study. It is an analytical survey that explores the many ways food manifests itself in classical Arabic literature, including pre-Islamic prose and poetry. While the literary texts are not treated as sources for food information, van Gelder still believes that his book will be of use to those interested in the Middle Eastern history of food. The texts he explores include a variety of descriptive epigrams, amusing anecdotes, parodies, satire, and even books on interpretations of dreams. He studies them from different angles to show "how food is depicted and shaped in literary contexts and how literary contexts are shaped by the theme of food." The theory that guides his analysis is based on the idea that "description of food and eating behavior in literary texts always function within a system that may be called the culinary semiotic code, knowledge of which helps the interpretation of these texts."[71] Van Gelder explores how foods in literary texts are utilized as symbols, metaphors, and markers—of time, place, class, status, religion, gender, character, and taste.

In addition to literature, Arab politics has emerged as another significant social activity deeply involved in food culture. This appears nowhere better than in the latest addition to food studies in the Arab world, which is Stacy Holden's *The Politics of Food in Modern Morocco* (2009). It deals with "politics from below," the emergence of an understanding of politics through food and the ways through which the power of food shapes politics. Holden's thesis works around the idea that "the challenge of feeding people," rather than religion, shapes state institutions and their political ideologies in the Islamic Arab world. Therefore, she proposes that "the study of food provisioning and the distribution of natural resources in a society—whether equitable or exploitive—merits attention for the insights it provides into the nature of political authority."[72]

Regional understanding, Holden suggests, would be "deepened if scholars—and US policymakers—focused on how governments deal with the unique shortcomings of geography and climate instead of on the ethnicity and religion of the peoples living there."[73] By way of example, she mentions that food issues in Cairo are highly politicized and cautions that a rise in the price of staples threatens riots, which is indeed exactly what happened in 2011. A National Public Radio story by Marilyn Geewax, "Rising Food Prices Can Topple Governments, Too" (aired January 30, 2011), tells how social media and governmental policies got the credit for spurring the uprising in Egypt, while a more compelling factor was at play: people's anger about the dramatic price hikes for basic foodstuffs, such as rice, cereals, cooking oil, and sugar.

For her case study, Holden chose Morocco in the late nineteenth and early twentieth centuries because it was the only country in the Arab world that remained politically stable during that time. Since flour, the staple of the poor, and meat, a luxury food beyond the means of many, were basic foods sold in urban markets, her study is based on flour mills and slaughterhouses, as both can be investigated as a prism though which relations and tensions between state and society may be viewed.

Conclusion

Writing the history of Arab cuisine has been enabled by pioneering generations of devoted scholars and food writers, like Maxime Rodinson, A. J. Arberry, Daoud Chelebi, Habeeb Zayyat, and Claudia Roden. The collective contribution of these generations has certainly increased public appreciation of Arab culinary culture and the Arab character itself since food is so intricately involved in human behavior. These pioneers' efforts have prepared the way for a better knowledge of Arabic writings on food. Although from this early epoch only one book has been available in English translation, al-Baghdadi's *Kitab al-Tabeekh*, Europeans had a taste of a different culinary tradition that proved strong enough to draw later further and deeper interest.

The 1980s saw that interest grow significantly and develop in the span of three decades into the kind of effort that eventually brought maturation to Arab culinary historiography, in books like *Patterns of Everyday Life* on the early period of the Abbasid era; *A Taste of Thyme* on contemporary food writing; *God's Banquet*, a study of food in classical Arabic literature; and *The Politics of Food in Modern Morocco*, which probes politics through the lens of food. Importantly, the Arab culinary tradition started to move from the confines of scholarly inquiry into mainstream interest. The dedicated work of two individuals, Charles Perry and David Waines, brought Arabic writings on food into wider English-language circulation.

Central to the appropriate repositioning of Arab culinary history so that it covers neighboring cultural activities, from food production, consumption, and cultivation of resources to the representations of food in the arts and belles lettres, is the availability of sources in European languages besides Arabic. Several key manuscripts are still in need of editing, and several important cookbooks and food studies remain known only to readers of Arabic. Now that food studies has a place in history and cultural studies, better knowledge of the Arab cuisine may well lead to better understanding of the Arab culture. Our perception and portrayal of Arab cuisine have certainly improved, and one hopes for a fuller view of it when manuscript sources make their way to publication.

Chronological Appendix of Old Cookbooks and Manuscripts

al-Jahiz, Abu 'Uthman (d. 869), *Al-Bukhala'* (Of misers), available in several Arabic editions, the most recent in 2008, ed. Muhammad al-Iskandarani (Beirut: Dar al-Kitab al-'Arabi); English translation 2000, trans. B. M. Serjeant, *The Book of Misers* (Ithaca, NY: Ithaca Press).

al-Isra'ili, Ishaq bin Sulayman (d. 932), *Kitab al-Aghdhiya* (Book of foods), 4 vols., 1986 facsimile of MS Fatih nos. 3604–07 in Sulaymaniyya Library, Istanbul (Frankfurt: Frankfurt University Press).

Ibn Wahshiyya, Abu Bakr al-Kisdani (tenth century), *Al-Filaha al-Nabatiyya* (Farming practices of the Nabateans), Arabic edition 1995, ed. Tawfeeq Fahd, 3 vols. (Damascus: Al-Ma'had al-'Ilmi al-Faransi li 'l-Dirasat al-'Arabiyya).

al-Warraq, Ibn Sayyar (tenth century), *Kitab al-Tabeekh* (Cookbook), Arabic edition 1987, ed. Kaj Ohrenberg and Sahban Mroueh, *Studia Orientalia* 60 (Helsinki: Finnish Oriental Society); English translation 2007, trans. Nawal Nasrallah, *Annals of the Caliphs' Kitchens: Ibn Sayyar al-Warraq's Tenth-Century Baghdadi Cookbook* (Leiden: Brill).

al-Baghdadi, Muhammad bin al-Hasan bin al-Kareem al-Katib (d. 1240), *Kitab al-Tabeekh* (Cookbook), Arabic edition 1934, ed. Daoud Chalabi; republished 1964 by Fakhri al-Barudi (Beirut: Dar al-Kitab al-Jadeed). English translation 1939, trans. A. J. Arberry, "A Baghdad Cookery-Book," *Islamic Culture* 13, no. 1: 21–47; no. 2: 189–214. Arberry's translation was republished in 2001 in *Medieval Arab Cookery* (Blackawton and Totnes, UK: Prospect Books): 275–465. Another English translation, by Charles Perry was published in 2005 as *A Baghdad Cookery Book* (Blackawton and Totnes, UK: Prospect Books).

An augmented version of al-Baghdadi's *Kitab al-Tabeekh* was written in the fourteenth century, entitled *Kitab Wasf al-At'ima al-Mu'tada* (Description of everyday foods). English translation directly from manuscript 2001, trans. Charles Perry, published in *Medieval Arab Cookery* (Blackawton and Totnes, UK: Prospect Books): 275–465.

Ibn al-'Adeem, Kamal al-Deen (d. 1262), *Kitab al-Wusla ila 'l-Habeeb fi Wasf al-Tayyibat wa 'l-Teeb* (Winning the lover's heart with delicious dishes and perfumes), Arabic edition 1986, ed. Sulayma Mahjoub and Durriyya al-Khateeb, 2 vols. (Aleppo: Ma'had al-Turath al-'Ilmi al-'Arabi).

Kitab al-Tabeekh fi 'l-Maghrib wa 'l-Andalus fi 'Asr al-Muwahhidin (Cookbook of al-Maghrib and Andalusia in the era of Almohads), known in English as *Anonymous Thirteenth-Century Andalusian Cookbook*. Arabic edited text by Huici Miranda in *RIEIM* 5 (1961–1962): 137–55; Miranda's Spanish translation of 1966 was reprinted and edited by Manuela Marin (2005), as *La Cocina Hispano-Magrebi* (Gijon: Trea). English translation by Charles Perry 1987, *Anonymous Andalusian Cookbook of the Thirteenth Century*, available online at http://www. daviddfriedman.com/Medieval/Cookbooks/Andalusian/andalusian_contents.htm (accessed August 2, 2011). Another Arabic edition based on a better manuscript than the one Miranda used has the title *Anwa' al-Saydala fi Alwan al-At'ima* (Varieties of dishes and their nutritious benefits), edited (2003) by 'Abdul Ghani Abu 'l-'Azm (Al-Dar al-Baydha': Matba'at al-Najah al-Jadida).

al-Tujibi, Ibn Razeen (thirteenth century), *Fidhalat al-Khiwan fi Tayyibat al-Ta'am wa 'l-Alwan* (The best of food offered at the table), Arabic edition 1984 by Muhammad bin Shaqroun (Beirut: Dar al-Gharb al-Islami); Spanish translation 2009 by Manuela Marin, *Relieves de las mesas, acerca de las delicias de la comida y los diferentes platos* (Austria: Trea).

Kanz al-Fawa'id fi Tanwee' al-Mawa'id, fourteenth century (The myriad benefits of variety at the table), Arabic edition 1993 by Manuela Marin and David Waines (Beirut: Franz Steiner Stuttgart).

Ibn al-Mubarrid (d. 1490), *Kitab al-Tibakha* (Cookbook), Arabic edition 1937 by Habeeb Zayyat, *Al-Mashriq* 35: 370–76; English translation 1985 by Charles Perry, "*Kitab al-Tibakha:* A Fifteenth-Century Cookbook," *Petits Propos Culinaires* 21: 17–22.

Notes

1. Ibn al-Mubarrid, 1937, 370–76.
2. The manuscript does not have a date. We now know, based on internal evidence, that it was most probably written at the beginning of the second half of the tenth century. See Nasrallah, 2007, 10–11.
3. al-Baghdadi, 1939.
4. Arberry, 1939, 30 n5.
5. In *Revue des études islamiques*, nos. 17 and 18. My quotations are from the English translation: Rodinson, 2001c.
6. Rodinson, 2001c, 94.
7. Rodinson, 2001c, 98.
8. Rodinson, 2001c, 113. See Robinson's note 3 for a full citation of Finkel's work.

9. I would translate it as "Winning the Lover's Heart with Delicious Dishes and Perfumes."

10. The articles are Rodinson, 2001b, originally published in *Romania* 71 (1950) and published in English translation in *Petits Propos Culinaires* 34 (1990); Rodinson, 2001a, originally published in *Etudes d'Orientalisme dédiées à la mémoire de E. Lévi-Provinçal* (1962) and published in English translation in *Petits Propos Culinaires* 33 (1989); and Rodinson, 2001d, originally an address at Il Primo Convegno dell' Accademia Italiana della Cucina in Venice (1967).

11. By Öhrnberg and Mroueh.

12. Nasrallah, 2007.

13. By the Syrian scholars Sulayma Mahjoub and Durriyya al-Khateeb; see Ibn al-'Adeem, 1986.

14. By David Waines and Manuela Marin; see *Kanz al-Fawa'id*, 1993.

15. I am in the process of translating it into English.

16. By Muhammad bin Shaqroun; see al-Tujibi, 1984. A Spanish translation by Manuela Marin was published in 2009. See review by Hayward, 2011, 118–20.

17. al-Baghdadi, 2001, 275–465.

18. Ibn al-Mubarrid, 1985, 17–22.

19. An English translation, available online, was executed in 1987 by Charles Perry.

20. Rodinson, 2001c, 91–163.

21. Roden, 2001, 9.

22. al-Isra'ili, 1986. Rodinson alludes to this work in his study "Studies in Arabic Manuscripts Relating to Cookery," discussed earlier in this chapter.

23. A useful website in this respect is http://www.alwaraq.net/Core/index.jsp?options=1.

24. Mez, 1937.

25. Lane, 1973 (facsimile of 1860 edition).

26. Lane, 2004, 135–85. The editor notes, "It may be objected to the title of the book that a considerable part of the notes is composed of recollections of Mr. Lane's personal experiences in Cairo in the early part of the present century [the nineteenth century]. The subject-matter, however, is really medieval," p. ix.

27. Fahad, 1967.

28. al-Shihabi, 1998.

29. Wright, 1999, 567.

30. Tannahill, 1973, 171–72.

31. Miller, 2007, 156.

32. Wright, 1999, 691.

33. Wright, 1999, 7.

34. C. A. Wilson, 1981, part 1, 13.

35. See, for instance, Peterson, 1980; Rosenberger, 1999.

36. Nabhan, 2008, 31.

37. Nabhan, 2008, 31.

38. Nabhan, 2008, 35.

39. See, for instance, Milstein, 1990, 1–5, 43; Hathaway, 2008.
40. M. Yerasimos, 2005, 11, 12.
41. M. Yerasimos, 2005, 19.
42. For details on the affinities between the Arab Abbasid cuisine and Ottoman cooking, see Nasrallah, 2012, 61–69.
43. Sancisi-Weerdenburg, 1995, 292.
44. See Rodinson, 2001c, 152.
45. See Bottéro, 1995, 21.
46. Waines, 2002a, xxxiii n46. See also Waines, 1999, 231–32; Waines, 2002b, 574. For a detailed analysis of affinities between the ancient Mesopotamian and the Arab Abbasid cuisines, see Nasrallah, 2012, 54–59.
47. al-Jahiz, 2008, 250–84.
48. Herodotus, 2004, book iii, sections 107, 110, 111, 112.
49. Zaouali, 2007, 22–25.
50. Hayward, 2011, 118.
51. See note 19.
52. See note 16.
53. Sánchez, 2002.
54. Marin, 2002.
55. Marin, 1994.
56. As Claudia Roden once noted. See Roden, 2001, 12.
57. See the discussion of cookbooks in the section "Arab Cuisine Comes to the Foreground."
58. The articles, along with the translation of *Kitab Wasf al-At'ima*, can be found in *Medieval Arab Cookery* (Rodinson, Arberry, and Perry, 2001).
59. See, for instance, Waines and Marin, 1989. In his 1948 article, Maxime Rodinson drew attention to the medieval medico-culinary tradition as a subject worthy of thorough probing; see earlier discussion of this article in this chapter.
60. Waines, 1999, 231–32.
61. Waines and Marin, 2002. See also Waines, 2002b.
62. Waines and Marin, 1998, 54.
63. Heine, 2004, vii.
64. Waines, 2002a, xxxviii.
65. Zubaida and Tapper, 1994a, 1.
66. Hafez, 1994, 257.
67. It was organized by the Center of Near and Middle Eastern Studies, School of Oriental and African Studies.
68. Allan, 1994, 19.
69. Zubaida, 1994, 36.
70. Zubaida, 1994, 39.
71. van Gelder, 2000, 4, 5.
72. Holden, 2009, 2.
73. Holden, 2009, 5.

Part III. South and East Asia

–10–

New Directions of Research on Indian Food

Krishnendu Ray

Agricultural production has been a legitimate area of academic research in the Western world at least since the Physiocrats in the eighteenth century, while culinary production has been outside the realm of rightful consideration, other than as episodes in now-dead disciplines such as home economics and domestic science. Once food enters the body, modern scientific disciplines of nutrition and public health take over the analysis, giving no quarter to local clinical practices, such as Ayurveda and Unani, and other cultural categories of illness and wellness. Food studies scholars are trying to challenge these cleavages, and in doing so they are reconfiguring Indian food studies to include issues inside and outside the body, within and beyond homes, and revivifying the conduit between folk medicine and high modern institutional therapeutics. Indian food studies, set in motion in the middle of the 1970s in the fields of anthropology and nutrition, is beginning to exceed the reach of those disciplines and surpass their durable dichotomies between the economic and the symbolic, the nutritional and the moral/aesthetic, the village and the city, materiality and the media. This chapter pays attention to interesting new studies that bridge these real and imagined categories in Indian food history.

Openings: From Political Economy to Cultures of Consumption

As India emerged from colonialism in 1947, with the recent memory of the 1943 Bengal Famine seared into middle-class consciousness, hunger dominated the public discussion on Indian food until nearly the end of the twentieth century. Michael Worboys and David Arnold have provided the history of concerns in British imperial conceptions about diet and malnutrition and its relationship to colonial science from the 1860s to the first decades of the twentieth century.[1] The nationalist response to this colonial "reconnaissance and categorization of India" developed hesitatingly and did not acquire full force until the 1930s.[2] By the late 1930s what had once clearly been "a branch of colonial science *about* Indians" was becoming part of an "Indian scientific research agenda *for* Indians."[3] A robust thread of that discussion continues in Amartya Sen's Nobel Prize–winning work on the political economy of hunger.[4]

166 • *Writing Food History*

Democracy and entitlements became the centerpieces of the discussion about access to food. In the United States, Mike Davis's *Late Victorian Holocausts* (2001), which deals with Indian famines in the late nineteenth and early twentieth centuries, is an inspired example of a critique of market-state relations within the frame of political ecology. In some ways Davis pursues the argument of the first generation of Indian nationalist economists such as Dadabhai Naoroji in *Poverty and Un-British Rule in India* (1901). Development of underdevelopment is the persistent thread in these discussions.[5]

The technological response to hunger and underdevelopment in India, by way of the green revolution—with its complex of dwarf hybrid wheat and rice varieties, heavy inputs of water, synthetic fertilizers, tractors, and large landholdings—has been developed by plant geneticists such as Norman Borlaug and M. S. Swaminathan of the Indian Agricultural Research Institute, along with chemists and agronomists. Swaminathan eventually occupied the chair of the UN World Food Congress in Rome in 1984 and continued the search for technological solutions to hunger.[6] Yet these technological approaches to hunger have provoked criticism, with Vandana Shiva emerging as the most vociferous critic of the ecological and social consequences of technical interventions such as the green revolution in India.[7] These directions of research, within the conceptual and disciplinary frame of political economy and political ecology, are quite well known in India and abroad. In this chapter I engage with what comes after that and take us toward cultures of consumption (and reproduction), a sphere that Mary Douglas and Baron Isherwood contend "is the very arena in which culture is fought over and licked into shape."[8] This dimension is less familiar to and more theoretically congruent with the interests of the audience of this book.

Proliferation: From Anthropology to Cultural Studies

Research into the cultural-aesthetic dimension of food acquired greater momentum by the 1980s and created new tributaries of discussion that eventually severed its connection to the more traditional scope of political economy and Indian anthropology's enduring concern with caste and commensality. For scholars working in the realm of interpretive cultural analysis, R. S. Khare's *The Hindu Hearth and Home* (1976) and Arjun Appadurai's "How to Make a National Cuisine: Cookbooks in Contemporary India" (1988) became important new touchstones.[9] Khare's work was produced within the frame of symbolic anthropology and was based on dense ethnographic description of the practices of Kanya-Kubja Brahmins of the Rae Bareli region. Appadurai's reconceptualization of the Indian social landscape—drawing on ethnography but eventually transcending its confines—allowed scholars to escape the burdens of the long-festering discussion on caste and commensality that had dominated Indian sociology since Louis Dumont's *Homo Hierarchicus* (1970).[10]

That escape may have been too fully executed, and the by-product was to divert the attention of emerging scholars from the work of Khare, the researcher who has done the most sustained work on Indian food.[11]

Curiously, a similar fate has befallen the equally original work of Francis Zimmermann, *The Jungle and the Aroma of Meats* (1987), which is increasingly confined to an audience of anthropologists working on ethnomedicine. Keeping Zimmermann's work in view could afford us the opportunity to develop a theory of taste and knowledge that is tethered to location, in this case the Doab between the Indus and the Ganges, prefiguring an Indic theory of terroir that could enrich the European conception. Zimmermann suggests that a different body and imagination may be at work here, reminding us that all classifications are local, although some have greater reach than others. In the process, he tries to retrace the Ayurvedic system of medico-gastronomic classification of the natural world that was superseded by the colonial episteme. It is promising notwithstanding two shortcomings. First, he is overenthusiastic about structuralism's binary oppositions, in this case, between *anupa* (wetlands) and *jangala* (drylands), and their relationship to disease and therapeutics in ancient Ayurvedic texts, which ignores the centrality of the third in-between position of *sadharana* (normal; average) that was central to clinical practice. Second, an excessively easy move is made from classical texts and their imaginary spiritual geography to modern empirical ecology and epidemiology. This unintentionally ends up caging the totality of Indic tradition within the scholastic and ideological against the putative scientific empiricism of the West, a posture that is popular in the French mode of Indology and in this case was perhaps borrowed from Zimmermann's teacher, Dumont.[12]

Zimmermann's method is similar to Charles Malamoud's sharp textual analysis in *Cooking the World: Ritual and Thought in Ancient India* (1996). Malamoud picks the Sanskrit phrase *lokapakti* in the Satapatha Brahmana, translating it as "cooking the world." At the heart of every Brahmanic rite, Malamoud asserts, is cooking the world. Every sacrificial operation employs a derivative of one of the roots signifying "to cook," "PAC or SRA (or one of their partial synonyms, such as US, GHR, TAP, or DAH)."[13] This is a powerful, almost magical claim that declares an unwillingness to place everything under the aegis of Western logic, intelligibility, and translatability. It clarifies much about both the ancient Vedic tradition and its contemporary Indic appropriation. Nevertheless, Malamoud's litany of rites is not exhaustive because it excludes the ultimate offering of the uncooked soma that the Vedas go on about. Yet in the case of the soma, too, it is food and food for thought. So it is not always cooking exactly, but at all times it is the offering of food that ties the world together across ritual cleavages. In my Oriya-Bengali world, food mediates between infancy and childhood through *annaprasanna* (eating-of-rice ceremony); between youthfulness and adulthood by way of the feast of *bou-bhat* during the marriage ceremony (daughter-in-law rice); and between this life and the after via death, where the body is cremated—cooked—to be offered to the gods. Zimmermann's and Malamoud's texts promise rich conceptual possibilities for contemporary analysts. Yet, eventually, both authors give in to speculation that ranges too widely from text to practice and between the past and the present. In contrast, Paul Toomey's ethnographic study *Food from the Mouth of Krishna* (1994) is less textual and more about everyday performance of ritual, zeroing in on Govardhan as an exemplary Vaishnava pilgrimage place in northern India. He targets the "kinds of food events observed at temple and feasts; food classification systems and coded sequences followed by ritual specialists in cooking, offering, and distributing food; and, finally, meanings conveyed by menu changes and changes in quantities of food offerings in different groups."[14] Nevertheless, the focus in most of these productive but traditional anthropological works is either on rural, ritual contexts or on textual analysis of scriptures. There is often a sharp division between economic and anthropological analyses, between studies of city and country (with the city mostly invisible), and between materialism and symbolism.

New scholarship in history, cultural studies, and postcolonial studies with greater attention to urban foodways, and approaches that bridge matter and sign, is pushing anthropologists from the center of the field.[15] The definitive two-volume *Oxford India Companion to Sociology and Social Anthropology* (2003), edited by Veena Das, has almost nothing pertaining to urban food consumption (less than half a page in a 1,600-page collection). Nevertheless, in the same volume Appadurai urges us to attend to certain spaces, institutions, and practices, such as "streets, bazaars and restaurants," that have been invisible to the disciplinary gaze.[16] Those attuned to the Indian intellectual space have not yet considered contemporary public and private eating a domain worthy of theoretical attention.[17] Perhaps academic attention to the contemporary urban aesthetics of food is something that comes with affluence and the end of public spectacles of hunger. Yet there is promising work in this direction.

Within the discipline of history, while K. T. Achaya's encyclopedic *Indian Food; A Historical Companion* (1998) remains the standard text to develop an overview, a new generation of scholars is beginning to produce highly theorized texts on the relationship between discourse and domesticities with some attention to dietary advice.[18] Bernard Cohn's attention to the materiality of clothes and bodies and related forms of explicit and implicit knowledge, and his productive harnessing of methodologies in anthropology and history, provides the opening to reconsider food, physiognomy, and body politics.[19] Nupur Chaudhuri's "Shawls, Jewelry, Curry and Rice in Victorian Britain" (1992) and Susan Zlotnick's "Domesticating Imperialism" (1996) afford templates of this direction of inquiry leading into food. A rich seam of research on domesticity and intimacy has subsequently been uncovered using new sources, such as domestic manuals in vernaculars (especially in Bengali), and revisiting old manuscripts in Persian and English.[20]

New kinds of work are beginning to emerge in two other directions. On one hand, edibles in semipublic spaces, such as restaurants and hotels in global cities, have come under the purview of scholars just within the last decade.[21] *Curried Cultures* (2012), a collection of essays edited by Tulasi Srinivas and myself, provides examples of this direction of inquiry.[22] We draw on the analyses of popular urban culture, restaurants, and the quest for status, which in some ways return us to the much older discussion of commensality and hierarchy, but here the focus is on the city through commerce rather than on the village and the community.[23] Both iterations of these themes—old concerns about caste and commensality and the new issues of city and consumption—have recently figured in special food issues of journals such as *South Asia Research* (2004), *China Report* (2007), and *South Asia* (2008).[24] Outside the academy a robust new direction is developing in popular food writing, mostly in the genres of travel and memoir. Chitrita Banerji has produced a number of works that combine these two superbly.[25] Two less poetic but much more comprehensive popular studies of Indian food are those by Colleen Taylor Sen.[26]

On the other hand, work on diets and diasporic domesticities is just emerging in studies of immigrant households, ethnic sensibilities, and questions of postcolonial identities.[27] These explore the unsettled boundaries between private and public, home and away, at multiple levels of analysis, from the individual to the ethnic group and the nation. They deal with shifting concepts of the domestic and the diasporic in urban foodways, exploring conceptions of belongingness and autonomy for networked Indian communities while simultaneously looking at narratives of health and fitness that such communities contend with and incorporate into their foodscapes.

The common use of terms such as *foodscapes*, *flows*, and *transnationalism* shows the immense debt owed to Appadurai's imaginative formulations, which frame almost any current discussion of globalization, modernity, and food. The task is to say something more than what is already argued in *Consuming Modernity* (edited by Breckenridge, 1995) and *Modernity at Large* (1996).[28] It is a challenge to go past the startling illumination of his suggestion to pay attention to movement by way of various *scapes* without, as he points out, sacrificing attention to the density of bodies, things in close proximity, and to communities that are still bounded in other ways. Food studies can draw attention to the weight of localized bodies caught in globalized motion, precisely because bodies are frictional and are always located in a place while consuming foods from all over the world. Appadurai makes a number of exemplary points about migrants and media reconstituting our worlds that must be brought to bear on food studies' tendency to territorialize taste and naturalize locality. For instance, he insists that ethnographers must find ways to represent the links between imagination and social life. If anthropology's traditional role was to fill the "savage slot in an internal Western dialogue about utopia," then, he proposes, a "recuperated anthropology must recognize that the genie is now out of the bottle and that speculations about utopia are everyone's prerogative."[29] He also forces us to rethink the relationship between diasporic publics and the private sphere of migrants where food plays a paramount role.[30]

An early and notable exception to the paucity of attention to urban public eateries in India is Frank Conlon's "Dining Out in Bombay" (1995). It is instructive that Conlon's work finds room within Appadurai and Breckenridge's capacious composition of "public culture" as the "space between domestic life and the projects of the nation state—where different social groups ... constitute their identities by their experience of mass-mediated forms in relation to the practices of everyday life."[31] Two instances of the richness of "Dining Out in Bombay" have to suffice here. First, Conlon was prophetic in paying attention to the intricate logistics of the lunch delivery system of the *dabbawallas* (lunch-box-carriers) of Bombay (now Mumbai) before their entrée into business school curricula as an instance of bottom-up, capillary networks of remarkable efficiency and robustness. Second, he warns us not to ignore recent developments in Bombay's elite restaurants, succumbing to the temptation to view them "merely as interesting, possibly amusing, manifestations of the cultural consumption on the periphery of a Euro-centered world capitalist system ... a comfortable assumption that Indian public culture is merely a derivative, if colorful, form of global modernity."[32] It is truer now than when Conlon was writing almost two decades ago that most of India's "population has existed between the extremes of great wealth and abject poverty and that at many intermediate levels people have experienced a growth of purchasing power ... [enabling] an ever widening popular participation in the phenomenon of restaurant dining."[33] Conlon's challenge has so far been taken up by too few scholars.

In "Public, Popular, and Other Cultures" (2001), Christopher Pinney points to the vivid materiality of popular visual culture in South Asia, decisively drawing it into the realm of academic analysis. Such a move is possible precisely because of popular culture's frisson of marginality, which makes it desirable for an academic fabrication of a countercultural posture. This is in part why films, television serials, and rickshaw and calendar art have been studied, yet the academic middle classes' own exemplary sites of everyday publicness, such as restaurants and coffeehouses, are rarely investigated. Another reason for ignoring eateries may be that the audiences they produce are smaller and more fragmented than those of a film or a television show, and thus less amenable to distant modes of representation and argumentation. However, restaurants, located as they are in the space between the public and the domestic, provide a view from the middle of those two unbridged categories. For this reason, analytical investigation of restaurants would be instructive as to the nature and means of transactions in literal tastes and how they shape aesthetic taste. Furthermore, urban eateries are worth paying attention to because, unlike cinema, television, cricket, and film music, restaurants might heighten the divergent trajectories of class-based spaces. That is to say, elite restaurants might re-cleave Indian public culture similar to Peter Burke's reading of early modern European culture as divided between two unbridgeable domains of elites and masses, replicated in nineteenth-century Calcutta (now Kolkata), studied by Sumanta Banerjee (1998), which would qualify, if not nullify, Ulf Hannerz's claim that postcolonial popular culture emerged as a "field of activity more or less uniting elites and masses in shared pastimes and pleasures."[34] Yet it is also true that, like cinema, street foods—*chaat, samosa, bhelpuri, vada, pakora, kebab*, and so on—are equally popular among elites, middle classes, and the poor. They are often consumed in shared spaces (produced by street vendors) in ways that elide and obscure such divisions, borrowing from high and low cultural universes at the same time and combining them in unexpected ways.

Analysis of urban eateries can teach us ways of reimagining and interrogating the strange but naturalized institution that we call a restaurant after the eighteenth-century institution popularized by Parisian tastemakers. The study of restaurants in India is worth pursuing in some detail not only because they are ubiquitous but also because it affords us theoretical insights that will complicate our ideas about cuisine, culture, and cities, which at present are mostly derived from Euro-American spaces. Hopefully, in the process we will also learn about what lies below the bourgeois restaurant, such as tea stalls, *dhabas* (roadside eateries), boiled-egg stands, *paan* and cigarette shops, and food vendors, which have not yet been the focus of academic analysis.

Current Conjuncture: Food, Globalization, and the Indian Middle Classes

South Asia is a new hub of intersecting global networks nourished by proliferating material and symbolic transactions pulling bodies, things, and conceptions across national boundaries. Food is a particularly good site to interrogate such processes, because it links the global to the local, and the mind to the body and beyond. The relationship of food to the body makes comestibles intensely local in spite of their long history of distant circulation.

Works such as *Globalization of Chinese Food* (2004), *Asian Food: The Global and the Local* (2001), *The Globalization of Food* (2009), and *Globalization, Food and Social Identities in the Asia Pacific Region* (2010) bear witness to transformations in the second half of the twentieth century as newer nodes in the global traffic in capital and culture from the Pacific Rim joined previous flows of the capitalist world economy from the edges of the Mediterranean and the Atlantic world.[35] Comparable work centering on the South Asian wellspring of unconventional flows of bodies, edible commodities, and cultural conceptions is just beginning to develop. Books such as *Alimentary Tracts* (2010), *Culinary Fictions* (2010), and *Curried Cultures* address gaps in our knowledge about South Asia, its connections to the larger world, and the cultural environment that urban middle classes almost everywhere face with increasing potency.[36] They draw attention to timeless processes of creolization and conservation, flow and counterflow, and the revaluation of the old and production of the new in the food cultures of a globalizing middle class. These works refer to the transaction between India and elsewhere, where dishes such as chicken tikka masala and curry raisu can be produced by people who do not wholly belong to the subcontinent but are oddly defined by it.

Interestingly, this new work indicates a certain practical proximity to dishes and diets that has often been missing in typical academic discussions—in political economy, within underdevelopment and agronomy, even in the anthropology that I have discussed—where food was considered only as a lens to investigate other things. These more contemporary works do look at food to comment on other things—such as globalization, nationalism, postcolonialism, hierarchy, taste, and so on—but the practices of cooking and eating also matter to these authors, who consider them as important forms of knowing the world and acting on it, drawing, I think, on the Heideggerian reorientation in current thinking that has moved the discussion from transcendental becoming to being-in-the-world. These authors bring a new kind of epistemic posture to the discussion, where it is no longer considered necessary to narrow sensory horizons to sharpen intellectual vision, which is contrary to what the dominant modern Western epistemology has assumed since Kant and Hegel.

In part what is new about the current conjuncture is that numerous spatially distributed urban middle classes (including academics) have been dramatically pulled into transnational transactions in taste, and they have inscribed a more legible imprint of their experience in Anglophone media. These works are often written by scholars who are themselves middle class and are writing about people who belong to the middle class and who know English as one language in a bi- or a multilingual world. Some of the brash assertion of middleness is probably the product of the novelty of their location in the emerging economic and cultural powerhouse that is India today.[37]

Work on the middle class has proliferated precisely because that class has emerged as a major player in issues contributing to globalization and to counterpositions to it. The field of cultural globalization is constituted by questions of the perimeter marked by the nation-state (what crosses national boundaries, at what cost, to whom), as well as by hierarchy in terms of class and profession (what are the differences between elites, middle classes, and the poor, between men and women, and so on, in terms of the opportunity and cost of such circulation?). These authors interrogate culinary cultures to address issues of globalization, nation-making, and beyond. Analysis based on the South Asian material posits that, in some ways, globalization makes national boundaries porous as people, goods, and signs move from one part of the world to another with greater velocity and ubiquity and, in the process, categories of the local and the global, which previously appeared to be distinct, now become increasingly interwoven and reproduce each other. In other ways, however, globalization solidifies the boundaries of the world and the mind, often by naming, codifying, and standardizing everyday practices that were rarely considered in previous epochs. Such analysis, too, explores changing ratios of legibility of everyday practices by interrogating culinary cultures in South Asia and among South Asians elsewhere. In the process, authors such as Roy, Mannur, and Ray and Srinivas examine dynamic formulations of identity and its maintenance in various uprooted "worlds"—a world of people who feel the pull of other worlds in taste and talk. Food is not only a lens here, but also something they pay particular attention to in both its material and its symbolic constitution.

For urban middle classes drawn into the vortex of global flows, national identity is no longer taken for granted but becomes an all-absorbing project that is often enacted through consumption. In Appadurai's cogent conception, "As group pasts become increasingly parts of museums, exhibits, and collections, both in national and transnational spectacles, culture becomes less what Pierre Bourdieu would have called a habitus (a tacit realm of reproducible practices and dispositions) and more an arena for conscious choice, justification, and representation, the latter often to multiple and spatially dislocated audiences."[38] Recent ethnographic works that describe cultural consumption among the Indian middle classes repeatedly link it to the shaping of a nation, imagined or otherwise.[39] But how this consumption, especially of comestibles, actually plays out in the everyday lives of South Asians, whether among the urban Indian middle classes or among their diasporic compatriots, and what it means to them and to others, is rarely explored.

Globalization has been seen by some theorists as the dominance of Euro-American culture.[40] That may be accurate regarding a number of things, such as restaurants and related standards of judgment filtered through the conception of French professional haute cuisine. For instance, elite restaurants in Indian cities can be treated as derivative forms of a metropolitan standard. Yet I think such instances could be engaged with more productively as vernacular forms of modernity, derived at some point and in many of its elements from the Euro-American West but exceeding it, much like the Anglophone Indian literature of Salman Rushdie, Amitav Ghosh, and Anita Desia. In other words, the superimposed cultural-linguistic matrix is appropriated as the "cosmopolitan vernacular," which is Sheldon Pollock's subtle, particularizing inflection of cosmopolitan cultural worlds that implies certain affiliations and summons the membership of certain locals in translocal networks.[41] That, of course, keeps open the possibility that the cosmopolitan vernacular may be challenged by more regional vernaculars with a far more proximate radius of usage, or by more dominant scripts with universalizing ambitions at the center of the global ecumene.

In the wake of the ethnic bloodbath that accompanied the collapse of Yugoslavia, followed by the virulence of terrorism and modes of counterterrorism, South Asianists, such as Carole Breckenridge, Sheldon Pollock, Homi Bhaba, and Dipesh Chakrabarty, argued for a minoritarian cosmopolitanism of refugees, migrants, and exiles as a critique of nationally constituted modern spaces.[42] These authors are typically attracted to a cosmopolitan ethic and aesthetic precisely because they are people who have come from elsewhere. For them it is also a pragmatic case of an existing cosmopolitanism that accounts for multiple national loyalties and attachment at a distance. As Bruce Robbins pointedly notes, "If people can get as emotional as [Benedict] Anderson says they do about relations with fellow nationals they never see face-to-face, then now that print-capitalism has become electronic- and digital-capitalism, and now that this system is so clearly transnational, it would be strange if people did *not* get emotional in much the same way, if not necessarily to the same degree, about others who are *not* fellow nationals, people bound to them by some transnational sort of fellowship."[43] So it is worth making the case against the "thousand gross and subtle ways in which we are told every day that people outside our borders are too distant to matter."[44]

Food studies, because of its genealogy in European scripts, is often too focused on Western national food cultures. On the other hand, sometimes as a retort to globalization, the making of food heritage can be seduced by a purifying provincialism, often visible in nationalized and racialized readings of the local that is territorialized as terroir (see, for instance, the discussions surrounding the sale of kebabs and curry in Lucca, Italy).[45] In contrast, we can draw on the South Asian imaginary for other kinds of relationships between the local and the supralocal that Pollock points to in *The Language of the Gods in the World of Men* (2006) in long-circulating elite networks of Sanskritic aesthetic cosmopolitanism that nevertheless permitted vernacular appropriations (e.g., Balinese Hinduism and Sinic Buddhism), allowing options beyond a bland homogenizing culture or a closed ethnolocalism. Such alternatives may also be possible again in contemporary patterns of circulation of peoples, commodities, and conceptions.[46] The discussion of culture and place as it pertains to South Asian cities and South Asians abroad can teach us alternative forms of cosmopolitanism that neither universalize a metropolitan culture nor posit a nativistic relationship between terrain, tongue, and taste. Like the feminist cosmopolitanism that preceded it, such work seeks to understand solidarities along with situatedness, while reaching across barriers of class, race, nation, and tribe. These kinds of postcolonial diasporic works take the problem of building translocal models of globalization seriously by fully engaging in meaningful dialogue that not only spans our gustatory differences but also makes inhabitance in a distant locale viable, while illuminating the poetics and politics of place-making through diet and desire.

Having outlined some sites of successful interrogations so far, in the remainder of the chapter I will provide a programmatic prospectus of directions in new research. In addition, I will point to three detailed analyses that attempt, with more or less success, to bridge the dichotomies of culture and commerce, science and experience, matter and symbol, and city and country, which have marked the literature on Indian food studies.

Present and Future: Cities and Bodies, Science and Tradition

Currently, even the gastronomic culture of large cities in India is understudied. For instance, the city of Kolkata—with a population of over thirteen million, thousands of eateries, 238 restaurants (in 2010, according to the *Telegraph* newspaper's Food Guide), and a number of gastronomic guides published in English and Bengali since the first decade of the twenty-first century—has not yet been the subject of any systematic academic work. But we are witnessing stirrings with some promise.[47] I believe we need studies of the food cultures of major Indian cities.

Second, scholarship needs to be developed on second- and third-tier cities, which are completely absent from the literature. In general, megacities dominate the discussion on urban studies and cultural analysis. On the other hand, anthropologists and folklorists have mastered narratives of the nonurban local. Food studies oscillates between these two polarities, skipping over the huge middle terrain. Big-city gastronomes and restaurant critics tend to naturalize the character of their own cities as ubiquitous to all forms of urbanism. Research projects must take their cue from Charles Tilly's recommendation not to treat all cities as interchangeable sites for analyzing modern life; he urges us to be attuned to the power of place without assuming that small towns are either scaled-down versions of the metropolis or stagnant provincial locales.[48] Scholars have successfully studied restaurant cultures in Paris, London, New York, Shanghai, Tokyo, and San Francisco.[49] In general, it is conceded that there is much to distinguish the culture of the city, as distinct from suburbia and the country, but it is assumed that urban cultures are similar across city size and location. There is reason to challenge that presumption and to consider peripheral cities—that is, cities under the double epistemological burden of smallness and location in developing countries—more closely, paying special attention to their gastronomic cultures.

Food's link to health through diet will be another dimension of increasing scholarly concern, especially with the globalization of the food system and cultural standards of consumption. A related route of inquiry with many interesting possibilities is food as a concern in the realm of ethnomedicine, especially Ayurveda. After the announced death of the humanist subject in postmodernism, the object has been revivified by studies in material culture, science studies, and food studies.[50] Bridging the gap between food and medicine, body and material, stuff and the senses, exciting new work is emerging that is transforming our ideas about the vitality of edible matter.[51]

Linking food to conceptions of health, yet getting past colonial epistemes, is Jean Langford's *Fluent Bodies: Ayurvedic Remedies for Postcolonial Imbalance* (2002).[52] It is a subtle meditation on folk practice that, rather than telling us how Ayurveda was superseded by modern, Western biomedicine, or how it represents resistance to colonizing modernity, or even how Ayurveda was modernized, instead tells us how modern medicine is reworked through Ayurvedic texts and practice. "As a result, this book breaks new ground in our understanding," argues Veena Das, a leading Indian sociologist, "of not only Ayurveda as a practice of healing but also its transformation into a national symbol through which the humiliation of colonialism is sought to be overcome. Langford's text is a layered description of the dispersed sites over which Ayurveda is being reconstructed in contemporary India."[53] First, Langford notes that the reframing of Ayurveda as a coherent medical system was a modern project that transformed the nature of Ayurvedic texts as cryptic aphorisms appropriated by experienced *vaidyas* (indigenous medical practitioners). She shows how the "vast project of codification" was a version of Orientalist longing that eventually became a nationalist imperative, underlining my previous claim that globalization feeds the codification of local forms of knowledge. As a result practitioners set themselves the task of systematizing and standardizing Ayurveda "to both compete with European medicine and offer a corrective for it." Implicated in the modern history of Ayurveda is the desire to be cured of illness, hegemonic desires of practitioners to emulate Europe, counter-hegemonic desires to reject all things European, contradictory desires for professionalism and for folk tradition, and demands to be modern and to be cured of illnesses associated with modernity.[54] Dr. Karnik, one of a handful of practicing physicians Langford interrogates intensively, notes that "the demarcation between modern medicine and Ayurveda is diffuse" and insists that there is no basic antagonism between Ayurveda and Western medicine. In the process the *vaidya* refused to construct the uniqueness of Ayurveda in spite of the ethnographer's desire for such an antagonistic construction. As a result Langford notes, "Frequently our conversations devolved into arguments in which I was embarrassed to find myself attempting to save Ayurveda as a form of ethnomedicine. ... For he would not permit Ayurveda to fill the empty category of tradition against which modernism is defined. He would not let me claim Ayurveda as a healing balm for modernity's excesses." As soon as we get comfortable with this construction, Langford quotes another practicing physician who avers that although Ayurvedic practice needs to be adjusted to fit the times, "Ayurvedic theory ... was already perfect."[55] Thus throughout the book she relentlessly shifts the terms of the debate between tradition and modernity, past and present, treating the whole patient and the diseased part, curing and preventing, science and culture, professional and quack, Western medicine and Ayurveda, without letting the reader settle down to a stable, comfortable dichotomy. This epistemic framing of Ayurveda and biomedicine brings us back full circle to concerns surrounding diet and disease, with which I began this chapter, and to ways of figuring out the relationships between food, health, system, and ideology, in a postcolonial, post-Orientalist, postmodern world that may have never been fully modern in the first place. This is the third domain where we will see interesting work on diet and desire coming out of India.

The two ends of seemingly incongruent polarities, from colonial famine to post-colonial gastronomic consumption, from health to disease, diets to diatribes, and rich empiricism to robust theorizing, are surprisingly tied together in Roy's remarkable book *Alimentary Tracts* (noted earlier). Heavily theorized and deeply entangled in the thicket of literary argument, it is chronologically selective, hopping, skipping, and jumping from the 1857 Indian Mutiny (against East India Company rule, the company that colonized India for a hundred years before direct takeover by the British state), to Gandhi's austere masculine vegetarianism, through hungers of the low-caste poor in Mahasweta Devi's novels, to the gastronomic reclamation of curry powder by Madhur Jaffrey. In traveling through the tangled web of such concerns, Roy tiptoes through the fertile borderlands of the ethical and the aesthetic consequences of eating the other, animal or human. In allowing the other to enter one's body without the desperate need of purgation, she expertly inverts the critique of hooks, Heldke, and Nandy, all of whom appear excessively cautious in their transactions with the other.[56] She does that by drawing on Jacques Derrida's suggestion of anthropophagy, not as an abomination, but as a "parabolic instantiation of unexpected somatic and ethical engagement with the other" where the "refusal to partake of the other is an important breakdown in or rejection of ethical reciprocity with the other."[57]

A book with a similar political-theoretical agenda and even more experimental in its narrative construction (the author invents a chorus, a dramatis personae, to pick up the thread of narration where there is inadequate empirical evidence) is Piya Chatterjee's *A Time for Tea: Women, Labor, and Post/Colonial Politics on an Indian Plantation* (2001). It addresses, perhaps even trips over, the central question faced most pointedly by self-declared third-world feminist, postcolonial theorists: how to make the silent subaltern speak and become the medium of that clairvoyance in spite of one's embeddedness in neoliberal networks. In *A Time for Tea* Chatterjee combines archival work, which she uses to tie metropolitan desire for tea over two centuries to the burdens of peripheral female labor managed through colonial and then nationalist patriarchy, with ethnographic observations at a tea plantation in northern Bengal in the twentieth century, where

> the history of the plantation is a history of desire. The history of tea is that of consuming desire. Imagine again the cup lifted to feminine lips. Consider the woman's body poised and posed, holding up the porcelain cup against the light. If you gaze closely against such painted light, the liquid is only an interior shadow. The body is not neutered but nubile, beckoning to the gaze of rule, its fleshy possibilities. The history of power is also the history of a woman's body bending to labor, captured by the scrutiny of desire that can claim her if it pleases.[58]

This attempt to yoke the political-economic to the symbolic-aesthetic dimension remains exceptional. The field of Indian food studies is polarized around a number of foci: one coalescing around crop science, another around development economics, one around culture and aesthetics, still another around nutrition and public health. I have attended to a few of these sites and pointed to the creative breaking of established analytical pots. I have urged more interdisciplinary work that can match the power of economics to the poetics of desire. I recommend greater interrogation of urban foodways with special attention to smaller towns and provincial capitals and advocate a robust approach to diet, health, and illness that engages as much with the experience of local empirics as with the expertise based on Western epistemologies. It would be productive to expand the category of public culture to accommodate studies of restaurants and roadside *dhabas* (truckstops).

Notes

This chapter has improved under the criticism of the editors of this volume and the detailed copyediting labor of Sierra Clark, who has saved me from a number of errors of substance, style, and grammar.

1. Warboys, 1988; Arnold, 1994. A rare recent work that bridges the historiography of indigenous and Western medicine is A. Digby, Ernst, and Muhkarji, 2010.
2. Arnold, 1994, 4.
3. Arnold, 1994, 26.
4. See, for instance, Sen's work in Drèze, A. Sen, and Hussain, 1995.
5. Currently, institutions such as the Food and Agriculture Organization (FAO) of the United Nations and nongovernmental organizations continue much of the routine empirical work on hunger and its amelioration through development. Food and Agriculture Organization (FAO), 2008; Fan and Brzeska, 2011; Newman, 2007. For examples of some local-level nongovernmental organizations working on hunger in India, such as Dapta, Karrtabya, IWD, NSS, Ankuran, Ayauskam, PIPAR, and PECUC, see *The Hunger Project*, n.d. Today there is a whole field at the intersection of the political economy of underdevelopment and malnutrition that I can only gesture toward here: Aradhna et al., 2010; Islam and Sarkar, 2010; Ratnawali, 2010.
6. Borlaug was accorded the second-highest civilian recognition—the Padma Vibhushan—by the government of India in 2006. For one recent example see Swaminathan, 2006.
7. Shiva, 1993; Shiva, 2005.
8. Douglas and Isherwood, 1996, 57.
9. Khare, 1976b; Appadurai, 1988; Zimmermann, 1987; Wujastyk and Meulenbeld, 2001; Wujastyk, 2003; Wujastyk and F. Smith, 2008.
10. See also Marriott, 1990.
11. Khare, 1966; Khare, 1976a; Khare, 1976b; Khare, 1992; Khare and Rao, 1986.
12. Obeyesekere, 1991.
13. Malamoud, 1996, 36–37.
14. Toomey, 1994, 4.
15. See special issues of the journals *South Asia* (Osella, 2008) and *South Asia Research* (2004); P. Roy, 2010; Mannur, 2010.
16. Appadurai, 2003, 654.
17. For journalistic pieces, essays, and works of fiction see N. Roy, 2004; Thieme and Raja, 2007.
18. Achaya, 1998; Arnold 1994; Chaudhuri and Strobel, 1992; Zlotnick, 1996; Harrison, 1999; E. M. Collingham, 2001; Prasad, 2005; Prasad, 2006.
19. Cohn, 1996.
20. Walsh, 1997; Walsh, 2004; S. M. Banerjee, 2004; Lal, 2005.
21. Conlon, 1995; Narayan, 1997; Srinivas, 2007; Buettner, 2008.
22. Ray and Srinivas, 2012.
23. Mukhopadhyay, 2004.
24. *South Asia Research*, 2004; T. Sen, 2007; Osella, 2008.
25. Banerji, 1997; Banerji, 2006; Banerji, 2007; Banerji, 2008.
26. C. Sen, 2004; C. Sen, 2009.

27. Narayan, 1997; Ganguly, 2001; Ray, 2004; Srinivas, 2006; Mannur, 2010; P. Roy, 2010.
28. Breckenridge, 1995; Appadurai, 1996.
29. Appadurai, 1996, 65.
30. For the discussion of public(s), see Fraser, 1993. Charles Taylor, in *Modern Social Imaginaries* (2004), underlines that public-ness cannot be exhausted by face-to-face meeting but could be mediated from a distance by print and electronic media. In *Flexible Citizenship: The Cultural Logics of Transnationality* (1999), Aiwha Ong theorizes the formation of ethnicized transnational publics that are dependent on neither critical rational face-to-face dialogue nor consumption, but on the proliferation of information technology.
31. Appadurai and Breckenridge, 1995, 4–5.
32. Conlon, 1995, 115.
33. Conlon, 1995, 116.
34. Burke, 1978; Hannerz, 1996, 240–41; S. Banerjee, 1998.
35. D. Wu and Cheung, 2004; Cwiertka and Walraven, 2001; Inglis and Gimlin, 2009; Farrer, 2010.
36. P. Roy, 2010; Mannur, 2010; Ray and Srinivas, 2012.
37. See Dickey, 2000; Dickey, 2011; Fernandes, 2006; Deshpande, 2003; Harriss, 2006; Fuller and Narasimhan, 2007; Fernandes and Heller, 2006; Dwyer, 2000; Derné, 2008.
38. Appadurai, 1996, 44.
39. F. Osella and C. Osella, C. 2000; Fernandes, 2006; Varma, 1998.
40. Barber, 1996; Berger, 1997; Friedman, 2000; Friedman, 2005.
41. Pollock, 2006.
42. Breckenridge et al., 2002.
43. Robbins, 1998, 7.
44. Robbins, 1998, 12.
45. The municipal council of Lucca (a town in Tuscany, Italy) ruled on January 26, 2009, that "with a view to safeguarding culinary traditions and the authenticity of structure, architecture, culture and history, establishments whose activities can be tracked to different ethnicities won't be allowed to operate." See Krause-Jackson, 2009.
46. Pollock confines that possibility to past instances of translocalism and not the current one.
47. See Liang, 2007; Mukhopadhyay, 2004; Ray, 2009; Srinivas, 2007; Siegel, 2010.
48. C. Tilly, 1996.
49. Spang, 2000; Schehr and Weiss, 2001; Capatti and Montanari, 2003; Rodinson, Arberry, and Perry, 2001; Ray, 2008; Swislocki, 2008; Burnett, 2004; Cwiertka, 2006a; Farrer, 2010.
50. To suggest just a handful of instances see Latour, 1992; Appadurai, 1986; Cadava, Connor, and Nancy, 1991; Daston, 2000.

51. See Bennet, 2010.
52. For an analysis of colonial epistemes see Arnold, 1993. For work on the post-colonial episteme see Langford, 2002.
53. Das, 2005, 849–50.
54. Langford, 2002, 10, 10–11.
55. Langford, 2002, 43, 94.
56. hooks, 1992; Heldke, 2003; Nandy, 2003.
57. Derrida, 1991; P. Roy, 2010, 14.
58. Chatterjee, 2001, 163.

The Shadow of Shinoda Osamu: Food Research in East Asia

Katarzyna Cwiertka and Yujen Chen

Shinoda Osamu and Food Research in East Asia

In his distinguished speaker lecture delivered at the meeting of the Council on Nutritional Anthropology at the 2001 annual meeting of the American Anthropological Association, Sidney Mintz stressed the importance of the work of pioneers in food anthropology with this statement:

> So rapidly has our field grown in recent decades that it seems ever more difficult to keep abreast of the work we do. Each time I must prepare a new syllabus for a food course, I feel like a pianist with extremely small hands, and legs too short to reach the pedals. Advances in research have enlarged our numbers and our readership; these days, students of food can contribute more effectively to ongoing discussions of major theoretical issues in anthropology. But I think we should also reflect more upon the contributions of our predecessors. That is, we need to build our understanding of the edifice of food studies: to broaden our perspectives, and to provide a clearer framework, both more inclusive and more coherent, for our field.[1]

These words not only reflect the state of the field of anthropology of food in Western academia but also pinpoint the stage that research on food has reached in East Asia. As elsewhere, research into food and eating in China, Hong Kong, Japan, (South) Korea, and Taiwan has experienced a genuine boost during the last two decades. In particular, the number of publications in English has skyrocketed after the turn of the century. In many respects these developments were part of the global expansion of interest in food in the humanities and social sciences. Yet they have also been propelled by the geopolitical changes in the region that have taken place since the rapid economic growth in China.

China has for centuries played a dominant role in shaping East Asian foodways. For example, the use of chopsticks and a widespread consumption of processed soybeans (soy sauce, soybean paste, and soybean curd) rank among the most vivid indicators of the common foundations that cuisines of East Asia rest on, which stem from the ancient Chinese civilization.[2] The crumbling of the ancient power structures triggered largely by the rise of Japan's imperialist ambitions in the late nineteenth century further strengthened the penetration of Chinese food throughout the region. This development was facilitated primarily by Chinese migration to Korea and Japan, and the Japanese settling in their newly acquired colonies of Formosa and Manchuria. This movement of people and culinary intermixing was further stimulated by the Asia-Pacific War (1937–1945) and its aftermath.[3] Although the American presence in the region intensified after 1945, its direct impact on East Asian foodways did not become prominent before the encroachment of American fast food that began in the 1970s.[4] Japan and Hong Kong were the first to embrace this new fashion, followed by Taiwan, South Korea, and China. The familiarity with global culinary trends that has intensified since the 1990s has in turn propelled the longing for the lost or vanishing foodways, and they are now widely utilized to reinforce national and local identities.[5]

To be sure, the economic growth that since the 1960s has gradually unfolded in different areas of East Asia has, in the first place, brought about dietary affluence. The populations of Japan, Hong Kong, Taiwan, (South) Korea, and, of late, China have never before eaten as well as they do now. Ironically, the culinary gentrification of recent years has inspired the nostalgic revival of (largely idealized) foods and consumption practices that had been abandoned on the way to affluence.

A growing attention to food and cuisine that can be witnessed throughout East Asia during the last two decades—in popular media as well as in academic circles—has been closely tied to these rapid shifts that the culinary cultures of the region have experienced since the 1980s. However, the foundation for research into East Asian foodways had been laid earlier, with Shinoda Osamu (1899–1978) clearly taking the lead as the uncontested pioneer.[6] Originally trained in biochemistry, Shinoda took up historical food research as his second career. In fact, his most important publications appeared only after his retirement.

Internationally, Shinoda is best known for his work on Chinese food history, *Chūgoku shokumotsu shi* (Food history of China), published in Japanese in 1974. It was awarded the prestigious Ema Tsutomu Prize, and a Chinese translation was published in Beijing in 1987. *Chūgoku shokkei sōsho* (Collected Chinese dietary manuals; 1972–1973), which attained the status of a seminal work on Chinese food history, is a two-volume compilation of forty ancient canonical texts concerning food, including agricultural manuals, private recipes, and treatises on tea, soup, and medicinal food. It is the latter work that earned Shinoda praise as a "tireless chronicler of the food canons of China"[7] who "carved out the field of Chinese food studies."[8]

Trained in chemistry and zoology at Kyoto Imperial University, Shinoda left for Europe in 1926 with a scholarship from the Rockefeller Foundation. By the age of thirty he held two PhD degrees, one from the Utrecht University (the Netherlands) and another from Kyoto University. Shinoda published widely on insect physiology, and this work received attention from the most unexpected corner—the engineers of the Japanese biological warfare program. Unit 731, also known under the name Ishii

Butai, was a biological and chemical warfare research and development unit of the Imperial Japanese Army that was set up in 1936 in the vicinity of Harbin, infamous for experimenting on humans.[9] Shinoda remained with Unit 731 for two years and in 1940 was transferred to the North China Army Hospital in Beijing, where he worked on the prevention and control of malaria, typhoid, bubonic plague, and other diseases transmitted by insects and vermin.[10]

The eight years in China proved a watershed in Shinoda's life, forcing him at the age of fifty to abandon his profession. A wartime wound made it physically impossible for him to carry out laboratory experiments, and his research notes and books shipped from Beijing after his repatriation to Japan were lost in transit. On the other hand, the Chinese experience provided the foundation for his future interest in food research. Field trips in Manchuria and North China undertaken for the sake of epidemic prevention research awakened the spirit of an ethnographer in him. During the eight years on the continent Shinoda also learned Chinese, a prerequisite in his research on Chinese food history. Ironically, Japan's imperialist expansion into China proved critical in turning a Japanese biochemist into a pioneer of Chinese food research.

Cancer prevented Shinoda from completing his research plans: a three-volume work on East Asian food history, each one dealing respectively with China, Korea, and Japan. He passed away at the age of seventy-nine while working on the manuscript of the second part of his trilogy. His best-known work on Japanese food is *Sushi no hon* (Book of sushi), published in 1966. This tiny booklet, which provides the reader with an overview of manifold local variations of sushi, was the result of over a decade of fieldwork and years of library research. It is written in a very accessible prose, contrasting with the overly sophisticated style of writing practiced in academic circles at the time. A biochemist by training, Shinoda strongly opposed the academic jargon that prevailed especially in historical works and his accessible writing contributed to the popularization of knowledge concerning Japanese food history among the general public.

Although Shinoda's work—particularly that on China—remains relevant today, his contribution to the field of East Asian food history goes beyond his publications. It can even be argued that his impact was greater in terms of inspiring people around him to consider food as a topic that deserves scholarly attention. It is in this respect that he was a true pioneer. Ishige Naomichi (b. 1937), the crowned king of food research in Japan,[11] and the pioneer of food research in Korea, Yi Song-u (1928–1992),[12] both developed their scholarly interest in food under Shinoda's influence.

Japanese Food History

Shinoda was not the first to publish about food in Japan. Yanagita Kunio (1875–1962) and other ethnographers had studied food habits since the early twentieth century in the context of Japanese folklore studies. Yet historians rather than ethnographers were the ones who published the first monographs on Japanese food. The work of Sasakawa Rinpū (1870–1949), Sakurai Shū (1885–1943), and Adachi Isamu (1901–1968), which appeared in the 1930s and 1940s, are still in print today.[13] They were actively involved in the formation of a new subfield of history, the so-called *fūzokushi*, which focused on the study of mundane social activities that hitherto had escaped the attention of historians.[14] Only two years after its inception in 1960, a separate food history section (Shokumotsushi bunkakai) was established within the Japan Society for Historical Research of Manners and Customs (Nihon fūzokushi gakkai). It became a central forum for intellectuals involved in food research, at first dominated by historians but soon joined by scholars with other disciplinary backgrounds, such as anthropology and home economics. Contrary to Sasakawa, Sakurai, and Adachi, who relied exclusively on written sources, Shinoda and Ishige insisted on the importance of ethnography in food research.

Sustained by the economic growth and gourmet boom of the 1980s, food research experienced a tremendous boost. As mentioned earlier, there was an explosion of popular and scholarly literature related to food history and cuisine. Some of the most influential publications were the edited proceedings of yearly symposia on food organized by the Ajinomoto Foundation for Dietary Culture (see Conclusion) launched by Domesu Shuppan in 1983; the twenty-seventh volume in this series appeared in 2009. In the late 1990s Yūzankaku issued *Zenshū: Nihon no shoku bunka* (Complete works on Japanese food culture), which is a high-quality, twelve-volume compilation of journal articles related to food published thus far.[15] Each volume covered a different topic. Volume 3, for example, was entirely devoted to staple foods; volume 6 to confectionery, sweets, and alcohol; and volume 9 to kitchen utensils and tableware. Definitely the most ambitious project was the monumental *Nihon no shokuseikatsu zenshū* (Complete works on Japanese food habits), published between 1986 and 1993 by the Rural Culture Association (Nōbunkyō). Stretched over fifty volumes, this series provides an overview of local food practices throughout Japan based on interviews with 5,000 individuals (predominantly elderly women) at 300 locations.[16]

Scholarly literature on food published during the last three decades in the Japanese language, based on both historical as well as ethnographic sources, undoubtedly ranks among the richest in the world. The overwhelming majority of these studies have one common characteristic: the emphasis on data collection and the relative lack of analysis.[17] If theoretical analysis has been present, it has tended to emphasize the uniqueness of the Japanese case, usually in comparison to "the West."[18]

This has not been the case with the literature on Japanese food written in English, perhaps with the exception of *The History and Culture of Japanese Food* (2001), a collage of Ishige's earlier work published in Japanese. The body of scholarship has grown steadily since the 1990s, the pace clearly accelerating during the last decade, with six monographs in English published (including Ishige's) at the time of writing. The very first monograph in English related to Japanese food was Ohnuki-Tierney's

Rice as Self (1993). The author convincingly demonstrates how rice and the technology for growing it, both of foreign origin, have been naturalized to symbolize quintessential *Japaneseness*, even today when, quantitatively, rice occupies a minor place in the diet. Ohnuki-Tierney's volume played a critical role in putting food on the research agenda as a serious object of inquiry in Japanese studies. *The Essence of Japanese Cuisine* (1998) by Ashkenazi and Jacob proved less successful. Based largely on anecdotal information, the authors pursue a highly outdated structuralist argument that there is a timeless "essence" that has the power to naturalize all the new elements that enter a cuisine. As Sidney Mintz argued a decade before the publication of *The Essence of Japanese Cuisine*, "human beings do create social structures, and do endow events with meaning; but these structures and meanings have historical origins that shape, limit, and help to explain such creativity."[19] *The Essence of Japanese Cuisine* is interesting, though, since it exemplifies the eagerness, particularly prevalent among the Japanese authors, to drape Japanese cuisine in an aura of exoticism, uniqueness, and traditionalism.

The first decade of the twenty-first century saw the publication of four monographs that are very likely to retain their position as seminal works on Japanese food for some time: Bestor's *Tsukiji: The Fish Market at the Center of the World* (2004), Cwiertka's *Modern Japanese Cuisine* (2006), Aoyama's *Reading Food in Modern Japanese Literature* (2008), and Rath's *Food and Fantasy in Early Modern Japan* (2010).

In essence, the focus of Bestor's volume is the social and economic organization of Tsukiji, the famous Tokyo fish market. However, it serves as an invaluable source for understanding the place seafood has attained in the Japanese cuisine and diet—both tangible and symbolic—and its historical development. Chapter 4 of Bestor's monograph, entitled "The Raw and the Cooked," provides a particularly useful analysis of Japanese culinary culture, engaging anthropological perspectives on food developed by scholars such as Claude Lévi-Strauss, Marvin Harris, and Sidney Mintz.[20] The chapter complements the historical analysis of Japanese cuisine since the late 1850s offered by Cwiertka's *Modern Japanese Cuisine*. She argues that Japanese cuisine, as it is projected and valued today, is a modern construct conceived in the midst of the twentieth-century historical dynamics. She identifies seven major processes in the dietary transformation of modern Japan: the embrace of the West as the model for political and economic development, the rise of the new urban mass gastronomy, the modernization of military catering and of home cookery, wartime food management, the dietary effects of Japanese imperialism, and the impact of the rapid economic growth.

Aoyama's *Reading Food in Modern Japanese Literature* approaches food in modern Japan from a very different angle. As the title indicates, *reading*—not food—is the focus of her monograph. Yet Aoyama's work contributes to food research in two respects. There is a high degree of correlation between the dietary reality and the depictions of food in literature. Literature can often serve as an ethnographic source in the study of food and eating. For example, detailed sketches of restaurant and home meals depicted as the backdrop of narratives not infrequently reveal important information for culinary historians. Aoyama's volume beams with such examples. The second contribution of this volume to the scholarship of food is even more significant. It lays bare the myth of Japan's literary obsession with food, clearly situating the food-focused media entertainment in Japan as a recent phenomenon. According to Aoyama, the preoccupation with food in Japan was directly inspired by the gourmet boom of the 1980s, which in turn emerged in reaction to "the repression and oppression of appetite" during the war and the immediate postwar period. Contrary to the common belief that is widespread today, the pursuit of edible delicacies occupied a very limited place in Japanese literature until recently. As the author points out, Tanizaki Jun'ichirō's *The Gourmet Club* (*Bishoku kurabu*, 1919), which was to become an exemplar for the gastronomic novel that is thriving today, was rediscovered only during the 1980s after being neglected by critics for nearly six decades.

Aoyama's statement contradicts the argument presented by Eric Rath in *Food and Fantasy in Early Modern Japan*, the most recently published monograph on Japanese food. Based on his analysis of cookbooks, recipe collections, and gastronomic writings from 1400 to 1868, Rath claims that there was a sophisticated understanding of cuisine as an intellectual and artistic practice that began with the medieval "fantasy food" rituals—where food was revered as symbol rather than consumed—and culminated in gastronomic texts written by early modern "foodies." Rath's contribution is essential since he introduces material that had thus far been available only in Japanese and, importantly, offers an interpretation. The overly descriptive character of Japanese research makes the engagement of foreign scholars like Rath of vital importance for the future of the field.

Along with the six monographs already mentioned, a number of English-language essays have a strong potential in mainstreaming Japanese cuisine in the field of food studies. Allison's article "Japanese Mothers and Obentōs" is in the lead as perhaps the most well-known piece on Japanese cuisine ever written.[21] Finally, the volume *Japanese Food Past and Present* (2010), edited by Rath and Assmann, represents the manifold topics that established and emerging scholars of Japanese food are currently engaged in and demonstrates a rich potential for growth.

Chinese Food Culture

One of the first studies on Chinese food history, published in 1911, was not a strictly scholarly exercise. *Zhongguo fengsu shi* (History of Chinese customs), written by Zhang Liang-cai (1870–1906), an intellectual with a traditional Chinese education, described the evolution of food habits from the age before the Yellow Emperor (ca. 2700 B.C.E.) to the Ming dynasty (1368–1644 C.E.) with a clear purpose in mind. The author strove to convince his readers to replace their luxurious customs with modest ones in the face of the economic problems that China was experiencing at the time, following the argument from Confucian canons such as *Liji* (Book of rites) and *Lunyu* (Edited conversations of Confucius), which claimed that feeding the people is the crucial responsibility of the ruler. Similarly, Lang's *Zhongguo minshi shi* (History of the Chinese people's food), published in 1933, emphasized the importance of food in maintaining social stability by examining how the Chinese people were fed throughout history.

The outbreak of the Asia-Pacific War in 1937 and the post-1945 turmoil did not provide a fertile ground for research of any kind. Furthermore, apart from a few exceptions, such as Hsu's "Zhoudai de yi shi zhu xing" (Clothes, food, living, and transportation in the Zhou dynasty), food has seldom been a subject of historical research in the Chinese world; politics and the economy remained the focus of scholarly concern.[22] It was not until the 1980s that serious research on Chinese food began to emerge. The foundation for the new research was provided by rich textual resources from the Chinese ancient and classical traditions, including Confucian philosophers' treatises related to ritual consumption of food, agricultural and technical manuals, recipes, cookbooks, and gourmand notes, many of which refer to the medicinal qualities of food and drink. Also, Chinese literature constitutes a rich source of information on a wide range of food-related themes. The extensive presence of food in Chinese literature is very well documented in *Zhongguo yinshi shiwen dadian* (Dictionary of food and drink in Chinese literature, 1995), which includes detailed citations from poetry and prose.[23]

Early studies published during the 1980s reveal particular interest in ancient times.[24] Moreover, more attention seems to have been paid at the time to food itself than to the social and historical contexts in which it was produced and consumed. For example, Zeng, Zhang, and Gao focused exclusively on neatly dividing Chinese food into categories: staple foods, vegetables, animal foods, drinks, condiments, snacks, and so on.[25] During the 1990s much effort was devoted to the publication of reference material, from reprints of classic texts to encyclopedias and dictionaries, including the monumental six-volume set *Zhongguo yinshi shi* (History of Chinese food and drink, 1999) edited by Xu.[26] Written by twenty-four authors, mostly historians, with each volume covering a period of several hundred years, the set treated a wealth of data concerning ingredients (staple foods, meats, vegetables, fruits, etc.) and their production, cooking methods, cooking utensils, dining manners, festivals and banquets, restaurants, and other related topics.

With the maturing of the field, in addition to these monumental volumes, more focused studies began to emerge. Some scholars narrowed their scope to a specific time span, a specific region, or a specific theme, such as the introduction of Western food into Chinese society.[27] The 1990s also marked the beginning of studies on single items, such as tea, ale, sugar, snacks, or banquet food.[28] Historical inquiry into agriculture and food technology also developed as an important category in Chinese food research. Along with classical works,[29] innovative studies that connected agriculture with ecological systems and regional food traditions began to emerge. A prime example is Tseng Pin-tsang's PhD thesis, entitled "Cong tianqi dao canzhuo" (From farm to table, 2006), in which he explores dietary patterns of Chinese Han society in Qing Taiwan in connection with their agricultural systems.

Generally speaking, however, the bulk of Chinese research on food remained descriptive rather than interpretative. Few studies seriously engaged in investigating the social meanings of food or analyzed the factors leading to dietary change. A notable exception was the subfield that emerged in Taiwan during the 1990s. Inspired by the French *Annales* school and the idea of "total history,"[30] young scholars called for a more comprehensive understanding of social change and incorporated anthropological and sociological concepts into historical research. In this context, life history, or the history of everyday life and consumption, increasingly became an important theme in academic circles. For example, the Taiwanese scholarly community composed mainly of specialists on the Ming and Qing dynasties (fourteenth to early twentieth centuries) began to study the consumer culture of the Chinese gentry, drawing on ideas generated by scholars such as Daniel Miller, Pierre Bourdieu, Craig Clunas, and Sidney Mintz.[31] Culinary culture became an important research theme, now not studied in isolation but taking into consideration wider historical and social contexts. This shift entailed not only a choice of different research topics but also a reliance on different research materials, which expanded from official archives and administrative documents to a wider range of sources related to daily life.

For example, Wu Jen-shu explored the fashion for luxurious eating in the Jiangnan region among the gentry since the late Ming dynasty and explained how this fashion led to the proliferation of private recipe books and dietary writings.[32] Wu suggests that these recipes reveal progress in the expression of sense perceptions and a higher demand for sensory enjoyment. Wang Hung-tai's research, in turn, revealed that the proliferation of drinking parlors and teahouses during the seventeenth century was a consequence of the growing social need for "communal spaces" for the gentry.[33] Chiu Chung-lin dealt with the preservation and consumption of seafood, linking refined dining with food production.[34] While quite revolutionary within Taiwanese academia, these studies relied heavily on the tradition of textual analysis, which restricted their subject matter to the upper class. This limitation of resources still leaves the food of the general public largely unexplored. A remarkable emerging trend is to employ diaries, account books, newspapers, and various folk resources to investigate the popular dietary culture, such as Tseng's research on the folk banquets in Taiwanese society.[35]

The most representative trend of the last decade is the emphasis on ethnographic fieldwork and anthropological and sociological approaches to historical research on food. For example, by combining textual analysis with fieldwork, Wang Ming-ke studied the social meanings of highland barley, buckwheat, and maize in Sichuan Province, exploring how their meanings altered with the changing ethnic boundaries of Qiang, a minor ethnic group in China.[36] Interpreting the transformation with

Bourdieu's theory of practice, he concluded that these food grains were endowed with social and cultural symbolism for their material qualities and their importance in the local economy.

In recent years a growing number of scholars of Chinese food have shifted their interest from historical to contemporary topics, including the role of food in the formation of (national) identity, the role of food in religion, ethnic groups, local culture, and globalization. Summarizing the anthropological studies on Chinese dietary culture, Hsu and Chien suggest that the Chinese dietary system is often viewed as a subsystem of the medical health system, which is closely associated with the operation of the universe.[37] Adopting theories of symbolism and structuralism, some researchers have analyzed Chinese dietary culture using the concepts of cold and hot, yin and yang, and the five elements (metal, wood, water, fire, and earth): these are key ideas in ancient Chinese cosmology and herbal medicine. In addition, sacrifices and offerings in Chinese society also acquired a great deal of attention from anthropologists: these activities have been interpreted as a symbolic language, serving as a communication channel between people and the gods. According to Hsu and Chien, understanding the role of food in religious festivals is essential for a deeper understanding of the spiritual life and social systems of the Han Chinese.

English-language research publications on Chinese food began to emerge from the late 1970s, with historians, anthropologists, and literary scholars approaching the topic with different concerns and frameworks. As the first English book focusing on Chinese food, the edited volume *Food in Chinese Culture* (1977) remains a crucial introduction to the general history of Chinese food. The editor, Chang Kwang-chih, explains his intention of exploring the change-within-tradition pattern and the underlying structure of Chinese society,[38] thus demonstrating the ambition of the volume to examine Chinese food culture from both a historical and a structural perspective.

Among the contributors to *Food in Chinese Culture*, the anthropologist E. N. Anderson is the only scholar who situates food as the core subject in his research. In his later work, he adopted cultural ecology as the main approach, seeking to investigate how Chinese people maximized their dietary adequacy with a minimum input of land and capital.[39] Expanding his focus from the southern provinces to the whole of China in *The Food of China* (1988), he details the efficiency of Chinese food production and how cultural practices, such as religious activities and medical systems, were embedded within food consumption.[40]

Since the 1990s, more scholars from various disciplines have participated in researching Chinese food history and have paid attention to increasingly diverse topics. For example, geographer Frederick Simoons has conducted an extensive study on the distribution and characteristics of the Chinese food system.[41] Huang's monumental volume in Joseph Needham's series *Science and Civilisation in China* (2000) focuses on the historical development of the fermentation technology used in Chinese food processing.[42] Literary scholars, such as David Knechtges and Stephen West, also began to play an active role in exploring Chinese food history. Their translations of China's plentiful ancient literature on food and eating highlighted for non-Chinese readers the core position that food had played in Chinese literary culture.[43]

Globalization of Chinese food, in Asia and beyond, is an important topic that emerged in recent literature on Chinese food published in English,[44] along with the encroachment of American fast food.[45] Attempts have also been made to approach the historical development of twentieth-century China in a systematic manner by using food and diet as a research focus. Mark Swislocki's *Culinary Nostalgia: Regional Food Culture and the Urban Experience in Shanghai* (2009) ranks among the most successful examples.[46]

While historians, literary researchers, and gastronomists are active writers in Chinese-language publications, anthropologists play a significant role in publications in English.[47] Moreover, historians are consciously moving to anthropological or sociological approaches, manifesting the interdisciplinary characteristics of food studies. For example, when exploring the continuities in Chinese food culture, the edited volume by Roel Sterckx has shown the shifting focus from "the material history of food and eating" to "ideas about food, cooking, banqueting, and diet within the social and religious context of the communities in which certain foods were consumed or eschewed."[48] Chen Yu-jen's research on the notion of "Taiwanese cuisine" also explored the history of Taiwanese cuisine across one century from the perspective of nationalism and "sense of body," combining historical and ethnographic methods as the main methodology. Through the interdisciplinary project, Chen examined the transformation of "Taiwanese cuisine" under different political regimes and suggested that national cuisine is a relational and performative concept as well as a commercial product.[49]

Korean Food History

As mentioned earlier, the pioneer of research into Korean food history, Yi Song-u, was greatly influenced by Shinoda Osamu and his followers in Japan. Yi's academic training began with undergraduate studies in the Department of Agriculture at Seoul National University and evolved during his graduate career in nutritional chemistry. In 1973, he received a PhD in this field from Pusan University, but under the impact of Shinoda's work, Yi soon began to publish extensively on food history.[50] His research was focused on the ancient and premodern periods. As was the case with the pioneering scholars in China, Yi paid particular attention to the classic treatises and manuals that dealt with food and diet. A one-volume compilation of such material, selected from over 2,500 texts written in Korea between the fourteenth and the twentieth centuries, was published under Yi's editorial supervision in 1981.[51] A full eight-volume edition of the entire compilation appeared eleven years later, coinciding with Yi's death.[52]

Yi was a founding member of two organizations that came to play a central role in the community of Korean food researchers today: the Korean Society of Food

Culture (Han'guk shingmunhwa hakhoe), founded in 1984, and the East Asian Society of Dietary Life (Tong asia siksaenghwal hakhoe), founded in 1991. Both have been quite active, organizing annual symposia and publishing journals.[53] Yet their focus remains largely fixed on nutritional issues and quantitative consumer research as the content of their publications testifies (see Table 1). This state of affairs is emblematic for food research in South Korea: the field became associated with home

Table 1. Table of Contents of February 2011 Issue of the *Journal of the East Asian Society of Dietary Life* (vol. 21, no. 1)

Study on Dietary Habits of North Korean Refugees

Nutritional Knowledge, Dietary Habits and Dietary Self-Efficacy of Childcare Major Students in Daegu

The Effect of Angelica keiskei Ethnol Extract on Proliferation, Apotosis and ROS Accumulation in Human Breast Cancer MDA-MB-231 Cells

Quality Characteristics of Pan Bread with Spirulina Powder

Quality Characteristics of Gochujang Dressing Containing Various Amounts of Maesil (Prunus mune) Concentrate

Quality Characteristics and Antioxidative Activity of Mung Bean Starch Gels Added with Carrot, Spinach and Mulberry Juice

Study on Rheological Properties of Wheat Flour Mixed with Buckwheat Powder

Antioxidative Ability of Some Produces in Ulleungdo and Quality Characteristics of the Taffy Made from the Produces

The Antioxidant and Nitrite Scavenging Activity of Wild Grape (Vitis coignetiea) Wine

Changes in Quality of Pork Meat Seasoned with Red Wine during Storage

Production of Sikhae Fermented Beverage using a Dextran Producing Isolate from Kimchi and Takju Yeast

A Comprehensive Study of Customers' Perceived Service Quality of Korean Restaurants II: The Effects of Perceived Service Quality in Korean Restaurants upon Customer Satisfaction— The Moderating Effect of Foreigners and Koreans

Research on the Dietary Habits and Satisfaction of School Meals of High School Students in Chungnam Area

Association between Educational Environment and Satisfaction with Learning in Students at Local Cooking Institutes -Focused on Pohang and Gyeongju Area

Menu Evaluation of Meal Boxes Delivered to Children from Low-Income Families during Summer Vacation

Study on the Current Status of Vegetable Utilization in the Development of Simple Pre-processed Foods

Comparison of Work Values of Undergraduate-level Foodservice Major Students

Nutrition Counseling Practice, Perception, and Nutrition Knowledge of Nutrition Counseling Participants and Non-Participants—Elementary Students in Gyeongbuk Province

Source: The East Asian Society of Dietary Life, http://ocean.kisti.re.kr/IS_mvpopo001P.do?method=multMain&poid=easdl&free (accessed June 27, 2011).

economics departments, with a very marginal role left to play by anthropologists and historians.

A typical example of home economics specialists taking over food historiography in South Korea is the case of royal cuisine. The process of defining, formalizing, and standardizing royal court cuisine has been studied by Hwang Hye-song (1920–2006), and in 1973 the government designated her a "Human Cultural Asset of Royal Cuisine" (Kungjung ŭmsik in'gan munhwajae). Hwang and her daughters Han Pok-chin and Han Pong-nyŏ even acquired a de facto monopoly for publishing about royal cuisine and its historical development. Han Pong-nyŏ succeeded her mother after her death as "Human Cultural Asset of Royal Cuisine." One might wonder if home economics education has provided these three individuals with sufficient qualifications to conduct historical research on the centuries-old practice of Korean royal cuisine. However, as Moon Okpyo argues in her analysis of the royal cuisine revival in South Korea and Hwang's role in this process, by ratifying the authenticity of Hwang's skills and knowledge the state's Intangible Cultural Asset system created a highly problematic circumstance in which historical research was subordinated to state policies.[54]

The number of publications in Korean on the topic of Korean food that have appeared since the mid-1980s is quite extensive, including dictionaries, ethnographic essays on Korean culinary heritage, descriptions of dining etiquette, and collections of historical recipes.[55] Han Pok-chin's overview of food in twentieth-century Korea, a detailed study of the food culture of Seoul by Chŏng and Yi, and the historical analysis of food in Korean paintings conducted by anthropologist/historian Chu Yng-ha stand out as particularly innovative works.[56]

As far as publications in English are concerned, the body of scholarship is very limited, especially in comparison to the large corpus on Chinese and Japanese food history, which has grown extensively during the last decade. So far, the only monograph in English entirely devoted to the topic of the historical development of Korean cuisine is Michael Pettid's *Korean Cuisine: An Illustrated History* (2008), while Cwiertka's *Cuisine, Colonialism and Cold War* will appear soon. Chapters in edited volumes and journal articles, while playing an important role in filling the void, are written by a relatively small circle of authors.[57] In contrast to the popularity of food studies among specialists on China and Japan, there seems to be a general lack of interest in, or at least long-term commitment to, studying Korean food among non-Korean scholars of Korea. Research published in English to date has largely been conducted by a handful of Korean scholars writing in English, with Han Kyung-koo and Bak Sangmee clearly in the lead, in addition to works translated into English for publication.[58]

Korean Cuisine: A Cultural Journey, an English-language translation of a Korean monograph done under the auspices of the Korean Foundation,[59] conveys very well the general spirit of Korean publications on food history, especially those targeted at a foreign audience: the glorification of the Korean culinary heritage and emphasis on the unique characteristics of time-honored traditions surrounding food production, preparation, and consumption in Korea. The foundation was established in affiliation with the Korean Ministry of Foreign Affairs to "promote a better understanding of Korea in the international community and to foster global friendship by conducting exchange activities between the Republic of Korea and foreign countries around the world."[60] Along with its quarterly mouthpiece *Koreana*, published in eight languages (English, German, Spanish, French, Arabic, Russian, Chinese, and Japanese) and distributed free of charge to universities, libraries, museums, research centers, and other cultural institutions in over a hundred countries, the Korean Foundation has increasingly invested in projects with a culinary focus, such as the *Korean Food Guide in English* (2003) and the translation of *Korean Cuisine: A Cultural Journey.*[61]

It remains to be seen whether a recent policy of the South Korean government aiming to popularize Korean cuisine globally, with an ultimate goal of elevating it to one of the world's five most popular cuisines by 2017, is going to include academic research as well. So far, the main strategies have involved financial incentives to increase the number of Korean restaurants abroad; plans to standardize the names, descriptions, and recipes of representative Korean dishes; dispatching of Korean chefs abroad to hold Korean cooking classes at renowned culinary schools; and intensification of promotional activities through Korean embassies and the Korea Tourism Organization.[62]

Conclusion

Shinoda Osamu passed away in 1978, approximately a decade before research into food history began to flourish in East Asia. It seems, however, that his spirit continues to have an influence on the field even today, with its highly interdisciplinary nature perhaps the most characteristic feature. Shinoda's legacy is not solely responsible for this development. Financial support from commercial enterprises played an important role in the inclusive character of food studies in this part of the world, and in particular in Japan and Taiwan, which created different conditions for growth than would have been the case in the closed setting of academia. In Japan companies such as Nissin Shokuhin, Asahi Beer, Suntory, and Ajinomoto have supported food-related research and a variety of activities aimed at spreading interest and knowledge on food and cuisine among the general public. The commitment of Ajinomoto[63] in this direction has proved particularly strong and long-standing. In 1979, at the occasion of the seventieth anniversary of the establishment of the company, Ajinomoto sponsored its first series of public symposia on food and has continued to support scholarly conferences on this topic. Ten years later, Ajinomoto established the Ajinomoto Centre for Dietary Culture (ACDC; Ajinomoto shoku no bunka sentā) in Tokyo, which became involved in organizing symposia, editing a journal, and running a library, along with administering research grants.[64]

The same year, 1989, a similar base of support for research into Chinese food was set up in Taipei by the Mercuries Group, named the Foundation of Chinese Dietary Culture (FCDC; Zhonghua yinshi wenhua jijinhui). A feature that clearly distinguishes FCDC in Taipei from ACDC in Tokyo is its international character. FCDC successfully runs international conferences on a biannual basis in different Asian cities, and its journal, *Zhongguo yinshi wenhua* (Journal of Chinese dietary culture), which was launched in 2005, includes both Chinese-language and English-language articles.[65] FCDC plays a key role in stimulating Chinese food research at both the national and the international level, while ACDC's parochial attitude remains unchanged.

No institution comparable to ACDC and FCDC has thus far emerged in South Korea. The Korean Food Foundation (KFF; Hansik Chaedan), set up in March 2010, is an organization of a very different nature; its main task is spearheading the efforts toward globalizing Korean cuisine rather than supporting research into Korean food historiography. However, the growing impact of historical imagery on the commercial revenues that a cuisine can generate is a point of concern, not only in South Korea. As argued elsewhere,[66] restaurant, food, and tourist industries time and again reinvent "national cuisines," not infrequently fabricating historical roots to make "ethnic cuisines" appear more exotic and time-honored than they are in reality. Manipulating the image of a culinary history to make it appear "traditional" and exotic—and more appealing for foreign consumption—is an issue that deserves attention in the food historiography of East Asia.

Notes

1. Mintz, 2002, 3.
2. Du Bois, Tan, and Mintz, 2007.
3. See Yang, 2005; Cwiertka, 2006a, 138–55.
4. J. Watson, 1997.
5. Swislocki 2009; Assmann, 2010; Moon, 2010.
6. Note that in this chapter, Asian names are given with the family name first, followed by the given name. Thus works by Shinoda Osamu, for example, will be found listed under Shinoda in the bibliography.
7. Huang, 2000, vii.
8. Chang, 1977, 5.
9. Barenblatt, 2004.
10. Information on Shinoda's work and life has been acquired during an interview with Ishige Naomichi (pers. comm., spring 2003) and from Shinoda's private documents, available at the Shinoda Collection; see Ishige, 1989. See also National Museum of Ethnology, n.d.
11. The database of the National Diet Library (http://opac.ndl.go.jp) lists 197 entries under Ishige's name. The bulk of this work is related to food.

12. For more detailed information on Yi see the later section on research into Korean food.
13. Sakurai and Adachi, 1934; Sasakawa and Adachi, 1935; Adachi, 1962.
14. It should be mentioned that the tradition of writing about *fūzoku* itself goes back to the late eighteenth century when popular writers (*gesakusha*) and men of letters often took up the topic of food and its history as a pastime.
15. Haga and Ishikawa, 1996–1999.
16. Nihon no shokuseikatsu zenshū henshū iinkai, 1986–1993.
17. For example, Shōwa Joshi Daigaku Shokumotsugaku Kenkyūshitsu, 1971, describes in more than 800 pages the details of modern Japanese food history without coming to any conclusion. See also Watanabe, 1986; Katō, 1977; Saitō, 1983; Kosuge, 1991; Ehara and Higashiyottsuyanagi, 2008.
18. See, for example, Kodama, 1980, 7–10; Ishige, 1984, 85; Tamura and Ishige, 1994, 141–43.
19. Mintz, 1985, xxx.
20. Lévi-Strauss, 1966; Lévi-Strauss, 1970; M. Harris, 1985; Mintz, 1985.
21. Allison, 1991. See also Noguchi, 1994; Sand, 2005; T. Holden, 2005.
22. Hsu C.-y., 1976.
23. Xiong, 1995. See also Knechtges, 1986, 54.
24. See, for example, Lin, 1989; Yao, 1989. Lin approached food history regionally, shifting the emphasis to the formation of regional cuisines. He argued that regional characteristics originated not only from local food resources but also from economic systems and cultural distribution.
25. Zeng, Zhang, and Gao, 1988.
26. For example, Xiao, 1992. There are also book series focusing on food, such as Zhonghua yinshi wenku (Collection of Chinese drink and food), published by Qingdao chubanshe during the 1990s.
27. For example, Chen W.-m., 1993, introduces the meal structure, food shops, and food processing during Tang and Song dynasties (seventh to thirteenth centuries C.E.). Li, 1998, suggests that medical and nutritional science had made amazing progress during Han and Tang dynasties.
28. Yao, 1994; Zhao, 1996.
29. Hong, 1984; Wang L.-h., 2000.
30. On the "new cultural history" see the preface of Bonnell and Hunt, 1999.
31. Chiu P.-s., 2006; Poo, 1992.
32. Wu J.-s., 2006.
33. Wang H.-t., 2000.
34. Chiu C.-l., 2005.
35. Tseng, 2010.
36. Wang M.-k., 2007.
37. Hsu M.-t. and Chien, 1996.
38. Chang, 1977, 20, 39.

39. E. Anderson, 1988, 380–81.

40. E. Anderson and M. Anderson, 1973; E. Anderson, 1988.

41. Simoons, 1991.

42. Huang, 2000.

43. Knechtges, 1986; Knechtges, 1997; West, 1997; Buell and Anderson, 2000.

44. Roberts, 2002; D. Wu and Cheung, 2002; Cheung and Tan, 2007.

45. J. Watson, 1997; Yan, 2000; Jing, 2000.

46. Swislocki, 2009. See also Lee, 2010; Schneider, 2011.

47. For example, J. Klein, 2007; J. Klein, 2009; Farquhar, 2002.

48. Sterckx, 2005, 3.

49. Chen Y.-j., 2010.

50. Yi, 1984; Yi, 1985; Yi, 1993.

51. Yi, 1981.

52. Yi, 1992.

53. See the Korean Society of Food Culture's website (http://www.food-culture.or.kr/index.html) and the East Asian Society of Dietary Life's website (http://society.kisti.re.kr/~easdl/1s_1.html).

54. Moon, 2010, 48–49.

55. Han P.-c., 1989a; Han P.-c., 1989b; Han P.-n., 1989; Yun S.-S., 1990; Han P.-n., 1995; Yun S.-k., 1996; Han P.-c., Han P.-n., and Hwang, 1998; Kim C.-s., 1998.

56. Han P.-c., 2001; Chŏng and Yi, 1996; Chu, 2005.

57. Pemberton, 2002; Walraven, 2002; Cwiertka, 2006b; Reinschmidt, 2007; Han K.-k., 2010a; Han K.-k., 2010b.

58. Bak, 1997; Bak, 2005; Jung, 2005; Yang, 2005; Han K.-k., 2010a; Han K.-k., 2010b; Bak, 2010.

59. Chung, 2009.

60. For details see the Korea Foundation website, http://www.kf.or.kr/.

61. The Korea Foundation, 2003; Chung, 2009.

62. Global Travel Media, 2010. For a detailed blueprint on the globalization of Korean food see Kim Y.-s., 2009, 458–600.

63. Before World War II, Ajinomoto was a leading producer of monosodium glutamate, which it first marketed in 1909. Currently, the company portfolio includes a wide range of activities, from manufacture of beverages and frozen foods to amino acids (monosodium glutamate and aspartame) and pharmaceuticals. See Ajinomoto, 2011.

64. Ajinomoto shoku no bunka sentā, 2009. See also the website of the center, http://www.syokubunka.or.jp/. Contrary to the Foundation for Chinese Dietary Culture (FCDC; see later on), the activities of the center never developed internationally, and the website is available only in Japanese.

65. See the Foundation of Chinese Dietary Culture's website for details: http://www.fcdc.org.tw/english/about/default.aspx.

66. Cwiertka, 2006a, 179.

Part IV. Africa

–12–

Writing on the African Pot: Recipes and Cooking as Historical Knowledge

James C. McCann

A chapter on the history of the cooking of Africa must cover an impossibly broad landscape of food, cooking, and culinary cultures found within the African continent, whose languages exceed 1,000 and whose named cultures number at least 2,000. Though Africa is a distinct landmass, its culinary expressions—like its political economies, local histories, and ecologies—have always reflected a wide cultural geography that includes the continent itself and its historical cultural diaspora. Can a traveler moving across such a vast continent make sense of culinary cultures that savor everything from pounded yam *fufu* in Ghana and southern Nigeria, to the spongy, sour *injera* of Ethiopia, to the rice-based *thiebou dienn* of Senegal? If a traveler on the ground would have trouble making generalizations about linguistic diversity, how much more difficult is it for writers about food and cuisine (i.e., cooking) to make coherent generalizations about the local ecologies of ingredients, trade, and the dietary ritual practice of Islam, mission Christianity, and local spiritual life.

What would a map of Africa's food geography look like? And what is the body of writing that can help us recognize distinctions of spice, texture, and sequence that mark African cooking? How might we understand ways that African women preserved primarily oral knowledge of culinary arts as their own body of knowledge? For Africa, in fact, the task has scarcely begun. Let us start by looking on the shelves of a modern urban bookstore, whether that is in London, Cambridge, New York, or Nairobi. In the section devoted these days to cookbooks in ethnic cuisine, African cooking occupies the smallest of spaces in even the most innovative bookshops or library collections.

Food—what people cook and what people eat—is the theme chosen for this chapter, and as a topic in African history it has two possible approaches. On the one hand would be food as a part of the daily struggle for sustenance contained within African origins of humankind or, a modern equivalent, the specter of famine that in the modern world has often featured Africa as its epicenter. In this view food is a means of filling the belly and sustaining life. This approach emphasizes struggle and heartbreak at the expense of recognizing Africa's fundamental energy and creativity in the history of its cooking, and the way the flavors and textures of food adds character and quality to life's daily rhythms. The second approach, the one I survey here, is food as a creative composition at the heart of all cultural expressions of ourselves as humans, that is to say, cuisine. Historically, in Africa, food grows in gardens, appears in bustling markets, in herds/flocks of sheep, goats, and cattle, and in small grocery shops that sell sacks of beans. In premodern times Africans, like all the world's peoples, ate in the rhythm of the seasons: the bearing of wild fruits, the movements of fish, the timing of harvests, and the migrations of domestic herds and animals in the wild. Modern African cooks choose ingredients from local ecologies but also from international trade that offers them macaroni, tins of tomato paste, or Maggi bouillon cubes.

I want to explore cuisine in Africa as something conceived, cooked, and consumed, first around home fires, cooking pots, griddles, and spits. But cuisine also appears in simmering market stall pots, in up-scale urban restaurants, and at political events, where food expresses power. Eating together, commensality, was thus not just nutrition but also a measure of particular human values, linking communities of kin, neighbors, and friends around tastes and sequences of taste expressing who they were on a daily basis: in a word, the mutually intelligibility of cuisine. Yet what are those things that make Africa's historical experiences with food distinctive, and how has scholarship or writing for a public audience included Africa? Where does Africa fit into the body of literature on food and cooking? Let us start with writing about food as history in a general sense. Cookbooks themselves make interesting reading as historical texts, but few readers are aware of their own value for reconstructing the past. It is worth a look at some classic texts that directly address food and cooking as a topic of history. One of the oldest, and most readable, books on food as a historical topic is Reay Tannahill's *Food in History* (1973). Tannahill's was the first of its kind for a general readership, but Africa gets exceedingly short shrift. She offers one page on "Arab Cooking" and comments for Africa that "cooking is only an art where food is consistently plentiful.... When shortages are a part of everyday life, filling the stomach is the only art."[1] That is a telling statement in many ways. Her disdainful comment about Africa probably applies more to social class than to geography. Would she say that about French or Italian rustic cooking? A more recent view of food and history, and more theoretically provocative one, would be Felipe Fernández-Armesto's *Food: A History* (2001); also see the edited volume by Jean-Louis Flandrin and Massimo Montanari, *Food: A Culinary History* (1999). Both of these books are the work of thoughtful historians who treat food as a serious topic for study and theoretical elaboration. Neither, however, addresses Africa as a cultural or geographic context except as a Mediterranean periphery.

Reading between the lines, a historian of Africa offers some insights into where Africa ought to fit and where we might expect new writing to appear. But at times writers about food just get it wrong: Linda Civitello's *Cuisine and Culture: A History of Food and People* (2004) argues, for example, that "much of modern African cuisine is the colonial cuisine that Europeans forced upon African in the 19th century."[2]

This comment suggests not so much a thoughtful conclusion but the dearth of serious literature on African cooking, a lack of culinary curiosity, and, more seriously, a failure to consult the historical record.

Of recent popular literature on food, the work that offers the most open-ended potential approaches to Africa's inclusion in culinary writing on history are journalist Michael Pollan's provocative books *The Botany of Desire* (2001) and *The Omnivore's Dilemma: A Natural History of Four Meals* (2006) because he sees food and cooking as a historical process, networks of food ingredients, that reflects wider trends of human action at a global level. Though he does not focus on Africa in any way, Pollan's writing on nature, human tastes, and the sensual at least invites the kinds of questions raised in this chapter. New writing on African foods and taste is likely to reflect some of his approaches.

Let us look more closely at food/cooking as a component of the study of Africa as a whole. Writing about African foodways, cooking, and links between household pots and farmers' fields is at a very early stage. For analysis of African cookery we need to look back at earlier ethnographic literature from anthropology, the study of food/cookery as an aspect of the material culture of particular African societies. For most of the continent that means the twentieth century. Food and cooking as culture and as a marker of cultural identity in world societies has more often concerned social anthropology than history. In the anthropology of diet in Africa, Audrey Richards's work stands out. In her 1939 work of classic Manchester School ethnography, *Land, Labour, and Diet in Northern Rhodesia: An Economic Study of the Bemba Tribe*, Richards was the first to present serious evidence about cooking techniques, ingredients, and the sensibilities of African women about the mechanics of cooking and the meaning of food. As a young woman anthropologist in a field of study at that time dominated by men, Richards began to explore an unusual approach to social anthropology by observing woman as the managers of nutrition and, then, cooking it. Her work showed clearly that what one African people—the Bemba of northern Rhodesia—ate changed radically over the year depending on the patterns of rain, movements of livestock, and Africa's peculiar wet/dry oscillations. *Land, Labour, and Diet in Northern Rhodesia* was to become a classic in social anthropology and in the field of food studies as a whole.

Richards became the best-known scholar on an African people's diet, but she was not the first to do it in a systematic fashion. Almost a decade earlier, another woman had undertaken a systematic study of cooking in British West Africa. For the Akan region of West Africa's Gold Coast (part of the Kwa language complex) a valuable benchmark of the study of cuisine is the 1931 pamphlet "General Survey of Gold Coast Food" by the anthropologist and physician Margaret Field.[3] Hers is the first such published survey, though, obviously, it drew on a long-standing and deep body of oral knowledge among women of common households and royal courts in West Africa.

Field's systematic description of the Gold Coast catalogs forty-three distinctive preparations that she divides into categories of starchy foods, stews, protein foods other than meat or fish, fruits, and oil seeds and nut foods. Her survey is not a collection of recipes but a comprehensive list of food preparations. It thus serves as a benchmark that primarily reflects the everyday cuisine of the compounds and streets of the Gold Coast's southern areas and offers names of preparations in the local languages of Twi/Fante (Akan), Ga, and Ewe. It is worthy of note that each of the dishes had distinct names in each of these local languages. What Field observed and described in 1931 was, in essence, a snapshot of the historical cuisine of the forest/savanna/coastal political and cultural ecology of West Africa. Variations of the culinary palette are found in the cultures of Benin (Dahomey), Togo, Cote d'Ivoire, Sierra Leone, Senegal, and, especially, southwestern Nigeria, but they share the culinary nuances evident in the Gold Coast at the historical moment of 1931, recording local innovation and adaptation, as well as personal preferences. Though recorded by a European observer, Field's synchronic list clearly reflected historical layering, generational experience, and bodies of oral communication accumulated over time. Many of these were, notably, the urbanization of rustic preparations.

From more recent scholarly writing we can reconstruct the diet and foodways of other African domestic cultures. African societies adapted to seasonality in ways that reflected a food system with livestock (that is, meat) or fish as a greater part of the mix than with the Bemba diet that Richards tells us about in the midcolonial era of the 1930s. For another society further south, historian Diana Wylie has described the nineteenth-century Zulu diet, a local menu that she assembled from accounts of observers of the time. There was a clear rhythm of seasonality evident in her reconstruction, but with the subtle differences of a society where cattle were a more important symbolic and nutritional focus than in Bembaland:

The staples of the 19th century Zulu diet were fermented milk, cereals boiled as porridge, and cultivated vegetables, eaten twice daily, first after milking and then before sunset. Zulus spoke of solid and watery foods. People stored their food by fermenting in the form of thick sour milk (*amazi*) and sorghum beer. Sour milk—extraordinarily rich in cream where the cattle graze on long grass, but low in yield after the calves had sucked—was ideally the basis of each of the two meals eaten daily. Only children drank fresh milk. Beer was a seasonal delight, the post-harvest reward for a good season's crops. People ate boiled or roasted maize every day, supplemented by pumpkins, beans, taro root, and sweet potatoes. The consistency of the porridges depended mainly on how coarsely the grain was ground and for how long it was boiled. When the grain and vegetable supply ran short in late winter and early spring, that is between June and August, people scoured the bush for wild spinaches (imfino), gathering greens perhaps three or four times a week in the spring, drying some leaves for winter meals when they might have to ration themselves to one daily meal. While looking for *imfino*, they could also hunt for bitter herbs to help their stomachs accommodate the radical shifts in diet brought by the changing seasons. Meat was rarely served.... By products of a slaughtered beast produced highly prized dishes of fatty dumplings and sausages and congealed blood. Only at such time and few others did nondairy animal fat enter the Zulu diet.[4]

The Bemba diet of the 1930s and the nineteenth-century Zulu food culture were seemingly unremarkable and monotonous compared to Cape Town and the East African coastal ports—and those of Field's southern Gold Coast. However, both Bemba and Zulu diets were then undergoing change through contact with the wider world of neighboring people, economic forces, and European intruders.[5] Though southern African societies, like Zulu and Bemba, are quite different in cultural and economic terms, by the mid-nineteenth century their foods nevertheless included New World plants like maize and groundnuts, but not yet cassava (see the following). Both societies consumed maize not as a grain but as a vegetable snack in the milky green stage, and not yet as a rough-milled flour used in porridges. Millet (for Bemba) and sorghum (for Zulu) were the dominant grains historically, and as a rural people not yet drawn into an urban orbit, both the Zulu and Bemba cooks also had access to a natural world of wild plants, game, and seasonal insects. Locusts, ants, and caterpillars were treats that broke the seasonal monotony. The rural diet depicted by Richards's pioneering study and Wylie's more recent one was also distinct from an older maritime and cosmopolitan culinary culture of the coastal urban cultures of the Indian Ocean and Atlantic Rim, where fish, fruit, and spicy curries brought a wide variety of flavors to local diets.

In the early years of independence, and primarily in Africa itself, women in groups and as individuals in African capitals began to publish cookbooks that sought to capture some of the flavor of local cooking. Some, like Sierra Leonean Pamela Greene's *Favourite Sierra Leone Recipes* (Freetown, 1970), assembled a collection of the author's own cooking practice, including a version of jollof rice that contains "two small cans tomato puree," a sign of her accommodation to global food markets. Greene's book tells us that she is a "Nutritionist–Home Economist." She tells us that she wrote the cookbook because her husband "was kind enough to tell me that he enjoys my cooking."[6] Despite her Anglophone name, Greene was a Sierra Leonean Krio speaker. Her small pamphlet was available in Freetown but was never distributed to a regional or international audience. Another collection of recipes, this time published locally in Malawi by a committee of European women, included a fascinating mélange of missionary comfort foods adapted to local ingredients, curries from Indian Ocean influences, and precise directions for the proper preparation of Malawi's diverse insect and larva ecology.[7] Still other informal publications, often undated, marked cooking in Ghana, Nigeria, Kenya, Mozambique, and South Africa. Gretchen Walsh, at Boston University's African Studies Library, collected a large number of informally published and distributed African literature on cooking. Those volumes, many undated, appear in the bibliography of this chapter. They are also listed in Boston University's Mugar Library online catalog.

After Richards's and Field's studies we had to wait more than a full generation for work on Africa that addressed food/cuisine as a topic. For Africa, the classics are Jack Goody's *Cooking, Cuisine, and Class: A Study in Comparative Sociology* (1982) and Jane Guyer's *Feeding African Cities: A Study in Regional Social History* (1987).

While both of these books are wonderful comparative studies and required reading for any would-be anthropologist of Africa, neither one directly engages the issue of food as either cooking or cultural knowledge. Guyer's edited volume treats the issue of urban food supply, not in cooking or cuisine, but its overall supply as a commodity. Its chapters, nonetheless, make important connections between urbanization and markets that lay a foundation for the commercialization of cooked food and women's entrepreneurship noted by writers a decade later. Goody, for his part, explicitly, and astonishingly, dismisses the idea of an African cuisine altogether. His point is that only certain societies actually had an elaborated food/cooking culture; he associated those societies that produced a cuisine with the technologies of the plow and literacy (such as Sudan and Ethiopia). His choice of northern Ghana as a research site prefigures his conclusion about African cuisine in general (or the absence of it) since he sought to find an economically isolated and small-scale ethnographic site that lay outside of the vibrant urban contexts that both Field and Guyer described.

In contrast to the insights into the diets and food cultures of particular ethnic groups or cooking itself, other studies of food commodities have taken a broader geography of particular key staples. Judith Carney's *Black Rice: The African Origins of Rice Cultivation in the Americas* (2001) traces not only the cultivation of rice in the Atlantic world but also the spread of particular African cooking techniques into Carolina and Caribbean pots. For maize, the most widespread cooked staple in Africa of the twentieth century, my *Maize and Grace: Africa's Encounter with a New World Crop, 1500–2000* (2005), tells of the spread of the crop, first as a vegetable and curiosity, and then as Africa's most widely produced ingredient in what African cooks and consumers describe variously as *miele pap* (South Africa, Lesotho), *ugali* (Kenya, Tanzania, Uganda), *sadza* (Zimbabwe), *bidia* (Congo), *gunfo* (Ethiopia), *xima* (Mozambique), *nsima* (Zambia, Malawi), and boiled maize porridge that Italians would call polenta. While neither of these books focuses primarily on cooking, they both suggest the importance of starchy staples as the major components of African meals. To rice and maize, we would also need to include *matooke* (plantain—boiled, fried, or pounded into flour), tubers (yams, cassava or manioc, potatoes, taro, ensete), grains (finger millet, sorghum, barley, wheat), peppers, squash, beans (including pigeon peas and cowpeas), and oil seeds. These key ingredients for African cooks appear in recipes and crop lists as imports or indigenous food types. *The Cambridge World History of Food* (2000), edited by Kiple and Ornelas, does a fine job of describing the origins, dissemination, and characteristics of these foods as ingredients of African cooking, though it says less about techniques and local variations. After all, it is the subtleties of the cook and the combinations of texture and flavor that differentiate the regions, ethnicity, and seasons that mark African culinary history.

In the mid-1980s food and cuisine emerged more fully into scholarly literature on Africa's history and culture. The most powerful and readable influence was Sidney Mintz (an anthropologist of the Caribbean) whose popular and pathbreaking monograph *Sweetness and Power* (1985) traced the role of sugar in the tropical societies that produced it and the global markets that obsessively consumed it. *Sweetness and Power* was not directly focused on Africa, but in many ways Mintz's work was the precursor to books that traced the history of single commodities as markers of globalized food consumption, including Africa.[8] A decade later, Mintz more fully explored the idea of food, cooking, and culture in his *Tasting Food, Tasting Freedom: Excursions into Eating, Culture, and the Past* (1996).

In the 1980s and 1990s, writing about Ghana has actually done the best job telling us what African cooking means, and it puts Field's compendium into its full social context. Claire Robertson's Herskovits Prize–winning book *Sharing the Same Bowl* (1984) is told via participant observation about women's lives and food in Accra as a window into both history and society. A decade later, Gracia Clark's *Onions Are My Husband* (1994) tells about both the meaning of cooking in modern society in Ghana and its implications for women's domestic strategies and marital sexuality. Those two works offered a glimpse of the social (and sexual) context of the recipes that we find in those compiled cookbooks that we occasionally find in bookshops in Africa's capital cities and on the shelves of used bookstores in London or East Lansing.

The best writing on African cooking and cuisine comes in the form of continent-wide presentations. The first and most visible of these was Laurens Van der Post's 1970 *African Cooking* in the Time-Life series, which attempted an impressively glossy set of recipes from Ethiopia, Ghana, Angola, and Mozambique; a large section on white South African *braai* (barbecue); and Cape Malay dishes of game pie, rock lobster, and pickled fish. More recently, Fran Osseo-Asare's book *Food Culture in Sub-Saharan Africa* (2005) is geographically comprehensive, suggesting common elements of regional cooking while conveying the depth of her knowledge of West Africa in particular.

More recent books on African cooking come out of interest in African American cultural history or out of an engagement with the African diaspora, or with diaspora cooking itself. Jessica Harris is probably the most widely read writer on African cooking; her goal is to present a comprehensive list of recipes with a decidedly West African tilt. *The Africa Cookbook: Tastes of the Continent* (1998) shares her personal journey, understandably, rather than a historian's search for meaning. Vertamae Smart-Grosvenor's writing on diaspora cooking, *Vibration Cooking*, adds a powerful measure of passion into the idea of cooking and African influence on black folk in North America. Poet Amiri Baraka's somewhat obscurely placed article on soul food traces a foundational component of food as identity within the black power movement. He does not write about recipes or techniques, but his lists of food preparations helped to establish soul food as a cultural marker. A more recent and fascinating study of African American diets and culinary geography is Robert Dirks and Nancy Duran's article "African American Dietary Patterns at the Beginning of the Twentieth Century" in the *Journal of Nutrition* (2001), which compares local foodways among African Americans living in different parts of the United States in the half century after the abolition of slavery.[9] While neither of these works specifically identifies African origins of African American cooking/cuisine, the evidence they offer of the foods themselves relates closely to Louisiana Creole cuisine, including jambalaya.[10] The newest writing on African cooking aesthetics comes from Africans who have immigrated in recent years to Europe and the United States and bring with them ideas of fusion now seen in a number of restaurants in major cities and university towns. The most influential of these writings has probably been Marcus Samuelsson's *The Soul of a New Cuisine: A Discovery of the Foods and Flavors of Africa* (2006). Samuelsson was born in Ethiopia, adopted by Swedish parents, and later emigrated to New York. His book takes readers on a virtual tour of African cooking via fusion recipes like "Trout with Spinach Sauce," "Harissa-Roasted Turkey Breast," and "Berbere-Crusted Rack of Lamb." His is a hip, globalized version of Van der Post's 1970 Time-Life volume.

In Africa itself there are many new examples of cookbooks as markers of a new middle class conscious of culinary roots and modern political identities. One such example is Bomme Basemzanzi, *South African Indigenous Foods: A Collection of Recipes of Indigenous Foods, Prepared by Generations of Women* (2004), a collection of quite simple regional recipes from women in South Africa that emphasizes local ingredients and basic staple grains (and almost no spice flavorings). This book offers recipes but virtually no analysis of the historical or ecological contexts for those foods.

Some of the most important treatments of food as an economic and social phenomenon are studies of foundational staple commodities that provide the texture and calories of African cooking across the continent. Some of those are classic economic studies of manioc (cassava), maize, and African staple crops.[11] More recently, studies of Africa's staple crops have more fully developed their social, political, and culinary contexts. Carney's book *Black Rice* has provided a pathbreaking insight into Africa's contributions to the techniques and substance of rice production that links the farmer to the trader to the cook. It also gives us the idea of cooking as a form of knowledge, and women's knowledge, at that. The subsequent work *In the Shadow of Slavery: Africa's Botanical Legacy in the Atlantic World* (2009), on food knowledge in the Atlantic world, coauthored by Carney and Richard Rosomoff, takes us even further. My own book, *Maize and Grace: Africa's Encounters with a New World Crop* (2005), explores maize's movement from fields to pots, and from its initial role as a vegetable garden crop to status as a grain commodity crop and also as a transformative agent in the agroecology of disease landscapes (malaria). Both books build on the Atlantic circulation of crop knowledge and exchange that has its roots in Alfred Crosby's classic study of the post-Columbus Atlantic networks. In the spirit of Crosby's book and studies of the Atlantic world, Robert Hall's chapter in the edited volume *Seeds of Change: Five Hundred Years since Columbus* (1991) emphasizes the role of food as one of Africa's contributions.[12]

Anthropology has also led itself into studies of food that have moved away from cooking and that use food as a metaphor for social dislocation. Jon Holtzman's recent book *Uncertain Tastes: Memory, Ambivalence, and the Politics of Eating in Samburu, Northern Kenya* (2009) uses the foodways of a self-sufficient pastoral people as a measure of their own alienation from traditional social norms. For Holtzman, food is a measure of material culture change but is, more important, a metaphor for what the Samburu themselves understand as a descent from the culinary textures of pastoralist foodways (blood, meat, and sour milk) to *loshorro*, their version of the ubiquitous East African maize porridge also known as *ugali*. For Holtzman's Samburu friends, the maize that comes from food aid or marginal plots is "gray food," sustenance with little cultural meaning.

On the face of it, *Uncertain Tastes* does not fit neatly into the new literature on food, cuisine, and cooking. That writing tends to choose sides between understanding food as bulk, as a commodity that offers the fullness of the belly that Wylie emphasized for nineteenth-century South African Zulu in *Starving on a Full Stomach*, and understanding food/cooking as an aesthetic expression whose elaboration denotes rank, ethnic identity, erudition of knowledge, and social class.[13]

Understanding food and cuisine as an aesthetic expression allows the clustering of mutually intelligible culinary cultures that are inclusive and comparable across time and space. West Africa is an example of such a zone, where dishes like jollof rice and groundnut stew have local variations but a fundamental consistency across a wide geography. Carney and Rosomoff's book *In the Shadow of Slavery* recounts the astonishingly rich food endowments of the black Atlantic world; it is a story of richness rather than despair across a wide swath of cultures related by historical experience and ecology.[14] My own 2009 book *Stirring the Pot: A History of African Cuisine* shares Carney and Rosomoff's argument about the circulation of African culinary practice as prima facie evidence of historical and cultural change and a form of exchangeable knowledge, and it expands the argument to the continent as a whole and its wider diaspora. In this view the African story of food includes cooking as a woman's art that includes pungent spices, powdered capsicum, exotic oils, and overlapping maritime cultures. This take on the history and anthropology of food in Africa is exciting and cosmopolitan.

By contrast, Holtzman's Samburu tale of food as a marker of the loss of livelihood in an economically marginal zone tells of food as a marker of social and political dystopia. If many studies of African food/cuisine focus, rightly, on women as the keepers of knowledge, Holtzman offers an important alternative focus. He writes the Samburu's food story with a fine personal, and subjective, touch of a small geographical and culturally homogeneous area. He describes food in a pastoral culture that is in the process of losing its economic and material base. Among other aspects, he tells the reader about the lives and diet of bachelors, the *murran*, young men coming of age for whom "gray" foods are a marker of dislocation in a modern world in which they are more marginal than their antecedents, who lived in a world of pastoral abundance. Meals made of milk, blood, and meat are a memory; porridge made from store-bought maize meal is the reality.

Both lines of argument—food as fullness or food as aesthetic expression—make up parts of an exciting and growing literature on food in African studies. Holtzman's study of the meanings of food in Samburu society enlivens the ethnographic present in a way that is effectively delivered and clear in its descriptions of change in pastoral livelihoods. Contrast Carney's beautifully illustrated and broadly based book and Holtzman's analytical ethnography to an under-the-radar body of primary Africa-based documents—cookbooks produced and distributed by mission wives, middle-class literate African women, and diplomatic women living in African capitals in the postindependence period. The latter category is a still-underappreciated body of historical knowledge on certain places and certain communities collecting local foods and techniques.

A further body of writing that reveals the substance and meaning of food in Africa is in its rich modern literature that is not consciously historical. Food allusions in appear several times in Achebe's classic work *Things Fall Apart*. But there is, of course, much more. Chris Albani's *Graceland* ends each chapter with an Igbo (southeastern Nigeria) recipe, invariably one of his mother's. Osuman Sembene's films (Mandabi or Xala) feature eating as a recurrent theme of domestic life and urban dislocation. African women's writing (Buchi Emecheta's *The Joys of Motherhood* or Mariama Bâ's *So Long a Letter*) offers rich insights for studies of both history and literature. In their own way, each of these books and renderings of African culture, including recipe lists and cookbooks, can take the reader further into the deeper structures and meanings of Africa's traditions of cooking. I urge the reader to think of them as historical and to enjoy the results.

Notes

1. Tannahill, 1973, 317.
2. Civitello, 2004, 218.
3. Field, 1993, 7–21. Field's survey of foods predated Audrey Richards's study of Bemba diets by eight years.
4. Wylie, 2001, 44.
5. For description of the African maritime cuisines see McCann, 2009, 153–60.
6. Greene, 1970, 3, 6.
7. Shaxon, Dickson, and Walker, 1979. The recipes include black flying ants, green caterpillars, sand crickets, and lake flies (pp. 21–23).
8. See, for example, Kurlansky, 1997; Kurlansky, 2002. For an African case of food commodity history, see McCann, 2005.
9. Baraka, 1962; Dirks and Duran, 2001, 1882–84.
10. See McCann, 2009, 166–71.
11. The first generation of these studies was done by economists and includes W. Jones, 1959; Miracle, 1966; and Johnston, 1958.
12. Crosby, 1972; Hall, 1991, 161–72.
13. Wylie, 2001; Mintz, 1996; McCann, 2009; Stoller, 1989; Appadurai, 1988.
14. Carney and Rosomoff, 2009.

Conclusion: Contours of Global Food Historiography

Peter Scholliers and Kyri W. Claflin

The preceding chapters provide impressive evidence of the richness and variety of ideas, approaches, sources, methods, and theories that have shaped the writing of food history in the traditions that this volume represents. The rapid rise of interest in food history since the 1990s embraces all of the periods and places touched on by the authors, although not in equal measure. We are clearly in the midst of a period of fast-growing academic and nonacademic attention to the field of food history and food studies more generally. This volume provides a starting point for conceptualizing differences and similarities in the development of food history in different nations and regions worldwide. It suggests, as well, the value of thinking comparatively as we continue to research the history of food.

Four chapters of twelve deal with Europe, and thus this continent is well represented.[1] While this is likely due to multiple factors, it appears that the modern tradition of scholarly writing about the history of food began earlier in the West and that a greater number of historians and social scientists have studied questions of Western food history. In addition, the language of the book is English and the audience Anglophone, which reinforces a bias toward the West. We also see traditions that originated in the West appear as well in the chapters on East Asia, the Ottoman Empire and modern Turkey, and the Arab and Jewish scholarly traditions, as well as Latin America and the Iberian world. Food history writing on Africa and India is also influenced by Western research, albeit less directly. In the chapter on India, Krishnendu Ray notes, "Food studies, because of its genealogy in European scripts, is often too focused on Western national food cultures," thus implying that the weight of the West in this book is no coincidence. On the other hand, non-Western influence on Western food history writing is not completely absent. Importantly, the non-Western chapters elucidate the great potential for future research in regions that have been too little studied.

Global Food History: The Commonalities

What can we say about patterns in the current global enterprise of writing food history? The chapters demonstrate that the traditional historical method of archival research has been and continues to be vital to the way historians work and make new discoveries. We see that food historians have also incorporated new kinds of primary sources and new ways of analyzing source materials. All of the chapters reveal that writing food history has drawn on methods and theoretical frameworks from across disciplines. There are as well mutual influences between scholars inside academia and those who are not. Most chapters testify to the value of second- and third-language acquisition for the practice of food history. The compiled bibliography contains over 1,000 works in a dozen languages. Almost across the board, our understanding of how to think about the place of food in human societies began in social and economic history and has shifted significantly in the direction of the cultural. The cultural turn informs the dominant working paradigm today; however, the social, the economic, and the political have not been abandoned. Indeed, these other approaches play important roles in most cultural analyses of food in history.

The West

Western food historiography agrees with the chronological developments in history writing in general. It is impossible to assert whether food historiography lagged behind or was ahead of developments in overall historiography because of the many diverse fields and subfields that emerged in the course of past decades (e.g., gender studies, urban history, business history, and environmental history). Food historians, too, have been engaged in very diverse aspects of food, including consumer practices, commodity biographies, markets and trade, nutrition, obesity, famine, institutions of urban provisioning, agriculture, restaurant menus, and questions of taste and disgust. All this implies the importance of diverse sources, approaches, and methodologies to the field of food history. Because of these wide interests and ensuing inspirations, these chapters suggest that food historiography has always been very close to taking the lead in fresh approaches, exploration of new sources, or application of innovative methods in Western history writing *tout court*. Of course it must be said that there are food historians who have obstinately rejected new ways of thinking, notably the cultural turn. In this, too, our field is like many others. The legitimacy of some kinds of sources used by many food historians, such as cookbooks or menu cards, is considered questionable by traditionalists (one critique being the lack of representativeness of such documents).

With regard to Western food historiography, the socioeconomic and ethnographic approach of the first half of the twentieth century was succeeded by social history (1960s–1980s) until the cultural turn (1990s), which challenged ingrained ways of thinking about history. The new emphasis on culture, semiotics, and representations was accompanied by shifts in the kinds of subjects being investigated and shifts in sources, methods, and interpretations. During what might be considered the first stage of the historiography of food, pioneers introduced the subject into academic history; socioeconomic historians Eileen Power and Marc Bloch, writing on medieval Europe, and Richard Cummings, writing on the United States, were among them. However, the influence of these pioneers was constrained by their small number. References in the 1960s, 1970s and early 1980s reflect the somewhat homogeneous influences of the French-based *Annales* school of history and its attention to history from below, quantification, and, later, *mentalités*. (Of course, the *Annales* style of social history was the result, to some degree, of the efforts of the pioneers.) *Annales* influence is not evident only in the four chapters on Europe and the one on the United States;[2] it emerges as well in the chapters on the Ottoman Empire and Turkey, the Iberian world, the Arab world, and East Asia. In the chapters on Europe and the United States there are references to, for example, Fernand Braudel, Georges Duby, Pierre Goubert, Jean-Jacques Hémardinquer, Paul Veyne, and Roland Barthes. In the non-European chapters, most mentions are simply to the *Annales* school, although particular *Annalistes* appear (e.g., Maxime Rodinson and Clifford Wright in the Arab chapter,[3] and François Chevalier and Ruggiero Romano in the chapter on Latin America). This does not mean that all food history writing in Europe made the *Annales* social turn in the 1960s, which is shown, for example, by the success of the emic approach of *Alltagsgeschichte* in the 1970s and 1980s.[4]

The 1990s cultural turn of Western food historiography was "prepared" by *Annalistes* of the so-called third generation, but it was particularly inspired by nonhistorians. With regard to the former, the chapters refer to Roger Chartier, Jean-Louis Flandrin, and Steven L. Kaplan, for example; with regard to nonhistorians, the works of Mary Douglas, Clifford Geertz, Claude Lévi-Strauss, Stephen Mennell, and Sidney Mintz receive numerous mentions in this book.[5] Sociologists, geographers, anthropologists, and ethnologists appear quite frequently in Western food historiography,[6] which demonstrates its multidisciplinary attitude. Yet two historians take the lead in the top-five cited authors in the book: Jean-Louis Flandrin (thirteen times) and Massimo Montanari (ten times). This is largely due to their pathbreaking co-edited volume *Histoire de l'alimentation*,[7] but also to their prolific output prior to and after this watershed publication. Yet their work is decidedly European; the chapters on the Iberian world, North America, East Asia, India, and the Ottoman Empire do not cite *Histoire de l'alimentation*.[8]

The preeminence of cultural and sociocultural approaches in present-day Western food historiography is reflected in the large and varied group of researchers that are referenced in the book. However, this group, so it seems at present, is without *maîtres-penseurs*. Each chapter on European and North American food history indeed quotes a quite varied group of people currently writing food history. Still, in each chapter some particular authors are prominent: with regard to antiquity, Andrew Dalby, Martin Pitts, Robin Nadeau, and Paul Erdkamp; with regard to the Middle Ages, Bruno Laurioux, Ernst Schubert, Trude Ehlert, and Johanna Maria van Winter; with regard to early modern Europe, Ken Albala, Joan Thirsk, Sara Pennell, and Emma Spary; with regard to modern Europe, Peter Atkins, Alessandro Stanziani, and

James Vernon; and with regard to North America, Warren Belasco, Roger Horowitz, Amy Trubek, and Hasia Diner. What seems to connect these authors, despite their very different interests in periods, approaches, and subjects, is their attention to the careful reading of a great diversity of sources and a greater emphasis on constructivism rather than seeking the truth of the past.

In American and European food history, consumerism currently holds the attention of a great many scholars. Despite this and other similarities, particular interests appear on each continent. North American food historiography, for example, developed with specific attention to food abundance (David Potter's *People of Plenty*) and its corollaries (overeating, anorexia, countercultural food movements). This seems to concur with Harvey Levenstein's two monographs on America's culture of copious eating (i.e., quantity in preference to quality), as well as with books (Michael Pollan) and movies (Morgan Spurlock) that criticize this culture. In Europe, the focus on culinary culture is related to diversity and identity. This showed up, for example, in a book published by the Council of Europe on the occasion of the fiftieth anniversary of the European Cultural Convention, in which forty countries were presented via food.[9]

Do non-Western researchers influence European and North American authors? This influence does not appear in the chapters on European and North American food history writing. An author like Arjun Appadurai, for example, who plays a significant role in non-Western food historiography, is not mentioned in the chapters on Europe and the United States. This absence here does not mean, however, that North American and European researchers do not use the concepts or insights of non-Western researchers. For example, in 1940 Fernando Ortiz launched the notion of transculturation (the mutual influence of encounters), which today appears regularly in studies of Western food history.[10] Appadurai himself is frequently cited in food histories of Europe and America. Amartya Sen's concept of food entitlement and famine has had a significant impact on European food history writing.[11]

The Non-*West*

The presence of Western historical views and of Western authors in the chapters on East Asia, the Ottoman Empire and Turkey, the Arab world, and the Iberian world clearly does not imply that there are no typical traits of food history writing in these parts of the world. Apart from the influence of particular Westerners (noted in the following), *Annales*, and the cultural turn (which had a dissimilar impact in each region with regard to rhythm and intensity), food history writing on each of these regions developed its own characteristics. Food historiography on Latin America shows a huge interest in (at times fiercely antagonist) interactions of different food regimes and classifications to which the work by Alfred Crosby and Fernando Ortiz is linked. This interest in exchanges entailed attention to fusion cuisines, which contributed to the debate on assimilation, acculturation, and bottom-up/trickle-down innovation (e.g., Marcy Norton), and, in turn, features questions about identity and about politics (e.g., Rebecca Earle or Natalia Milanesio). Recently, Chinese, Japanese, and Korean food historiography keenly rediscovered "traditional" food (e.g., Stephanie Assmann), which follows a new interest in cultural contexts (e.g., Wu Jenshu) and in anthropology, as shown by Chiu P.-s. on material culture in everyday life in China, or Chu Yong-ha on food representations in paintings in South Korea. This came after a period of skyrocketing attention to food history since about 1980, which had primarily led to the collection of large amounts of data without much analysis or interpretation. Just like in China, food historiography on the Ottoman Empire and Turkey has paid much attention to the origins of present-day food culture. This implied knowledge of different languages, religious rules, and ethnic cuisines. Current investigation focuses largely on elite cookbooks and court cuisine (e.g., Tülay Artan, Suraiya Faroqhi and Christoph Neumann, Özge Samancı), which reveals an interest in the multicultural aspect of Turkish cuisine (e.g., Sula Bozis, 2000). Reading Samancı's chapter in connection to the chapter on food in the Arab world reveals similarities as well as differences with regard to approaches and focus. Arab food historiography seems to be in need of more attention from within the Arab world (going through "an isolated growth," in the words of Nawal Nasrallah), although the research by Orientalists (e.g., Arthur Arberry and Maxime Rodinson[12]) pays attention to the role of the Arab world in the transcultural exchanges between the Far East and Europe (in particular, Andalusia, with research by David Waines and Manuela Marin). Still, although national or local sentiments are palpably present in the Arab world today, food studies have so far not contributed to constructing identities as it has done in the case of modern Turkey.

The chapter on Africa (in this book, actually sub-Saharan Africa) poses even more problems of grabbing common features with regard to global food historiography: after all, this continent has a myriad of languages and cultures. More seriously, written sources are largely lacking. It is no surprise that anthropologists' research (Audrey Richards and Margaret Field in the 1930s, and Jack Goody and Jane Guyer in the 1980s) is of great importance. Just as it was with food history writing on the Ottoman Empire and Turkey, the Arab world, and East Asia, the 1980s saw the proliferation of research on Africa, in which Mintz's and Crosby's works opened the way for other scholars (e.g., Fran Osseo-Asare on West African food).[13] As was also the case with Arab cuisine, American researchers studied the history of the diaspora of sub-Saharan African food (e.g., Vertamae Smart-Grosvenor's *Vibration Cooking*, 1992). Recently, African consciousness of regional culinary traditions has emerged, as evidenced in the publishing of local cookbooks. Paradoxically, food history writing on Africa now presents two distinct features: attention to starvation, inequality, and failure on the one hand, and to food as an aesthetic expression on the other.

The case of Jewish food historiography is very particular because of the duality between text-oriented historians and "sociologists," the former dealing primarily with religion and prescriptions, the latter with modern developments and actual consumption.

Yet both groups are influenced by methods of literary criticism, and both pay great attention to sentiments of belonging. More than with regard to historians' role in other regions, scholars who research Jewish food history contribute to the ongoing construction of Jewish identity. This chapter also touches on transgression, acculturation, and negotiating interactions, which appear in most other chapters of this book.

In India, food history writing circumvented, so to speak, the *Annales* approach when budging from political economy (particularly, hunger and the riposte, the so-called green revolution) in the 1970s to cultural studies in the 1980s. Rather than Braudel, sources of inspiration were Ravindra Khare and Arjun Appadurai. A growing trend regards the cultural-aesthetic dimension of food, which addresses issues of commensality, intimacy, and, particularly, public eateries (Frank Conlon's 1995 "Dining Out in Bombay" being a forerunner). In general, this trend focuses on urban spaces and middle classes, which is a shift away from the previous heavy emphasis on rural communities. Importantly, in India as in the chapters on the Arab world and Africa, the question of the diaspora in relation to postcolonial identity also comes to the fore.

There are more common features between food history writing on India, the Arab and Jewish worlds, and Africa. First, food research broke through thoroughly in the 1970s, although there were predecessors in each region prior to 1960. Second, in all regions Westerners contributed to this success, either directly or indirectly. Third, just like in other regions of the world, food researchers became fully aware of their own regions and their culinary habits (whether of recent making or not). And, finally, surveying the chapters on Africa, India, and the Arab and Jewish worlds, it becomes very clear that transcultural exchanges are, more than ever, part of local foodscapes.

Writing Food History: The Future

According to the authors in this book, the future of food historiography is definitely interdisciplinary. The fortune of working with insights from other disciplines and, primarily, of having sociologists, anthropologists, geographers, and representatives of many other disciplines working on the history of food is an unquestionable luxury. The interdisciplinarity of food will continue to offer historians fruitful theoretical frameworks and diverse methodologies. Historians writing about food contribute to the interdisciplinary endeavor an emphasis on temporality and on historical context as indispensable for understanding change.

Some of the chapters note that issues of food and identity construction are still in need of further research. Questions about identity include the national, transnational, regional, and urban perspectives as well as class, religion, and gender. A related theme is the diffusion of culinary culture. Diffusion has introduced debates, including the influence of Arabic cuisine on medieval European cooking. Continued investigation of culinary influences is needed in all time periods as there has been continual movement of people, ideas, and goods. The essays also note that the areas of science, medicine, food politics and policy, and social hierarchies need further study. The authors recognize the value of using new methods more extensively for researching consumption of food in many times and places, including material culture, archaeology, and unconventional historical texts (such as cookbooks).

This volume has considered the question "How has the history of food been studied?" from a global perspective. We may recall a more basic question from the Introduction: "Why study the history of food?" The authors here say, in their different ways, that food tells us who we are and even who we want to be. The history of food puts such inquiries into context, showing us the great variety of social, cultural, and material reasons how and why we are also what our ancestors ate.

Notes

1. This book does not cover some parts of the world (such as Russia and Australia), where food historiography may be well developed.
2. Forster and Ranum, 1979.
3. Wright refers directly to Braudel's *histoire totale* in writing his *Mediterranean Feast* (1999).
4. Teuteberg, 2008.
5. Sociologists Pierre Bourdieu, Carole Counihan, and Alan Warde, for example, are hardly mentioned in this book, which may appear strange in light of their work on everyday social hierarchies, identity and gender, and eating (out) habits.
6. This assertion is based on the total number of citations that appear in this book (about 1,260 titles). S. Mintz comes first (with 8 mentions), followed by M. Douglas (5), P. Ferguson (3), J. Goody (3), C. Lévi-Strauss (3), C. Geertz (3), S. Mennell (2), and G. Wiegelmann (2). Naturally, these authors may be cited more than appears from this little bibliometric exercise; for example, work by S. Mintz is referred to fifteen times in eight chapters of this book (which means that his *Sweetness and Power* or other writing not only appears in various chapters but also is cited several times in one or more chapters). Moreover, some authors are mentioned in chapters of this book, without a bibliographic reference (including Norbert Elias, Jürgen Habermas, Daniel Miller, Michel Foucault, and Jack Goody).
7. Flandrin and Montanari, 1996. Some of our authors denounce the Eurocentric approach of *Histoire de l'alimentation*, which contributes to the number of times it is mentioned.
8. The chapter "Les Occidentaux et les autres," however, addresses the contacts/confrontations between European and "non-European" food.
9. Goldstein and Merkle, 2005.
10. E.g., Bröck, 2008, who compares food magazines on both sides of the Atlantic in search for signs (the food) and metasigns (the narratives on food) (following Barthes).

Bibliography

Abad, R. 2002. *Le grand marché.* Paris: Fayard.

'Abd al-'Azeez, N. 1957. *Al-Matbakh al-Sultani Zaman al-Ayyubeen wa 'l-Mamaleek.* Cairo: Maktabat al-Anglo al-Misriyya.

Abusch-Magder, R. 2002. "Eating 'Out': Food and the Boundaries of Jewish Community and Home in Germany and the United States." *Nashim: A Journal of Jewish Women's Studies & Gender Issues* 5: 53–82.

Achaya, K. T. 1998. *Indian Food: A Historical Companion.* Delhi: Oxford University Press.

Adachi, I. 1962. *Nihon shokumotsu shi gaisetsu* [Outline of Japanese food history]. Tokyo: Ishiyaku shuppan.

Adams, N., and Smith, B. G., eds. 2001. *History and the Texture of Modern Life: Selected Essays of Lucy Maynard Salmon.* Philadelphia: University of Pennsylvania Press.

Adams, R. 1986. "The Egregious Feasts of the Chester and Towneley Shepherds." *Chaucer Review* 21: 96–107.

Adamson, M. W. 2000. *Buch von guter Speise, Daz buch von guter Spise: The Book of Good Food: A Study, Edition and English Translation of the Oldest German Cookbook.* Krems, Austria: Medium Aevum Quotidianum.

Adamson, M. W. 2002. *Regional Cuisines of Medieval Europe.* New York: Routledge.

Aguilar-Rodríguez, S. 2008. "Cooking Modernity: Food, Gender, and Class in 1940s and 1950s Mexico City and Guanajuato." PhD diss., University of Manchester.

Ahsan, M. 1979. *Social Life under the Abbasids.* London: Longman.

Ajinomoto. 2011. "Corporate Data." http://www.ajinomoto.com/about/corporatedata/index.html (accessed June 29, 2011).

Ajinomoto shoku no bunka sentā. n.d. http://www.syokubunka.or.jp/ (accessed April 20, 2011).

Ajinomoto shoku no bunka sentā. 2009. *Shoku no bunka 20nen no ayumi* [The 20-year progress of food culture]. Tokyo: Ajinomoto shoku no bunka sentā.

Ajmar-Wollheim, M., and Dennis, F., eds. 2006. *At Home in Renaissance Italy.* London: Victoria and Albert Publications.

Albala, K. 2002. *Eating Right in the Renaissance.* Berkeley: University of California Press.

Albala, K. 2007a. *The Banquet.* Chicago and Urbana: University of Illinois Press.

Albala, K. 2007b. *Beans: A History.* Oxford and New York: Berg.

Albala, K. 2007c. "The Use and Abuse of Chocolate in 17th-Century Medical Theory." *Food and Foodways* 15: 53–74.

Albala, K. 2009. "History on a Plate." *Historically Speaking* 10, no. 5: 6–8.

Albala, K., ed. 2011. *Food Cultures of the World Encyclopedia.* Westport, CT: Greenwood.

Alexandre, A., et al. 2010. "The Co-creation of a Retail Innovation: Shoppers and the Early Supermarket in Britain." *Enterprise & Society* 10, no. 3: 529–58.

Alexandre-Bidon, D. 2005. *Une archéologie du goût: Céramique et consommation (Moyen Âge–Temps modernes).* Paris: Picard.

Alexis of Piedmont. 1562. *The Secrets of the Reverend Maister Alexis of Piemont.* Translated by W. Warde. London: Rouland Hall.

Allan, T. 1994. "Food Production in the Middle East." In *A Taste of Thyme: Culinary Cultures of the Middle East.* Edited by S. Zubaida and R. Tapper. London: I. B. Taurus: 19–31.

Allen, G., Albala, K., and Nestle, M., eds. 2007. *The Business of Food: Encyclopedia of the Food and Drink Industries.* Westport, CT: Greenwood.

Allison, A. 1991. "Japanese Mothers and Obentōs: The Lunch Box as Ideological State Apparatus." *Anthropological Quarterly* 4: 195–208.

Alston, R., and Van Nijf, O., eds. 2008. *Feeding the Ancient Greek City.* Leuven, Belgium: Peeters.

Altıntaş, A. 2002. "Osmanlı Sarayı İçin Bursa'da Yaptırılan Turşu, Sirke ve Nar Ekşileri." In *Bursa Halk Kültürü Sempozyumu Bildiri Kitabı. Cilt I.* Bursa: Uludağ Üniversitesi: 91–109.

Amenda, L. 2009. "Food and Otherness: Chinese Restaurants in West European Cities in the 20th Century." *Food & History* 7, no. 2: 157–79.

Amigues, S. 2003. "Pour la table du Grand Roi." *Journal des savants* 1: 3–80.

Amigues, S. 2006. *Théophraste: Recherches sur les plantes. Livre IX.* Paris: Belles Lettres.

Anderson, B. 1991. *Imagined Communities: Reflections on the Origins and Spread of Nationalism.* Rev. ed. London: Verso.

Anderson, E. N. 1988. *The Food of China.* New Haven, CT: Yale University Press.

Anderson, E. N., and Anderson, M. L. 1973. *Mountains and Water: Essays on the Cultural Ecology of South Coastal China.* Taipei: Chinese Association for Folklore/Orient Cultural Service.

André, J. 1974. *L'Art culinaire.* Paris: Belles Lettres.

André, J. 1981. *L'Alimentation et la cuisine à Rome.* Paris: Belles Lettres.

André, J. 1985. *Les noms des plantes dans Rome Antique.* Paris: Belles Lettres.

Anwa' al-Saydala fi Alwan al-At'ima. 2003. Edited by 'Abdul Ghani Abu 'l-'Azm. Al-Dar al-Baydha': Matba'at al-Najah al-Jadida.

Aoyama, T. 2008. *Reading Food in Modern Japanese Literature.* Honolulu: Hawaii University Press.

Appadurai, A., ed. 1986. *The Social Life of Things: Commodities in Cultural Perspective.* Cambridge: Cambridge University Press.

Appadurai, A. 1988. "How to Make a National Cuisine: Cookbooks in Contemporary India." *Comparative Studies in Society and History* 30, no. 1: 3–24.

Appadurai, A. 1996. *Modernity at Large: Cultural Dimensions of Globalization.* Minneapolis: University of Minnesota Press.

Appadurai, A. 2003. "Public Culture." In *The Oxford India Companion to Sociology and Social Anthropology.* Edited by V. Das. Oxford: Oxford University Press: 654–74.

Appadurai, A., and Breckenridge, C. A. 1995. "Public Modernity in India." In *Consuming Modernity: Public Culture in a South Asian World.* Edited by C. A. Breckenridge. Minneapolis: University of Minnesota Press: 1–22.

Apple, R. 1987. *Mothers and Medicine: A Social History of Infant Feeding, 1890–1950.* Madison: University of Wisconsin Press.

Appleby, A. B. 1979. "Diet in Sixteenth-Century England: Sources, Problems, Possibilities." In *Health, Medicine and Mortality in the Sixteenth Century.* Edited by C. Webster. Cambridge: Cambridge University Press: 97–116.

Appleby, J., Hunt, L., and Jacob, M. 1994. *Telling the Truth about History.* New York: W. W. Norton.

Aradhna, A. V., Kandpal, V., Murry, B., and Saraswathy, K. N. 2010. "G6PD Deficiency and Haptoglobin Polymorphism among Gaddis of Palampur, Himachal Pradesh." *South Asian Anthropologist* 10, no. 2: 109–10.

Arberry, A. J. 1939. "Preface." In "A Baghdad Cookery-Book," by Muhammad bin al-Hasan bin al-Kareem al-Katib al-Baghdadi. *Islamic Culture* 13, no. 1: 21–47.

Arcondo, A. 2002. *Historia de la alimentación en Argentina: Desde los orígenes hasta 1920.* Córdoba, Spain: Ferreyra Editor.

Argunşah, M., and Çakır, M. 2005. *15. Yüzyıl Osmanlı Mutfağı Muhammed bin Mahmud Şirvani.* Istanbul: Gökkubbe.

Arnold, D. 1993. *Colonizing the Body: State Medicine and Epidemic Disease in Nineteenth Century India.* Berkeley: University of California Press.

Arnold, D. 1994. "The 'Discovery' of Malnutrition and Diet in Colonial India." *Indian Economic and Social History Review* 31, no. 1: 1–26.

Arnott, G. 2000. "Athenaeus and the Epitome." In *Athenaeus and His World: Reading Greek Culture in the Roman Empire.* Edited by D. Braund and J. Wilkins. Exeter, UK: University of Exeter Press: 39–52.

Aron, J.-P. 1976. *Le mangeur du XIXe siècle.* Paris: Laffont. Translated as *The Art of Eating in France.* London: Harper and Row, 1976.

Artan, T. 2000. "Aspects of the Ottoman Elite's Food Consumption: Looking for 'Staples', 'Luxuries' and 'Delicacies' in a Changing Century." In *Consumption Studies and the History of the Ottoman Empire 1550–1922.* Edited by D. Quataert. New York: State University of New York Press: 107–201.

Artan, T. 2011. "Ahmed I's Hunting Parties: Feasting in Adversity, Enhancing the Ordinary." In *Starting with Food: Culinary Approaches to Ottoman History.* Edited by A. Singer. Princeton, NJ: Markus Wiener: 93–138.

Ashkenazi, M., and Jacob, J. 1998. *The Essence of Japanese Cuisine: An Anthropological Essay into Food and Culture.* Richmond, UK: Curzon.

Assmann, S. 2010. "Reinventing Culinary Heritage in Northern Japan: Slow Food and Traditional Vegetables." In *Japanese Foodways Past and Present*. Edited by E. C. Rath and S. Assmann. Urbana: University of Illinois Press: 243–56.

Association for the Study of Food & Society (ASFS). n.d. "Food Studies Program List." http://www.food-culture.org/programs.php.

Atkins, P. 2010. *Liquid Materialities: A History of Milk, Science and the Law.* Farnham, UK, and Burlington, VT: Ashgate.

Atkins, P., Lummel, P., and Oddy, D., eds. 2007. *Food and the City in Europe.* Aldershot, UK: Ashgate.

Auberger, J. 2010. *Manger en Grèce classique.* Quebec, Canada: Presses de l'Université de Laval.

Audoin-Rouzeau, F., and Sabban, F., eds. 2007. *Un aliment sain dans un corps sain: Perspectives historiques.* Tours, France: Presses Universitaires François Rabelais.

Auslander, L. 1996. *Taste and Power: Furnishing Modern France.* Berkeley: University of California Press.

Austin, T. 1888. *Two Fifteenth-Century Cookbooks.* Early English Text Society, vol. 91. London: N. Trubner.

Avakian, A. V., ed. 1997. *Through the Kitchen Window: Women Explore the Intimate Meanings of Food and Cooking.* Boston: Beacon.

Aymard, M., Grignon, C., and Sabban, F. 1996. "Introduction." In "Food Allocation of Time and Social Rhythms." Special issue, *Food and Foodways* 6: 161–85.

Aynural S. 2001. *İstanbul Değirmenleri ve Fırınları Zahire Ticareti (1740–1840).* Istanbul: Tarih Vakfı Yurt Yayınları.

Ayora-Díaz, S. 2010. "Regionalism and the Institution of the Yucatecan Gastronomic Field." *Food, Culture & Society* 13: 397–420.

Baer, Yitzhak. 1968. *Yisra'el ba-amim: iyunim be-toldot yeme ha-bayit ha-sheni u-tekufat he-Mishnah uvi-yesodot ha-halakhah ve-ha-emunah.* Jerusalem: Mosad Byalik.

al-Baghdadi, Muhammad bin al-Hasan bin al-Kareem al-Katib. 1939. "A Baghdad Cookery-Book." Translated by A. J. Arberry. *Islamic Culture* 13, no. 1: 21–47; no. 2: 189–214.

al-Baghdadi, Muhammad bin al-Hasan bin al-Kareem al-Katib. 1964. *Kitab al-Tabeekh.* Reprint of Daoud Chelebi's 1934 edition. Beirut: Dar al-Kitab al-Jadeed.

al-Baghdadi, Muhammad bin al-Hasan bin al-Kareem al-Katib. 2001. *Kitab Wasf al-At'ima al-Mu'tada* (fourteenth-century augmented version of *Kitab al-Tabeekh*). Translated by C. Perry. In *Medieval Arab Cookery*, by M. Rodinson, A. J. Arberry, and C. Perry. Totnes, UK: Prospect Books: 275–465.

al-Baghdadi, Muhammad bin al-Hasan bin al-Kareem al-Katib. 2005. *A Baghdad Cookery Book.* Translated by C. Perry. Totnes, UK: Prospect Books.

Bahya Ben Asher Hlava. 2010. *Shulhan Shel Arba.* Translated by Jonathan Brumberg-Kraus. Wheaton College. http://acadblogs.wheatoncollege.edu/jbk/ (accessed January 30, 2012).

Bailyn, B. 1982. "The Challenge of Modern Historiography." *American Historical Review* 87, no. 1: 1–24.

Bak, S. 1997. "McDonald's in Seoul: Food Choices, Identity, and Nationalism." In *Golden Arches East: McDonald's in East Asia.* Edited by J. L. Watson. Stanford, CA: Stanford University Press: 126–60.

Bak, S. 2005. "From Strange Bitter Concoction to Romantic Necessity: The Social History of Coffee Drinking in South Korea." *Korea Journal* 2: 37–59.

Bak, S. 2010. "Exoticizing the Familiar, Domesticating the Foreign." *Korea Journal* 1: 110–32.

Bak-Geller Corona, S. 2009. "Los recetarios 'afrancesados' del siglo XIX en México: La construcción de la nación mexicana y de un modelo culinario nacional." *Anthropology of Food* S6 (December). http://aof.revues.org/index6464.html (accessed December 2010).

Balbi, M. 1999. *Los chifas en el Perú: Historia y recetas.* Lima, Peru: Universidad San Martín de Porres.

Bancroft, G. 1878. *History of the United States of America, From the Discovery of the American Continent.* Boston: Little, Brown.

Bancroft-Marcus, R. 2000. "A Dainty Dish to Set before a King." In *Athenaeus and His World: Reading Greek Culture in the Roman Empire.* Edited by D. Braund and J. Wilkins. Exeter, UK: University of Exeter Press: 53–69.

Banerjee, S. 1998. *The Parlor and the Streets: Elite and Popular Culture in Nineteenth-Century Calcutta.* Calcutta: Seagull Books.

Banerjee, S. M. 2004. *Men, Women, and Domestics: Articulating Middle-Class Identity in Colonial Bengal.* New Delhi: Oxford University Press.

Banerji, C. 1997. *Bengali Cooking: Seasons and Festivals.* London: Serif.

Banerji, C. 2006. *Feeding the Gods: Memories of Food and Culture in Bengal.* London and New York: Seagull Books.

Banerji, C. 2007. *Land of Milk and Honey: Travels in the History of Indian Food.* Oxford and New York: Seagull Books.

Banerji, C. 2008. *Eating India: Exploring the Food and Culture of the Land of Spices.* London: Bloomsbury.

Baraka, A. [LeRoi Jones]. 1962. "Soul Food." In *Home: Social Essays.* New York: Morrow: 121–23.

Barber, B. R. 1996. *Jihad vs. McWorld.* New York: Ballantine Books.

Barenblatt, D. 2004. *A Plague upon Humanity: The Secret Genocide of Axis Japan's Germ Warfare Operation.* New York: Harper Collins.

Barkan, Ö. L. 1962–1963. "Saray Mutfağının 894–895 (1489–1490) yılına ait muhasebe bilançosu." *İstanbul Üniversitesi İktisat Fakültesi Mecmuası* 22, no. 1–2: 380–98.

Barkan, Ö. L. 1964. "Edirne ve civarındaki bazı imaret tesislerinin yıllık muhasebe bilançoları." *Belgeler* 1: 235–377.

Barkan, Ö. L. 1971. "Süleymaniye Cami ve İmareti Tesislerine ait yıllık bir muhasebe bilançosu 993/994 (1585/1586)." *Vakıflar Dergisi* 9: 109–61.

Barkan, Ö. L. 1979. "İstanbul Saraylarına Ait Muhasebe Defterleri." *Belgeler* 9: 2–380.

Barker, H. 2009. "A Grocer's Tale: Gender, Family and Class in Early-Nineteenth-Century Manchester." *Gender & History* 21, no. 2: 340–57.

Barlösius, E. 1992. "The History of Diet as Part of the *vie matérielle* in France." In *European Food History: A Research Review.* Edited by H.-J. Teuteberg. Leicester: Leicester University Press, 90–108.

Barlösius, E. 1999. *Soziologie des Essens: Eine sozial- und kulturwissenschaftliche Einführung in die Ernährungsforschung.* Weilheim, Germany, and Munich: Juventa.

Barona, J. 2008. "Nutrition and Health. The International Context during the Inter-War Crisis." *Social History of Medicine* 21: 87–105.

Barron, J. 2011. "With Latest Donation, NYU Food Library Joins Big Leagues." *New York Times,* April 5. http://cityroom.blogs.nytimes.com/2011/04/05/with-latest-donation-n-y-u-food-library-joins-big-leagues/?scp=1&sq=Marvin%20Taylor&st=cse (accessed May 2011).

Barthes, R. 1970. "Pour une psycho-sociologie de l'alimentation contemporaine." In *Pour une histoire de l'alimentation.* Edited by J. J. Hémardinquer. Paris: Librairie Armand Colin: 307–15.

Barthes, R. 1979. "Toward a Psychosociology of Contemporary Food Consumption." In *Food and Drink in History.* Edited by R. Forster and O. Ranum. Baltimore: John Hopkins University Press: 166–73.

Basemzanzi, B. 2004. *South African Indigenous Foods: A Collection of Recipes of Indigenous Foods, Prepared by Generations of Women.* Pretoria, South Africa: IndiZAFoods.

Bauer, A. 1975. *Chilean Rural Society from the Conquest to 1930.* New York: Cambridge University Press.

Bauer, A. 2001. *Goods, Power, History: Latin America's Material Culture.* Cambridge: Cambridge University Press.

Baumann, N. 2008. " 'Sonnenlichtnahrung' versus gutbürgerliche Fleischeslust. Die richtige Ernährung im Spannungsfeld von Ernährungswissenschaft, Körpervermessung und Lebensreformbewegung im schweizerischen Raum zwischen 1890 und 1930." *Schweizerische Zeitschrift für Geschichte* 58, no. 3: 298–317.

Bayart, J. 2007. *Global Subjects: A Political Critique of Globalization.* Cambridge, UK: Polity.

Beard, C. A. 1913. *An Economic Interpretation of the Constitution of the United States.* New York: Macmillan.

Beer, M. 2010. *Taste or Taboo.* Totnes, UK: Prospect Books.

Bekker-Nielsen, T., ed. 2005. *Ancient Fishing and Fish Processing in the Black Sea Region.* Aarhus, Denmark: Aarhus University Press.

Belasco, W. J. 1989. *Appetite for Change: How the Counterculture Took On the Food Industry.* New York: Pantheon.

Belasco, W. J., and Horowitz, R., eds. 2009. *Food Chains: From Farmyard to Shopping Cart.* Philadelphia: University of Pennsylvania Press.

Belasco, W. J., and Scranton, P., eds. 2002. *Food Nations: Selling Taste in Consumer Societies.* London: Routledge.

Beldiceanu, N., and Beldiceanu-Steinherr, I. 1978. "Riziculture dans l'empire ottoman (XIVe–XVe siècle)." *Turcica Revue d'études turques* 9/2X: 9–28.

Belgrano, L. T. 1875. *Della vita privata dei Genovesi.* 2nd ed. Genoa, Italy: R. Istituto Sordo-Muti.

Bennet, J. 2010. *Vibrant Matter: A Political Ecology of Things.* Durham, NC: Duke University Press.

Benporat, C. 1996. *Cucina italiana del quattrocento.* Florence, Italy: Olschki.

Bentley, A. 1998. *Eating for Victory: Food Rationing and the Politics of Domesticity.* Urbana: University of Illinois Press.

Bentley, A. 2008. "Introduction." *Food and Foodways* 16: 111–16.

Berg, M. 1992. "The First Women Economic Historians." *Economic History Review* 45, no. 2: 308–29.

Berg, M. 1996. *A Woman in History: Eileen Power 1889–1940.* Cambridge: Cambridge University Press.

Berg, M., and Clifford, H., eds. 1999. *Consumers and Luxury.* Manchester, UK: Manchester University Press.

Berger, P. L. 1997. "Four Faces of Global Culture." *National Interest* 49: 23–29.

Bernabeu-Mestre, J., and Barona-Vilar, J., eds. 2008. "Nutrition and Health during the First Half of the 20th Century: A Spanish Perspective of Community Nutrition." *Food & History* 6, no. 1: 117–276.

Bertier, J. 1972. *Mnésithée et Dieuchès.* Leiden: Brill.

Bestor, T. C. 2004. *Tsukiji: The Fish Market at the Center of the World.* Berkeley: University of California Press.

Better Life Programme (Nigeria). 1990. *Plateau State, Traditional Dishes, Snacks, Drinks and Herbs from Plateau State.* Jos: Fab Anieh Nigeria.

Beye, A. K. n.d. *Etude de L'Art Culinaire Senegambien Traditionnel.* Vol. 1. Dakar, Senegal: Clairafrique.

Beyers, L. 2008. "Creating Home: Food, Ethnicity and Gender among Italians in Belgium since 1946." *Food, Culture & Society* 11, no. 1: 7–27.

Bhabha, H. K. 1994. *The Location of Culture.* London: Routledge.

Biarnès, M. 1978. *La cuisine sénégalaise.* Dakar, Senegal: Société Africaine d'Edition.

Bieleman, J., Buyst, E., and Segers, Y., eds. 2009. *Exploring the Food Chain: Food Production and Food Processing in Western Europe, 1850–1980.* Turnhout, Belgium: Brepols.

Bilgin, A. 2004. *Osmanlı Saray Mutfağı.* Istanbul: Kitabevi.

Bilgin, A., and Samancı, Ö., eds. 2008. *Turkish Cuisine.* Ankara: Turkish Ministry of Culture and Tourism.

Birlinger, A. 1865. "Ein alemannisches Büchlein von guter Speise." *Sitzungsberichte der Königlichen bayerischen Akademie der Wissenschaften zu München. Phil.- Hist. Kl.,* 2: 171–99.

Blau, E., et al. 1990. *Spice and Spirit: The Complete Kosher Jewish Cookbook.* Brooklyn: Lubavitch Women's Cookbook Publications.

Bloch, M. 1964. *Feudal Society.* 2 vols. Chicago: University of Chicago Press.

Bloisy, W., and Hoel, H. 2008. "Abusive Work Practices and Bullying among Chefs: A Review of the Literature." *International Journal of Hospitality Management* 28, no. 4: 649–56.

Blondé, B. 2005. "Cities in Decline and the Dawn of a Consumer Society, Antwerp in the 17th–18th Centuries." In *Retailers and Consumer Changes in Early Modern Europe: England, France, Italy, and the Low Countries.* Edited by B. Blondé et al. Tours, France: Presses Universitaires François-Rabelais: 37–52.

Blue, G. 1991. "Marco Polo et les pâtes." *Médiévales* 20: 91–98.

Bohstedt, J. 2010. *The Politics of Provisions: Food Riots, Moral Economy, and Market Transition in England, c. 1550–1850.* Burlington, VT: Ashgate.

Bokser, B. M. 1984. *The Origins of the Seder: The Passover Rite and Early Rabbinic Judaism.* Berkeley: University of California Press.

Bonnell, V. E., and Hunt, L., eds. 1999. *Beyond the Cultural Turn: New Directions in the Study of Society and Culture.* Berkeley: University of California Press.

Bookmann, H. 1996. "Süßigkeiten im finsteren Mittelalter: Das Konfekt des Deutschordenshochmeisters." In *Mittelalterliche Texte: Überlieferung, Befunde, Deutungen: Kolloquium der Zentraldirektion der Monumenta Germaniae Historica am 28.29. Juni 1996.* Edited by R. Schieffer. MGH Schriften, vol. 42. Hannover: Hahn: 173–88.

Boorstin, D. 1973. *The Americans: The Democratic Experience.* New York: Random House.

Borau, C. 1995. "*D'Aparellar de menjar:* Un altre receptari de cuina medieval en català." In *Ier Colloqui d'història de l'alimentació a la Corona d'Aragó, Edat Mitjana.* Lleida, Spain: Institut d'Estudis Ilerdencs: 2: 801–12.

Boston University Libraries. n.d. "Gastronomy Research Guide." http://www.bu.edu/ library/guides/gastronomy.html.

Bottéro, J. 1995. *Mesopotamian Culinary Texts.* Translated by J. Cooper. Winona Lake, IN: Eisenbrauns.

Boudreau, F. G. 1942. "Review of Cummings's The American and His Food." *American Journal of Public Health* 32, no. 4: 432.

Bourdieu, P. 1984. *Distinction: A Social Critique of the Judgement of Taste.* Cambridge, MA: Harvard University Press.

Bower, A., ed. 1997. *Recipes for Reading: Community Cookbooks, Stories, Histories.* Amherst: University of Massachusetts Press.

Bowie, E. 1986. "Early Greek Elegy, Symposium and Public Festival." *Journal of Hellenic Studies* 106: 13–35.

Boyer, P. 2001. "American Historiography." In *The Oxford Companion to United States History.* Edited by P. Boyer. Oxford: Oxford University Press. http://www. encyclopedia.com/topic/American_Historiography.aspx#2–1O119:Historiography American-full/ (accessed April 13, 2011).

Bozis, S. 2000. *İstanbul Lezzeti: İstanbullu Rumların Mutfak Kültürü.* Istanbul: Tarih Vakfı Yurt Yayınları.

Bradford, W. 1856. *History of Plimouth Plantation, 1650.* Edited by C. Deane. Boston: Massachusetts Historical Society.

Braudel, F. 1970. "Alimentation et catégories de l'histoire." In *Pour une histoire de l'alimentation.* Edited by J.-J. Hémardinquer. Paris: Librairie Armand Colin: 15–19.

Braudel, F. 1981. *The Structures of Everyday Life: Civilization and Capitalism, 15th–18th Centuries.* Vol. 1. New York: Harper and Row.

Braund, D., and Wilkins, J., eds. 2000. *Athenaeus and His World.* Exeter, UK: University of Exeter Press.

Braund, S. M. 1996. "The Solitary Feast: A Contradiction in Terms?" *Bulletin of the Institute of Classical Studies* 41: 37–52.

Breckenridge, C. A., ed. 1995. *Consuming Modernity: Public Culture in a South Asian World.* Minneapolis: University of Minnesota Press.

Breckenridge, C. A., et al., eds. 2002. *Cosmopolitanism.* Durham, NC: Duke University Press.

Breen, T. H. 2004. *Marketplace of Revolution: How Consumer Politics Shaped American Independence.* London: Oxford University Press.

Brejon de Lavergnée, M. 2007. "Alimentation populaire et secours charitables: L'exemple parisien (1840–1870)." *Food & History* 5, no. 2: 95–127.

Brenner, A., and van Henten, J. W., eds. 1999. "Food and Drink in the Biblical Worlds." Special issue, *Semeia: An Experimental Journal of Biblical Criticism* 86.

Brewer, J., and Porter, R., eds. 1993. *Consumption and the World of Goods.* London and New York: Routledge.

Briant, P. 1996. *Histoire de l'Empire perse.* Paris: Fayard.

Brillat-Savarin, J. A. 1999. *The Physiology of Taste or Meditations on Transcendental Gastronomy.* Translated by M.F.K. Fisher. Washington, DC: Counterpoint Press.

British Library. n.d. "Medieval Food." *Books for Cooks.* http://www.bl.uk/learning/ langlit/booksforcooks/med/medievalfood.html.

Brodnitz, G. 1928. "Bibliography: Recent Work in German Economic History (1900–1927)." *Economic History Review* 1, no. 2: 322–45.

Bröck, S. 2008. "Global Gourmets: Food Writing and its Fancies of Transculturation." In *Transcultural Visions of Identities in Images and Texts.* Edited by W. Raussert and R. Isensee. Heidelberg, Germany: Winter: 155–67.

Brothwell, D., and Brothwell, P. 1969. *Food in Antiquity.* Baltimore: Johns Hopkins University Press.

Brown, G. 2002. "Social Encounters and Self-Image in the Age of Enlightenment: Norbert Elias in Eighteenth-Century French Cultural Historiography." *Journal of Early Modern History* 6, no. 1: 24–51.

Brumberg, J. J. 1988. *Fasting Girls: The History of Anorexia Nervosa.* Boston: Harvard University Press.

Brumberg-Kraus, J. 1999a. "Meat-Eating and Jewish Identity: Ritualization of the Priestly Torah of Beast and Fowl (Lev 11:46) in Rabbinic Judaism and Medieval Kabbalah." *AJS Review* 24, no. 2: 227–62.

Brumberg-Kraus, J. 1999b. "'Not by Bread Alone...... ': The Ritualization of Food and Table Talk in the Passover Seder and in the Last Supper." *Semeia: An Experimental Journal of Biblical Criticism* 86: 165–91.

Brumberg-Kraus, J. 2001. "The Ritualization of Scripture in Rabbenu Bahya's *Shulhan Shel Arba.*" *World Congress of Jewish Studies* 13: 1–17. http://www.lekket. com/Site_ViewDocument.asp?id=913&idPage=1 (accessed July 24, 2011).

Brumberg-Kraus, J. 2005. "Meals as Midrash: A Survey of Ancient Meals in Jewish Studies Scholarship." In *Food and Judaism.* Edited by L. J. Greenspoon et al. Omaha and Lincoln: Creighton University Press/University of Nebraska Press: 297–317.

Brumberg-Kraus, J. 2010. "'Truly the Ear Tests Words as the Palate Tastes Food' (Job 12:11): Synaesthetic Food Metaphors for the Experience of the Divine in Jewish Tradition." In *Food and Language: Proceedings of the Oxford Symposium on Food and Cookery 2009.* Edited by R. Hosking. Totnes, UK: Prospect Books: 42–51.

Bruyérin-Champier, J. 1998. *L'alimentation de tous les peuples et de tous les temps jusqu'au XVI siècle.* Translated by Sigurd Amundsen. Paris: Intermédiaire des Chercheurs et Curieux. (Orig. pub. 1560.)

Buccheim, C. 2010. "Der Mythos vom 'Wohlleben': Der Lebensstandard der deutschen Zivilbevölkerung im Zweiten Weltkrieg." *Vierteljahrshefte für Zeitgeschichte* 58, no. 3: 299–328.

Buell, P. D., and Anderson, E. N. 2000. *A Soup for the Qan.* London: Kegan Paul International.

Buettner, E. 2008. "'Going for an Indian': South Asian Restaurants and the Limits of Multiculturalism in Britain." *Journal of Modern History* 80, no. 4: 865–901.

Bulgaru, A.-D., and Matilda, M. 1957. "Contribution à l'étude de l'approvisionnement en blé de Constantinople au XVIIIe siècle." *Studia et Acta Orientalia,* no. 1: 13–37.

Burke, P. 1978. *Popular Culture in Early Modern Europe.* New York: Harper Torchbook.

Burke, P. 1992. *The Fabrication of Louis XIV.* New Haven, CT: Yale University Press.

Burke, P. 2001. "The New History: Its Past and Its Future." In *New Perspectives on Historical Writing.* Edited by P. Burke. University Park: Pennsylvania State University Press: 1–24.

Burke, V. E., and Gibson, J., eds. 2004. *Early Modern Women's Manuscript Writing.* Aldershot, UK: Ashgate.

Burkert, W. 1977. *Griechische Religion.* Stuttgart, Germany: Kohlhammer. Translated by John Raffan as *Greek Religion.* Oxford: Blackwell, 1977.

Burkert, W. 1979. *Structure and History in Greek Mythology and History.* Berkeley: University of California Press.

Burnett, J. 2004. *England Eats Out 1830–Present.* London: Longman Pearson.

Bynum, C. W. 1987. *Holy Feast and Holy Fast: The Religious Significance of Food to Medieval Women.* Berkeley: University of California Press.

Bynum, C. W. 1991. *Fragmentation and Redemption: Essays on Gender and the Human Body in Medieval Religion.* New York and Cambridge, MA: Zone Books. Distributed by MIT Press.

Cadava, E., Connor, P., and Nancy, J.-L., eds. 1991. *Who Comes after the Subject?* London: Routledge.

Le café en Méditerranée. Histoire, anthropologie, économie, XVIIIe–XXe siécle. 1980. Aix-en Provence, France: Institut de recherches méditerranéennes— Groupement d'intérêt scientifique.

Calhoun, C. 2007. *Nations Matter: Culture, History, and the Cosmopolitan Dream.* London: Routledge.

Camargo da Heck, M. 1998. *Cozinha dos imigrantes: Memorias & recetas.* São Paulo, Brazil: DBA Melhoramentos.

Camp, C. 1982. "Foodways in Everyday Life." *American Quarterly* 34, no. 3: 278–89.

Camp, C. 1989. *American Foodways: What, When, Why and How We Eat in America.* Atlanta: August House.

Camporesi, P. 1989. *Bread of Dreams: Food and Fantasy in Early Modern Europe.* Cambridge, UK: Polity.

Capatti, A., and Montanari, M. 2003. *Italian Cuisine: A Cultural History.* Translated by Aine O'Healy. New York: Columbia University Press.

Carlin, M. n.d. Professor Martha Carlin's home page. https://pantherfile.uwm.edu/carlin/www/.

Carney, J. 2001. *Black Rice: The African Origins of Rice Cultivation in the Americas.* Cambridge, MA: Harvard University Press.

Carney, J., and Rosomoff, R. 2009. *In the Shadow of Slavery: Africa's Botanical Legacy in the Atlantic World.* Berkeley: University of California Press.

Castillero-Calvo, A. 1987. "Niveles de vida y cambios de dieta a fines del periodo colonial en América." *Anuario de Estudios Americanos* 44: 427–76.

Çevik, N., ed. 2000. *Hünkar Beğendi 700 Years of Culinary Culture: Ottoman Palace Cuisine.* Ankara: Kültür Bakanlığı Yayınları.

Chang, K. C., ed. 1977. *Food in Chinese Culture: Anthropological and Historical Perspectives.* New Haven, CT: Yale University Press.

Chartier, R. 1985. "Texts, Symbols, and Frenchness." *Journal of Modern History* 57, no. 4: 682–95.

Chastanet, M., Fauvelle-Aymar, F.-X., and Juhé-Beaulaton, D., eds. 2002. *Cuisine et société en Afrique: Histoire, saveurs, savoir-faire.* Paris: Éditions Karthala.

Chatterjee, P. 2001. *A Time for Tea: Women, Labor, and Post/Colonial Politics on an Indian Plantation.* Durham, NC: Duke University Press.

Chaudhuri, N. 1992. "Shawls, Jewelry, Curry and Rice in Victorian Britain." In *Western Women and Imperialism: Complicity and Resistance.* Edited by N. Chaudhuri and M. Strobel. Bloomington: Indiana University Press: 231–46.

Chaudhuri, N., and Strobel, M., eds. 1992. *Western Women and Imperialism: Complicity and Resistance.* Bloomington: Indiana University Press.

Chen, W.-m. 1993. *Tang song yinshi wenhua chutan* [Exploration of the dietary culture in the Tang and Song dynasties]. Beijing: Zhongguo shangye chubanshe.

Chen, Y. 2010. "Food as World History: Broadening the Horizon and Reach of Historical Research." *Journal of World History* 21, no. 2: 297–304.

Chen, Y.-j. 2010. "Embodying Nation in Food Consumption: Changing Boundaries of 'Taiwanese Cuisine' (1895–2008)." PhD diss., Leiden University.

Cheung, S.C.H., and Tan, C.-B., eds. 2007. *Food and Foodways in Asia: Resource, Tradition and Cooking.* London and New York: Routledge.

Chevalier, F. 1970. *Land and Society in Colonial Mexico: The Great Hacienda.* Edited by L. Byrd Simpson. Translated by A. Eustis. Berkeley: University of California Press.

Chiquart. 1986. *Chiquart's On Cookery, A Fifteenth-Century Savoyard Culinary Treatise.* Edited and translated by T. Scully. New York: P. Lang.

Chiu, C.-l. 2005. "Bingjiao, bingchuan yu bingxian: Mingdai yijiang jiangzhe de bingxian yuye yu haixian xiaofei" [Ice houses, frozen ships, and fresh seafood: The frozen fishery and seafood consumption in Jiangsu-Zhejiang China, 1368–1930s]. *Journal of Chinese Dietary Culture* 2: 31–95.

Chiu, P.-s. 2006. "Wuzhi wenhua yu richang shenghuo de bianzheng" [The dialectic of material culture and everyday life]. *New History* 4: 1–14.

Cho, L. 2010. *Eating Chinese: Culture on the Menu in Small Town Canada.* Toronto: University of Toronto Press.

Chŏng, H.-k., and Yi, C.-h. 1996. *Sŏul-e ŭmsik munhwa: Yŏngyanghak-kwa illyuka mannam* [The food culture of Seoul: Encounter between nutritional science and anthropology]. Seoul: Sŏulhak yŏn'guso.

Chu, Y.-h. 2005. *Kŭrimsok-e ŭmsik, ŭmsiksok-e yŏksa* [Food in paintings, history in food]. Seoul: Sagyejŏl ch'ulpansa.

Chung, H. 2009. *Korean Cuisine: A Cultural Journey.* Seoul: Thinking Tree.

Cinotto, S. 2001. *A Family That Eats Together: Food and Community in the Italian American Community of New York, 1920–1940.* Turin, Italy: Otto.

Cinotto, S. 2008. *Soft Soil, Black Grape: Labor, Social Captial, and Race in the Experience of Italian Winemakers in California.* Turin, Italy: Otto.

Civitello, L. 2004. *Cuisine and Culture: A History of Food and People.* Hoboken, NJ: Wiley.

Claflin, K. W. 2006. "Culture, Poltics, and Modernization in Paris Provisioning, 1880–1920." PhD diss., Boston University.

Claflin, K. W. 2007. "Le 'retour à la terre' après la Grande Guerre: politique agricole, cuisine et régionalisme." In *Gastronomie et Indentité Culturelle Française: Discours et représentations (XIX–XXI siècles)*. Edited by F. Hache-Bissette and D. Saillard. Paris: Nouveau Monde Editions: 215–37.

Claflin, K. W. 2008a. "Les Halles and the Moral Market." In *Food and Morality, Proceedings of the Oxford Symposium on Food and Cookery 2007*. Totnes, UK: Prospect Books: 82–92.

Claflin, K. W. 2008b. "La Villette: City of Blood (1867–1914)." In *Meat, Modernity, and the Rise of the Slaughterhouse*. Edited by P. Y. Lee. Lebanon, NH: University Press of New England: 27–45.

Claiborne, C. 1968. "Debut for a Series of International Cookbooks." *New York Times*, February 19: 46.

Claridge, A. 1999. *Rome*. Oxford: Oxford University Press.

Clark, A. 1919. *Working Life of Women in the Seventeenth Century*. London: G. Routledge & Son. Repr., 1982.

Clark, G. 1994. *Onions Are My Husband: Survival and Accumulation by West African Market Women*. Chicago: University of Chicago Press.

Clark, G. 1999. *On Abstinence from Killing Animals*. London: Duckworth.

Clark, S. 1983. "French Historians and Early Modern Popular Culture." *Past & Present* 100: 62–99.

Cleary, M. C. 1988. "French Agrarian History after 1750: A Review and Bibliography." *Agricultural History Review* 37: 65–74.

Clement, A. 1999. *Nourrir le peuple: Entre Etat et marché, XVI–XIX siècle*. Paris: L'Harmattan.

Coatsworth, J. 1976. "Anotaciones sobre la producción de alimentos durante el Porfiriato." *Historia Mexicana* 26: 167–87.

Coe, S. 1994. *America's First Cuisines*. Austin: University of Texas Press.

Coe, S., and Coe, M. 1996. *The True History of Chocolate*. London: Thames and Hudson.

Cohn, B. S. 1996. *Colonialism and Its Forms of Knowledge: The British in India*. Princeton, NJ: Princeton University Press.

Collingham, E. M. 2001. *Imperial Bodies: Physical Experience of the Raj, c.1800– 1947*. Cambridge: Polity.

Conlon, F. 1995. "Dining Out in Bombay." In *Consuming Modernity: Public Culture in a South Asian World*. Edited by C. Breckenridge. Minneapolis: University of Minnesota Press: 90–127.

Connolly, J. 2008. "Decentering Urban History. Peripheral Cities in the Modern World." *Journal of Urban History* 35, no. 1: 3–14.

Cook, S., and Borah, W. 1960. *The Indian Population of Central Mexico, 1531– 1610*. Berkeley: University of California Press.

Cook, S., and Borah, W. 1963. *The Aboriginal Population of Central Mexico on the Eve of the Spanish Conquest.* Berkeley: University of California Press.

Cook, S., and Borah, W. 1979. "Indian Food Production and Consumption in Central Mexico before and after the Conquest (1500–1650)." In *Essays in Population History: Mexico and California.* Edited by S. Cook and W. Borah. Berkeley: University of California Press: 129–77.

Cool, H.E.M. 2006. *Eating and Drinking in Roman Britain.* Cambridge: Cambridge University Press.

Cooper, J. 1993. *Eat and Be Satisfied: A Social History of Jewish Food.* Northvale, NJ: Jason Aronson.

Corbier, M. 1989. "The Ambiguous Status of Meat in Ancient Rome." *Food and Foodways* 3: 223–64.

Corcuera de Mancera, S. 1991. *Entre gula y templanza: Un aspecto de la historia mexicana.* 3rd ed. Mexico City: Fondo de Cultura Económica.

Corner, S. 2010. "Transcendent Drinking: The Symposium at Sea Reconsidered." *Classical Quarterly* 60: 352–80.

Corti, P. 1997. "Emigración y alimentación: Representaciones y autorrepresentaciones en la experiencia de una corriente migratoria regional italiana." *Estudios Migratorios Latinoamericanas* 12: 103–28.

Counihan, C., and Van Esterik, P. 1997. *Food and Culture: A Reader.* New York: Routledge.

Cowan, B. 2005. *The Social Life of Coffee: The Emergence of the British Coffeehouse.* New Haven, CT: Yale University Press.

Cowan, B. 2007. "New Worlds, New Tastes: Food Fashions after the Renaissance." In *Food: The History of Taste.* Edited by P. Freedman. Berkeley: University of California Press: 197–231.

Cressy, D. 1993. "Literacy in Context: Meaning and Measurement in Early Modern England." In *Consumption and the World of Goods.* Edited by J. Brewer and R. Porter. London: Routledge: 305–19.

Cronon, W. 1991. *Nature's Metropolis: Chicago and the Great West.* New York: Norton.

Cronon, W. 1992. "A Place for Stories: Nature, History, and Narrative." *Journal of American History* 78, no. 4: 1347–76.

Crosby, A. 1972. *The Columbian Exchange: Biological and Cultural Consequences of 1492.* Westport, CT: Greenwood.

Cross, H. 1978. "Living Standards in Nineteenth Century Mexico." *Journal of Latin American Studies* 10: 1–19.

Crowston, C. H. 2011. "Credit and the Metanarrative of Modernity." *French Historical Studies* 34, no. 1: 7–19.

Cummings, R. O. 1940. *The American and His Food: A History of Food Habits in the United States.* Chicago: University of Chicago Press.

Curren, P. 1989. *Grace before Meals: Food Ritual and Body Discipline in Convent Culture.* Urbana: University of Illinois Press.

Curtis, R. 1991. *Garum and Salsamenta.* Leiden: Brill.

Curtis, R. 2001. *Ancient Food Technology.* Leiden: Brill.

Cwiertka, K. J. 2005. "From Ethnic to Hip: Circuits of Japanese Cuisine in Europe." *Food and Foodways* 13, no. 4: 241–72.

Cwiertka, K. J. 2006a. *Modern Japanese Cuisine: Food, Power and National Identity.* London: Reaktion Books.

Cwiertka, K. J. 2006b. "The Soy Sauce Industry in Korea." *Asian Studies Review* 30: 389–410.

Cwiertka, K. J. Forthcoming. *Cuisine, Colonialism and Cold War: Food in Twentieth Century Korea.* London: Reaktion Books.

Cwiertka, K. J., and Walraven, B.C.A., eds. 2001. *Asian Food: The Global and the Local.* Honolulu: University of Hawaii Press.

da Camara Cascudo, L. 1967. *História da Alimentação no Brasil.* 2 vols. São Paulo, Brazil: Companhia Editora Nacional.

Dalby, A. 1993. "Food and Sexuality in Classical Greece." In *Food, Culture and History.* Edited by G. Mars and V. Mars. London: London Food Seminar: 165–90.

Dalby, A. 1996. *Siren Feasts.* London: Routledge.

Dalby, A. 1998. *Cato: On Farming.* Totnes, UK: Prospect Books.

Dalby, A. 2000. *Empire of Pleasures.* London: Routledge.

Dalby, A. 2003. *Food in the Ancient World from A to Z.* London: Routledge.

Dalby, A. 2010. *Geoponika.* Totnes, UK: Prospect Books.

Dalby, A., and Grainger, S. 1996. *The Classical Cookbook.* London: British Museum.

Daly, S., and Forman, R., eds. 2008. "Cooking Culture: Situating Food and Drink in the 19th Century." *Victorian Literature and Culture* 36, no. 2: 363–602.

Danbom, D. B. 2010. "Reflections: Whither Agricultural History." *Agricultural History* 84: 166–75.

Das, V., ed. 2003. *The Oxford India Companion to Sociology and Social Anthropology.* New Delhi: Oxford University Press.

Das, V. 2005. "Review: Fluent Bodies." *Bulletin of the History of Medicine* 79, no. 4: 849–50.

Daston, L., ed. 2000. *Biographies of Scientific Objects.* Chicago: University of Chicago Press.

Davidson, A. 1972. *Mediterranean Seafood.* Harmondsworth, UK: Penguin.

Davidson, A. 1992. "Europeans' Wary Encounter with Tomatoes, Potatoes, and Other New World Foods." In *Chilies to Chocolate: Food the Americas Gave the World.* Edited by N. Foster and L. Cordell. Tucson: University of Arizona Press: 1–14.

Davidson, A. 1999. *The Oxford Companion to Food.* Oxford and New York: Oxford University Press.

Davidson, J. 1997. *Courtesans and Fishcakes.* London: Harper Collins.

Davies, R. 1971. "The Roman Military Diet." *Britannia* 2: 122–42.

Davis, J. 2004. "Men of Taste: Gender and Authority in the French Culinary Trades, 1730–1830." PhD diss., Pennsylvania State University.

Davis, J. 2009. "Masters of Disguise." *Gastronomica* 9, no. 1: 36–49.

Davis, M. 2001. *Late Victorian Holocausts: El Niño Famines and the Making of the Third World.* London: Verso.

Davis, N. Z. 1988. "History's Two Bodies." *American Historical Review* 93, no. 1: 1–30.

Dawson, M. 2009. *Plenty and Grase.* Totnes, UK: Prospect Books.

Day, I. 2000. *Eat, Drink and Be Merry.* London: Philip Wilson.

Day, I. 2002. *Royal Sugar Sculpture: 600 Years of Splendor.* Barand Castle, UK: Bowes Museum.

Day, I. *Historic Food.* http://www.historicfood.com.

de Carcer y Disdier, M. 1953. *Apuntes para la historia de la transculturación indo-español.* Mexico City: Instituto de Historia.

de Castro, T. 2002. "L'émergence d'une identité alimentaire: Musulmans et chrétiens dans le royaume de Grenade." In *Histoire et identités alimentaires en Europe.* Edited by M. Bruegel and B. Laurioux. Paris: Hachette: 199–216.

De Vooght, D. 2006. "Culinary Networks of Power: Dining with King Leopold II of Belgium (1865–1909)." *Food & History* 4: 85–104.

De Vooght, D. 2011. *Display at the Dining Table? Culinary Networks of Power at the Belgian Royal Court of the 19th Century.* Brussels: P. Lang.

de Vos, P. 2006. "The Science of Spices: Empiricism and Economic Botany in the Early Spanish Empire." *Journal of World History* 17: 399–427.

De Vries, J. 2008. *The Industrious Revolution: Consumer Behavior and the Household Economy, 1650 to the Present.* Cambridge: Cambridge University Press.

Del Arco Blanco, M. 2010. "Hunger and the Consolidation of the Francoïst Regime (1939–1951)." *European History Quarterly* 40, no. 3: 458–83.

del Río Moreno, J. 1991. *Los inicios de la agricultura europea en el nuevo mundo (1492–1542).* Sevilla, Spain: ASAJA-Sevilla.

Delaveau, P. 1987. *Les épices: Histoire, description et usage des différents épices, aromates et condiments.* Paris: Albin Michel.

Demirel, F. 2007. *Dolmabahçe ve Yıldız Saraylarında Son Ziyaretler Son Ziyafetler.* Istanbul: Doğan Kitap.

Demirtaş, M. 2008. *Osmanlıda Fırıncılık 17. Yüzyıl.* Istanbul: Kitap Yayınevi.

Dennis, A. 2008. "From Apicius to Gastroporn: Form, Function, and Ideology in the History of Cookery Books." *Studies in Popular Culture* 31, no. 1: 1–17.

Dentzer, J.-M. 1982. *Le motif du Banquet couché dans le Proche-Orient et le monde grec du VII au IV siècle av. JC.* Rome and Paris: Ecole française de Rome.

Derby, L. 1998. "Gringo Chickens with Worms: Food and Nationalism in the Dominican Republic." In *Close Encounters of Empire: Writing the Cultural History of U.S.-Latin American Relations.* Edited by G. Joseph, C. LeGrand, and R. Salvatore. Durham, NC: Duke University Press: 451–93.

Derné, S. 2008. *Globalization on the Ground: New Media and the Transformation of Culture, Class, and Gender in India.* New Delhi: Sage.

Derrida, J. 1991. "Eating Well, or the Calculation of the Subject: An Interview with Jacques Derrida." In *Who Comes after the Subject?* Edited by E. Cadava, J.-L. Nancy, and P. Conner. New York: Routledge: 96–119.

Deshpande, S. 2003. *Contemporary India: A Sociological View.* New Delhi: Viking.

DeSilva, C. 1996. *In Memory's Kitchen: A Legacy from the Women of Terezín.* Northvale, NJ: J. Aronson.

Desmet-Grégoire, H. 2002. "Les boissons non alcoolisées en Turquie: Approche ethnologique." Documents de travail: Etudes Turques et Ottomanes Documents de travail, no. 11–12. Centre d'études turques, ottomanes, balkaniques et centrasiatiques (Paris). http://cetobac.ehess.fr/document.php?id=101.

Desmet-Grégoire, H., and Georgeon, F., eds. 1997. *Cafés d'Orient revisités.* Paris: Centre National de la Recherche Scientifique.

Detienne, M. 1972. *Les jardins d'Adonis.* Paris: Gallimard. Translated by Janet Lloyd as *The Gardens of Adonis.* Princeton, NJ: Princeton University Press, 1994.

Detienne, M., and Vernant, J.-P., eds. 1979. *La cuisine du sacrifice en pays grec.* Paris: Gallimard. Translated as *The Cuisine of Sacrifice among the Greeks.* Chicago: University of Chicago Press, 1989.

Deubner, L. 1932. *Attische Feste.* Berlin: H. Keller.

Deutsch, J. 2008. *Jewish American Food Culture.* Food Cultures in America. Westport, CT: Greenwood.

Dew, N. 2006. "Reading Travels in the Culture of Curiosity: Thévenot's Collection of Voyages." *Journal of Early Modern History* 10, no. 1–2: 39–59.

Dickey, S. 2000. "Permeable Homes: Domestic Service, Household Space, and the Vulnerability of Class Boundaries in Urban India." *American Ethnologist* 27, no. 2: 462–89.

Dickey, S. 2011. "The Pleasures and Anxieties of Being in the Middle: Emerging Middle Class Identities in Urban South India." *Modern Asian Studies* 45, no. 6: 1–41.

Digby, A., Ernst, W., and Muhkarji, P. B., eds. 2010. *Crossing Colonial Historiographies: Histories of Colonial and Indigenous Medicines in Transnational Perspective.* Cambridge: Cambridge University Press.

Digby, K. 1677. *The Closet of the Eminently Learned Sir Kenelm Digby Kt. Opened.* London: H.C. for H. Brome.

Diner, H. R. 2001. *Hungering for America: Italian, Irish, and Jewish Foodways in the Age of Migration.* Cambridge, MA: Harvard University Press.

Dirks, R. 1987. *The Black Saturnalia: Conflict and Its Ritual Expression on British West Indian Slave Plantations.* Gainesville: University of Florida Press.

Dirks, R. n.d. *World Food Habits: English-Language Resources for the Anthropology of Food and Nutrition.* http://lilt.ilstu.edu/rtdirks/.

Dirks, R., and Duran, N. 2001. "African American Dietary Patterns at the Beginning of the Twentieth Century." *Journal of Nutrition* 131: 1882–84.

Donahue, J. 2004. *The Roman Community at Table during the Principate.* Ann Arbor: University of Michigan Press.

Douglas, M. 1966. *Purity and Danger: An Analysis of Concepts of Pollution and Taboo.* London: Routledge and Kegan Paul.

Douglas, M. 1972. "Deciphering a Meal." *Daedalus* 101, no. 1: 61–81.

Douglas, M., and Isherwood, B. 1996. *The World of Goods: Towards an Anthropology of Consumption.* New York: Basic Books.

Drèze, J., Sen, A., and Hussain, A., eds. 1995. *The Political Economy of Hunger.* Oxford: Clarendon.

Drinot, P. 2005. "Food, Race and Working-Class Identity: Restaurantes Populares and Populism in 1930s Peru." *The Americas* 62: 245–70.

Driver, E. 2008. *Culinary Landmarks: A Bibliography of Canadian Cookbooks, 1825–1949.* Toronto: University of Toronto Press.

Driver, E. 2009. "Cookbooks as Primary Sources for Writing History." *Food, Culture & Society* 12, no. 3: 257–74.

Drouard, A. 2007. *Histoire des cuisiniers en France, XIXe–XXe siècle.* 2nd ed. Paris: CNRS Editions.

Du Bois, C. M., Tan, C.-B., and Mintz, S. W., eds. 2007. *The World of Soy.* Urbana: University of Illinois Press.

Duby, G. 1962. *L'économie rurale et la vie des compagnes dans l'occident médiéval.* Paris: Aubier.

Duby, G. 1973. *Guerriers et paysans: Essai sur la première croissance économique de l'Europe.* Paris: Gallimard.

Dumont, L. 1970. *Homo Hierarchicus: The Caste System and Its Implications.* Chicago: University of Chicago Press.

Dunbabin, K. 2003. *The Roman Banquet: Images of Conviviality.* Cambridge: Cambridge University Press.

Dupont, F. 1977. *Le Plaisir et la Loi.* Paris: Maspero.

Duran, N. 2000. "Dietary Studies Related to the United States Diet prior to World War II: A Bibliography for the Study of Changing American Food Habits over Time." *Journal of Nutrition* 130, no. 8: 1881–86.

Duru, M. 2005. "When Signifying Goodwill Is No Longer Enough: The Kola Nut and Gender among Igbos in Nigeria and Belgium." *Food and Foodways* 13: 201–20.

Dwyer, R. 2000. *All You Want Is Money, All You Need Is Love: Sex and Romance in Modern India.* London: Cassell.

Dyer, C. 1983. "English Diet in the Later Middle Ages." In *Social Relations and Ideas: Essays in Honour of R. H. Hilton.* Edited by T. H. Aston et al. Cambridge: Cambridge University Press: 191–216.

Dyer, C. 1989. *Standards of Living in the Later Middle Ages: Social Change in England, c. 1200–1520.* Cambridge: Cambridge University Press.

Dyer, C. 1998. "Did the Peasants Really Starve in the Middle Ages?" In *Food and Eating in Medieval Europe.* Edited by M. Carlin and J. Rosenthal. London: Hambledon Press: 53–71.

Eamon, W. 1994. *Science and the Secrets of Nature: Books of Secrets in Medieval and Early Modern Culture.* Princeton, NJ: Princeton University Press.

Earle, R. 2010. "'If You Eat Their Food......': Diets and Bodies in Early Colonial Spanish America." *American Historical Review* 115: 688–713.

Earle, R. 2012. *The Body of the Conquistador: Food, Race and the Colonial Experience in Spanish America, 1492–1700.* Chicago: University of Chicago Press.

Earle, R. Forthcoming. "The Columbian Exchange." In *The Oxford Handbook of the History of Food.* Edited by J. Pilcher. New York: Oxford University Press.

East Asian Society of Dietary Life. http://society.kisti.re.kr/~easdl/1s_1.html (accessed June 27, 2011).

Edelstein, L. 1931. "Antike Diëtetik." *Die Antike* 7: 255–70. Repr. as "The Dietetics of Antiquity." In *Ancient Medicine.* Edited by O. Temkin and C. L. Temkin. Baltimore: Johns Hopkins University Press, 1967: 303–16.

Edge, J. T. 2006. *Donuts: An American Passion.* New York: Putnam.

Edwards, G., and Mason, J. 1981. *Onje Fun Orisa* [Food for the gods]. New York: Yoruba Theological Archministry.

Ehara, A., and Higashiyottsuyanagi, S. 2008. *Kindai ryōrisho no sekai* [The world of the modern cookbook]. Tokyo: Domesu Shuppan.

Ehlert, T. 1991. *Das Kochbuch des Mittelalters: Rezepte aus alter Zeit.* Munich and Zurich: Artemis und Winkler.

Ehlert, T. 1996a. *Maister hannsen des von wirtenberg Koch, Transkription, Übersetzung, Glossar und kulturhistorischer Kommentar.* Frankfurt: Tupperware.

Ehlert, T. 1996b. "Das Reichenauer Kochbuch aus der Badischen Landesbibliothek [Aug. Pap. 125]. Edition und Kommentar." *Mediaevistik* 9: 135–88.

Ehlert, T. 1999. *Münchener Kochbuchhandschriften aus dem 15. Jahrhundert.* Donauwörth, Germany: Auer.

Ehlert, T. 2000. "Handschriftliche Vorläufer der 'Küchenmeisterei' und ihr Verhältnis zu den Drucken: der Codex S 490 der Zentralbibliothek Solothurn und die Handschrift G. B. 4o 27 des Stadtarchivs Köln." In *De consolatione philologiae: Studies in Honor of Evelyn S. Firchow.* Edited by A. Grotans et al. Göppingen, Germany: Kümmerle: 41–65.

Eley, G. 1989. "Labor History, Social History, 'Alltagsgeschichte': Experience, Culture, and the Politics of the Everyday—a New Direction for German Social History?" *Journal of Modern History* 61, no. 2: 297–343.

Elias, N. 1978. *The Civilizing Process: The History of Manners.* Translated by Edmund Jephcott. New York: Urizen Books.

Erdkamp, P. 2005. *The Grain Market in the Roman Empire: A Social, Political and Economic Study.* Cambridge: Cambridge University Press.

Erdkamp, P., ed. 2011. *A Cultural History of Food in Antiquity 800 BCE–500 CE.* Vol. 1, *A Cultural History of Food.* Oxford and New York: Berg.

Evans, S. 2007. *Bound in Twine: The History and Ecology of the Henequen-Wheat Complex for Mexico and the American and Canadian Plains, 1880–1950.* College Station: Texas A & M University Press.

Eyeoyibo, M. O. 1993, *Cookery Book in Isekiri (Warri Kingdom).* Benin City, Nigeria: Mofe Press.

Faas, P. 2003. *Around the Roman Table.* New York: Palgrave Macmillan.

Fabre-Vassas, C. 1997. *The Singular Beast: Jews, Christians, and the Pig.* European Perspectives. New York: Columbia University Press.

Fabricant, F. 2011. "A Book of Recipes Gathered from Holocaust Survivors." *New York Times,* April 26. http://www.nytimes.com/2011/04/27/dining/27survivors. html (accessed July 24, 2011).

Fahad, B. 1967. *Baghdad fi 'l-Qarn al-Khamis al-Hijri.* Baghdad: Matba'at al-Irshad.

Fan, S., and Brzeska, J. 2011. *The Nexus between Agriculture and Nutrition: Do Growth Patterns and Conditional Factors Matter?* New Delhi, India: International Food Policy Research Institute (IFPRI). http://www.ifpri.org/sites/default/files/publications/2020anhconfpaper01.pdf.

Faroqhi, S. 1984. *Towns and Townsmen of Ottoman Anatolia: Trades, Crafts and Food Production in an Urban Setting 1520–1620.* Cambridge: Cambridge University Press.

Faroqhi, S. 1995. *Kunst und Alltagsleben im Osmanischen Reich.* Munich: C. H. Beck. Translated into Turkish by Elif Kılıç as *Osmanlılarda Gündelik Yaşam, Ortaçağdan Yirminci Yüzyıla.* Istanbul: Tarih Vakfı Yurt Yayınları, 1997.

Faroqhi, S. 2000. *Subjects of the Sultan: Culture and Daily Life in the Ottoman Empire.* London: I. B. Tauris.

Faroqhi, S., and Neumann, C. K. 2003. *The Illuminated Table, the Prosperous House.* Würzburg, Germany: Ergon.

Farquhar, J. 2002. *Appetites: Food and Sex in Postsocialist China.* Durham, NC: Duke University Press.

Farr, J. R. 1988. *Hands of Honor: Artisans and Their World in Dijon, 1550–1650.* Ithaca, NY: Cornell University Press.

Farrer, J., ed. 2010. *Globalization, Food and Social Identities in the Asia Pacific Region.* Tokyo: Sophia University. http://icc.fla.sophia.ac.jp/global%20food%20 papers/ (accessed on September 13, 2011).

Fattacciu, I. 2009. "Cacao: From an Exotic Curiosity to a Spanish Commodity. The Diffusion of New Patterns of Consumption in Eighteenth-Century Spain." *Food & History* 7: 53–78.

Fenton, A., ed. 2000. *Order and Disorder: The Health Implications of Eating and Drinking in the Nineteenth and Twentieth Centuries.* East Linton, UK: Tuckwell.

Ferguson, P. 2004. *Accounting for Taste: The Triumph of French Cuisine.* Chicago: University of Chicago Press.

Ferguson, P. 2005. "Eating Orders: Market, Menus, and Meals." *Journal of Modern History* 77, no. 3: 679–700.

Fernandes, L. 2006. *India's New Middle Class: Democratic Politics in an Era of Economic Reform.* Minneapolis: University of Minnesota Press.

Fernandes, L., and Heller, P. 2006. "Hegemonic Aspirations." *Critical Asian Studies* 38, no. 4: 495–522.

Fernández-Armesto, F. 2001. *Food: A History.* London: MacMillan.

Fernández-Armesto, F. 2008. "Global Histories of Food." *Journal of Global History* 3: 459–64.

Ferrières, M. 2002. *Histoire des peurs alimentaires du Moyen Âge à l'aube du XIXe siècle.* Paris: Le Seuil. Translated by Jody Gladding as *Sacred Cow, Mad Cow: A History of Food Fears.* New York: Columbia University Press, 2006.

Ferrières, M. 2007. *Nourritures Canailles.* Paris: Editions du Seuil.

Ferst, D. 2011. "Recipes Recall Darker Days." *Jewish Daily Forward*, June 24. http://www.forward.com/articles/138605/ (accessed on July 24, 2011).

Field, M. 1993. "Gold Coast Food." *Petits Propos Culinaires* 43: 7–21.

Fifth International Food Congress. Turkey 1–3 September 1994. 1999. Edited by F. Halıcı. Ankara: Atatürk Kültür Merkezi Başkanlığı Yayınları.

Findlen, P. 1994. *Possessing Nature: Museums, Collecting and Scientific Culture in Early Modern Italy.* Berkeley: University of California Press.

Finlay, M. 2001. "New Sources, New Themes, and New Organizations in the New Germany: Recent Research on the History of German Agriculture." *Agricultural History* 75, no. 3: 279–307.

Fiorato, A. C., and Baratto, A. F., eds. 1999. *La Table et ses Dessous.* Paris: Presses de la Sorbonne Nouvelle.

First International Food Congress. Turkey 25–30 September 1986. 1988. Edited by F. Halıcı. Ankara: Kültür ve Turizm Bakanlığı Yayını, Nurol Matbaacılık.

Fisher, F. J. 1935. "The Development of the London Food Market, 1540–1640." *Economic History Review* 5, no. 2: 46–64.

Fisher, N. 2000. "Symposiasts, Fish-Eaters and Flatterers: Social Mobility and Moral Concerns." In *The Rivals of Aristophanes.* Edited by D. Harvey and J. Wilkins. London: Duckworth and The Classical Press of Wales: 355–96.

Fishkoff, S. 2010. *Kosher Nation.* New York: Schocken Books.

Fiske, J. 1892. *The Discovery of America.* Cambridge, MA: Riverside.

Fitzgerald, D. 2003. *Every Farm a Factory: The Industrial Ideal in American Agriculture.* New Haven, CT: Yale University Press.

Fitzgerald, G., and Petrick, G. 2008. "In Good Taste: Rethinking American History with Our Palates." *Journal of American History* 95, no. 2: 392–404.

Flandrin, J.-L. 1981. "Différences et différenciation des goûts: réflexion sur quelques exemples européens entre le 14e et le 18e siècles." In *National and Regional Styles of Cookery: Proceedings of the Oxford Symposium 1981.* Edited by Alan Davidson. Totnes, UK: Prospect Books: 191–207.

Flandrin, J.-L. 1984. "Internationalisme, nationalisme et régionalisme dans la cuisine des XIVe et XVe siècles: le témoignage des livres de cuisine." In *Manger et boire au moyen age. Actes du Colloque de Nice.* Edited by D. Manjot. Nice, France: Les Belles Lettres: 2: 75–91.

Flandrin, J.-L. 1987. "Jack Goody, Cooking, Cuisine and Class. A Study in Comparative Sociology, Stephen Mennell, All Manners of Food. Eating and Taste in

England and France from the Middle Ages to the Present." *Annales* 42 (1987): 645–51.

Flandrin, J.-L. 1989. "Distinction through Taste." In *A History of Private Life: Passions of the Renaissance.* Edited by R. Chartier. Translated by A. Goldhammer. Cambridge, MA: Harvard University Press: 265–307.

Flandrin, J.-L. 1999a. "Dietary Choices and Culinary Technique, 1500–1800." In *Food: A Culinary History.* Edited by J.-L. Flandrin and M. Montanari. Translated by C. Botsford. New York: Columbia University Press: 403–17.

Flandrin, J.-L. 1999b. "Préface." In *Tables d'hier, tables d'ailleurs.* Edited by J.-L. Flandrin and J. Cobbi. Paris: Odile Jacob: 17–36.

Flandrin, J.-L. 2007. *Arranging the Meal: A History of Table Service in France.* Translated by J. E. Johnson. Berkeley: University of California Press.

Flandrin, J.-L., and Cobbi, J., eds. 1999. *Tables d'hier, tables d'ailleurs.* Paris: Odile Jacob.

Flandrin, J.-L., and Hyman, P. 1986. "Regional Tastes and Cuisines: Problems, Documents, and Discourses on Food in Southern France in the 16th and 17th Centuries." *Food and Foodways* 1: 221–51.

Flandrin, J.-L., Hyman, P., and Hyman, M., eds. 1983. *Le cuisinier françois.* Paris: Montalba.

Flandrin, J.-L., and Montanari, M., eds. 1996a. *Histoire de l'alimentation.* Paris: Fayard.

Histoire de l'alimentation. Edited by J.-L. Flandrin and M. Montanari. Paris: Fayard: 7–15.

Flandrin, J.-L., and Montanari, M., eds. 1999. *Food: A Culinary History.* Translated by C. Botsford. New York: Columbia University Press.

Flandrin, J.-L., and Redon, O. 1981. "Les livres de cuisine italiens des XIVe et XVe siècles." *Archaeologia medievale* 8: 393–408.

Flemming, R. 2000. *Medicine and the Making of Roman Women.* Oxford: Oxford University Press.

Fletcher, R. 1988. "History from Below Comes to Germany: The New History Movement in the Federal Republic of Germany." *Journal of Modern History* 60, no. 3: 557–68.

Florescano, E. 1969. *Precios de maíz y crisis agrícolas en México (1708–1810).* Mexico City: El Colegio de México.

Flower, B., and Rosenbaum, E. 1958. *Apicius: The Roman Cookery Book.* London: Harrap.

Fogel, R. 2004. *The Escape from Hunger and Premature Death, 1700–2100: Europe, America, and the Third World.* Cambridge and New York: Cambridge University Press.

Fogel, R., and Engerman, S. 1974. *Time on the Cross.* Boston: Little, Brown.

Food and Agriculture Organization (FAO). 2008. *The State of Food Insecurity in the World.* Rome, Italy: Food and Agriculture Organization. http://www.fao.org/docrep/011/i0291e/i0291e00.htm/.

The Foodblog.Com, A Healthy Serving of Food Blogs. 2007–. http://www.foodblog blog.com/.

Food First. http://www.foodfirst.org/en/about/programs/.

Foods of the World. 1968–1971. New York: Time-Life Books.

Forbes, H., and Foxhall, L. 1982. "*Sitometreia:* The Role of Grain as a Staple Food in Classical Antiquity." *Chiron* 12: 41–90.

Forbes, H., and Foxhall, L. 1995. "Ethnoarchaeology and Storage in the Ancient Mediterranean: Beyond Risk and Survival." In *Food in Antiquity.* Edited by J. Wilkins, D. Harvey, and M. Dobson. Exeter, UK: University of Exeter Press: 69–86.

Forster, R., and Ranum, O., eds. 1979. *Food and Drink in History: Selections from the* Annales. Vol. 5. Baltimore: Johns Hopkins University Press.

Foundation of Chinese Dietary. http://www.fcdc.org.tw/english/about/default.aspx (accessed February 10, 2011).

Fourth International Food Congress. Turkey 3–6 September 1992. 1993. Edited by F. Halıcı. Ankara: Konya Kültür ve Turizm Vakfı Yayını.

Franc, M. 2006. "Merry and Abundant: Celebrating Christmas in the Czech Lands in the 1950s and 1960s." *Food & History* 4, no. 2: 237–51.

Franklin, A. 1894. *La vie privée d'autrefois: arts et métiers, modes, mœurs, usages des Parisiens, du XIIème au XVIIème siècles, après des documents originaux ou inédits.* Paris: Plon et Nourrit.

Frasca-Spada, M., and Jardine, N., eds. 2000. *Books and the Sciences in History.* Cambridge: Cambridge University Press.

Fraser, N. 1993. "Rethinking the Public Sphere: A Contribution to the Critique of Actually Existing Democracy." In *Habermas and the Public Sphere.* Edited by C. Calhoun. Cambridge, MA: MIT Press: 109–42.

Frati, L. 1900. *La vita privata in Bologna dal secolo XIII al XVII.* Bologna, Italy: Zanichelli.

Frayn, J. 1979. *Subsistence Farming in Roman Italy.* London: Open Gate Press.

Frayn, J. 1993. *Markets and Fairs in Roman Italy.* Oxford: Clarendon.

Freedman, P. 1999. *Images of the Medieval Peasant.* Stanford, CA: Stanford University Press.

Freedman, P., ed. 2007. *Food: The History of Taste.* Berkeley: University of California Press.

Freedman, P. 2008. *Out of the East: Spices and the Medieval Imagination.* New Haven, CT: Yale University Press.

Freidberg, S. 2010. "Ambiguous Appetites: A Modern History." *Food, Culture & Society* 13, no. 4: 477–91.

Freidenreich, D. 2011. *Foreigners and Their Food: Constructing Otherness in Jewish, Christian, and Islamic Law.* Berkeley: University of California Press.

Freyre, G. 1956. *The Masters and the Slaves: A Study in the Development of Brazilian Civilization.* Translated by S. Putnam. New York: Alfred A. Knopf.

Friedlander, M. S., and Kugelmann, C., eds. 2009. *Koscher & Co.: über Essen und Religion: eine Ausstellung des Jüdischen Museums Berlin, 9. Oktober 2009 bis 28. Februar 2010.* Berlin: Jüdisches Museum.

Friedman, T. L. 2000. *The Lexus and the Olive Tree: Understanding Globalization.* New York: Anchor.

Friedman, T. L. 2005. *The World Is Flat: A Brief History of the Twenty-First Century.* New York: Farrar, Straus and Giroux.

Fry, P. 1977. "Feijoada e soul food: Notas sobre a manipulaçao de símbolos étnicos e nacionais." *Ensaios de Opinião* 2: 44–47.

Fuller, C. J., and Narasimhan, H. 2007. "Information Technology Professionals and the New-Rich Middle Class in Chennai (Madras)." *Modern Asian Studies* 41, no. 1: 121–50.

Furnivall, F. J. 1868. *The Babees Book.* London: Early English Text Society. Repr., New York: Greenwood, 1969.

Fussell, B. 1983. *Masters of American Cookery: M. F. K. Fisher, James Andrews Beard, Raymond Craig Claiborne, Julia McWilliams Child.* New York: Times Books.

Fussell, B. 1984. *I Hear America Cooking: The Cooks, Regions, and Recipes of American Regional Cuisine.* New York: Viking.

Fussell, B. 1992. *The Story of Corn.* New York: Knopf.

Fussell, B. 2000. *My Kitchen Wars: A Memoir (At Table).* San Francisco: Northpoint.

Futselaar, R. 2010. "Incomes, Class, and Coupons: Black Markets for Food in the Netherlands during the Second World War." *Food & History* 8, no. 1: 171–98.

Gabaccia, D. 2000. *We Are What We Eat: Ethnic Food and the Making of Americans.* Cambridge, MA: Harvard University Press.

Gabaccia, D. 2001. "Review of Food, a Culinary History." *Journal of Social History* 34, no. 4: 985–87.

Gaddis, J. L. 2002. *The Landscape of History.* Oxford: Oxford University Press.

Gallant, T. 1984. *A Fisherman's Tale: An Analysis of the Potential Productivity of Fishing in the Ancient World.* Ghent, Belgium: Miscellanea Graeca, University of Ghent Press.

Gallant, T. 1991. *Risk and Survival in Ancient Greece: Reconstructing the Rural Domestic Economy.* Stanford, CA: Stanford University Press.

Gallo, L. 1983. "Alimentazione et Classi Sociali: una nota su orzo e frumento in Grecia." *Opus* 2: 449–72.

Ganguly, K. 2001. *States of Exception: Everyday Life and Postcolonial Identity.* Minneapolis: University of Minnesota Press.

García Acosta, V. 1988. *Los precios del trigo en la historia colonial de México.* Mexico City: Centro de Investigaciones y Estudios Superiores en Antropología Social.

García Acosta, V. 1989. *Las panaderías, sus dueños, y trabajadores: Ciudad de México, siglo XVIII.* Mexico City: Centro de Investigaciones y Estudios Superiores en Antropología Social.

García Sánchez, E. G. 2002. "Dietetic Aspects of Food in al-Andalus." In *Patterns of Everyday Life*. Edited by D. Waines. Hampshire, UK: Ashgate: 275–88.

Gardner, A. 1992. *Karibu: Welcome to the Cooking of Kenya*. Nairobi: Kenway.

Garnsey, P.D.A. 1988. *Famine and Food Supply in the Greco-Roman World: Responses to Risk and Crisis*. Cambridge: Cambridge University Press.

Garnsey, P.D.A. 1996. "Les raisons de la politique." In *Histoire de l'alimentation*. Edited by J.-L. Flandrin and M. Montanari. Paris: Fayard: 302–22.

Garnsey, P.D.A. 1998. *Cities, Peasants and Food in Classical Antiquity: Essays in Social and Economic History*. Cambridge: Cambridge University Press.

Garnsey, P.D.A. 1999. *Food and Society in Classical Antiquity*. Cambridge: Cambridge University Press.

Garnsey, P.D.A., and Rathbone, D. 1985. "The Background to the Grain Law of Gaius Gracchus." *Journal of Roman Studies* 75: 20–25.

Gately, I. 2008. *Drink, A Cultural History of Alcohol*. New York: Gotham Books.

Geertz, C. 1973. *The Interpretation of Cultures: Selected Essays*. New York: Basic Books.

Geertz, C. 1983. *Local Knowledge: Further Essays in Interpretive Anthropology*. New York: Basic Books.

Geleneksel Türk Tatlıları Sempozyumu Bildirileri (17–18 Aralık 1983 Ankara). 1984. Ankara: Kültür ve Turizm Bakanlığı, Milli Folklor Araştırma Dairesi Yayınları.

Gélinet, P. 2008. *2000 ans d'histoire gourmande*. Paris: Perrin.

Genç, R. 1982. "XI. Yüzyılda Türk Mutfağı." In *Türk Mutfağı Sempozyumu Bildirileri (31 Ekim–1 Kasım 1981 Ankara)*. Ankara: Kültür ve Turizm Bakanlığı, Milli Folklor Araştırma Dairesi Yayınları: 57–69.

Gentilcore, D. 2010. *Pomodoro! A History of the Tomato in Italy*. New York: Columbia University Press.

Georgeon, F. 2002. "Ottomans and Drinkers: The Consumption of Alcohol in Istanbul in the Nineteenth Century." In *Outside In: On the Margins of the Modern Middle East*. Edited by E. Rogan. London: I. B. Tauris: 7–30.

Germov, J., and Williams, L., eds. 2008. *A Sociology of Food and Nutrition: The Social Appetite*. New York and Oxford: Oxford University Press.

Gernet, L. 1909. *L'Approvisionnement d'Athènes en blé au V et IV siècle*. Paris: Faculté des Lettres.

Geyzen, A. 2011. "Popular Discourse on Nutrition, Health and Indulgence in Flanders, 1945–1960." *Appetite* 54: 278–83.

Giacosa, I. G. 1999. *A Taste of Ancient Rome*. Translated by A. Herklotz. Chicago: University of Chicago Press. (Orig. pub. as *A cena di Lucullo: come cucinare oggi I piatti dell'antica Roma*. Casale Monferrato, Italy: Edizioni Piemme, 1986.)

Gibson, C. 1964. *The Aztecs under Spanish Rule: A History of the Indians of the Valley of Mexico, 1519–1810*. Stanford, CA: Stanford University Press.

Girard, A. 1977. "Le triomphe de 'La cuisinière bourgeoise': Livres culinaires, cuisine et société en France aux XVII et XVIII siècles." *Revue d'histoire moderne et contemporaine* 26: 497–523.

Girard, A. 1982. "Du manuscrit à l'imprimé: le livre de cuisine en Europe aux 15 et 16 siècles." In *Pratiques & Discours Alimentaires à la Renaissance, Actes du Colloque de Tours 1979.* Edited by J.-C. Margolin and R. Sauzet. Paris: Maisonneuve et Larose: 107–17.

Gitlitz, D. M., and Davidson, L. K. 1999. *A Drizzle of Honey: The Lives and Recipes of Spain's Secret Jews.* New York: St. Martin's.

Global Travel Media. 2010. "Win A Trip to Korea and Feast Like a King." March 23. http://www.eglobaltravelnews.com.au/tourist-office/win-a-trip-to-korea-and-feast-like-a-king.html (accessed February 20, 2011).

Gloning, T. n.d. "Bibliographical Notes on the History of Cookery, Food, Wine, etc." http://www.uni-giessen.de/gloning/bib/cookbib.pdf.

Gloning, T. Culinary and dietetic texts. http://www.uni-giessen.de/gloning/kobu.htm.

Godley, A., and Williams, B. 2009. "Democratizing Luxury and the Contentious Invention of the Technological Chicken in Britain." *Business History Review* 83, no. 2: 267–90.

Gökyay, O. Ş. 1985. "Sohbetname." *Tarih ve Toplum* 14: 56–64.

Gold, B., and Donahue, F., eds. 2005. *Roman Dining.* Baltimore: American Philological Society.

Goldstein, D. 2006. "Rus Yemeklerinin Kültürel Tarihine Doğru." Translated by N. Pişkin. *Yemek ve Kültür* 5: 52–87.

Goldstein, D., and Merkle, K., eds. 2005. *Culinary Cultures of Europe: Identity, Diversity and Dialogue.* Strasbourg: Council of Europe.

Goldstein, J. 2001. "The Future of French History in the United States: Unapocalyptic Thoughts for the New Millennium." *French Historical Studies* 24, no. 1: 1–10.

Gonahasa, J. 2002. *Taste of Uganda.* Kampala, Uganda: Fountain.

Goody, J. 1982. *Cooking, Cuisine, and Class: A Study in Comparative Sociology.* Cambridge: Cambridge University Press.

Goody, J. 1989. "Symposium Review on Cooking, Cuisine and Class." *Food and Foodways* 3: 175–90.

Goshgarian, R. 2011. "Blending In and Separating Out: Sixteenth-Century Anatolian Armenian Food and Feasts." In *Starting with Food: Culinary Approaches to Ottoman History.* Edited by A. Singer. Princeton, NJ: Markus Wiener: 49–68.

Goubert, P. 1960. *Beauvais et le Beauvaisis de 1600 à 1730.* Paris: S.E.V.P E N.

Goubert, P. 1991. *Louis XIV et vingt millions de Français.* Paris: Fayard.

Gourevitch, D. 1985. "L'Obésité et son traitement dans le monde romain." *History and Philosophy of the Life Sciences* 7: 195–215.

Gowers, E. 1993. *The Loaded Table.* Oxford: Oxford University Press.

Grainger, S. 2006. *Cooking Apicius: Roman Recipes for Today.* Totnes, UK: Prospect Books.

Grandjean, C., Hugoniot, C., and Lion, B., eds. Forthcoming. *Le Banquet du Monarque dans le Monde antique: Orient, Grèce, Rome.* Rennes and Tours, France: Presses Universitaires de Rennes and Presses Universitaires François-Rabelais.

Grant, M. 1996. *Anthimus: On the Observance of Foods.* Totnes, UK: Prospect Books.

Grant, M. 1997. *Dieting for an Emperor.* Leiden: Brill.

Grant, M. 2000. *Galen in Food and Diet.* London: Routledge.

Gratzer, W. 2005. *Terrors of the Table: The Curious History of Nutrition.* Oxford and New York: Oxford University Press.

Green, R. 1951. *Galen: Hygiene.* Springfield: Thomas.

Greene, P. 1970. *Favourite Sierra Leone Recipes.* Freetown, MA: Commercial Printers Company.

Greenspoon, L. J., et al., eds. 2005. *Food and Judaism.* Studies in Jewish Civilization 15. Omaha: Creighton University Press.

Greenwood, A. 1988. "Istanbul's Meat Provisioning: A Study of the Celebkeşan System." PhD diss., University of Chicago.

Grewe, R. 2004. *Llibre de Sent Sovi. Llibre de totes maneres de potatges de menjar, Llibre de totes maneres de confits.* Revised by A.-J. Soberanes and J. Santanach. Barcelona, Spain: Barcino.

Grieco, A. J. 1987. "Classes sociales, nourriture et imaginaire alimentaire en Italie (XIVe–XVe siècle)." Thesis, École des Hautes Études en Sciences Sociales.

Grieco, A. J. 1992. "Food and Social Classes in Late Medieval and Renaissance Italy." In *Food: A Culinary History.* Edited by J.-L. Flandrin and M. Montanari. Translated by C. Botsford. New York: Columbia University Press: 302–12.

Grieco, A. J. 2006. "Meals." In *At Home in Renaissance Italy.* Edited by M. Ajmar-Wollheim and F. Dennis. London: V&A Publications: 244–53.

Grieco, A. J. n.d. *The Food Bibliography, Food History, a Bibliographic Database.* http://www.foodbibliography.eu/index_en.asp.

Grieco, A. J., and Scholliers, P., eds. 2008. "In corpore sano? Food Fears and Health in Past and Present." *Appetite* 51: 5–33.

Griffin, R., Pitts, M., Smith, R., and Brook, A. 2011. "Inequality at Late Roman Baldock: The Impact of Social Factors on Health and Diet." *Journal of Anthropological Research* 67: 533–56.

Grignon, C. 2007. "Préface. Histoire et sociologie." In *Alimentation populaire et réforme sociale. Les consommations ouvrières dans le second XIXe siècle,* by A. Lhuissier. Paris: Maison des sciences de l'homme: 1–10.

Grimaudo, S. 2008. *Difendere la Salute.* Palermo: Bibliopolis.

Grimm, V. 1996. *From Feasting to Fasting: The Evolution of a Sin.* London: Routledge.

Grocock, C., and Grainger, S. 2006. *Apicius.* Totnes, UK: Prospect Books.

Grossmann, A. 2010. "Grams, Calories, and Food: Languages of Victimization, Entitlement, and Human Rights in Occupied Germany, 1945–1949." *Central European History* 44, no. 1: 118–48.

Grover, K., ed. 1988. *Dining in America, 1850–1900.* Amherst: University of Massachusetts Press.

Grupo Interdisciplinario de Cultura Alimentaria Andalucía-América. 1996. "El ayuno como ritual de paso. El ayuno eclesiástico en España y América." In *Cultura alimentaria Andalucía-América.* Edited by A. Garrido Aranda. Mexico City: Universidad Nacional Autónoma de México: 74–175.

Güçer, L. 1949–1950. "XVIII. Yüzyıl ortalarında Istanbul'un iaşesi için lüzumlu hububatın temini meselesi." *İstanbul Üniversitesi Iktisat Fakültesi Mecmuası*, no. 11: 397–416.

Güçer, L. 1964. *16. ve 17. Asırlarda Osmanlı İmparatorluğu'nda Hububat Meselesi ve Hububattan Alınan Vergiler.* Istanbul: İstanbul Üniversitesi İktisat Fakültesi Yayınları.

Gudmundson, L. 1995. *Coffee, Society, and Power in Latin America.* Baltimore: Johns Hopkins University Press.

Guerreau-Jalabert, A. 1992. *Index des motifs narratifs dans les romans Arthuriens français en vers (XIIe–XIIIe siècles).* Geneva: Droz.

Güran, T. 1984–1985. "The State Role in the Grain Supply of Istanbul: The Grain Administration, 1793–1839." *International Journal of Turkish Studies* 3: 27–41.

Gurney, P. 2009. "Rejoicing in Potatoes: The Politics of Consumption in England during the 'Hungry Forties.'" *Past & Present* 203, no. 1: 99–136.

Guthman, J. 2004. *Agrarian Dreams: The Paradox of Organic Farming in California.* Berkeley: University of California Press.

Gutman, H. 1975. *Slavery and the Numbers Game: A Critique of Time on the Cross.* Urbana: University of Illinois Press.

Guyer, J., ed. 1987. *Feeding African Cities: A Study in Regional Social History.* London: International African Institute.

Gymnich, M., Lennartz, N., and Scheunemann, N. K. 2010. *The Pleasures and Horrors of Eating: The Cultural History of Eating in Anglophone Literature.* Göttingen and Bonn, Germany: V&R—Bonn University Press.

Hache-Bissette, F., and Saillard, D., eds. 2007. *Gastronomie et identité culturelle française: discours et représentations (XIXe–XXIe siècles).* Paris: Nouveau Monde.

Hadiye Fahriye. 2002. *Tatlıcıbaşı.* Istanbul: Bateş Kültür Yayınları.

Hafez, S. 1994. "Food as a Semiotic Code in Arabic Literature." In *A Taste of Thyme: Culinary Cultures of the Middle East.* Edited by S. Zubaida and R. Tapper. London: I. B. Taurus: 257–80.

Haga, N., and Ishikawa, H., eds. 1996–1999. *Zenshū: Nihon no shoku bunka* (Japanese food culture series). Tokyo: Yūzankaku.

Hall, R. L. 1991. "Savoring Africa in the New World." In *Seeds of Change: Five Hundred Years since Columbus.* Edited by H. Viola and C. Margolis. Washington, DC: Smithsonian Institution Press: 161–72.

Halstead, P., and O'Shea, J. 1989. *Bad Year Economics: Cultural Responses to Risk and Uncertainty.* Cambridge: Cambridge University Press.

Hamilton, E. 1934. *American Treasure and the Price Revolution in Spain, 1501–1650.* Cambridge, MA: Harvard University Press.

Hamilton, E. 1976. "What the New World Gave the Economy of the Old." In *First Images of America: The Impact of the New World on the Old.* Edited by F. Chiapelli. 2 vols. Berkeley: University of California Press: 2: 853–84.

Hamilton, S. 2009. "Analyzing Commodity Chains: Linkages or Restraints?" In *Food Chains: From Farmyard to Shopping Cart.* Edited by W. Belasco and R. Horowitz. Philadelphia: University of Pennsylvania Press: 16–25.

Han, K.-k. 2010a. "Noodle Odyssey: East Asia and Beyond." *Korea Journal* 1: 60–83.

Han, K.-k. 2010b. "The Kimchi 'Wars' in Globalizing East Asia: Consuming Class, Gender, Health." In *Consuming Korean Tradition in Early and Late Modernity.* Edited by L. Kendall. Honolulu: University of Hawaii Press: 21–38.

Han, P.-c. 1989a. *Chŏnt'ong ŭmsik* [Traditional food]. Seoul: Daewonsa.

Han, P.-c. 1989b. *P'aldo ŭmsik* [Food of Korea]. Seoul: Daewonsa.

Han, P.-c. 2001. *Uri saenghwal 100 nyŏn: ŭmsik* [Hundred years of our lifestyle: Food]. Seoul: Hyŏnamsa.

Han, P.-c., Han, P.-n., and Hwang, H.-s. 1998. *Uri ŭmsik paekkaji* [The hundred kinds of our food]. Vols. 1 and 2. Seoul: Hyŏnamsa.

Han, P.-n. 1989. *Ttŏk-kwa kwaja* [Confectionery]. Seoul: Daewonsa.

Han, P.-n. 1995. *Kungjung ŭmsik-kwa Soul ŭmsik* [Royal cuisine and the food of Seoul]. Seoul: Daewonsa.

Han, P.-n. 1999. *Uri-ga chŏngmal araya hal uri kimch'i paek kaji* [The hundred kinds of kimchi we really should know]. Seoul: Hyŏnamsa.

Hannerz, U. 1996. *Transnational Connections: Culture, People, Places.* New York: Routledge.

Harkness, D. E. 1997. "Managing an Experimental Household: The Dees of Mortlake and the Practice of Natural Philosophy." *Isis* 88, no. 2: 247–62.

Harkness, D. E. 2007. *The Jewel House: Elizabethan London and the Scientific Revolution.* New Haven, CT: Yale University Press.

Harland, P. 2010. *Meals in the Greco-Roman World: A Seminar of the Society of Biblical Literature.* http://www.philipharland.com/meals/GrecoRomanMealsSeminar.htm/ (accessed July 24, 2011).

Harner, M. 1977. "The Ecological Basis for Aztec Sacrifice." *American Ethnologist* 4: 117–35.

Haro Cortés, M. 2010. "Et no andedes tras vuestra voluntad en comer ni en bever ni en fornicio: De gula y lujuria en la literatura sapiencial." In *Être à table au Moyen Âge.* Edited by N. Labère. Madrid: Casa de Velázquez: 51–62.

Harris, J. B. 1998. *The Africa Cookbook: Tastes of the Continent.* New York: Simon and Schuster.

Harris, M. 1975. *Cows, Pigs, Wars and Witches: The Riddles of Culture.* London: Hutchinson.

Harris, M. 1985. *The Sacred Cow and the Abominable Pig: Riddles of Food and Culture.* New York: Simon and Schuster.

Harris, M. 1998. *Good to Eat: Riddles of Food and Culture.* Long Grove, IL: Waveland.

Harrison, M. 1999. *Climates and Constitutions: Health, Race, Environment and British Imperialism in India, 1600–1850.* New Delhi: Oxford University Press.

Harriss, J. 2006. "Middle-Class Activism and the Politics of the Informal Working Class: A Perspective on Class Relations and Civil Society in Indian Cities." *Critical Asian Studies* 38, no. 4: 445–65.

Harvey, D. 2001. *Spaces of Capital: Towards a Critical Geography.* New York: Routledge.

Hathaway, J. 2008. *The Arab Lands under Ottoman Rule, 1516–1800.* London: Pearson Education Limited Longman.

Hauser, H. 1933. "The Characteristic Features of French Economic History from the Middle of the Sixteenth to the Middle of the Eighteenth Century." *Economic History Review* 4, no. 3: 257–72.

Hayward, V. 2011. "Review of Ibn Razin al-Tujibi: *Relieves de las mesas, acerca de las delicias de la comida y los diferentes platos.*" *Petits Propos Culinaires* 92: 118–20.

Hazelton, N. 1971. "Because All Men Eat." *New York Times*, June 6: BR40.

Hecker, J. 2005. *Mystical Bodies, Mystical Meals: Eating and Embodiment in Medieval Kabbalah.* Detroit: Wayne State University Press.

Heine, P. 1994a. "Marzipan und manches mehr: Rezeption der arabischen Kochkunst und Getränke in Europa." In *Kommunikation zwischen Orient und Okzident: Alltag und Sachkultur.* Vienna: Österreichische Akademie der Wissenschaften: 379–92.

Heine, P. 1994b. "The Revival of Traditional Cooking in Modern Arab Cookbooks." In *A Taste of Thyme: Culinary Cultures of the Middle East.* Edited by S. Zubaida and R. Tapper. London: I. B. Taurus: 143–52.

Heine, P. 2004. *Food Culture in the Near East, Middle East, and North Africa.* Westport, CT: Greenwood.

Heldke, L. 2003. *Exotic Appetites: Ruminations of a Food Adventure.* New York: Routledge.

Hémardinquer, J.-J., ed. 1970. *Pour une histoire de l'alimentation.* Paris: Librairie Armand Colin.

Hémardinquer, J.-J. 1979. "The Family Pig of the Ancien Régime: Myth or Fact?" In *Food and Drink in History.* Edited by R. Forster and O. Ranum. Baltimore: Johns Hopkins University Press: 50–72.

Herodotus. 2004. *The Histories.* New York: Barnes and Noble Classics.

Hersh, J. F. 2011. *Recipes Remembered: A Celebration of Survival.* New York: Ruder Finn Press/Museum of Jewish Heritage.

Herzfeld, M. 2001. *Anthropology: Theoretical Practice in Culture and Society.* Oxford: Blackwell.

Hess, K., and Hess, J. L. 1977. *The Taste of America.* New York: Grossman.

Hesse, C., and Laqueur, T. 1994. "Introduction, National Cultures before Nationalism." *Representations* 47: 1–12.

Hieatt, C. B., ed. 1988. *An Ordinance of Pottage. An Edition of the Fifteenth Century Culinary Recipes in Yale University's MS Beinecke 163.* London: Prospect Books.

Hieatt, C. B. 1996. "The Middle English Culinary Recipes in MS. Harley 5401, an Edition and Commentary." *Medium Aevum* 65: 54–71.

Hieatt, C. B., and Butler, S., eds. 1985. *Curye on Inglysch. English Culinary Manuscripts of the Fourteenth Century (Including the Forme of Cury).* London: Early English Text Society.

Hieatt, C. B., and Butler, S. 1997. *Pleyn delit: Medieval Cookery for Modern Cooks.* 2nd ed. Toronto: University of Toronto Press.

Hieatt, C. B., and Jones, R. F. 1986. "Two Anglo-Norman Culinary Collections Edited from BL Manuscripts Additional 32085 and Royal 12, C. xii." *Speculum* 61: 859–82.

Hieatt, C. B., Lambert, C., Laurioux, B., and Prentki, A. 1992. "Répertoire des manuscrits médiévaux contenant des recettes culinaires." In *Du manuscrit à la table.* Edited by C. Lambert. Paris: Champion-Slatkine: 315–88.

al-Hijjiyya, 'Aziz Jasim. 1967–1999. *Baghdadiyyat.* 7 vols. Baghdad: Mudiriyyat al-Funun wa 'l Thaqafa al-Sha'biyya fi Wizarat al-Thaqafa wa 'l-Irshad.

Hitch, S. 2009. *King of Sacrifice: Ritual and Royal Authority in the Iliad.* Cambridge, MA: Harvard University Press.

Ho, P. 1955. "The Introduction of American Food Plants into China." *American Anthropologist* 57: 191–201.

Hochstrasser, J. B. 2007. *Still Life and Trade in the Dutch Golden Age.* New Haven, CT: Yale University Press.

Hoepfner, W., and Schwandner, E. L. 1994. *Haus und Stadt im klassischen Griechenland.* Munich: Deutscher Kunstverlag.

Holden, S. 2009. *The Politics of Food in Modern Morocco.* Gainesville: University Press of Florida.

Holden, T.J.M. 2005. "The Undercooked and Overdone: Masculinities in Japanese Food Programming." *Food and Foodways* 2: 39–65.

Holtzman, J. 2009. *Uncertain Tastes: Memory, Ambivalence, and the Politics of Eating in Samburu, Northern Kenya.* Berkeley and Los Angeles: University of California Press.

Hong, G.-z. 1984. *Zhongguo shipin keji shigao (shang)* [Historical draft of Chinese food technology, vol. 1]. Beijing: Zhongguo shangye chubanshe.

Honig, E. A. 1998. *Painting and the Market in Early Modern Antwerp.* New Haven, CT: Yale University Press.

Hooker, R. J. 1981. *Food and Drink in America: A History.* Indianapolis: Bobbs-Merrill.

hooks, b. 1992. "Eating the Other." In *Black Looks: Race and Representation.* Boston: South End Press: 121–39.

Hordern, P., and Purcell, N. 2000. *The Corrupting Sea.* Oxford: Blackwell.

Horowitz, R. 2006. *Putting Meat on the American Table: Taste, Technology, Transformation.* Baltimore: Johns Hopkins University Press.

Horwitz, R. P. 1998. *Hog Ties: Pigs, Manure and Mortality in American Culture.* New York: St. Martin's.

Houghton, W. E., Jr. 1941. "The History of Trades: Its Relation to Seventeenth-Century Thought: As Seen in Bacon, Petty, Evelyn, and Boyle." *Journal of the History of Ideas* 2, no. 1: 33–60.

Hsu, C.-y. 1976. "Zhoudai de yi shi zhu xing" [Clothes, food, living and transportation in the Zhou dynasty]. *Bulletin of the Institute of History and Philology Academia Sinica* 3: 503–35.

Hsu, M.-t., and Chien, M.-l. 1996. "Yinshi yu wenhua: Renleixue guandian de huigu yu zhanwang" [Diet and culture: An overview from anthropological perspectives]. In *Paper Collection of the 4th Symposium on Chinese Dietary Culture.* Edited by Foundation of Chinese Dietary Culture. Taipei: Foundation of Chinese Dietary Culture: 65–82.

Huang, H.-t. 2000. *Fermentations and Food Science*, part 5 of *Biology and Biological Technology*, vol. 6 of *Science and Civilisation in China.* Edited by J. Needham. Cambridge: Cambridge University Press.

Huizinga, J. 1954. *The Waning of the Middle Ages.* New York: Doubleday.

The Hunger Project. n.d. "Overview of Local NGO Partners in Orissa, India." http://www.thp.org/where_we_work/south_asia/india/map/orissa/ngo_partners.

Hunt, K. 2010. "The Politics of Food and Women's Neighborhood Activism in First World War Britain." *International Labor and Working-Class History* 77: 8–16.

Hunt, L. 1986. "French History in the Last Twenty Years: The Rise and Fall of the Annales Paradigm." *Journal of Contemporary History* 21: 209–24.

Hunt, L., ed. 1989. *The New Cultural History.* Berkeley: University of California Press.

Huntington, S. 1993. "The Clash of Civilizations?" *Foreign Affairs* 72, no. 3: 22–49.

Hyldtoft, O. 2007. "Food as Social Markers: A Copenhagen Hospital c. 1800." *Food & History* 5, no. 2: 131–51.

Hyman, P., and Hyman, M. 1992. "Les livres de cuisine et le commerce des recettes en France aux XV et XVI siècles." In *Du Manuscrit à la Table.* Edited by C. Lambert. Montréal, Canada, and Paris: Presses de l'Université de Montréal/Champion-Slatkine: 59–68.

Hyvernat-Pou, G. 1984. "Un repas princier à la fin du XVe siècle d'après *le romain de Jehan de Paris.*" In *Manger et boire au Moyen Age. Actes du Colloque de Nice (15–17 octobre 1982).* Edited by D. Manjot. Paris: Les Belles Lettres: 1: 261–64.

Ibn al-'Adeem, Kamal al-Deen. 1986. *Kitab al-Wusla ila 'l-Habeeb fi Wasf al Tayyibat wa 'l-Teeb.* Edited by Sulayma Mahjoub and Durriyya al-Khateeb. Vol. 2. Aleppo, Syria: Ma'had al-Turath al-'Ilmi al-'Arabi.

Ibn al-Mubarrid. 1937. *"Kitab al-Tibakha."* Edited by Habeeb Zayyat. *Al-Mashriq* 35: 370–76.

Ibn al-Mubarrid. 1985. *"Kitab al-Tibakha:* A Fifteenth-Century Cookbook." Translated by C. Perry. *Petits Propos Culinaires* 21: 17–22.

Ibn Wahshiyya, Abu Bakr al-Kisdani. 1995. *Al-Filaha al-Nabatiyya.* Edited by Tawfeeq Fahd. 3 vols. Damascus: Al-Ma'had al-'Ilmi al-Faransi li'l-Dirasat al 'Arabiyya.

İnalcık, H. 1982. "Rice Cultivation and the Çeltükci-Reaya System in the Ottoman Empire." *Turcica Revue d'études turques* 14: 69–141.

İnalcık, H. 1991. "Matbakh." In *Encylopédie de l'Islam.* Leiden: Brill: 6: 799–803.

Inglis, D., and Gimlin, D. L., eds. 2009. *The Globalization of Food.* Oxford: Berg.

Ishige, N. 1984. "Civilization without Models." In *Japanese Civilization in the Modern World: Life and Society.* Edited by U. Tadao et al. Osaka: National Museum of Ethnology: 77–86.

Ishige, N., ed. 1989. *Catalog of the Shinoda Collection at the National Museum of Ethnology.* Vol. 1. Bulletin of the National Museum of Ethnology no. 8. Osaka: National Museum of Ethnology.

Ishige, N. 2001. *The History and Culture of Japanese Food.* London: Kegan Paul.

Işın, M. 1998. *Mahmud Nedim Bin Tosun, Aşçıbaşı.* Istanbul: Yapı Kredi Yayınları.

Islam, A., and Sarkar, P. C. 2010. "Linking Food Security and Nutrition: Conceptual Issues." *South Asian Anthropologist* 10, no. 2: 129–34.

al-Isra'ili, Ishaq bin Sulayman. 1986. *Kitab al-Aghdhiya.* 4 vols. Facsimile of MS Fatih nos. 3604–07, in Sulaymaniyya Library in Istanbul. Frankfurt: Frankfurt University Press.

Jaboulet-Vercherre, A. 2011. *Wine, the Physician and the Drinker: Late Medieval Medical Views on Wine's Uses, Pleasures and Problems.* PhD diss., Yale University.

Jacob, J. 2001. "Ateneo, o il Dedalo delle parole, introduzione." In *I Deipnosofisti: I dotti a banchetto/Ateneo.* Edited by L. Canfora. Rome: Salerno: xi–cxvi.

Jaffee, M. S. 2006. *Early Judaism: Religious Worlds of the First Judaic Millenium.* Bethesda: University Press of Maryland.

al-Jahiz, Abu 'Uthman. 2008. *Al-Bukhala'.* Edited by Muhammad al-Iskandarani. Beirut: Dar al-Kitab al-'Arabi.

Jaine, T. 2008. "Warwick Conference." *Petits Propos Culinaires* 86: 9–10.

Jameson, M. H. 1988. "Sacrifice and Animal Husbandry in Classical Greece." In *Pastoral Economies in Classical Antiquity.* Edited by C. R. Whittaker. Cambridge, UK: Cambridge Philological Society: 87–119.

Janer, Z. 2006. "Culinary Crossings." In "A Symposium on the Globalization of Indian Cuisine." Special issue, *Seminar,* no. #566. http://www.india-seminar.com/semsearch.htm/ (accessed September 13, 2011).

Januarius, J. 2008. "Feeling at Home: Interiors, Domesticity, and Everyday Life of Belgian Limburg Miners in the 1950s." *Home Cultures* 6, no. 1: 43–70.

Jardine, L. 1996. *Worldly Goods: A New History of the Renaissance*. New York: Norton.

Jasny, N. 1944. *The Wheats of Classical Antiquity*. Baltimore: Johns Hopkins Press.

Jenkins, V. 2000. *Bananas: An American History*. Washington, DC: Smithsonian Institution.

Jenner, M.S.R., and Wallis, P., eds. 2007. *Medicine and the Market in England and Its Colonies, c. 1450–c. 1850*. Basingstoke, UK, and New York: Palgrave Macmillan.

"The Jew and the Carrot: Jews, Food, and Contemporary Issues." 2010. *Jew and the Carrot. Forward.com.* http://blogs.forward.com/the-jew-and-the-carrot/about/ (accessed July 24, 2011).

Jing, J., ed. 2000. *Feeding China's Little Emperors: Food, Children, and Social Change*. Stanford, CA: Stanford University Press.

Johns, A. 1998. *The Nature of the Book: Print and Knowledge in the Making*. Chicago: University of Chicago Press.

Johnson, L., and Tandeter, E., eds. 1990. *Essays on the Price History of Eighteenth-Century Latin America*. Albuquerque: University of New Mexico Press.

Johnston, B. 1958. *The Staple Food Commodities of Western Tropical Africa*. Palo Alto, CA: Stanford University Press.

Johnston, J., and Baumann, S. 2007. "Democracy versus Distinction: A Study of Omnivorousness in Gourmet Food Writing." *American Journal of Sociology* 113, no. 1: 165–204.

Jones, C., and Spang, R. 1999. "Sans-culottes, sans café, sans tabac: Shifting Realms of Necessity and Luxury in Eighteenth-Century France." In *Consumers and Luxury*. Edited by M. Berg and H. Clifford. Manchester, UK: Manchester University Press: 37–62.

Jones, G. F. 1960. "The Function of Food in Medieval German Literature." *Speculum* 35: 78–86.

Jones, W. O. 1959. *Manioc in Africa*. Palo Alto, CA: Stanford University Press.

Joselit, J. W. 1994. *The Wonders of America: Reinventing Jewish Culture 1880–1950*. New York: Hill and Wang.

Joselit, J. W., et al., eds. 1990. *Getting Comfortable in New York: The American Jewish Home, 1880–1950*. New York: Jewish Museum.

Joseph, N. B., ed. 2002. "Gender, Food, and Survival." Special issue, *Nashim: A Journal of Jewish Women's Studies and Gender* 5.

Jouanna, J., and Villard, L., eds. 2002. *Vin et Santé en Grèce ancienne*. Supplement to *Bulletin de Correspondance hellénique* 40.

Joyner, C. 1986. *Down by the Riverside: A South Carolina Slave Community*. Urbana: University of Illinois Press.

Juárez López, J. 2008. *Nacionalismo culinario: La cocina mexicana en el siglo XX*. Mexico City: CONACULTA.

Judt, T. 1979. "A Clown in Regal Purple: Social History and the Historians." *History Workshop* 7: 66–94.

Juhé-Beaulaton, D. 1990. "La diffusion du maïs sur les côtes de l'or et des esclaves aux XVII et XVIII siècles." *Revue Française d'Histoire d'Outre-Mer* 77: 188–90.

Jung, K.-S. 2005. "Colonial Modernity and the Social History of Chemical Seasoning in Korea." *Korea Journal* 2: 9–36.

Kadletz, E. 1998. *Animal Sacrifice in Greek and Roman Religion*. Ann Arbor: University of Michigan Press.

Kamminga, H., and Cunningham, A., eds. 1997. *The Science and Culture of Nutrition (1840–1940)*. Amsterdam: Rodopi.

Kamp, R. 2006. *United States of Arugula: How We Became a Gourmet Nation*. New York: Clarkson Potter.

Kanz al-Fawa'id fi Tanwee' al-Mawa'id. 1993. Edited by M. Marin and D. Waines. Beirut: Franz Steiner Stuttgart.

Kaplan, S. L. 1984. *Provisioning Paris: Merchants and Millers in the Grain and Flour Trade during the Eighteenth Century*. Ithaca, NY: Cornell University Press.

Kaplan, S. L. 1996. *The Bakers of Paris and the Bread Question, 1700–1775*. Durham, NC: Duke University Press.

Kaplan, S. L. 2008. *Le pain maudit: retour sur la France des années oubliées, 1945–1958*. Paris: Fayard.

Katō, H. 1977. *Meiji, Taishō, Shōwa shokuseikatsu sesōshi* [Popular history of food in the Meiji, Taishō, and Shōwa periods]. Tokyo: Shibata Shoten.

Katz, S. H., and Weaver, W. W., eds. 2002. *Encyclopedia of Food and Culture*. New York: Charles Scribner's Sons.

Kenneally, R., and Lebel, K. 2009. "Childhood Memories of the Domestic Landscape: The Home as the Site of Mindful Eating." *Material Culture Review* 70: 69–81.

Kenny, N. 2004. *The Uses of Curiosity in Early Modern France and Germany*. Oxford: Oxford University Press.

Khare, R. S. 1966. "A Case of Anomalous Values in Indian Civilization: Meat-Eating among the Kanya-Kubja Brahmans of Katyayan Gotra." *Journal of Asian Studies* 25, no. 2: 229–40.

Khare, R. S. 1976a. *Culture and Reality: Essays on the Hindu System of Managing Foods*. Simla: Indian Institute of Advanced Study.

Khare, R. S. 1976b. *The Hindu Hearth and Home*. Delhi: Vikas Publishing House.

Khare, R. S. 1992. *The Eternal Food: Gastronomic Ideas and Experiences of Hindus and Buddhists*. Albany: State University of New York Press.

Khare, R. S., and Rao, M.S.A., eds. 1986. *Food, Society, and Culture: Aspects in South Asian Food Systems*. Durham, NC: Carolina Academic Press.

Kim, C.-s. 1998. *Chejudo ŭmsik* [The food of Chejudo]. Seoul: Daewonsa.

Kim, Y.-s., ed. 2009. *Han'guk oesik yŏn'gam* [Yearbook of Korean food service]. Seoul: Han'guk oesik chŏngbo chusik hoesa.

Kiple, K. 1984. *The Caribbean Slave: A Biological History.* Cambridge: Cambridge University Press.

Kiple, K., and Ornelas, K. C., eds. 2000. *The Cambridge World History of Food.* Cambridge: Cambridge University Press.

Kirkby, D., and Luckins, T., eds. 2007. *Dining on Turtles: Food Feasts and Drinking in History.* Basingstoke, UK, and New York: Palgrave.

Kirkby, D., Luckins, T., and Santich, B. 2007. "Introduction: Of Turtles, Dining and the Importance of History in Food, Food in History." In *Dining on Turtles: Food Feasts and Drinking in History.* Edited by D. Kirkby and T. Luckins. Basingstoke, UK, and New York: Palgrave: 1–11.

Kirshenblatt-Gimblett, B. 1987. "The Kosher Gourmet in the Nineteenth-Century Kitchen: Three Jewish Cookbooks in Historical Perspective." *Journal of Gastronomy* 2, no. 4: 51–89.

Kjaernes, U., Harvey, M., and Warde, A. 2007. *Trust in Food: A Comparative and Institutional Analysis.* Hampshire, UK, and New York: Palgrave MacMillan.

Klein, J. 2007. "Redefining Cantonese Cuisine in Post-Mao Guangzhou." *Bulletin of the School of Oriental and African Studies* 3: 511–37.

Klein, J. 2009. "Chinese Meals: Diversity and Change." In *Meals in Science and Practice: Interdisciplinary Research and Business Applications.* Edited by H. L. Meiselman. Cambridge, UK: Woodhead: 452–82.

Klein, U. 2008. "The Laboratory Challenge: Some Revisions of the Standard View of Early Modern Experimentation." *Isis* 99: 769–82.

Klein, U., and Spary, E. C., eds. 2010. *Materials and Expertise in Early Modern Europe: Between Market and Laboratory.* Chicago: University of Chicago Press.

Knechtges, D. R. 1986. "A Literary Feast: Food in Early Chinese Literature." *Journal of the American Oriental Society* 106, no. 1: 49–63.

Knechtges, D. R. 1997. "Gradually Entering the Realm of Delight: Food and Drink in Early Medieval China." *Journal of the American Oriental Society* 117, no. 2: 229–39.

Kodama, S. 1980. *Nihon no shokuji yōshiki* [The pattern of the Japanese meal]. Tokyo: Chūō Kōronsha.

Kogman-Appel, K. 2006. *Illuminated Haggadot from Medieval Spain: Biblical Imagery and the Passover Holiday.* University Park: Pennsylvania State University Press.

König, J. Forthcoming. *Saints and Symposiasts: The Literature of Food and the Symposium in Greco-Roman and Early Christian Culture.* Cambridge: Cambridge University Press.

König, J., and Whitmarsh, T. 2007. *Ordering Knowledge in the Roman Empire.* Cambridge: Cambridge University Press.

The Korea Foundation. n.d. http://www.kf.or.kr/.

The Korea Foundation, ed. 2003. *Korean Food Guide in English.* Seoul: Cookand.

Korean Society of Food Culture. n.d. http://www.food-culture.or.kr/index.html (accessed June 27, 2011).

Koşay, H. Z. 1935. "Yiyinti İşleri, yemek adları, hazırlama yolları ve mutfak." In *Ankara Budun Bilgisi.* Ankara: Ankara Halkevi Neşriyatı: 221–40.

Koşay, H. Z., and Ülkücan, A. 1961. *Anadolu Yemekleri ve Türk Mutfağı.* Ankara: Milli Eğitim Basımevi.

Kosuge, K. 1991. *Nippon daidokoro bunka shi* [The cultural history of the Japanese kitchen]. Tokyo: Yūzankaku.

Köymen, M. A. 1982. "Selçuklular Zamanında Beslenme Sistemi." In *Türk Mutfağı Sempozyumu Bildirileri (31 Ekim–1 Kasım 1981 Ankara).* Ankara: Kültür ve Turizm Bakanlığı, Milli Folklor Araştırma Dairesi Yayınları: 35–47.

Kracauer, S. 2005. *The Mass Ornament: Weimar Essays.* Cambridge, MA: Harvard University Press.

Kraemer, D. C. 2009. *Jewish Eating and Identity through the Ages.* Routledge Advances in Sociology 29. London: Routledge.

Kraidy, M., and Murphy, P. D. 2008. "Shifting Geertz: Towards a Theory of Translocalism in Global Communication Studies." *Communication Theory* 18, no. 3: 335–55.

Krassen, M., trans. 1992. *Peri Ez Hadar: Fruit of the Tree of Splendor.* Shomrei Adamah Archives. http://ellenbernstein.org/shomrei-periezhadar.htm (accessed July 24, 2011).

Krause-Jackson, F. 2009. "Tuscan Town Accused of Culinary Racism for Ethnic Food Ban." *Bloomberg,* January 27. http://www.bloomberg.com/apps/news?pid=20601092&sid=aSqb1ksisZaI&refer; (accessed January 26, 2012).

Krieger, M. 2009. *Tee: Eine Kulturgeschichte.* Cologne, Germany: Böhlau.

The Kudeti Book of Yoruba Cookery. 1961. Lagos: C.M.S. (Nigeria) Bookshops.

Kuh, P. 2001. *The Last Days of Haute Cuisine: America's Culinary Revolution.* New York: Viking.

Kümin, B. 2003. "Eating Out before the Restaurant: Dining Cultures in Early-Modern Inns." In *Eating Out in Europe: Picnics, Gourmet Dining and Snacks since the Late Eighteenth Century.* Edited by M. Jacobs and P. Scholliers. Oxford: Berg: 71–87.

Kümin, B., and Tlusty, B. A. 2002. "The World of the Tavern: An Introduction." In *The World of the Tavern: Public Houses in Early Modern Europe.* Edited by B. Kümin and B. A. Tlusty. Aldershot, UK: Ashgate: 3–11.

Kurlansky, M. 1997. *Cod: A Biography of a Fish That Changed the World.* New York: Walker.

Kurlansky, M. 2002. *Salt: A World History.* New York: Penguin Books.

Kut, G. 1986. *Et-Terkibat Fi Tabhi'l-Hulviyyat.* Ankara: Kültür ve Turizm Bakanlığı, Milli Folklor Araştırma Dairesi.

Kut, G. 1987. "Şehzade Cihangir ve Beyazıd'ın Sünnet Düğünlerindeki Yemekler Üzerine." *III. Milletlerarası Türk Folklor Kongresi Bildirileri 5. cilt: Maddi Kültür.* Ankara: Kültür ve Turizm Bakanlığı: 227–38.

Kut, G. 1988. "Şirvani'nin Yemek Kitabı Çevirisine Eklediği Yemekler Üzerine." In *I. Milletlerarası Türk Folklor Kongresi Bildirileri.* Ankara: Milli Folklor Araştırma Dairesi: 170–75.

Kut, G. 1996. "Turkish Culinary Culture." In *Timeless Tastes: Turkish Culinary Culture.* Edited by E. Pekin and A. Sümer. Istanbul: Vehbi Koç: 38–71.

Kut, G. 2008. "Banquet Dinners at Festivities." In *Turkish Cuisine.* Edited by A. Bilgin and Ö. Samancı. Ankara: Minister of Culture & Tourism: 93–115.

Kut, T. 1985. *Açıklamalı Yemek Kitapları Bibliyografyası (Eski Harfli Yazma ve Basma Eserler).* Ankara: Kültür ve Turizm Bakanlığı, Milli Folklor Araştırma Dairesi.

Kut, T. 1990. "A Bibliography of Turkish Cook Books up to 1927." *Petits Propos Culinaires* 36: 29–48.

Kütükoğlu, M. 1978. "1009 (1600) tarihli Narh Defterine Göre Istanbul'da Çeşitli Eşya ve Hizmet Fiyatları." In *Tarih Enstitüsü Dergisi IX.* Istanbul: İstanbul Üniversitesi Edebiyat Fakültesi: 1–85.

Kütükoğlu, M. 1983. *Osmanlılarda Narh Müessesesi ve 1640 Tarihli Narh Defteri.* Istanbul: Enderun Kitabevi.

LaCombe, M. 2012. *"Never Wanting Government, They Never Wanted Bread": Food and Authority in the English Atlantic World, 1570–1650.* Philadelphia: University of Pennsylvania Press.

Lafortune-Martel, A. 1984. *Fête noble en Bourgogne au XVe siècle: Le Banquet du Faisan (1454): Aspects politiques, sociaux et culturels.* Montreal, Canada: Bellarmin.

Lal, R. 2005. *Domesticity and Power in the Early Mughal World.* Cambridge: Cambridge University Press.

Lambert, C., ed. 1992. *Du Manuscrit à la Table.* Montréal, Canada, and Paris: Presses de l'Université de Montréal/Champion-Slatkine.

Lane, E. W. 1973. *Account of the Manners and Customs of the Modern Egyptians.* Facsimile of 1860 edition. New York: Dover.

Lane, E. W. 2004. *Arab Society in the Times of the Thousand and One Nights.* Edited by S. Lane-Poole. New York: Dover. (Orig. pub. as *Arabian Society in the Middle Ages.* London: Chatto and Windus, 1883.)

Lang, Q.-x. 1933. *Zhongguo minshi shi* [History of the Chinese people's food]. Shanghai: Shangwu yinshuguan.

Langer, W. 1963. "Europe's Initial Population Explosion." *American Historical Review* 69: 1–17.

Langford, J. M. 2002. *Fluent Bodies: Ayurvedic Remedies for Postcolonial Imbalance.* Durham, NC: Duke University Press.

Latour, B. 1992. "Where Are the Missing Masses? The Sociology of a Few Mundane Artifacts." In *Shaping Technology/Building Society: Studies in Sociotechnical Change.* Edited by W. Bijker and J. Law. Cambridge, MA: MIT Press: 225–58.

Latour, B. 1993. *We Have Never Been Modern.* Cambridge, MA: Harvard University Press.

Lauden, R. 2004. "The Mexican Kitchen's Islamic Connection." *Saudi Aramco World*, May/June: 32–39.

Lauden, R. 2011. "Diana Kennedy's Oaxaca." *Zester Daily*, April 22. http:// zesterdaily.com/media-a-entertainment/901-diana-kennedys-oaxaca (accessed May 31, 2011).

Laurence, R. 1994. *Roman Pompeii: Space and Society.* London: Routledge.

Laurioux, B. 1983. "De l'usage des épices dans l'alimentation médiévale." *Médiévales* 3: 15–31.

Laurioux, B. 1993. "La cuisine des médecins à la fin du Moyen Age." In *Maladie, médecines et sociétés: Approches historique pour le Présent, Actes du VI colloque d'Histoire au Présent.* Paris: L'Harmattan: 136–48.

Laurioux, B. 1996. "I libri di cucina italiani alla fine del Medioevo; un nuovo bilancio." *Archivio storico italiano* 154: 33–58.

Laurioux, B. 1997a. *Les livres de cuisine médiévaux.* Turnhout, Belgium: Brepols.

Laurioux, B. 1997b. *Le règne de Taillevent: Livres pratiques culinaires à la fin du Moyen Âge.* Paris: Publications de la Sorbonne.

Laurioux, B. 2005. *Une histoire culinaire du Moyen Âge.* Paris: Honoré Champion.

Lavandier, M., et al. 2005. *La table à l'Elysée. Réceptions officielles des présidents depuis la IIIe République.* Paris: Cinq Continents.

Le Roy Ladurie, E. 1964. "Voies nouvelles pour l'histoire rurale (XVI–XVIII siècles)." *Etudes rurales* 13–14: 79–95.

Leach, W. 1986. "Review of *Perfection Salad: Women and Cooking at the Turn of the Century* by Laura Shapiro." *Journal of American History* 73, no. 3: 784–85.

Lee, S.-j. 2010. *Gourmets in the Land of Famine: The Culture and Politics of Rice in Modern Canton.* Stanford, CA: Stanford University Press.

Lehmann, G. 2003. *The British Housewife: Cookery Books, Cooking and Society in Eighteenth-Century Britain.* Totnes, UK: Prospect Books.

Leimgruber, V., ed. 1996. *Mestre Robert, Libre del coch: Tractat de cuina medieva/.* Barcelona, Spain: Curial.

León García, M. 2002. *La distinción alimentaria de Toluca: El delicioso valle y los tiempos de escasez, 1750–1800.* Mexico City: Porrúa.

Leonardi, S. J. 1989. "Recipes for Reading: Summer Pasta, Lobster à la Riseholme, and Key Lime Pie." *PMLA: Journal of the Modern Language Association of America* 104, no. 3: 340–47.

Leong, E. 2005. "Medical Recipe Collections in Seventeenth-Century England: Knowledge, Text and Gender." D. Phil. thesis, University of Oxford.

Leong, E. 2008. "Making Medicines in the Early Modern Household." *Bulletin of the History of Medicine* 82, no. 1: 145–68.

Leong, E., and Pennell, S. 2007. "Recipe Collections and the Currency of Medical Knowledge in the Early Modern Medical Marketplace." In *Medicine and the Market in England and Its Colonies, c. 1450–c. 1850.* Edited by M. Jenner and P. Wallis. Basingstoke, UK: Palgrave Macmillan: 133–52.

Levenstein, H. 1988. *Revolution at the Table: The Transformation of the American Diet.* New York: Oxford University Press.

Levenstein, H. 2002. *Paradox of Plenty: A Social History of Eating in Modern America.* Oxford: Oxford University Press.

Lévi-Strauss, C. 1966. "The Culinary Triangle." *Partisan Review* 33: 586–95.

Lévi-Strauss, C. 1970a. *Introduction to a Science of Mythology: The Raw and the Cooked.* London: Jonathan Cape.

Lévi-Strauss, C. 1970b. *The Raw and the Cooked.* New York: Harper and Row.

Levy, F. 2000. *1,000 Jewish Recipes.* Foster City, CA: IDG Books Worldwide.

Lhuissier, A. 2007. *Alimentation populaire et réforme sociale. Les consommations ouvrières dans le second XIXe siècle.* Paris: Maison des sciences de l'homme.

Li, H., ed. 1998. *Han tang yinshi wenhuashi* [History of the dietary culture in the Han and Tang dynasties]. Beijing: Beijing shifan daxue chubanshe.

Liang, J. 2007. "Migration Patterns and Occupational Specialisations of Kolkata Chinese: An Insider's History." *China Report* 43, no. 4: 397–410.

Lin, N.-s. 1989. *Zhongguo yinshi wenhua* [Chinese dietary culture]. Shanghai: Shanghai renmin chubanshe.

Lindorfer, B. 2009. "Discovering Taste: Spain, Austria, and the Spread of Chocolate Consumption among the Austrian Aristocracy, 1650–1700." *Food & History* 7: 35–51.

Linne, K. 2010. "Hunger und Kannibalismus bei sowjetischen Kriegsgefangenen im Zweiten Weltkrieg." *Zeitschrift für Geschichtswissenschaft* 58, no. 3: 243–62.

Lissarrague, F. 1987. *Un flot d'images.* Paris: Biro. Translated as *The Aesthetics of the Greek Banquet.* Princeton, NJ: Princeton University Press, 1990.

Livres en bouche: Cinq siècles d'art culinaire français. 2001. Paris: Bibliothèque nationale de France & Hermann.

Long, P. O. 2001. *Openness, Secrecy, Authorship: Technical Arts and the Culture of Knowledge from Antiquity to the Renaissance.* Baltimore: Johns Hopkins University Press.

Longo, O., and Scarpi, P. 1989. *Homo Edens.* Verona, Italy: Diapress.

López-Lázaro, F. 2007. "Sweet Food of Knowledge: Botany, Food, and Empire in the Early Modern Spanish Kingdoms." In *At the Table: Metaphorical and Material Cultures of Food in Medieval and Early Modern Europe.* Edited by T. J. Tomasik and J. M. Vitullo. Turnhout, Belgium: Brepols: 3–28.

Luce, J.-M., ed. 2000. *Paysage et Alimentation dans le monde grec.* Toulouse, France: Presses Universitaires du Mirail.

Maclagan, I. 1994. "Food and Gender in the Yemeni Community." In *A Taste of Thyme: Culinary Cultures of the Middle East.* Edited by S. Zubaida and R. Tapper. London: I. B. Taurus: 159–72.

Mahjoub, Sulayma. 1986. *Kitab al-Wusla ila 'l-Habeeb fi Wasf al Tayyibat wa 'l-Teeb.* Vol. 1. Aleppo, Syria: Ma'had al-Turath al-'Ilmi al-'Arabi.

Maixé-Altès, J. C. 2009. "La modernización de la distribución alimentaria en España, 1947–1995." *Revista de Historia Industrial* 18, no. 3: 125–60.

Malamoud, C. 1996. *Cooking the World: Ritual and Thought in Ancient India.* New Delhi: Oxford University Press.

Mannur, A. 2010. *Culinary Fictions: Food in South Asian Diasporic Culture.* Philadelphia: Temple University Press.

Mantran, R. 1962. *Istanbul dans la deuxième moitié du XVIIe siècle: Essai d'histoire institutionnelle, économique et sociale.* Paris: Maisonneuve.

Marcus, I. G. 1996. *Rituals of Childhood: Jewish Acculturation in Medieval Europe.* New Haven, CT: Yale University Press.

Margairaz, D. 2005. "Enjeux et Pratiques des Classifications du Commerce en France. Les Trois Figures de Différentiation Gros/Détail 1673–1844." In *Retailers and Consumer Changes in Early Modern Europe: England, France, Italy, and the Low Countries.* Edited by B. Blondé et al. Tours, France: Presses Universitaires François-Rabelais: 213–34.

Margolin, J.-C., and Sauzet, R., eds. 1982. *Pratiques & Discours Alimentaires à la Renaissance.* Paris: Maisonneuve et Larose.

Marin, M. 1994. "Beyond Taste: The Complements of Color and Smell in the Medieval Arab Culinary Tradition." In *A Taste of Thyme: Culinary Cultures of the Middle East.* Edited by S. Zubaida and R. Tapper. London: I. B. Taurus: 204–14.

Marin, M. 2002. "Pots and Fire: The Cooking Processes in the Cookbooks of al-Andalus and the Maghrib." In *Patterns of Everyday Life.* Edited by D. Waines. Hampshire, UK: Ashgate: 289–302.

Marks, C. 1992. *Sephardic Cooking: 600 Recipes Created in Exotic Sephardic Kitchens from Morocco to India.* New York: Donald I. Fine.

Marks, G. 1996. *The World of Jewish Cooking.* New York: Simon & Schuster.

Marks, G. 2010. *Encyclopedia of Jewish Food.* Hoboken, NJ: John Wiley & Sons.

Maroney, S. R. 2011. "'To Make a Curry the India Way': Tracking the Meaning of Curry across Eighteenth-Century Communities." *Food and Foodways* 19, no. 1: 122–34.

Marriott, M. 1990. *India through Hindu Categories.* New Delhi: Sage.

Matalas, A.-L. 2006. "Dietary Patterns in Pre-World War II Greece: Disparities within Peasant and Urban Foodways." *Food & History* 4, no. 1: 221–36.

Matthaiou, A. 1997. *Aspects de l'Alimentation en Grèce sous la domination ottomane. Des Réglementations au discours normatif.* Frankfurt: Peter Lang.

Mazumdar, S. 1999. "The Impact of New World Food Crops on the Diet and Economy of China and India, 1600–1900." In *Food in Global History.* Edited by R. Grew. Boulder, CO: Westview: 58–78.

McCann, J. 2005. *Maize and Grace: Africa's Encounter with a New World Crop, 1500–2000.* Cambridge, MA: Harvard University Press.

McCann, J. C. 2009. *Stirring the Pot: A History of African Cuisine.* Athens: Ohio University Press.

McNeill, W. 1991. "American Food Crops in the Old World." In *Seeds of Change: A Quincentennial Commemoration.* Edited by H. Viola and C. Margolis. Washington, DC: Smithsonian Institution Press: 43–59.

McQueen, A., ed. n.d. *The Liberian Way of Cooking.* Monrovia: Committee on International Club Women's Project (typescript).

Mead, W. E. 1931. *The Medieval English Feast.* London: Allen & Unwin.

Mehmet Kamil. 1844. *Melceü't-Tabbahin (Aşçıların Sığınağı).* Edited by C. Kut. Istanbul: Duran Ofset, 1997.

Le ménagier de Paris: Traité de morale et d'économie domestique. 1846. Edited by J. Pichon. 2 vols. Paris: Imprimerie de Crapelet.

Le ménagier de Paris. 1981. Edited by G. E. Brereton and J. Ferrier. Oxford: Oxford University Press.

Menjot, D., ed. 1984. *Manger et boire au Moyen Âge. Actes du Colloque de Nice (15–17 octobre 1982).* 2 vols. Paris: Les Belles Lettres.

Mennell, S. 1985. *All Manners of Food: Eating and Taste in England and France from the Middle Ages to the Present.* Oxford: Basil Blackwell. Repr., Urbana: University of Illinois Press, 1996.

Mennell, S. 1987. "On the Civilizing of Appetite." *Theory, Culture & Society* 4: 373–403.

Menon, F. 1750. *La Science du Maître d'Hôtel, Confiseur, á l'usage des Officiers.* Paris: Chez Paulus-du-Mesnil.

Mesfin, D. J., ed. 2004. *Exotic Ethiopian Cooking: Society, Culture, Hospitality, and Traditions.* Falls Church, VA: Ethiopian Cookbook Enterprises.

Metcalfe, F. 1844. *Gallus: Or Roman Scenes in the Time of Augustus.* Translated by W. Bekker. New York: Appleton.

Meyers, C. 2002. "Having Their Space and Eating There Too: Bread Production and Female Power in Ancient Israelite Households." *Nashim: A Journal of Jewish Women's Studies & Gender Issues* 5: 14–44.

Meyzie, P. 2007. *La Table du Sud-Ouest et l'émergence des cuisines régionales (1700–1850).* Rennes, France: Presses Universitaires de Rennes.

Meyzie, P. 2010. *L'alimentation en Europe à l'époque modern.* Paris: A. Colin.

Mez, A. 1937. *The Renaissance of Islam.* Translated by S. K. Bakhsh and D. S. Margoliouth. Patna, India: Jubilee. (Orig. pub. in German as *Die Renaissance des Islams,* 1922.)

Milanesio, N. 2010. "Food Politics and Consumption in Peronist Argentina." *Hispanic American Historical Review* 90: 75–108.

Miller, H. D. 2007. "The Pleasures of Consumption." In *Food: The History of Taste.* Edited by P. Freedman. Berkeley: University of California Press: 135–61.

Miller, J., and Deutsch, J. 2009. *Food Studies: An Introduction to Research Methods.* Oxford and New York: Berg.

Miller, J. I. 1969. *The Spice Trade of the Roman Empire.* Oxford: Oxford University Press.

Miller, S. 1978. *The Prytaneion: Its Form and Architecture.* Berkeley: University of California Press.

Milstein, R. 1990. *Miniature Painting in Ottoman Baghdad.* Costa Mesa, CA: Mazda.

Mintz, S. W. 1985. *Sweetness and Power: The Place of Sugar in Modern History.* New York: Viking.

Mintz, S. W. 1987. "Symposium Review on Sweetness and Power." *Food and Food-ways* 2: 107–50.

Mintz, S. W. 1993. "The Changing Roles of Food in the Study of Consumption." In *Consumption and the World of Goods*. Edited by J. Brewer and R. Porter. London and New York: Routledge: 261–73.

Mintz, S. W. 1996. *Tasting Food, Tasting Freedom: Excursions into Eating, Culture, and the Past*. Boston: Houghton Mifflin.

Mintz, S. W. 2002. "Heroes Sung and Unsung: Toward a History of the Anthropology of Food." *Council on Nutritional Anthropology Newsletter* 2: 3–8.

Mintz, S. W., and Dubois, C. 2002. "The Anthropology of Food and Eating." *Annual Review of Anthropology* 31: 99–119.

Miracle, Marvin P. 1966. *Maize in Tropical Africa*. Madison: University of Wisconsin Press.

Mitchell, S. 1993. *Anatolia I*. Oxford: Oxford University Press.

Moffat, T., and Prowse, T., eds. 2010. *Human Diet and Nutrition in Biocultural Perspective: Past Meets Present*. Oxford and New York: Berghahn.

Molina Enríquez, A. 1978. *Los grandes problemas nacionales*. Mexico City: Editorial Era. (Orig. pub. 1909.)

Montanari, M. 1979. *L'alimentazione contadina nell' alto Medioevo*. Naples: Liguori.

Montanari, M. 1988. *Alimentazione e cultura nel medioevo*. Rome: Laterza.

Montanari, M. 1993. *La fame e l'abbondanza. Storia dell'alimentazione in Europa*. Rome: Laterza.

Montanari, M 1994. *The Culture of Food*. Translated by C. Ipsen. Oxford: Blackwell.

Montanari, M. 2003. "A New History Journal. A Journal about New History?" *Food & History* 1: 14–17.

Montanari, M. 2010. *L'identità Italiana in cucina*. Rome: Laterza.

Montenach, A. 2009. *Espaces et pratiques du commerce alimentaire à Lyon au XVII siècle: L'économie du quotidien*. Grenoble, France: Presses Universitaires de Grenoble.

Moon, O. 2010. "Dining Elegance and Authenticity." *Korea Journal* 1: 36–58.

Mouré, K. 2010. "Food Rationing and the Black Market in France (1940–1944)." *French History* 24, no. 2: 262–82.

Moxey, K. 1989. "Festive Peasants and the Social Order." In *Peasants, Warriors, and Wives: Popular Imagery in the Reformation*. Edited by K. Moxey. Chicago: University of Chicago Press: 35–66.

Mukhopadhyay, B. 2004. "Between Elite Hysteria and Subaltern Carnivalesque: The Politics of Street-Food in the City of Calcutta." *South Asia Research* 24, no. 1: 37–50.

Murphey, R. 1988. "Provisioning Istanbul: The State and Subsistence in the Early Modern Middle East." *Food and Foodways* 2: 217–63.

Murray, O., ed. 1990. *Sympotica*. Oxford: Oxford University Press.

Murray, O., and Tecusan, M. 1995. *In Vino Veritas*. London: British School at Rome.

Murrell, J. 1617. *A Daily Exercise for Ladies and Gentlewomen*. London: Widow Helme.

al-Musawi, M. 2000. *Mujtama'Alf Layla wa Layla*. Tunis, Tunisia: Markaz al-Nashr al-Jami'i.

Mutch, A. 2010. "Improving the Public House in Britain, 1920–1940: Sir Sydney Neville and Social Work." *Business History* 52, no. 4: 517–35.

Mylona, D. 2008. *Fish-Eating in Greece from the Fifth Century BC to the Seventh Century AD*. Oxford: British Archaeological Reports.

Nabhan, G. P. 2008. *Arab/American: Landscape, Culture, and Cuisine in Two Great Deserts*. Tucson: University of Arizona Press.

Nadeau, R. 2010a. *Les Manières de Table dans le monde gréco-romain*. Rennes and Tours, France: Presses Universitaires de Rennes and Presses Universitaires Francois-Rabelais.

Nadeau, R. 2010b. "Penser les banquets grec et romain." *Ktèma* 35: 3–10.

Nadeau, R. 2010c. "Les pratiques sympotiques à l'époque impériale." *Ktèma* 35: 11–26.

Nandy, A. 2003. "Ethnic Cuisine: The Significant Other." In *India: A National Culture?* Edited by G. Sen. New Delhi: Sage: 246–51.

Naoroji, D. 1901. *Poverty and Un-British Rule in India*. London: S. Sonnenschein.

Narayan, U. 1997. *Dislocating Cultures: Identities, Traditions, and Third-World Feminism*. New York: Routledge.

Naso, I., ed. 1990. *Formaggi del Medioevo: la "Summa lacticiniorum" di Pantaleone da Confienza*. Turin, Italy: Slow Food.

Nasrallah, N., trans. 2007. *Annals of the Caliphs' Kitchens: Ibn Sayyar al Warraq's Tenth-Century Baghdadi Cookbook*. Leiden: Brill.

Nasrallah, N. 2012. *Delights from the Garden of Eden: A Cookbook and a History of the Iraqi Cuisine*. 2nd ed. Sheffield: Equinox.

National Diet Library. n.d. Public access catalog. http://opac.ndl.go.jp.

National Museum of Ethnology. n.d. "Collection Information." http://www.minpaku.ac.jp/english/library/material/collection.html (accessed June 7, 2011).

Nestle, M. 2002. *Food Politics: How the Food Industry Influences Nutrition and Health*. Berkeley: University of California Press.

Nestle, M., and McIntosh, W. A. 2010. "Writing the Food Studies Movement." *Food, Culture & Society* 13, no. 2: 159–79.

Neumann, C. 2003. "Spices in the Ottoman Palace: Courtly Cookery in the Eighteenth Century." In *The Illuminated Table, the Prosperous House*. Edited by S. Faroqhi and C. K. Neumann. Würzburg, Germany: Ergon: 127–61.

Neuschel, K. B. 2011. "Teaching and the 'Telescoping' of History." *French Historical Studies* 34, no. 1: 47–55.

Neusner, J. 1979. *Method and Meaning in Ancient Judaism*. Missoula, MT: Scholars Press.

Neusner, J. 2010. "Review of *Food and Identity in Early Rabbinic Judaism* by Jordan D. Rosenblum." *Midwest Jewish Studies Association—Shofar Book Reviews.* http://www.case.edu/artsci/jdst/reviews/Food.htm (accessed July 24, 2011).

Neustadt, K. 1992. *Clambake: A History and Celebration of an American Tradition.* Amherst: University of Massachusetts Press.

Newman, B. 2007. *Development Report # 15: A Bitter Harvest. Farmer Suicide in India.* Oakland, CA: Food First/Institute for Food and Development Policy.

Newmyer, S. 2006. *Animals, Rights and Reason and Plutarch and Modern Ethics.* London: Routledge.

Newson, L., and Minchin, S. 2007. "Diets, Food Supplies, and the African Slave Trade in Early Seventeenth-Century Spanish America." *The Americas* 63: 517–50.

Ngude, M. 1978. *Mapishi Yetu.* Dar Es Salaam: Longman Tanzania.

Nihon no shokuseikatsu zenshū henshū iinkai, ed. 1986–1993. *Nihon no shokuseikatsu zenshū* [Complete works on Japanese food habits]. 50 vols. Tokyo: Nōsangyosan bunka kyōkai.

Noguchi, P. 1994. "Savor Slowly: Ekiben—the Fast Food of High Speed Japan." *Ethnology* 4: 317–30.

Norton, M. 2008. *Sacred Gifts, Profane Pleasures: A History of Tobacco and Chocolate in the Atlantic World.* Ithaca, NY: Cornell University Press.

Nussbaum, M. C. 1996. *For Love of Country: Debating the Limits of Patriotism.* Boston: Beacon.

Nützenadel, A., and Trentmann, F., eds. 2008. *Food and Globalization. Consumption, Markets and Politics in the Modern World.* Oxford and New York: Berg.

Nyaho Chapman, E., Amarteifio, E., and Asare, J. 1970. *Ghana Recipe Book.* Tema: Ghana Publishing Corporation.

Oberling, G., and Smith, G. M. 2001. *The Food Culture of the Ottoman Palace.* Istanbul: Society of Friends of Topkapı Palace Museum.

Obeyesekere, G. 1991. "Review: Hindu Medicine and the Aroma of Structuralism." *Journal of Religion* 73, no. 1: 419–25.

Ochoa, E. 2000. *Feeding Mexico: The Political Uses of Food since 1910.* Wilmington, DE: Scholarly Resources.

Oddy, D. 2008. "Review of *Hunger: A Modern History.*" *Reviews in History*, November. http://www.history.ac.uk/reviews/paper/oddyd.html (accessed January 2, 2011).

Oddy, D., Atkins, P., and Amilien, V., eds. 2009. *The Rise of Obesity in Europe: A Twentieth Century Food History.* Farnham, UK, and Burlington, VT: Ashgate.

Ögel, B. 1978. *Türk Kültür Tarihine Giriş, cilt 4, Türklerde yemek Kültürü.* Ankara. Kültür ve Turizm Bakanlığı.

Oğuz, B. 1976. *Türkiye Halkının Kültür Kökenleri Giriş Beslenme Teknikleri.* Vol. 1. Istanbul: Istanbul Matbaası.

Ohnuki-Tierney, E. 1993. *Rice as Self: Japanese Identities through Time.* Princeton, NJ: Princeton University Press.

Oliver, G. 2007. *War, Food and Politics in Early Hellenistic Athens.* Oxford: Oxford University Press.

Oliver, S. 2006. "Ruminations on the State of American Food History." *Gastronomica* 6, no. 4: 91–98.

Olson, S. D. 2007. *Broken Laughter.* Oxford: Oxford University Press.

Olson, S. D., and Sens, A. 1999. *Matro of Pitane and the Tradition of Epic Parody in the 4th Century BC.* Atlanta: Scholars Press.

Olson, S. D., and Sens, A. 2000. *Archestratos.* Oxford: Oxford University Press.

Ong, A. 1999. *Flexible Citizenship: The Cultural Logics of Transnationality.* Durham, NC: Duke University Press.

Önler, Z. 1990. *Müntahab-ı Şifa I.* Ankara: Türk Dil Kurumu.

Önler, Z. 1999. *Müntahab-ı Şifa II Sözlük.* Istanbul: Simurg.

Orfanos, C., and Carrière, J.-C., eds. 2003. *Symposium, Banquet et Représentations en Grèce et à Rome.* Toulouse, France: Presses Universitaires du Mirail.

Orland, B. 2010. "The Invention of Nutrients: William Prout, Digestion and Alimentary Substances in the 1820s." *Food & History* 8, no. 1: 149–68.

Ortiz, F. 1993. "Los factores humanos de la cubanidad." In *Etnia y sociedad.* Edited by I. Barreal. Havana: Editorial de Ciencias Sociales: 1–20.

Ortiz, F. 1995. *Cuban Counterpoint: Tobacco and Sugar.* 2nd ed. Durham, NC: Duke University Press.

Ortíz Cuadra, C. 2006. *Puerto Rico en la olla, ¿somos aún lo que comimos?* Madrid: Ediciones Doce Calles.

Osborne, C. 2006. *Dumb Beasts and Dead Philosophers.* Oxford: Oxford University Press.

Osella, C. 2008. "Food: Memory, Pleasure and Politics." *South Asia: Journal of South Asian Studies* 31, no. 1.

Osella, F., and Osella, C. 2000. *Social Mobility in Kerala: Modernity and Identity in Conflict.* London: Pluto.

Osseo-Asare, F. 2005. *Food Culture in Sub-Saharan Africa.* Westport, CT: Greenwood.

Özveren, E. 2003. "Black Sea and the Grain Provisioning of Istanbul in the Longue Durée." In *Nourrir les cités de Mediterranée: Antiquité–Temps Modernes.* Edited by B. Marin and C. Virlouvet. Paris: Maisonneuve & Larose: 223–49.

Panayi, P. 2008. *Spicing Up Britain: The Multicultural History of British Food.* London: Reaktion Books.

Parasecoli, F., and Scholliers, P., eds. 2011. *A Cultural History of Food.* 6 vols. Oxford and New York: Berg.

Pardailhé-Galabrun, A. 1991. *The Birth of Intimacy.* Philadelphia: University of Pennsylvania Press.

Park Redfield, M. 1929. "Notes on the Cookery of Tepoztlan, Morelos." *American Journal of Folklore* 42: 167–96.

Parker, R. 1983. *Miasma.* Oxford: Oxford University Press.

Parkin, K. 2006. *Food Is Love: Advertising and Gender Roles in Modern America.* Philadelphia: University of Pennsylvania Press.

Parkman, F. 1869. *La Salle and the Discovery of the Great West.* Boston: Little, Brown.

Parrington, V. L. 1927. *Main Currents in American Thought.* New York: Harcourt Brace.

Pegge, S., ed. 1780. *The Forme of Cury, a Roll of Ancient English Cookery.* London: Nichols.

Peiss, K. 2007. "Studying Gender, Studying Food." Radcliffe Conference on Gender and Food (unpublished manuscript).

Pekin, E., and Sümer, A., eds. *Timeless Tastes: Turkish Culinary Culture.* Istanbul: Vehbi Koç.

Peloso, V. 1985. "Succulence and Sustenance: Region, Class, and Diet in Nineteenth-Century Peru." In *Food, Politics, and Society in Latin America.* Edited by J. Super and T. Wright. Lincoln: University of Nebraska Press: 46–54.

Peltre, J., and Thouvenot, C., eds. 1989. *Alimentations & Regions.* Nancy, France: Presses Universitaires de Nancy.

Pemberton, R. 2002. "Wild-Gathered Food as Countercurrents to Dietary Globalisation in South Korea." In *Asian Food: The Global and the Local.* Edited by K. J. Cwiertka with Boudewign C.A. Walraven. Honolulu: University of Hawaii Press: 76–94.

Pennell, S. 1997. "The Material Culture of Food in Early Modern England, circa 1650–1750." PhD diss., Oxford University.

Pennell, S. 1998. "'Pots and Pans History': The Material Culture of the Kitchen in Early Modern England." *Journal of Design History* 11, no. 3: 201–16.

Pennell, S. 1999. "Consumption and Consumerism in Early Modern England." *Historical Journal* 42, no. 2: 549–64.

Pennell, S. 2004. "Perfecting Practice? Women, Manuscript Recipes and Knowledge in Early Modern England." In *Early Modern Women's Manuscript Writing.* Edited by V. E. Burke and J. Gibson. Aldershot, UK: Ashgate: 237–58.

Pennell, S. 2012. "Professional Cooking, Kitchens and Service Work: 'Accomplisht' Cookery." In *The Cultural History of Food.* Edited by B. Kümin. Oxford and New York: Berg: 4: 103–21.

Percy, G. 1907. "A True Relation of the Proceedings and Occurrences of Moment which have Happened in Virginia From the Time Sir Thomas Gates was Shipwrecked Upon the Bermudes Ano 1609 Until My Departure Out of the Country Which was in Ano Domini 1612." In *Narratives of Early Virginia, 1607–1625.* Edited by L. G. Tyler. New York: Scribner: 1–22.

Perry, C., trans. 1987. *Anonymous Andalusian Cookbook of the Thirteenth Century.* http://www.daviddfriedman.com/Medieval/Cookbooks/Andalusian/andalusian_contents.htm (accessed August 2, 2011).

Perry, C. 2001a. "Elements of Arab Feasting." In *Medieval Arab Cookery,* by M. Rodinson, A. J. Arberry, and C. Perry. Totnes, UK: Prospect Books: 227–31.

Perry, C. 2001b. "Shorba: A Linguistic-Chemico-Culinary Enquiry." In *Medieval Arab Cookery,* by M. Rodinson, A. J. Arberry, and C. Perry. Totnes, UK: Prospect Books: 257–59.

Perry, C. 2001c. "What to Order in Ninth-Century Baghdad." In *Medieval Arab Cookery,* by M. Rodinson, A. J. Arberry, and C. Perry. Totnes, UK: Prospect Books: 219–24.

Perry, C. 2001d. "A Thousand and One Fritters: The Food of the Arabian Nights." In *Medieval Arab Cookery,* by M. Rodinson, A. J. Arberry, and C. Perry. Totnes, UK: Prospect Books: 487–96.

Peterson, T. 1980. "The Arab Influence on Western European Cooking." *Journal of Medieval History* 6: 317–40.

Pettid, M. J. 2008. *Korean Cuisine: An Illustrated History.* London: Reaktion Books.

Pilcher, J. 1996. "Tamales or Timbales: Cuisine and the Formation of Mexican National Identity, 1821–1911." *The Americas* 53: 193–216.

Pilcher, J. 1998. *¡Que vivan los tamales! Food and the Making of Mexican Identity.* Albuquerque: University of New Mexico Press.

Pilcher, J. 2004. "Empire of the 'Jungle': The Rise of an Atlantic Refrigerated Beef Industry, 1880–1920." *Food, Culture & Society* 7: 63–78.

Pilcher, J. 2006a. *Food in World History.* New York and London: Routledge.

Pilcher, J. 2006b. *The Sausage Rebellion: Public Health, Private Enterprise, and Meat in Mexico City, 1890–1917.* Albuquerque: University of New Mexico Press.

Pilcher, J. 2010. "Food Scholarship and Food Writing." *Food, Culture & Society* 13, no. 3: 322–26.

Pilcher, J. 2012. *Planet Taco: A Global History of Mexican Food.* New York: Oxford University Press.

Pillsbury, R. 1998. *No Foreign Food: The American Diet in Time and Place.* Boulder, CO: Westview.

Pinkard, S. 2009. *A Revolution in Taste: The Rise of French Cuisine.* Cambridge: Cambridge University Press.

Pinney, C. 2001. "Public, Popular, and Other Cultures." In *Pleasure and the Nation: The History, Politics and Consumption of Popular Culture in India.* Edited by C. Dwyer and C. Pinney. New Delhi: Oxford University Press: 1–34.

Piranyan B. 2008. *Aşçının Kitabı.* Translated by T. Tovmasyan. Istanbul: Aras Yayıncılık.

Pite, R. E. 2007. "Creating a Common Table: Doña Petrona, Cooking, and Consumption in Argentina, 1928–1983." PhD diss., University of Michigan.

Pitts, M. 2005. "Pots and Pits: Drinking and Deposition in Late Iron Age South-East Britain." *Oxford Journal of Archaeology* 24: 143–61.

Pitts, M. 2008. "Globalizing the Local in Roman Britain: An Anthropological Approach to Social Change." *Journal of Anthropological Archaeology* 27: 493–506.

Planche, A. 1984. "La table comme signe de la classe: le témoignage du *Roman du Comte d'Anjou* (1316)." In *Manger et boire au Moyen Age.* Nice, France: Les Belles Lettres: 1: 239–60.

Plat, H. 1602. *Delightes for Ladies.* London: Peter Short.

Plummer, G. n.d. *Ibo Cookery Book.* Lagos, Nigeria: C.M.S. Bookshops.

Pollan, M. 2001. *The Botany of Desire: A Plant's-Eye View of the World.* New York: Random House.

Pollan, M. 2006. *The Omnivore's Dilemma: A Natural History of Four Meals.* New York: Random House.

Pollan, M. 2008. *In Defense of Food: An Eater's Manifesto.* New York: Penguin.

Pollock, S. 2006. *The Language of the Gods in the World of Men: Sanskrit, Culture and Power in Pre-Modern India.* Berkeley: University of California Press.

Pommeranz, K. 2000. *The Great Divergence: China, Europe and the Making of the Modern World Economy.* Princeton, NJ: Princeton University Press.

Poo, M.-c. 1992. "Xifang jinnianlai de shenghuoshi yanjiu" [Recent research on life history in the West]. *New History* 4: 139–53.

Poppendieck, J. 1986. *Breadlines Knee Deep in Wheat: Food Assistance in the Great Depression.* New Brunswick, NJ: Rutgers University Press.

Portincasa, A. 2008. "La pasta come stereotipo della cucina italiana." *Storicamente (Laboratorio di storia).* http://www.storicamente.org/03portincasa.htm (accessed December 23, 2010).

Potter, D. M. 1954. *People of Plenty: Economic Abundance and the American Character.* Chicago: University of Chicago Press.

Poulain, J.-P. 2002. *Sociologies de l'alimentation.* Paris: Presses Universitaires de France.

Powell, O. 2003. *Galen: On the Properties of Foodstuffs.* Cambridge: Cambridge University Press.

Power, E. 1934. "On Medieval History as a Social Study." *Economica* 1, no. 1 (February): 13–29.

Power, E., trans. 2006. *The Goodman of Paris* (Le Ménagier de Paris). Woodbridge, Suffolk, UK: Boydell. (Orig. pub., London: George Routledge and Sons, 1928.)

Prasad, S. 2005. "Sanitising the Domestic: Gender, Hygiene and Health in Bengal/India, 1885–1935." *Wellcome History* 28: 6–7.

Prasad, S. 2006. "Social Production of Hygiene: Domesticity, Gender, and Nationalism in Late Colonial Bengal and India." PhD diss., University of Illinois at Urbana-Champaign.

Prestwich, P. 2007. "Histoire de la qualité alimentaire by A. Stanziani." *Journal of Social History* 40, no. 3: 756–58.

Purcell, N. 1985. "Wine and Wealth in Ancient Italy." *Journal of Roman Studies* 75: 1–19.

Quellier, F. 2007. *La Table des Français: une histoire culturelle (XVe–début XIXe siècle).* Rennes, France: Presses Universitaire de Rennes.

Quiroz, E. 2005. *Entre el lujo y la subsistencia: Mercado, abastecimiento y precios de la carne en la ciudad de México, 1750–1812.* Mexico City: El Colegio de México.

Rabinovitch, L. Forthcoming. "Feeding Identity: Romanian Jewish Immigrants in New York City and Montreal, 1900–1939." PhD diss., New York University.

Rambourg, P. 2005. *De la cuisine à la gastronomie: Histoire de la table française.* Paris: Audibert.

Raphael, C. 1993. *A Feast of History: The Drama of Passover through the Ages: With a New Translation of the Haggadah for Use at the Seder.* London: Weidenfeld.

Rath, E. 2010. *Food and Fantasy in Early Modern Japan.* Berkeley: California University Press.

Rath, E., and Assmann, S., eds. 2010. *Japanese Food Past and Present.* Urbana: University of Illinois Press.

Ratnawali. 2010. "Supplementary Nutrition to Women and Children: A Situational Analysis of Anganwadis in Tribal Areas of Gujarat." *Social Change* 40, no. 3: 319–43.

Raven, J. 2007. *The Business of Books: Booksellers and the English Book Trade.* New Haven, CT: Yale University Press.

Raviv, Y. 2003. "Falafel: A National Icon." *Gastronomica* 3, no. 3: 20–25.

Ravoir, F., and Dietrich, A., eds. 2009. *La cuisine et la table dans la France de la fin du Moyen Âge: Contenu et contenants du XIVe au XVIe siècle.* Caen, France: Centre de recherche d'archéologie et d'histoire medievale.

Ray, K. 2004. *The Migrant's Table: Meals and Memories in Bengali-American Households.* Philadelphia: Temple University Press.

Ray, K. 2008. "Nation and Cuisine: The Evidence from American Newspapers ca. 1830–2003." *Food and Foodways* 16, no. 4: 259–97.

Ray, K. 2009. "Sabina Sehgal Saikia." *Gastronomica* 9, no. 2: 1–4.

Ray, K., and Srinivas, T., eds. 2012. *Curried Cultures.* Berkeley: University of California Press.

Reader, J. 2009. *Potato: A History of the Propitious Esculent.* New Haven, CT, and London: Yale University Press.

Redon, O., et al., eds. 2005. *Le Désir et le Goût.* Saint-Denis: Presses Universitaires de Vincennes.

Redon, O., and Laurioux, B. 2003. "Histoire de l'alimentation entre Moyen Âge et temps modernes: Regard sur trente ans de recherches." In *Le Désir et le Goût: Une autre histoire (XIIIe–XVIII siècles).* Edited by O. Redon, L. Sallmann, and S. Steinberg. Paris: Presses Universitaires de Vincennes: 64–75.

Reindl-Kiel, H. 2003. "The Chickens of Paradise Official Meals in the Mid-Seventeenth Century Ottoman Palace." In *The Illuminated Table, the Prosperous House.* Edited by S. Faroqhi and C. K. Neumann. Würzburg, Germany: Ergon: 59–89.

Reinschmidt, M. 2007. "Estimating Rice, Agriculture, Global Trade and National Food Culture in South Korea." In *Food and Foodways in Asia.* Edited by S. Cheung and C.-B. Tan. London: Routledge: 96–111.

Remedi, F. 1998. *Los secretos de la olla. Entre el gusto y la necesidad: la alimentación en la Córdoba de principios del siglo XX.* Córdoba, Spain: Centro de Estudios Históricos.

Renfrew, J. 1973. *Palaeoethnobotony.* New York: Columbia University Press.

Revel, J. 1979. "A Capital City's Privileges: Food Supplies in Early-Modern Rome." In *Food and Drink in History.* Edited by R. Forster and O. Ranum. Baltimore: Johns Hopkins University Press: 37–49.

Richards, A. 1939. *Land, Labour, and Diet in Northern Rhodesia: An Economic Study of the Bemba Tribe.* Oxford: Oxford University Press.

Rickman, G. 1980. *The Corn Supply of Ancient Rome.* Oxford and New York: Clarendon and Oxford University Press.

Riera i Melis, A. 1991. "El sistema alimentario como elemento de diferenciación social en la alta edad media Occidente, siglos VIII–XII." In *Representaciones de la sociedad en la historia: De la autocomplacencia a la utopía.* Edited by A. Riera i Melis et al. Valladolid, Spain: Universidad de Valladolid: 81–107.

Riera i Melis, A. 1995–1996. "Jerarquía social y desigualdad alimentaria en el Mediterráneo noroccidental en la baja edad media." *Acta mediaevalia* 16–17: 181–205.

Riera i Melis, A. 1997. *Senyors, monjos i pagesos: Alimentació i identitat social als segles XII i XIII.* Barcelona, Spain: Institut d'Estudis Catalans.

Riley, G. 1993. "Tainted Meat." In *Spicing Up the Palate: Studies of Flavourings—Ancient and Modern. Proceedings of the Oxford Symposium on Food and Cookery.* Totnes, UK: Prospect Books: 1–6.

Riley, G., ed. 2007. *The Oxford Companion to Italian Food.* Oxford: Oxford University Press.

Rittersma, R. 2010. "'Ces pitoyables truffes d'Italie'. Die französisch-italienische Rivalität auf dem europäischen Trüffelmarkt seit 1700, oder: wie entsteht Gastrochauvinismus. Die historischen Tiefendimensionen des Terroir." *Österreichische Zeitschrift für Geschichtswissenschaften* 21, no. 2: 80–104.

Riu, M. C. 1999–2000. "El retablo de San Miguel y San Juan Bautista de la iglesia parroquial de Sant Llorenç de Morunys (s. XV)." *Acta mediaevalia* 20–21: 737–54.

Robbins, B. 1998. "Introduction Part I: Actually Existing Cosmopolitanism." In *Cosmopolitics: Thinking and Feeling beyond the Nation.* Edited by P. Cheah and B. Robbins. Minneapolis: University of Minnesota Press: 1–19.

Roberts, J.A.G. 2002. *China to Chinatown: Chinese Food in the West.* London: Reaktion Books.

Robertson, C. 1984. *Sharing the Same Bowl: A Socioeconomic History of Women and Class in Accra, Ghana.* Bloomington: Indiana University Press.

Robinson, D. M., and Graham, J. W. 1938. *Excavations at Olynthus,* Vol. 8, *The Hellenic House.* Baltimore: Johns Hopkins Press.

Robinson, M. Forthcoming. Publications of the Herculaneum Conservation Project. The British School at Rome. http://www.bsr.ac.uk/research/publications/italiano-publications-in-print.

Roche, D. 2000. *A History of Everyday Things.* Cambridge: Cambridge University Press.

Roche, D. 2003. *Humeurs vagabondes.* Paris: Fayard.

Roden, C. 1968. *Middle Eastern Food.* London: Thomas Nelson and Sons.

Roden, C. 1996. *The Book of Jewish Food: An Odyssey from Samarkand to New York.* New York: Knopf.

Roden, C. 2001. "Foreword." In *Medieval Arab Cookery*, by M. Rodinson, A. J. Arberry, and C. Perry. Totnes, UK: Prospect Books: 9–14.

Rodinson, M. 2001a. "Ma'muniya East and West." In *Medieval Arab Cookery*, by M. Rodinson, A. J. Arberry, and C. Perry. Totnes, UK: Prospect Books: 185–97.

Rodinson, M. 2001b. "Romania and Other Arabic Words in Italian." In *Medieval Arab Cookery*, by M. Rodinson, A. J. Arberry, and C. Perry. Totnes, UK: Prospect Books: 165–82.

Rodinson, M. 2001c. "Studies in Arabic Manuscripts Relating to Cookery." In *Medieval Arab Cookery*, by M. Rodinson, A. J. Arberry, and C. Perry. Totnes, UK: Prospect Books: 91–163.nnn

Rodinson, M. 2001d. "Venice, the Spice Trade and Eastern Influences on European Cooking." In *Medieval Arab Cookery*, by M. Rodinson, A. J. Arberry, and C. Perry. Totnes, UK: Prospect Books: 199–215.

Rodinson, M., Arberry, A. J., and Perry, C. 2001. *Medieval Arab Cookery.* Totnes, UK: Prospect Books.

Rojas, R. 2005. "Transculturation and Nationalism." In *Cuban Counterpoints: The Legacy of Fernando Ortiz.* Edited by M. Font and A. Quiroz. Lanham, MD: Lexington Books: 65–71.

Roller, M. 2006. *Dining Posture in Ancient Rome: Bodies, Values and Status.* Princeton, NJ: Princeton University Press.

Romano, E. 2000. "La Dietetica di Galeno." In *Studi su Galeno.* Edited by D. Manetti. Firenze, Italy: Scienze Antichità de la Università di Firenze: 31–44.

Romano, R. 1972. *Les mécanismes de la conquête coloniale: les conquistadores.* Paris: Flammarion.

Romeri, L. 2002. *Philosophes entre Mots et Mets: Plutarque, Lucienet Athénée autour de la table de Platon.* Grenoble, France: Millon.

Root, W., and De Rochemont, R. 1976. *Eating in America: A History.* New York: Morrow.

Rose, P. G. 1989. *The Sensible Cook: Dutch Foodways in the Old and New World.* Syracuse, NY: Syracuse University Press.

Rosenberger, B. 1999. "Arab Cuisine and Its Contribution to European Culture." In *Food: A Culinary History from Antiquity to the Present.* Edited by A. Sonnenfeld. New York: Columbia University Press: 207–23.

Rosenblum, J. 2010. *Food and Identity in Early Rabbinic Judaism.* New York: Cambridge University Press.

Roth, L. 2010. "Toward a Kashrut Nation in American Jewish Cookbooks, 1990–2000." *Shofar: An Interdisciplinary Journal of Jewish Studies* 28, no. 2: 65–91.

Rothenberg, D. 2000. *With These Hands: The Hidden World of Migrant Farmworkers Today.* Berkeley: University of California Press.

Rotherham, R. 2009. *Simmering through the Ages: A Culinary Journey through History.* Stratford-upon-Avon, UK: S. Brookes.

Rotroff, S. I., and Oakley, J. H. 1992. *Debris from a Public Dining Place in the Athenian Agora.* Hesperia, Suppl. 25. Princeton, NJ: American School of Classical Studies at Athens.

Rowan, M. 1998. *Flavours of Mozambique.* Maputo, Mozambique: Marielle Rowan.

Rowley, A. 2006. *Une histoire mondiale de la table: stratégies de bouches.* Paris: O. Jacob.

Roxborough, I. 1986. "Review of *Sweetness and Power.*" *Man* 21, no. 3: 575.

Roy, N., ed. 2004. *A Matter of Taste: The Penguin Book of Indian Writing on Food.* New Delhi: Penguin.

Roy, P. 2010. *Alimentary Tracts: Appetites, Aversions, and the Postcolonial.* Durham, NC: Duke University Press.

Rozin, P. 1991. "Food Is Fundamental, Fun, Frightening, and Far-Reaching." *Social Research* 66: 9–30.

Rozin, P., et al. 1997. "Disgust: Preadaptation and the Cultural Evolution of a Food-Based Emotion." In *Food Preferences and Taste: Continuity and Change.* Edited by H. Macbeth. Providence, RI: Berghahn Books, 65–82.

Ruark, J. K. 1999. "A Place at the Table: More Scholars Focus on Historical, Social, and Cultural Meanings of Food, but Some Critics Say It's Scholarship-Lite." *Chronicle of Higher Education*, July 9.

Sahlins, M. 1978. "Culture as Protein and Profit." *New York Review of Books*, November 23.

Saitō, T. 1983. *Nihon shokuseikatsushi nenpyō* [The chronological table of Japanese food history]. Tokyo: Gakuyu Shobō.

Sakurai, S., and Adachi, I. 1934. *Nihon shokumotsu shi* [Japanese food history]. Tokyo: Yūzankaku.

Salaman, R. 1949. *The Social History and Influence of the Potato.* London: Cambridge University Press.

Sallares, R. 1991. *The Ecology of the Ancient Greek World.* London: Duckworth.

Samancı, Ö. 1998. "Continuity and Change in the Culinary Culture of the Ottoman Palace in the Nineteenth Century." Master's thesis, Bogazici University, Istanbul.

Samancı, Ö. 2003. "Culinary Consumption Patterns of the Ottoman Elite during the First Half of the 19th Century." In *The Illuminated Table, the Prosperous House.* Edited by S. Faroqhi and C. K. Neumann. Würzburg, Germany: Ergon: 161–85.

Samancı, Ö. 2006. "19. Yüzyılda Osmanlı Saray Mutfağı." *Yemek ve Kültür* 4: 36–59.

Samancı, Ö. 2006a. "19. yüzyıl Osmanlı Mutfağında Yeni Lezzetler." *Yemek ve Kültür* 6: 86–98.

Samancı, Ö. 2006b. "Vegetable Patrimony of the Ottoman Culinary Culture." In *Proceedings of the Fourth International Congress of Ethnobotany (ICEB 2005).* Istanbul.

Samancı, Ö. 2009. "La Culture Culinaire d'Istanbul au XIXe Siècle: l'alimentation, les techniques culinaires et les manières de table." PhD diss., Ecole des Hautes Etudes en Sciences Sociales, Paris.

Samancı, Ö. 2011. "Pilaf and Bouchées: The Modernization of Official Banquets at the Ottoman Palace in the Nineteenth Century." In *Royal Taste, Food, Power and Status at the European Courts after 1789*. Edited by D. De Vooght. Farnham, UK: Ashgate: 111–42.

Samuelsson, M. 2006. *The Soul of a New Cuisine: A Discovery of the Foods and Flavors of Africa*. New York: Wiley and Sons.

Sancisi-Weerdenburg, H. 1995. "Persian Food: Stereotypes and Political Identity." In *Food in Antiquity*. Edited by J. Wilkins et al. Exeter, UK: University of Exeter Press: 286–302.

Sand, J. 2005. "Good Science, Bad Science and Taste Cultures." *Gastronomica* 4: 38–49.

Santucci, M. 1984. "Nourritures et symboles dans le *banquet du Faisan* et dans *Jehan de Saintrè.*" In *Manger et boire au Moyen Age. Actes du Colloque de Nice*. Edited by D. Manjot. Nice, France: Les Belles Lettres: 1: 429–40.

Sarasúa, C. 2001. "Upholding Status: The Diet of a Noble Family in Early Nineteenth-Century La Mancha." In *Food, Drink and Identity: Cooking, Eating and Drinking in Europe since the Middle Ages*. Edited by P. Scholliers. Oxford: Berg: 37–62.

Sarasúa, C., Scholliers, P., and Van Molle, L., eds. 2005. *Land, Shops and Kitchens: Technology in the Food Chain in Twentieth-Century Europe*. Turnhout, Belgium: Brepols.

Sarı, N. 2008. "Food as Medicine." In *Turkish Cuisine*. Edited by A. Bilgin and Ö. Samancı. Ankara: Turkish Ministry of Culture and Tourism: 137–52.

Sasakawa, R., and Adachi, I. 1935. *Kinsei nihon shokumotsu shi* [Food history of early modern Japan]. Tokyo: Yūzankaku.

Sauner, M. H. 2001. "Les Traditions culinaires de la Méditerranée: modèles, emprunts, permanences." In *L'anthropologie de la Méditerranée*. Edited by D. Albera, A. Blok, and C. Bromberger. Paris: Maisonneuve & Larose: 491–510.

Sauner-Nebioğlu, M. H. 1995. *Evolution des pratiques alimentaires en Turquie: Analyse comparative*. Berlin: Klaus Schwarz.

Şavkay, T. 1999. *Osmanlı Mutfağı*. Istanbul: Şekerbank Kültür Yayınları.

Scarborough, J. 2010. *Pharmacy and Drug Lore in Antiquity: Greece, Rome, Byzantium*. Farnham, UK: Ashgate.

Schehr, L. R., and Weiss, A. S., eds. 2001. *French Food: On the Table, on the Page, and in French Culture*. New York: Routledge.

Scheid, J. 2005. *Quand faire, c'est croire: Les rites sacrificielles des Romains*. Paris: Aubier.

Schlesinger, A. 1918. *The Colonial Merchants and the American Revolution, 1763–1776*. New York: Columbia University Press.

Schlosser, E. 2001. *Fast Food Nation: The Dark Side of the All-American Meal.* New York: Houghton Mifflin.

Schmitt-Pantel, P. 1992. *La Cité au Banquet.* Paris: Publications de la Sorbonne. Repr., 3rd ed., Paris: Publications de la Sorbonne, 2011.

Schneider, H. M. 2011. *Keeping the Nation's House: Domestic Management and the Making of Modern China.* Vancouver: University of British Columbia Press.

Scholliers, P., ed. 2001. *Food, Drink and Identity. Cooking, Eating and Drinking in Europe since the Middle Ages.* Oxford and New York: Berg.

Scholliers, P. 2007. "Twenty-Five Years of Studying *un phénomène social total:* Food History Writing on Europe in the Nineteenth and Twentieth Centuries." *Food, Culture and Society* 10: 449–71.

Scholliers, P., and Grieco, A., eds. 2009. "Food Exchanges in History: People, Products, and Ideas." *Food & History* 7, no. 1: 105–226.

Scholliers, P., and Van den Eeckhout, P. 2011. "Hearing the Consumer? The Laboratory, the Public, and the Construction of Food Safety in Brussels (1840s–1910s)." *Journal of Social History* 44, no. 4: 1139–55.

Schroter, H. 2008. "The Americanization of Distribution and Its Limits: The Case of the German Retail System, 1950–1975." *European Review of History* 15, no. 4: 445–58.

Schubert, E. 2006. *Essen und Trinken im Mittelalter.* Darmstadt, Germany: Primus.

Schwartz, S. 1985. *Sugar Plantations in the Formation of Brazilian Society: Bahia, 1550–1835.* New York: Cambridge University Press.

Schwartz, S., ed. 2004. *Tropical Babylons: Sugar and the Making of the Atlantic World, 1450–1680.* Chapel Hill: University of North Carolina Press.

Scobie, J. 1964. *Revolution on the Pampas: A Social History of Argentine Wheat, 1860–1910.* Austin: University of Texas Press.

Scott, J. 1993. "A Biting Analysis of Society." *Los Angeles Times*, November 18. http://articles.latimes.com/1993-11-18/news/mm-58159_1_cultural-history.

Scully, T. 1992. "The Sickdish in Early French Recipe Collections." In *Health, Disease and Healing in Medieval Culture.* Edited by S. Campbell et al. New York: St. Martin's: 132–40.

Scully, T., ed. 2000. *The Neapolitan Recipe Collection. Cuoco Napoletano.* Ann Arbor: University of Michigan Press.

Scully, T. 2006. *La Varenne's Cookery.* Totnes, UK: Prospect Books.

Scully, T. 2008. *The Opera of Bartolomeo Scappi (1570).* Toronto: University of Toronto Press.

Seaford, R. 2006. *Dionysos.* London: Routledge.

Second International Food Congress. Turkey 3–10 September 1988. 1989. Edited by F. Halıcı. Ankara: Konya Kültür ve Turizm Vakfı yayını, Güven Matbaası.

Sée, H. 1927. "Bibliography: Recent Work in French Economic History (1905–1925)." *Economic History Review* 1, no. 1: 137–53.

Sefercioğlu, N. 1985. *Türk Yemekleri XVIII. Yüzyıla Ait bir Yemek Risalesi.* Ankara: Kültür ve Turizm Bakanlığı Milli Folklor Araştırma Dairesi Yayınları.

Sen, C. T. 2004. *Food Culture in India.* Westport, CT: Greenwood.

Sen, C. T. 2009. *Curry: A Global History.* London: Reaktion Books.

Sen, T., ed. 2007. "Kolkata (India) and China." Special issue, *China Report* 43, no. 4.

Sengupta, J. 2010. "Nation on a Platter: The Culture and Politics of Food and Cuisine in Colonial Bengal." *Modern Asian Studies* 44: 81–98.

Sewell, W. H., Jr. 2001. "Whatever Happened to the 'Social' in Social History?" In *Schools of Thought.* Edited by J. W. Scott and D. Keates. Princeton, NJ: Princeton University Press: 209–26.

Sewell, W. H., Jr. 2005. *Logics of History: Social Theory and Social Transformation.* Chicago: University of Chicago Press.

Shammas, C. 1993. "Changes in English and Anglo-American Consumption from 1550 to 1800." In *Consumption and the World of Goods.* Edited by J. Brewer and R. Porter. London: Routledge: 177–205.

Shapin, S. 1988. "The House of Experiment in Seventeenth-Century England." *Isis* 79, no. 3: 373–404.

Shapiro, L. 1986. *Perfection Salad: Women and Cooking at the Turn of the Century.* New York: Farrar, Strauss and Giroux.

Sharp, M. 1998. "The Food Supply in Roman Egypt." DPhil. thesis, Oxford University.

Shaw, J. E. 2002. "Retail, Monopoly, and Privilege: The Dissolution of the Fishmongers' Guild of Venice, 1599." *Journal of Early Modern History* 6, no. 4: 396–427.

Shaxon, A., P. Dickson, and J. Walker. 1979. *The Malawi Cookbook.* Zomba, Malawi: The Government Printer.

al-Shihabi, Qutaiba. 1998. *Tareef al-Nida' fi Dimashq al-Fayha'.* 2 vols. Damascus: Ministry of Culture.

Shinoda, O. 1966. *Sushi no hon* [Book of sushi]. Tokyo: Shibata shoten.

Shinoda, O. 1974. *Chūgoku shokumotsu shi* [Food history of China]. Tokyo: Shibata shoten.

Shinoda, O., and Seiichi, T., eds. 1972–1973. *Chūgoku shokkei sōsho* [Collected Chinese dietary manuals]. Tokyo: Shoseki bunbutsu ryūtsū kai.

Shiratori, K., ed. 2005. *African Kitchen.* Addis Ababa: Shama Books.

Shiva, V. 1993. *Monocultures of the Mind: Perspectives on Biodiversity and Biotechnology.* New Delhi: Zed Books.

Shiva, V. 2005. *Earth Democracy: Justice, Sustainability, and Peace.* London: South End Press.

Shōwa Joshi Daigaku Shokumotsugaku Kenkyūshitsu. 1971. *Kindai nihon shokumotsu shi* [Food history of modern Japan]. Tokyo: Kindai Bunka Kenkyūjo.

Siegel, B. 2010. "Learning to Eat in a Capital City: Constructing Public Eating Culture in Delhi." *Food, Culture and Society* 13, no. 1: 71–90.

Simmons, D. 2007. "Alessandro Stanziani, Histoire de la qualité alimentaire." *Journal of Modern History* 79, no. 1: 173–75.

Simoons, F. J. 1991. *Food in China: A Cultural and Historical Inquiry.* Boca Raton, FL: CRC Press.

Singer, A. 2011a. "The 'Michelin Guide' to Public Kitchens in the Ottoman Empire." In *Starting with Food: Culinary Approaches to Ottoman History*. Edited by A. Singer. Princeton, NJ: Markus Wiener: 69–92.

Singer, A., ed. 2011b. *Starting with Food: Culinary Approaches to Ottoman History*. Princeton: Markus Wiener.

Slater, W., ed. 1991. *Dining in a Classical Context*. Ann Arbor: University of Michigan Press.

Smail, D. L. 2011. "Introduction: History and the Telescoping of Time: A Disciplinary Forum." *French Historical Studies* 34, no. 1: 1–6.

Smart, N. 2000. *Worldviews: Crosscultural Explorations of Human Beliefs*. Upper Saddle River, NJ: Prentice Hall.

Smart-Grosvenor, V. 1992. *Vibration Cooking or the Travel Notes of a Geechee Girl*. New York: Ballantine.

Smith, A. F. 1994. *The Tomato in America: Early History, Culture and Cookery*. Columbia: University of South Carolina Press.

Smith, A. F. 2001. "False Memories: The Invention of Culinary Fakelore and Food Fallacies." In *Proceedings of the Oxford Symposium on Food & Cookery 2000*. Edited by Harlan Walker. Totnes, UK: Prospect Books: 254–60.

Smith, A. F., ed. 2004. *Oxford Encyclopedia of Food and Drink in America*. London: Oxford University Press.

Smith, A. F., Pilcher, J. M., and Goldstein, D. 2010. "Food Scholarship and Food Writing." *Food, Culture & Society* 13, no. 3: 319–29.

Smith, B. G. 1984. "The Contribution of Women to Modern Historiography in Great Britain, France, and the United States, 1750–1940." *American Historical Review* 89, no. 3: 709–32.

Smith, D. E. 2003. *From Symposium to Eucharist*. Minneapolis: Augsburg Fortress.

Söderlind, U. 2010. *The Nobel Banquets: A Century of Culinary History (1901–2001)*. Translated by M. Knight. Hackensack, NJ: World Scientific Publishing.

Soler, J. 1997. "The Semiotics of Food in the Bible." In *Food and Culture: A Reader*. Edited by C. Counihan and P. Van Esterik. New York: Routledge: 55–66.

Soluri, J. 2005. *Banana Cultures: Agriculture, Consumption, and Environmental Change in Honduras and the United States*. Austin: University of Texas Press.

Sönmez, E. 2010. *Annales Okulu ve Türkiye'de Tarih Yazımı*. Ankara: Tan Kitabevi Yayınları.

South Asia Research. 2004. Special food issue. *South Asia Research* 24, no. 1.

Spang, R. 2000. *The Invention of the Restaurant: Paris and Modern Gastronomic Culture*. Cambridge, MA: Harvard University Press.

Sparkes, B. 1962. "The Greek Kitchen." *Journal of Hellenic Studies* 82: 121–37.

Spary, E. C. 2005. "Ways with Food." *Journal of Contemporary History* 40: 763–71.

Spary, E. C. 2010. "Liqueurs and the Luxury Marketplace in Paris." In *Materials and Expertise in Early Modern Europe: Between Market and Laboratory*. Edited by U. Klein and E. C. Spary. Chicago: University of Chicago Press: 225–55.

Spiekermann, U. 2011. "Redefining Food: The Standardization of Products and Production in Europe and the United States, 1880–1914." *History & Technology* 27: 11–37.

Spurlock, M. 2004. *Supersize Me: A Film of Epic Proportions.* New York: Roadside Attractions/The Con and Samuel Goldwyn Films.

Srinivas, T. 2006. "'As Mother Made It': The Cosmopolitan Indian Family, 'Authentic' Food and the Construction of Cultural Utopia." *International Journal of Sociology of the Family* 32, no. 2: 199–221.

Srinivas, T. 2007. "Everyday Exotic: Transnational Spaces and Contemporary Foodways in Bangalore." *Food, Culture & Society* 10, no. 1: 85–107.

Staller, J., Tykot, R., and Benz, B. 2006. *Histories of Maize: Multidisciplinary Approaches to the Prehistory, Linguistics, Biogeography, Domestication, and Evolution of Maize.* San Diego: Elsevier Academic.

Standage, T. 2009. *An Edible History of Humanity.* Waterville, ME: Thorndike.

Stanziani, A. 2005. *Histoire de la qualité alimentaire.* Paris: Le Seuil.

Stanziani, A. 2007. "Negotiating Innovation in a Market Economy: Foodstuffs and Beverages Adulteration in 19th-Century France." *Enterprise & Society* 8: 375–412.

Stearns, P. N. 1985. "Social History and History: A Progress Report." *Journal of Social History* 19, no. 2: 319–34.

Steele, C. 2008. *Hungry City.* London: Chatto and Windus.

Steere-Williams, J. 2010. "The Perfect Food and the Filth Disease: Milk-Borne Typhoid and Epidemiological Practice in Late-Victorian Britain." *Journal of the History of Medicine and Allied Sciences* 65, no. 4: 514–45.

Stein, S., and Stein, B. 1970. *The Colonial Heritage of Latin America: Essays on Economic Dependence in Perspective.* New York: Oxford University Press.

Stein-Hölkeskamp, E. 2005. *Das römische Gastmahl, Eine Kulturgeschichte.* Munich: Beck.

Sterckx, R., ed. 2005. *Of Tripod and Palate: Food, Politics, and Religion in Traditional China.* New York and Basingstoke, UK: Palgrave Macmillan.

Stocks, C. 2008. *Forgotten Fruits: A Guide to Britain's Disappearing Fruits and Vegetables.* New York: Random House.

Stoll, S. 2002. *Larding the Lean Earth: Soil and Society in Nineteenth-Century America.* New York: Hill and Wang.

Stoller, P. 1989. *The Taste of Ethnographic Things.* Philadelphia: University of Pennsylvania Press.

Stouff, L. 1970. *Ravitaillement et alimentation en Provence aux XIVe et XVe siècles.* Paris and The Hague: Mouton.

Strachey, W. 1969. *For the Colony in Virginea Britannia: Laws Divine, Moral and Martiall, 1612.* In *The Basis of "Martial Law" in the Colony.* Edited by D. H. Flaherty. Charlottesville: University Press of Virginia: 9–25.

Strauss, G. 1991. "The Dilemma of Popular History." *Past & Present* 132: 130–49.

Sullivan, M. A. 1999. "Aertsen's Kitchen and Market Scenes: Audience and Innovation in Northern Art." *Art Bulletin* 81, no. 2: 236–66.

Super, J. 1988. *Food, Conquest, and Colonization in Sixteenth-Century Spanish America.* Albuquerque: University of New Mexico Press.

Super, J. 1996. "Libros de cocina y cultura en la América Latina temprana." In *Conquista y comida: Consecuencias del encuentro de dos mundos.* Edited by J. Long. Mexico City: UNAM: 451–68.

Super, J. 2002. "Food History." *Journal of Social History* 36: 165–78.

Swaminathan, M. S. 2006. "An Evergreen Revolution." *Crop Science* 46: 2293–303.

Swislocki, M. 2009. *Culinary Nostalgia: Regional Food Culture and the Urban Experience in Shanghai.* Stanford, CA: Stanford University Press.

Tabory, J. 1996. *Pesah dorot: perakim be-toldot Lel ha-Seder* [The Passover ritual throughout the generations]. Tel Aviv: ha-Kibuts ha-me'uhad.

Taillevent, Guillaume Tirel dit. 1892. *Le Viandier de Guillaume Tirel dit Taillevent.* Edited by J. Pichon and G. Vicaire. Paris: Techener. Repr., Geneva: Slatkine, 1967.

Taillevent, Guillaume Tirel dit. 1988. *The Viandier of Taillevent, An Edition of All Extant Manuscripts.* Edited by T. Scully. Ottawa, Canada: University of Ottawa Press.

Tamura, S., and Ishige, N., eds. 1994. *Kokusaika jidai no shoku* [Food in the age of globalization]. Tokyo: Domesu Shuppan.

Tanizaki, J. 2001. *The Gourmet Club: A Sextet.* Tokyo: Kodansha.

Tannahill, R. 1973. *Food in History.* New York: Stein and Day.

Taylor, C. 2004. *Modern Social Imaginaries.* Durham, NC: Duke University Press.

Taylor, W. 1979. *Drinking, Homicide and Rebellion in Colonial Mexican Villages.* Stanford, CA: Stanford University Press.

Tchernia, A. 1986. *Le vin de l'Italie romaine: essai d'histoire économique d'après les amphores.* Rome: Ecole française de Rome.

Teughels, N. 2010. "Marketing Food, Marketing a Necessity? Belgian Food Retailing and the Concept of Luxury in Advertising, 1870–1940." In *Luxury in the Low Countries.* Edited by R. Rittersma. Brussels: Pharo: 213–37.

Teuteberg, H.-J., ed. 1992. *European Food History: A Research Review.* Leicester, UK: Leicester University Press.

Teuteberg, H.-J. 2008. "Kulturhistorische Ernährungsforschungen: Ziele, Theorien und Methoden seit dem 19. Jahrhundert." *Rheinisch-Westfälische Zeitschrift für Volkskunde* 53: 17–46.

Teuteberg, H.-J., and Wiegelmann, G. 1986. *Unsere tägliche Kost: Geschichte und regionale Prägung.* Münster, Germany: Coppenrath.

Tezcan, S. 1997. "Bir Ziyafet Defteri." In *Das Osmannische Reich in seinen Archivalien und Chroniken. Nejat Göyünç: zu Ehren.* Edited by K. Kreiser and C. Neumann. Stuttgart: Franz Steiner: 261–97.

Tezcan, S. 1998. *Bir Ziyafet Defteri.* Istanbul: Simurg.

Theophano, J. 2003. *Eat My Words: Reading Women's Lives through the Cookbooks They Wrote.* New York: Palgrave Macmillan.

Thick, M. 2010. *Sir Hugh Plat.* Totnes, UK: Prospect Books.

Thieme, J., and Raja, I., eds. 2007. *The Table Is Laid. The Oxford Anthology of South Asian Food Writing.* New Delhi: Oxford University Press.

Third International Food Congress Turkey 7–12 September 1990. 1991. Edited by F. Halıcı. Ankara: Konya Kültür ve Turizm Vakfı Yayını.

Thirsk, J. 1955. "The Content and Sources of English Agrarian History after 1500." *Agricultural History Review* 3, no. 2: 66–79.

Thirsk, J. 1978. *Economic Policy and Projects: The Development of a Consumer Society in Early Modern England.* Oxford: Clarendon.

Thirsk, J. 1985. "Foreword." In *Women in English Society, 1500–1800.* Edited by M. Prior. London and New York: Routledge: 1–21.

Thirsk, J. 2007. *Food in Early Modern England: Phases, Fads, Fashions 1500–1760.* London: Hambledon Continuum.

Thompson, E. P. 1971. "The Moral Economy of the English Crowd in the Eighteenth Century." *Past and Present* 50: 76–136.

Thompson, H. A., and Wycherley, R. A. 1972. *The Agora of Athens.* The Athenian Agora 14. Princeton, NJ: Princeton University Press.

Thrupp, S. 1933. "The Grocers of London." In *Studies in English Trade in the Fifteenth Century.* Edited by E. Power. London: Routledge: 247–92.

Tilly, C. 1996. "What Good Is Urban History?" *Journal of Urban History* 22, no. 6: 702–19.

Tilly, L. 1983. "Food Entitlement, Famine, and Conflict." *Journal of Interdisciplinary History* 14, no. 2: 333–49.

Tomasik, T. J., and Vitullo, J. M., eds. 2007. *At the Table: Metaphorical and Material Cultures of Food in Medieval and Early Modern Europe.* Turnhout, Belgium: Brepols.

Toomey, P. M. 1994. *Food from the Mouth of Krishna: Feasts and Festivities in a North Indian Pilgrimage Center.* Delhi: Hindustan Publishing Corporation.

Topik, S. 1998. "Coffee." In *The Second Conquest of Latin America: Coffee, Henequen, and Oil during the Export Boom, 1850–1930.* Edited by S. Topik and A. Wells. Austin: University of Texas Press: 37–84.

Tourist Company of Nigeria, Food Research Committee. n.d. *Nigerian Dishes.* Ogunkoya Press.

Tower, J. 2004. *California Dish: What I Saw (and Cooked) at the American Culinary Revolution.* New York: Free Press.

Trentmann, F., and Flemming, J., eds. 2006. *Food and Conflict in Europe in the Age of the Two World Wars.* Basingstoke, UK, and New York: Palgrave.

Trubek, A. 2008. *The Taste of Place: A Culinary Journey into Terroir.* Berkeley: University of California Press.

Tseng, P.-t. 2006. "Cong tianqi dao canzhuo: Qingdai Taiwan hanren de nongye shengchan yu shiwu xiaofei" [From farm to table: The agricultural production and food consumption of the Taiwanese Han people in Qing dynasty]. PhD diss., National Taiwan University.

Tseng, P-t. 2010. "Banzhuo: Qingdai Taiwan de yanhui yu hanren shehui" [Banzhuo: Banquets and Han society in Qing Taiwan]. *New History* 4: 1–55.

Türk Mutfağı Sempozyumu Bildirileri (31 Ekim–1 Kasım 1981 Ankara). Ankara: Kültür ve Turizm Bakanlığı Milli Folklor Araştırma Dairesi Yayınları.

al-Tujibi, Ibn Razeen. 1984. *Fidhalat al-Khiwan fi Tayyibat al-Ta'am wa 'l-Alwan.* Edited by Muhammad bin Shaqroun. 2nd ed. Beirut: Dar al-Gharb al-Islami.

Turner, F. J. 1921. *The Frontier in American History.* New York: Holt.

Tyrrell, A., Hill, P., and Kirkby, D. 2007. "Feasting on National Identity: Whisky, Haggis and the Celebration of Scottishness in the Nineteenth Century." In *Dining on Turtles: Food Feasts and Drinking in History.* Edited by D. Kirkby and T. Luckins. Basingstoke, UK, and New York: Palgrave: 46–63.

University of Adelaide Library. n.d. *Gastronomy and Food Studies Library.* http://libguides.adelaide.edu.au/foodstudies.

Ünsal, A. 1997. *Süt Uyuyunca—Türkiye Peynirleri.* Istanbul: Yapı Kredi Yayınları.

Ünsal, A. 2003a. *Nimet Geldi Ekine / Türkiye'nin Ekmeklerinin Öyküsü.* Istanbul: Yapı Kredi Yayınları.

Ünsal, A. 2003b. *Ölmez Ağacın Peşinde, Türkiye'de Zeytin ve Zeytinyağı.* Istanbul: Yapı Kredi Yayınları.

Ünsal, A. 2007. *Silivrim Kaymak—Türkiye'nin Yoğurtları.* Istanbul: Yapı Kredi Yayınları.

Ünver, S. 1948. *Tarihte 50 Türk Yemeği.* Istanbul: İstanbul Üniversitesi Tıp Tarihi Enstitüsü.

Ünver, S. 1952. *Türkiye Gıda Hijyeni Tarihinde Fatih Devri Yemekleri.* Istanbul: Istanbul Üniversitesi Tıp Tarihi Enstitüsü.

Ünver, S. 1982. "Selçuklular, Beylikler ve Osmanlılarda Yemek Usulleri ve Vakitleri." In *Türk Mutfağı Sempozyumu Bildirileri (31 Ekim–1 Kasım 1981 Ankara).* Ankara: Kültür ve Turizm Bakanlığı Milli Folklor Araştırma Dairesi Yayınları: 1–13.

Uzun, A. 2006. *Istanbul'un Iaşesinde Devletin Rolü Ondalık Ağnam Uygulaması 1783–1857.* Ankara: TTK.

Vağinag Pürad. 2010. *Mükemmel Yemek Kitabı 1926.* Edited by A. Margosyan. Translated by T. Tovmasyan. Istanbul: Aras Yayınları.

Vais, R. 2010. *Okhlim la-da'at* [Meal tests]. Tel Aviv: ha-Kibuts ha-me'uhad.

Van Aert, L., and Van Damme, I. 2005. "Retail Dynamics of a City in Crisis: The Mercer Guild in Pre-industrial Antwerp." In *Retailers and Consumer Changes in Early Modern Europe: England, France, Italy, and the Low Countries.* Edited by Bruno Blondé, Eugénie Briot, Natacha Coquery, and Laura van Aert. Tours, France: Presses Universitaires François-Rabelais.

Van den Eeckhout, P., and Scholliers, P. 2011. "The Belgian Multiple Food Retailer Delhaize Le Lion and Its Clientele, 1867–1914." *Essays in Economic and Business History* 29: 87–100.

Van Den Heuvel, D. 2008. "Partners in Marriage and Business? Guilds and the Family Economy in Urban Food Markets in the Dutch Republic." *Continuity and Change* 23, no. 2: 217–36.

Van der Eijk, P. 2000–2001. *Diocles of Carystus.* Leiden: Brill.

Van der Post, L. 1970. *African Cooking.* New York: Time-Life Books.

Van Gelder, G. J. 2000. *God's Banquet: Food in Classical Arabic Literature.* New York: Columbia University Press.

Van Winter, J. M. 2007. *Spices and Comfits: Collected Papers on Medieval Food.* Totnes, UK: Prospect Books.

Van Young, E. 1981. *Hacienda and Market in Eighteenth-Century Mexico: The Rural Economy of the Guadalajara Region.* Berkeley: University of California Press.

Van Young, E. 1999. "The New Cultural History Comes to Old Mexico." *Hispanic American Historical Review* 79: 211–47.

Vandenbroeck, P. 1984. "Verbeeck's Peasant Weddings: A Study of Iconography and Social Function." *Simiolus* 14: 79–124.

Varma, P. K. 1998. *The Great Indian Middle Class.* New York: Viking.

Vega Jiménez, P. 2004. *Con sabor a tertulias. Historia del consumo del café en Costa Rica (1840–1940).* San José: Editorial de la Universidad de Costa Rica.

Vega Jiménez, P. 2012. "*El Gallo Pinto*: Afro-Caribbean Rice and Beans Conquer the Costa Rican National Cuisine." *Food, Culture & Society* 15, no. 2: 223–40.

Vernon, J. 2007. *Hunger: A Modern History.* Cambridge, MA, and London: Harvard University Press.

Vernon, J. 2008. "Author's Response to Review no. 695." *Reviews in History*, November. http://www.history.ac.uk/reviews/paper/oddydresp.html (accessed January 2, 2011).

Veyne, P. 1976. *Le pain et le cirque: sociologie historique d'un pluralisme politique.* Paris: Editions du Soleil.

Viallon-Schoneveld, M., ed. 2004. *Le boire et le manger au XVI siècle.* Saint-Etienne: Publications de l'Université de Saint-Etienne.

Vidal-Naquet, P. 1981. "Land and Sacrifice in the Odyssey: A Study of Religious and Mythical Meaning." In *Religion and Society.* Edited by R. Gordon. Cambridge: Cambridge University Press.

Viola, H., and Margolis, C. 1991. *Seeds of Change: Five Hundred Years since Columbus.* Washington, DC: Smithsonian Institution Press.

Vössing, K. 2004. *Mensa Regia: Das Bankett beim hellenistischen König und beim römischen Kaiser.* Munich: K. G. Saur.

Waddington, K. 2006. *The Bovine Scourge: Meat, Tuberculosis and Public Health, 1850–1914.* Woodbridge and Rochester, UK: Boydell.

Waines, D. 1987. "Cereals, Bread and Society: An Essay on the Staff of Life in Medieval Iraq." *Journal of Economic and Social History of the Orient* 30, no. 3: 255–85.

Waines, D. 1989. *In a Caliph's Kitchen.* London: Riad el-Rayyes.

Waines, D. 1999. "Dietetics in Medieval Islamic Culture." *Medical History* 43: 228–40.

Waines, D. 2002a. "Introduction." In *Patterns of Everyday Life*. Edited by D. Waines. Hampshire, UK: Ashgate: xi–xlviii.

Waines, D. 2002b. "Luxury Foods in Medieval Islamic Societies." *World Archaeology* 34, no. 3: 571–79.

Waines, D. 2010. *The Odyssey of Ibn Battuta: Uncommon Tales of a Medieval Adventurer.* Chicago: Chicago University Press.

Waines, D., and Marin, M. 1989. "The Balanced Way: Food for Pleasure and Health in Medieval Islam." *Manuscripts of the Middle East* 4: 123–32.

Waines, D., and Marin, M. 1998. "Foodways and the Socialization of the Individual." In *Individuals and Society in the Mediterranean Muslim World: Issues and Sources.* Edited by R. Deguilhem. Aix-en-Provence, France: European Science Foundation: 48–55.

Waines, D., and Marin, M. 2002. "*Muzawwar:* Counterfeit Fare for Fasts and Fevers." In *Patterns of Everyday Life.* Edited by D. Waines. Hampshire, UK: Ashgate: 303–15.

Wallerstein, I. 1974. *The Modern World-System.* Vol. 1, *Capitalist Agriculture and the Origins of the European World-Economy in the Sixteenth Century.* New York and London: Academic Press.

Walraven, B.C.A. 2002. "Bardot Soup and Confucians' Meat: Food and Korean Identity in Global Context." In *Asian Food: The Global and the Local.* Edited by K. J. Cwiertka with B.C.A. Walraven. Honolulu: University of Hawaii Press: 95–115.

Walsh, J. E. 1997. "What Women Learned When Men Gave Them Advice: Rewriting Patriarchy in Late-Nineteenth-Century Bengal." *Journal of Asian Studies* 56, no. 3: 641–77.

Walsh, J. E. 2004. *Domesticity in Colonial India: What Women Learned When Men Gave Them Advice.* Lanham, MD: Rowman & Littlefield.

Wang, H.-t. 2000. "Cong xiaofei de kongjian dao kongjian de xiaofei: Ming Qing chengshi zhong de jiulou yu chaguan" [From consumer space to the consumption of space: Drinking parlors and tea houses in Ming and Qing cities]. *New History* 3: 1–48.

Wang, L.-h. 2000. *Zhonggu huabei yinshi wenhua de bianqian* [Transformation of the drink and food of medieval northern China]. Beijing: Zhongguo shehui kexue chubanshe.

Wang, M.-k. 2007. "Qingke, qiaomai yu yumi" [Highland barley, buckwheat, and maize]. *Journal of Chinese Dietary Culture* 2: 23–71.

Warboys, M. 1988. "The Discovery of Colonial Malnutrition between the Wars." In *Imperial Medicine and Indigenous Societies.* Edited by D. Arnold. Manchester, UK: Manchester University Press: 208–22.

Warde, A. 2009. "Imagining British Cuisine: Representations of Culinary Identity in the Good Food Guide, 1951–2007." *Food, Culture & Society* 12, no. 1: 151–71.

Warman, A. 2003. *Corn and Capitalism: How a Botanical Bastard Grew to Global Dominance.* Translated by N. L. Westrate. Chapel Hill: University of North Carolina Press.

Warner, Richard. 1791. *Antiquitates culinariae, or, Curious Tracts Relating to the Culinary Affairs of the Old English.* London: Printed for R. Blamire.

al-Warraq, Ibn Sayyar. 1987. *Kitab al-Tabeekh.* Edited by Kaj Ohrenberg and Sahban Mroueh. *Studia Orientalia* 60. Helsinki: Finnish Oriental Society.

al-Warraq, Ibn Sayyar. 2007. *Annals of the Caliphs' Kitchens: Ibn Sayyar al Warraq's Tenth-Century Baghdadi Cookbook.* Translated by N. Nasrallah. Leiden: Brill.

Wason, B. 1962. *Cooks, Gluttons, and Gourmets: A History of Cookery.* New York: Doubleday.

Watanabe, M. 1986. *Nihon shokuseikatsu shi* [The history of Japanese foodways]. Tokyo: Yoshikawa Kōbunkan.

Watson, A. 1983. *Agricultural Innovation in the Early Islamic World: The Diffusion of Crops and Farming Techniques, 700–1100.* Cambridge: Cambridge University Press.

Watson, J. L., ed. 1997. *Golden Arches East: McDonald's in East Asia.* Stanford, CA: Stanford University Press.

Watson, J. L., and Caldwell, M. L., eds. 2005. *The Cultural Politics of Food and Eating: A Reader.* Malden, MA: Blackwell.

Watts, S. 2006. *Meat Matters: Butchers, Politics, and Market Culture in Eighteenth-Century Paris.* Rochester, NY: University of Rochester Press.

Weatherill, L. 1988. *Consumer Behavior and Material Culture in Britain 1660–1760.* London and New York: Routledge.

Weber, E. 1976. *Peasants into Frenchmen: The Modernization of Rural France, 1870–1914.* Stanford, CA: Stanford University Press.

Weindling, P. 1986. "Medicine and Modernization: The Social History of German Health and Medicine." *History of Science* 24: 277–301.

Weiner, M. 1996. "Consumer Culture and Participatory Democracy: The Story of Coca-Cola during WWII." *Food and Foodways* 6, no. 2: 109–29.

Weingarten, S. 2003. "A Feast for the Eyes: Women and Baking in the Talmudic Literature." In *To Be a Jewish Woman; Proceedings of the Second International Conference: Woman and Her Judaism.* Edited by M. Shilo. Jerusalem, Israel, and Waltham: Kolech—Religious Women's Forum—and Urim: 45–54.

Weingarten, S. 2005a. "Children's Foods in the Talmudic Literature." In *Feast, Fast or Famine, Food and Drink in Byzantium.* Edited by M. Mayer and S. Trzcionka. Brisbane: Australian Association for Byzantine Studies: 147–60.

Weingarten, S. 2005b. "'Magiros', 'nahtom' and Women at Home: Cooks in the Talmud." *Journal of Jewish Studies* 56, no. 2: 285–97.

Weingarten, S. 2009. "Milch und Honig? Essen in der Bibel." In *Koscher & Co.: über Essen und Religion: eine Ausstellung des Jüdischen Museums Berlin, 9. Ok-*

tober 2009 bis 28. Februar 2010. Edited by M. S. Friedlander and C. Kugelmann. Berlin: Jüdisches Museum: 270–75.

Weinreb, A. 2011. "The Tastes of Home: Cooking the Lost Heimat in West Germany in the 1950s and 1960s." *German Studies Review* 34: 345–64.

Weis, R. 2008. "Las panaderías en la Ciudad de México de Porfirio Díaz: Los empresarios vascos-navarros y la movilización obrera." *Revista de Estudios Sociales* 29: 70–85.

Welch, E. 2005. *Shopping in the Renaissance: Consumer Cultures in Italy 1400–1600.* New Haven, CT: Yale University Press.

West, S. H. 1997. "Playing with Food: Performance, Food, and the Aesthetics of Artificiality in the Sung and Yuan." *Harvard Journal of Asiatic Studies* 1: 67–106.

Wheaton, B. K. 1983. *Savoring the Past: The French Kitchen and Table from 1300 to 1789.* Philadelphia: University of Pennsylvania Press.

White, E., ed. 2007. *The English Kitchen.* Totnes, UK: Prospect Books.

Whitmarsh, T. 2004. *Ancient Greek Literature.* Oxford: Polity.

Whittaker, C. R., ed. 1988. *Pastoral Economies in Classical Antiquity.* Cambridge, UK: Cambridge Philological Society.

Wiegelmann, G. 1967. *Alltags- und Festspeisen.* Marburg: Elwert. Repr. as volume 11 of the Münsteraner Schriften zur Volkskunde, 2006.

Williamson, J. 2009. "History without Evidence: Latin American Inequality since 1491." NBER working paper, no. 14766.

Wilk, R. 2006. *Home Cooking in the Global Village: Caribbean Food from Buccaneers to Ecotourists.* Oxford and New York: Berg.

Wilkins, J. 2000. *The Boastful Chef: The Discourse of Food in Ancient Greek Comedy.* Oxford: Oxford University Press.

Wilkins, J. 2003. "Banquets sur la scène comique et tragique." In *Symposium, Banquet et Représentations en Grèce et à Rome.* Edited by C. Orfanos and J.-C. Carrière. Toulouse, France: Presses Universitaires du Mirail: 167–74.

Wilkins, J. 2004. "The Social and Cultural Context of Regimen II." In *Hippocrates in Context.* Edited by P. Van der Eijk. Leiden: Brill: 121–33.

Wilkins, J. 2007. "Galen and Athenaeus in the Hellenistic Library." In *Ordering Knowledge in the Roman Empire.* Edited by J. König and T. Whitmarsh. Cambridge: Cambridge University Press: 69–87.

Wilkins, J. Forthcoming. *Galien: Sur les facultés des aliments.* Paris: Belles Lettres.

Wilkins, J., Harvey, D., and Dobson, M., eds. 1995. *Food in Antiquity.* Exeter, UK: University of Exeter Press.

Wilkins, J., and Hill, S. 1994. *Archestratus: The Life of Luxury.* Totnes, UK: Prospect Books. Repr., 2011.

Wilkins, J., and Hill, S. 2006. *Food in the Ancient World.* Malden, MA, and Oxford: Wiley- Blackwell.

Wilkins, J., and Nadeau, R., eds. Forthcoming. *The Blackwell Companion to Food in the Ancient World.* Malden, MA, and Oxford: Wiley.

Williams-Forson, P. 2006. *Building Houses out of Chicken Legs: Black Women, Food and Power.* Chapel Hill: University of North Carolina Press.

Williot, J.-P. 2006. "De l'innovation industrielle à l'excellence gastronomique: l'apparition de la cuisine à gaz." In *Histoire des innovations alimentaires XIXe et XXe siècles.* Edited by A. Drouard and J.-P. Williot. Paris: L'Harmattan: 216–39.

Wilson, B. 2008. *Swindled: The Dark History of Food Fraud, from Poisoned Candy to Counterfeit Coffee.* Princeton, NJ: Princeton University Press.

Wilson, C. A. 1981. "The Saracen Connection: Arab Cuisine and the Medieval West." *Petits Propos Culinaires* 7: 13–22; 8: 19–28.

Wilson, C. A., ed. 1986. *Banquetting Stuffe.* Edinburgh: University of Edinburgh Press.

Wilson, C. S. 1973. "Food Habits: A Selected Annotated Bibliography." *Journal of Nutrition Education* 5, no. 1: 41–71.

Wilson, T., ed. 2006. *Food, Drink and Identity in Europe.* Amsterdam and New York: Rodopi.

Wissowa, G., et al. 1893–1972. *Paulys Real-Encyclopädie der classischen Altertumswissenschaft.* Stuttgart, Germany: Metzler.

Wood, G. S. 2010. "In Defense of Academic History Writing." *Perspectives on History* 48, no. 4: 19–20.

Wood, M. W. 1981. "Paltry Peddlers or Essential Merchants? Women in the Distributive Trades in Early Modern Nuremberg." *Sixteenth Century Journal* 12, no. 2: 3–13.

Woolgar, C. M., et al. 2006. *Food in Medieval England: Diet and Nutrition.* Oxford: Oxford University Press.

Wright, Clifford. 1999. *A Mediterranean Feast.* New York: William Morrow.

Wu, D.Y.H., and Cheung, S.C.H., eds. 2002. *The Globalization of Chinese Food.* Richmond, UK: Curzon.

Wu, J.-s. 2006. "Ming Qing yinshi wenhua zhong de ganguan yanhua yu pinwei suzao: yi yinshan shuji yu shipu wei zhongxin de tantao" [Changes in sense perception and the construction of taste in the dietary culture of Ming and Qing China: An investigation centered on dietary writings and recipe books]. *Journal of Chinese Dietary Culture* 2: 45–95.

Wujastyk, D. 2003. *The Roots of Ayurveda: Selections from Sanskrit Medical Writings.* New York: Penguin Books.

Wujastyk, D., and Meulenbeld, G. J. 1987. *Indian Medical History.* Delhi: Motilal Banarsidass.

Wujastyk, D., and Meulenbeld, G. J., eds. 2001. *Studies in Indian Medical History.* Delhi: Motilal Banarsidass.

Wujastyk, D., and Smith, F. M. 2008. *Modern and Global Ayurveda: Pluralism and Paradigms.* Albany: State University of New York Press.

Wylie, D. 2001. *Starving on a Full Stomach: Hunger and the Triumph of Cultural Racism in Modern South Africa.* Charlottesville: University of Virginia Press.

Xiao, F., ed. 1992. *Zhongguo pengren cidian* [Dictionary of Chinese cookery]. Beijing: Zhongguo shangye chubanshe.

Xiong, S.-z., ed. 1995. *Zhongguo yinshi shiwen dadian* [Dictionary of food and drink in Chinese literature]. Qingdao, China: Qingdao chubanshe.

Xu, H.-r., ed. 1999. *Zhongguo yinshi shi* [History of Chinese food and drink]. Beijing: Huaxia chubanshe.

Yan, Y.-x. 2000. "Of Hamburger and Social Space: Consuming McDonald's in Beijing." In *The Consumer Revolution in Urban China.* Edited by D. S. Davis. Berkeley: University of California Press: 201–25.

Yang, Y.-k. 2005. "Jajangmyeon and Junggukjip." *Korea Journal* 2: 60–88.

Yao, W.-j. 1989. *Zhongguo yinshi wenhua tanyuan* [Exploring the origin of Chinese dietary culture]. Nanning, China: Guangxi renmin chubanshe.

Yao, W.-j. 1994. *Yupan zhenxiu zhiwanqian: gongting yinshi* [Valuable and precious dishes: Court diets]. Wuhan, China: Huazhong ligong daxue chubanshe.

Yerasimos, M. 2002. *500 Yıllık Osmanlı Yemek Kültürü.* Istanbul: Boyut.

Yerasimos, M. 2005. *500 Years of Ottoman Cuisine.* Translated by S. Bradbrook. Istanbul: Boyut.

Yerasimos, M. 2009. "Evliya Çelebi'nin Seyehatnamesi'ndeki Balıklar ve Diğer Su Ürünleri." *Yemek ve Kültür* 16: 49–72.

Yerasimos, S. 2001. *A la table du Grand Turc.* Paris: Actes Sud.

Yerasimos, S. 2002. *Sultan Sofraları 15. ve 16. Yüzyılda Osmanlı Saray Mutfağı.* Istanbul: Yapı Kredi Yayınları.

Yi, S.-u. 1981. *Han'guk sikkyŏng taejŏn* [Compilation of Korean dietary texts]. Seoul: Suhaksa.

Yi, S.-u. 1984. *Han'guk sikpum sahwesa* [Social history of Korean foods]. Seoul: Kyomunsa.

Yi, S.-u. 1985. *Han'guk yori munhwasa* [Social history of Korean cuisine]. Seoul: Kyomunsa.

Yi, S.-u. 1992. *Han'guk koshik munhŏn chipsŏng* [Compilation of old Korean food-related sources]. Seoul: Suhaksa.

Yi, S.-u. 1993. *Han'guk siksaenghwal-e yŏksa* [The history of Korean foodways]. Seoul: Suhaksa.

Yıldırım, N. 2008. "Soups, Main Dishes and Desserts Recommended to Sick People as Represented in 14th and 15th Century Turkish Medicinal Manuscripts." In *Turkish Cuisine.* Edited by A. Bilgin and Ö. Samancı. Ankara: Turkish Ministry of Culture and Tourism: 153–78.

Yıldırım, O. 2003. "Bread and Empire: The Workings of Grain Provisioning in Istanbul during the 18th Century." In *Nourrir les cités de Mediterranée: Antiquité– Temps Modernes.* Edited by B. Marin and C. Virlouvet. Paris: Maisonneuve & Larose: 251–71.

Yoder, D. 1972. "Folk Cookery." In *Folklore and Folklife: An Introduction.* Edited by R. M. Dorson. Chicago: University of Chicago Press: 325–50.

Young Lee, P., ed. 2005. "The Slaughterhouse and the City." Special issue, *Food & History* 3, no. 2.

Yun, S.-k., ed. 1996. *Uri mal choriŏ sajŏn* [Dictionary of culinary vocabulary in our language]. Seoul: Sinkwang ch'ulp'an.

Yun, S.-S. 1974. *Han'guk sikpumsa yŏn'gu* [Study of the history of Korean foods]. Seoul: Singwang ch'ulpansa.

Yun, S.-S. 1990. *Han'guk sikpumsa yŏn'gu* [Study of the history of Korean foods]. Seoul: Minūmsa.

Zaouali, L. 2007. *Medieval Cuisine of the Islamic World: A Concise History with 175 Recipes.* Translated by M. B. Debevoise. Berkeley: University of California Press.

Zayyat, H. 1947. "Fann al-Tabkh wa Islah al-At'ima fi 'l-Islam." *Al-Mashriq* 41: 1–26.

Zayyat, H. 1952a. "Duhn al-Narjeel." In *Min al-Khizana al-Sharqiyya.* Beirut: Al-Matba'a al-Katholikiyya: 382–83.

Zayyat, H. 1952b. "Khubz al-Abazeer." In *Min al-Khizana al-Sharqiyya.* Beirut: Al-Matba'a al Katholikiyya: 380–81.

Zayyat, H. 1952c. "Khubz al-Aruzz." In *Min al-Khizana al-Sharqiyya.* Beirut: Al-Matba'a al Katholikiyya: 377–80.

Zayyat, H. 1952d. "Kitab al-Hisba." In *Min al-Khizana al-Sharqiyya.* Beirut: Al-Matba'a al-Katholikiyya: 384–90.

Zayyat, H. 1952e. "Mishmish Dimashq." In *Min al-Khizana al-Sharqiyya.* Beirut: Al-Matba'a al Katholikiyya: 365–69.

Zecchini, G. 1989. *La cultura storica di Ateneo.* Milan: Vita e pensiero.

Zeldin, T. 1977. *France 1848–1945.* Vol. 2, *Intellect, Taste and Anxiety.* Oxford: Clarendon.

Zeng, Z.-y., Zhang, Z.-l., and Gao, J. 1988. *Zhongguo yinzhuanshi* [History of Chinese drinks and dishes]. Beijing: Zhongguo shangye chubanshe.

Zhang, L-c. 1911. *Zhongguo fengsu shi* [History of Chinese customs]. Shanghai: Shangwu yinshuguan.

Zhao, R.-g. 1996. *Manzu shiwenhua bianqian yu manhan quanxi wenti yanjiu* [Transformation of the dietary culture of Manzhu and study of the Man-Han banquet]. Haerbin, China: Heilongjiang renmin chubanshe.

Zimmermann, F. 1987. *The Jungle and the Aroma of Meats: An Ecological Theme in Hindu Medicine.* Berkeley: University of California Press.

Zlotnick, S. 1996. "Domesticating Imperialism: Curry and Cookbooks in Victorian England." *Frontiers: A Journal of Women Studies* 16, no. 3: 51–68.

Zubaida, S. 1994. "National, Communal and Global Dimensions in Middle Eastern Food Cultures." In *A Taste of Thyme: Culinary Cultures of the Middle East.* Edited by S. Zubaida and R. Tapper. London: I. B. Taurus: 33–45.

Zubaida, S., and Tapper, R. 1994a. "Introduction." In *A Taste of Thyme: Culinary Cultures of the Middle East.* Edited by S. Zubaida and R. Tapper. London: I. B. Taurus: 1–17.

Zubaida, S., and Tapper, R., eds. 1994b. *A Taste of Thyme: Culinary Cultures of the Middle East.* London: I. B. Taurus.

Index

Columbian exchange, 77–8, 91, 94, 96–7

commodity (ies): biography, 52, 62–3, 113, 210; chains, 99; circulation of, 40; crops, 206; economic, 133; exports, 93; food as, 77, 171, 206; food history and, 72; geography of, 204; globalization and, 99, 205; knowledge as, 50; luxury, 43; meat as, 48; price and, 40; production, 93; as a social denominator, 154; studies of, 44; sugar as, 44, 81; urban food supply as a, 204

Conlon, F., 169–70, 214

consumer(s), 1–2, 65; African, 204; associations, 64; coffee and, 99; culture; 46, 48, 101, 188; goods, 45; power relations and, 65; practices, 210; recipes and, 28; research, 191; revolution, 45; tastes, 49, 99

consumption: alcohol and, 114; American caloric, 76; ancient, 15; *Annales* and, 188; approaches to, 27; Chinese ritual, 187; class and, 31, 147; class identity and, 100; coffee and, 114; conspicuous, 46; as a cultural activity, 156; cultures of, 166, 170; dangers, 100; elite, 97, 115; emulation theory and, 55; European historians and, 43; food history and, 72, 155; food or commodity chains and, 2, 99; food retailing and, 63; globalization and, 94, 175, 205; guilds and, 48; historians of, 45; history of, 82, 188; Indian cities and, 169; Jewish identity and, 132, 134, 213; journal articles and, 75; luxury, 44; mapping of, 93; Mintz and, 46, 80; national identity and, 173; Ottoman patterns of, 109, 113; politics and, 43–4; post-colonial, 176; practices, 182; processed soybeans and East Asian cuisines, 181; rabbinic texts and, 129; social acts and, 97; sociocultural approach and, 117; Teuteberg and, 61

Cook, S. F., 92

cookbooks: African, 203, 205, 208, 213; ancient, 11, 13, 17; Andalusian, 152–3; books of secrets and, 52; Chinese, 187;

discursive analysis of, 97; as a genre, 50, 132; as historical artifacts, 81–2; historical texts, 79, 200, 215; Jewish, 122, 125, 131–3; library collections of, 74; manuscript, 28–9, 34, 43, 50, 107, 109–13, 115–17, 141–5, 150, 152–4, 158, 168, 183; as markers of class, 206; medieval Arab, 111, 141–3, 146–7, 150, 153; medieval European, 24–5, 27–9, 32–4, 38, 148; modern Arab, 156; Ottoman, 111–13, 150; as primary sources, 43, 46, 49, 50, 66, 79, 82, 107, 111, 116–17, 144, 210, 213; study or analysis of, 155, 186; women and, 82, 84; writers of, 74, 98, 101; writing and publishing history, 51

cooking: as an aesthetic expression, 207; African, 199–201, 204–6, 208; African-American, 206; in antiquity, 18–19; appliances, 101; Arabic influence on European, 214; Arab influence in America, 138; Arab influence on Ottoman, 149; diaspora, 205; diet and, 21; Greek houses and, 16; hearth, 51; as a historical process, 201; implements or utensils, 45, 60, 64, 187; Indian, 11; Irish, 87; Jewish, 132; as knowledge, 204–5; literature on, 200, 203, 207; local, 203; manuals, 147; manuscripts, 107, 110–11, 115; as a marker of cultural identity, 201; medicine and, 34, 52, 155; medieval, 25, 32; methods or techniques, 27–8, 52, 73, 94, 96, 110, 117, 187, 201; nutrition and, 14; peasant, 45; practices, 172, 203; public, 49; regional, 60, 205; ritual and, 167–8; Strauss's writings on, 41; study of, 50, 66, 109; systems, 97; traditional, 63; Turkish, 113; women and, 98

Cool, H.E.M., 19

Cooper, J., 124

Corner, S., 16

court(s): celebrations and ceremony, 30; cooking/cuisine, 143, 147; cooks, 28; dining, 12, 24, 44, 46; Henry II, 24; influence on consumption, 50; life, 142; power, 44; records, 116–17; Renaissance,